THE PURSUIT OF
Godly Seed

Denny Kenaston

Home Fires Publishers
P.O. Box 256, Reamstown PA 17567-0256
www.homefirespub.com

THE PURSUIT OF GODLY SEED
by Denny Kenaston

Copyright 2003 © by Denny Kenaston
All Rights Reserved

Published by
Home Fires Publishers
P.O. Box 256
Reamstown PA 17567-0256
www.homefirespub.com

Library of Congress Control Number: 2003109221

Softcover Edition
ISBN 0-9742751-0-7
Hardcover Edition
ISBN 0-9742751-1-5

All Scripture References are from the King James Bible

Printed in the United States of America

Cover photo by Alpine Portraits, Ellensburg WA 98926

Contents

About the Author V

About the Family VI

Acknowledgements VII

Introduction... 9

1. *The Holy Art of Child Training* 15

2. *Clear Conversion*.. 19

3. *The Eternal Value of a Child*............................. 29

4. *A Vision That Motivates*................................... 39

5. *The Heritage of the Generation to Come*............. 45

6. *A Godly Heritage Today*................................... 55

7. *The Influence of a Godly Home*......................... 65

8. *Bring the Fathers Home* 75

9. *Bible Pictures of a Godly Home* 81

10. *More Pictures of Promise* 93

11. *Wholehearted Households* 103

12. *Garden Rules for Raising Children* 113

13. *Blessings: The Key to Obedience*...................... 123

14. *The Hearts of the Fathers Must Turn*................ 137

15. *The Rod is Love*.. 153

16. *A Sacred Exercise* 169

17. *The Training of the Will*	181
18. *The Bondage of Foolishness*	193
19. *Father: An Anointed Teacher*	201
20. *Train Up a Child*	219
21. *A Quiet Ordered Life*	237
22. *Three Mysterious Influences*	247
23. *A Dwelling Place for the Living God*	261
24. *Father: The Watchman*	277
25. *The Fulfilled Woman*	287
26. *The Hidden Woman*	295
27. *My Lord and My lord*	309
28. *Motherhood: The Highest Place of Honor*	325
29. *Where are the Men*	333
30. *Happy Radiant Wives*	345
31. *The Spirit of Law and the Spirit of Grace*	359
32. *Youth: Anointed Disciples of Jesus Christ*	369
33. *Joining the Next Generation*	385
34. *Eternal Tragedy: Offending the Little Ones*	395
35. *Fighting For the Next Generation*	405
36. *Revival and Godly Homes*	413
Bibliography	425

About the Author

Denny Kenaston has been preaching on the home and child training for twenty-two years. God has used his tape series, The Godly Home, to challenge and transform homes all over America in every major denomination. Tens of thousands of this set have been distributed over the last 15 years.

He and his wife Jackie have eight children. Five of them are at home yet, and the other three are married, and out serving God on the mission fields of the world.

Denny is a graduate of Hyles Anderson College, in Crown Point, Indiana, a Baptist Bible College.

In 1982, he became founding Pastor of Charity Christian Fellowship in Leola, Pennsylvania.

In 1987, God stepped down from heaven and visited the church with revival fires. From those glory filled days, the influence of the church has grown to national and international levels. You can see more about the ministry of the church on the back pages of this book. Brother Denny's burden for godly homes grew out of many years of pastoral experiences. Today, he continues to serve as an elder in this church and preaches there regularly. He is also traveling in revival ministry, and church planting work.

About the Family

The children continue to grow, marry, and go out from us to serve God and their generation. This leaves Mama and I with only five at home. Samuel is twenty-one, Hannah is sixteen, Esther is fourteen, Joshua is eleven, and David is eight. We live in Lancaster County Pennsylvania, where we continue to prepare these last five arrows. We live joyfully on a 15 acre farm. We have lots of homeschooling opportunities in this rural setting. Lots of "unit studies." Anything from butchering a cow, to managing a business, to publishing a book, even cleaning the manure out of the barn. Pray for us, there are many adversaries, but God's grace is absolutely always all sufficient.

I have inserted pictures and an explanation of what the older three children are doing in chapter 32.

Come visit us any Sunday morning. Services start at 9:00 AM.

Charity Christian Fellowship
59 S. Groffdale Rd. • Leola PA, 17540
Call (717) 656-4155 for details

Acknowledgements

I thank God for my dear parents who cared for me during my growing up years. I didn't always make their job an easy one I know. I especially treasure the adult friendship my father and I have developed in our latter years.

My precious wife Jackie gave support and counsel all the way through the book, while my sweet daughters, Hannah and Esther, willingly lent their eyes and fingers to many a task. My sons, Samuel, Joshua, and David carried the load in the shop for me and all of them bore the sacrifice of time without their Papa. I thank my married children for how they bless me from afar.

My Uncle Don and Aunt Pearl led me to Christ and discipled me the first year of my Christian life; the late Jack Hyles provided inspirational influence in evangelism; Bill Gothard, taught clear simple teachings on family order; Lou and Ralph Sutera, and the late Leonard Ravenhill, emphasized revival. I also owe a special debt to Mose Stoltzfus for his friendship and counsel over the last twenty-one years of ministry together.

As the busyness of ministry threatened to overwhelm me, these men met specific needs in my life: Gerhard DuToit, by praying for me and inspiring me to pray, also by keeping me accountable; Keith Daniel, by living and lifting up an example of consistent Bible reading and devotional life; and Zac Poonen, for his friendship and clear instructions on the difference between the Old and New Covenants. Lastly, I want to give credit to the late Andrew Murray whose writings have been my mentors in the truths of the deeper Christian life.

I am indebted to many faithful servants who have contributed their time, talents, and encouragements into this endeavor. I cannot possibly list them all, but will highlight a few of the major ones: My church family at Charity Christian Fellowship, Robert and Kitty Stills, the entire John Weaver and David Mong families, Sheree Hostetter, Amy Smoker, John D. Martin, Harold Herr, Jason and Rebekah Mohler, Carl and Esther Swartzentruber, Dean Taylor, Eric Wenger, Roger Weaver, and Rachel Metzler.

Meditations

Press On

*For those whose lives are linked to thee.
Whose hearts seek e'er true faith to see.
For all who'd stumble if you should fall.
Stay faithful to the upward call.*

*When fears assail to turn thee back
When courage you most sorely lack.
Look onward, upward to thy King.
And from that glance thy heart can sing.*

*Be pressing onward for their sake.
And from thy God thy courage take.
For though thy struggles weigh thee down.
Thy perseverance wins thy crown.*

*So be found faithful for those you love;
Keep fixed thy heart on God above;
And ne'er look back tho' the night be long.
But look to Christ and still press on!*

Shelly Hendry 2002

Introduction

That He might seek a godly seed.
                                    Malachi 2:15

As I sit down to write an introduction for this book several thoughts pass through my mind. I think of the hundreds of times I have prayed about writing this book, and now, here I am, sitting in front of the keyboard, beginning to type. I do not know of anything I have prayed more about except my own family. I have received many requests to take the material from the *Godly Home* tape series and put it in print. I appreciate each request, for they have forced me to keep praying about it.

You might ask, "Why so much prayer?"

A few reasons come to my mind. First, I do not want to make a mistake and just write another book on the home. There are already many books on the home, and I do not want to add one more book to the list unless God is in it. The second reason I prayed so much is simple: I do not know how to write a book. Each time I thought about starting, I remembered my lack of knowledge. How do you write a book? So, as I begin, I move ahead with much trembling. I beg your patience with me as you read, for I am a beginner. In addition, I often felt it was not time to write a book on the home yet, because I needed some more years of experience. I remember the words of one of my heroes, Leonard Ravenhill. He said, "Don't write a book until you are older than fifty, or you will probably regret some of what you wrote and have to go back and change it." These were guiding words for this novice, and I have reflected on them many times. The last reason I have prayed much about this book is that I myself have lots of room to grow in the many areas of home life and child training. Who am I, writing a book about raising godly children? Nevertheless, alas, God has the last word, and I simply obey.

As I am pressing quickly toward the fifty-five age mark in my pilgrimage here on earth, it seems like the proper time. Three of our eight children are married now, and they are having their own children ("Oh glory!", say Grandma and Grandpa Kenaston). Rebekah, our first-born, is twenty-seven, and David, our last-born so far, is eight. This gives me a wide range of experiences to draw from, and a unique perspective. I can write as an older man, and yet Jackie and I are still very much involved in the whole process of child training. I am not just dreaming dreams as a young man does and should, but I now know by experience that these things work.

The title of this book, *The Pursuit of Godly Seed*, expresses the burden I carry for the homes of this our land, and for homes all over the world. God is brooding over our homes with jealousy. He is seeking a godly seed as it says in Malachi 2:15, and nobody seeks more diligently than God does. I enter into that burden and desire to labor together with Him for precious godly children, children who will rise up, love Him, and serve Him with all their hearts.

I reference (Mal. 4:5-6) often as we move through the many aspects of child training. Many applications flow from the truths revealed in these verses. The Spirit of God is moving on the hearts of fathers, mothers, and children alike in these last days. There is a mysterious work of God taking place in multitudes of homes. All across America and the world God is literally causing men everywhere to repent of their unscriptural focus on other things, and turning their hearts to see the family as He sees it. This is the burden of this book. I join my heart with God's heart in calling homes back to His beautiful order and the blessing He intended them to be.

Introduction

Our Confession

My precious wife, Jackie, and I were converted out of the hippy culture in the early 1970's. We started our Christian home with limited knowledge. The truths I share in the pages of this book, we have learned out of much failure. We took our failures to God and to His Word and began to meditate. We looked at the needs in our home and began to cry out to God for answers. "Lord, why are the children this way, and what can we do about it?" We brought many questions to God in faith, searching the Scriptures for insights, and God gave clear answers for our home.

This process of meditation and application is the most effectual way to find answers. Every one of you can do the same thing. I encourage you to keep track of all the scriptures covered in this child-training manual and chew on them for months and months to come. If you do this, God will transform your heart and your home.

I want to say again, we are sharing out of failure, not out of success. Do not think that there is no hope for you. Jackie and I did not have a very good start. As we look back at our heritage, neither one of us had clear patterns to follow in our homes. I did not know how to be a Christian husband; Jackie did not know how to be a Christian wife; and neither one of us knew how to raise children! Therefore, there is hope for you.

I close this introduction with an experience I had in Africa that I will never forget. It illustrates the cry of a parent's heart in every culture of this world. Humanity is looking for answers to the problems in their closest relationships, that is their marriage and their experience with their children.

I visited a large village in West Africa about six years ago with others from our church. The purpose for our visit to this village was to explore the possibilities of planting a mission there. I wish I could personally take each one of you to a village like this because I know it would change your life forever. I know I cannot do this, so I will try to take you there with these words.

In many African villages the tribal chief is still the man in authority. Although there has been much progress in Africa, still much of the government of the people is by chiefs, just as in the old days. When you go to visit a village you must always get permission from the Chief. My unforgettable experience flows from this African order of government.

It was a hot January day when we arrived in the village where we hoped to plant a church. We made our request to talk with the Chief, and were waiting under a shaded area for his ascent to his throne. This Chief had fifteen wives and sixty children. That's right. I didn't make a mistake in typing. As the Chief came out of his palace of mud and grass, dressed in his royal robes, everyone began to bow. He took his seat in the shade on his throne and looked our way for a spokesman to present the group and explain why we were there. I was the oldest one there, so I stepped forward. I wasn't feeling very bold at the time, but we were there on a greater King's business, so I knelt down near his throne and began to talk. I explained to him that we wanted to start a church in his village. He was very pleased and promised to give us land when we arrived.

At this time, I introduced the rest of the party to him. Three of my children were in Africa at the time. I explained to him that these were my children, and that I had five more at home.

He exclaimed in surprise, "From one wife?"

I smiled and nodded my head.

He then turned his head and began to look at the children intently. Turning back to me, he said with a puzzled look on his face, "Your children, they follow your ways." He paused for a moment, and I could tell he was thinking. Then he looked at my children again and said, "My children are rebellious. They won't do what I say."

The look on his face spoke volumes to me. His heart was saying, "How do you get them to follow your ways? How do you get them to leave the comforts of America and come over here to Africa? It is hot, it is full of malaria, it has all kinds of discomforts, and yet they are here."

I'm sure he had no idea how long I could talk to him on that subject.

His words ring in the ears of my heart repeatedly, "Your children, they follow your ways."

Introduction

God says in His Word, *"Train up a child in the way he should go."* He has given us ways and means to bring this to pass. These treasures of wisdom lie hidden in His Word. As parents, we can go mine them out and use them, and the children will follow our ways, which are God's ways.

In the pages of this book, I try to answer the Chief's questioning heart. "How do you get your children to follow your ways?" Maybe you have a heart that is longing for answers to the same question.

This is a long book, thirty-six chapters. I have not written a book that you can sit down and read in one sitting. It is more like a manual that you can refer to repeatedly. I present it in Jesus Christ's name. Come, let us reason together about our homes and our many responsibilities. I offer this simple prayer at the presentation of this book.

Prayer

Oh Father in heaven, here we are before You. You know us all so very well. You know the state of our different homes, and You know what we need. In Jesus Christ's name, open the understanding of our hearts. Let us begin to see our homes the way You do, even if that is painful. Renew our vision, engage our wills, and empower us to obey whatever the cost. Create in us a desire to change, and give us the grace to do it. In Jesus Christ's name. Amen.

Brother Denny

Meditations

I never cease to be in awe as I gaze into the open face of an innocent child. When God gives them to us, they come as a blank sheet of paper, clean, pure, and waiting to be inscribed upon. They trust us, open themselves up to us, and receive whatever we give them, whether it be good or bad. Lord, teach us how to guide and train them.

1

The Holy Art of Training Children

That our sons may be as plants grown up in their youth;
that our daughters may be as cornerstones,
polished after the similitude of a palace.

Psalm 144:12

Watch the artist with his paintbrush in hand. Watch him as he creates a beautiful painting that captivates and motivates those who gaze upon it. He moves with order and purpose, each stroke of his brush creating more of the scene he desires to display. Now look deeper into the heart of this man, this artist, and you will find that he has more in mind than a picture. He is trying to say something. He is attempting to express some deep thought of his heart. As we watch him paint, he makes painting look very simple. The colors flow together to show one image after another, until we look with wonder on the finished extension of the artist's heart and hands. You might stop and ask him the question he has often heard, "How did you learn to do that?" We all know what he would say. "It is a gift, an ability that God gave me, but it is a gift I had to develop."

This illustration explains the title of this first chapter very well. The artist's answer to the oft-asked question is a clear revelation of the art of raising children. It is an ability given to us by a loving God, but we must learn to develop this gift.

There are several reasons why I have chosen the words "holy art" to illustrate child training. Child training:

> **A Holy Art**--because we find in the Bible a revelation of sanctified principles that, if followed, all work together to form a beautiful soul filled with Christlike character.
> **A Holy Art**--because these principles are disciplines for the parents, not for the children. They are rigorous at times, but if we will follow them, we will find ourselves becoming proficient in them.
> **A Holy Art**--because the subject of child training is a subject that must be studied, learned, practiced, and mastered. Oh the joyful results that come as we learn the nuts and bolts of everyday nurturing.
> **A Holy Art**--because many go about it in a very haphazard way. It is a sort of hit and miss thing to them, here a little, there a little, and of course, they get the same kind of results.
> **A Holy Art**--because we need to lift these principles up out of the commonplace, where many have laid them, and set them in the realms of the holy again.

Let us pause for a moment of reflection on the definition of the word "art," and see how much encouragement we can draw from it for our homes. A dictionary definition of this word can be summed up as follows.

Art: A skill that is attained by study, practice, and observation. A system of principles and methods employed in the creation of some form of beauty.

My, what a lovely definition of training children. Again, consider the artist and his marvelous ability to create on canvas what he sees and feels in his heart. It is a natural talent given by God the creator. There probably was a point in time when he realized "I have an ability to draw." Maybe at first his parents or a teacher made him aware of the gift. Like most of us, he probably didn't agree with them at first. Once this realization was clear to him, he began to practice. He spent extra time studying the art of drawing and painting. He started observing pictures with a new interest. Trips to the art museum and books on how to draw were his delight. When he had a chance to watch a mature artist draw a picture, he was right there with open eyes and many questions. This is an excellent analogy for our subject at hand. This is a perfect way to approach the following chapters in this book. You must have the spirit of a learner.

God has given you an ability. You may question these words as the young unknown artist did but stay with me a while yet. I know we have to deal with the fall of man in the Garden of Eden. However, remember, we are looking at this ability through the glasses of our "so great salvation."

Come reason with me for a moment. From what you know of our great God, would He give us children and then not provide a way for us to train them? In all of His Creation, we see that He has given each animal the instinctive ability to care for and train its young. Well, what about us?

Yes, I know and I agree that man is a fallen being because of sin. A separation from God took place. The creature is not what he used to be. Sin and failure are the normal way for a man on this earth now. *"But God, who is rich in mercy, for his great love wherewith he loved us"* (Eph. 2:4). This God *"Commendeth his love toward us, in that, while we were yet sinners, Christ died for us"* (Rom. 5:8). There is a way that man can be salvaged, praise God! There is a way for man to train the next generation of children. We have a salvation presented to us in the Holy Bible that provides a way to be saved, delivered, justified, sanctified, and many other such things.

Maybe you feel that your home is in need of a salvage job. God can do it, for He is in the salvage business. That transformation may begin with a change in your own heart called the "new birth."

On the other hand, maybe you have lost the reality of the grace of God that is in Christ Jesus our Lord. God has the answers to the needs of your home. We simply need to get under His blessings, and the rest will come.

If you are a child of God, washed in the blood, set apart unto God, He has given you an ability to raise your children in the nurture and admonition of the Lord. That ability is there, even though

The Pursuit of Godly Seed

it may be lying dormant, needing an awakening. Will you allow me to be the teacher who comes alongside the student and joins in with your heavenly Father to say, "The ability is there?" It is there. I know it is. It needs only to be stimulated and motivated. Just like the artist, who set his heart to learn all he could, you need to rise up and develop it. Turn the focus of your heart toward your precious children, and begin to study, learn, and observe how you can train them to the glory of God.

I have already referred to God's heart for our children which was spoken by the prophet Malachi. God is seeking a godly seed. This is the deep longing of His heart and a major theme of revelation in the Scriptures. He is pursuing godly children for Himself. He is intensely interested in your child. You can't go wrong if you turn your attention to something that is very near to God's heart.

As I see it, we are to co-labor with God in the rearing of little ones and big ones. We are not alone. We have not been left without an instruction manual. We are not without a teacher in this awesome task. What an exciting prospect, working together with the glorious, omnipotent, all-wise God of heaven to raise my children.

Are you listening? You have a gift. Open your heart and believe. Let us step into the water and see if the Jordan River parts. It will. I know it will.

Prayer

Heavenly Father, we come to You in Jesus Christ's name. You know that many feel undone right now as they read these words. We doubt, Lord, we doubt. Please forgive us, help our unbelief. Father, we do accept Your word as truth, and we choose to believe the many promises written about our children. Sit with us Lord as we read the pages of this book, and be our Teacher, Comforter, and Guide. We need Your divine help, for we do not know how to do all of this. In Jesus Christ's name. Amen.

2

Clear Conversion

If any man be in Christ, he is a new creature: old things are passed away; behold all things are become new.
II Corinthians 5:17

First things first, Amen? As we begin to examine the subject of a godly home and the children that come forth from it, it is good to remember an old American proverb, "Don't put the cart before the horse." Although the picture represented by these words is rather odd, the reality of them happens all the time in many areas of life.

To set out on a journey to raise our children for the Lord Jesus Christ without knowing Him, without having a vital relationship with Him, is to place the cart ahead of the horse. We won't get very far. Many parents are in this very frustrating position, wondering why they are having so many problems getting it all together.

Recently, I was working with a couple who were at their wits' end in their home. I share more about them later, but they were trying to have a godly home without God. Oh, they thought they were all right until they stopped to examine themselves honestly. Their conclusion? "We have never been born again." What a staggering thought. Could this be your case?

The Pursuit of Godly Seed

Now I know that I need to tread softly on this subject, but I feel urgently that it is a place where we must tread. I know that most who read this book are true, sincere Christians. However, as we consider the mixture in Christianity today, we dare not pass over it.

Many look back on their "conversion" with uncertainty. You may be one of them. As a youth you may have attended a meeting in which the preacher said, "If you want to be saved please stand up." You stood to your feet, and then sat down again. Everyone rejoiced with you and told you that you were now saved. Please don't misunderstand me. There are many different ways that God can save us. I know a man who was under such conviction that when he stood to his feet in a meeting, his whole life was forever changed. But many others stood and nothing changed. Let us examine ourselves.

We come from many different backgrounds. Maybe you responded to an altar call and went forward. A counselor met you and asked you if you wanted to be saved, and you said "yes." He showed you a few verses and led you to pray a prayer, and you did. He may even have told you what to pray. Everyone was happy for you, and you even felt good about it. But as you look back over the years, alas very little changed in your life. This is the concern that I have. We must have a right foundation to begin our godly home. Jesus Christ Himself is the foundation of a true Christian life.

Maybe you are one of those who heard a sermon on hell when you were 5 or 6 years old. You were afraid, and didn't want to go there. No child wants to go to hell. You responded, and the worker asked you if you wanted to go to heaven when you die. Well yes, of course you did. He asked you if you knew that you were a sinner. You knew you were because of your failings at home. Then he said, "Just ask Jesus to come into your heart." You did, and everyone was happy for you. However, as the years go by, and you look at your life, you have a sense of uncertainty because there was very little change. Multitudes of religious people joined the church through baptism in their youth, but there never was a change in their heart.

Clear Conversion

Many people who claim to be Christians today have these kinds of salvation experiences, but show very little fruit in their lives. This is not the salvation revealed in the Bible. According to the Bible, nothing short of a personal encounter with Jesus Christ will do. Paul challenged the Corinthian church with words that are fitting for today's Christian, *"Examine yourselves, whether ye be in the faith; prove your own selves"* (II Cor. 13:5). We live in an age when many are trying to live the Christian life without Christ. This is impossible. In fact, what a burden life must be trying to make all these home responsibilities work without Him who makes His commandments a joy.

These words may apply to only a few people. Nevertheless, it is good groundwork for all of us if we are going to get back to the basics. How can we ever expect to enter into one of the most holy, awesome tasks this side of glory, which is raising godly children for the Lord, without Him who gives us grace? How could we enter into this work without a vibrant relationship with Jesus Christ? Some parents attempt to do it, but they stumble along. They hear some tapes, they go to a seminar, and they apply some of what they learn. When they get home, they make some changes. These changes do affect their home. All this is good for the children, but deep down at the bottom of the whole thing, it is just not going very well.

Some time ago, I was preaching at some meetings in a distant state. It was quite an interesting combination of meetings. Revival, missions, and the home were the three subjects. The couple I mentioned earlier came to the meetings to get their home straightened out. Earlier, they had listened to the *Godly Home* tapes. They were really encouraged by them, but things were not going well at home. So they thought, "We are going to these meetings, and we will surely get our home straightened out."

Each day of these meetings there was a session on the home, with a revival message every evening. The brother preaching the revival message at that time was led by God to preach a salvation message. In his message, he spoke about the false, phony, and sometimes weak conversions in America. At the end of the message, the wife came to the altar weeping. When her husband saw that she was weeping, he didn't know what was wrong, but he fol-

The Pursuit of Godly Seed

lowed her and knelt beside her. He thought, "Something is very wrong with my wife, and I'm going to stay with her."

In the prayer room, the leader asked, "Is there anybody here who is not sure if he or she is born again?" The wife's hand went up quickly, and her husband just looked on in shock. I happened to be the next counselor in line, and we ended up together. We found a room and started talking and sharing.

She broke down weeping and said, "It doesn't work. I'm tired of trying. I'm tired of pumping myself up." She went on, "I'm tired of dead devotions. I'm tired of praying and nothing ever happens. The whole thing just doesn't work. I'm not born again."

She spoke these words in utter despair, and I could see a burden of hypocrisy roll off her back, as she finally got honest and shared the long-standing feelings of her heart.

Her husband said, "Honey, don't you remember that you've been baptized, and don't you remember that seminar we went to and the leader had us pray this prayer and you prayed it?" He tried to console her and make her feel better.

Then she talked again, and pretty soon this thing just came gushing back out of her heart, "I've got to get this thing settled."

We went back and forth like this for a little while, and finally I just said to the husband, "Friend, I think your wife needs to get born again. Could you trust me and wait, and maybe we can talk about it later?"

"Okay, okay," he said, "I'll stay out of the way."

I began to deal with her. I asked, "Do you feel you need to be born again?"

Her answer was a deep-felt "yes."

Then I asked her, "Are you willing to sell out to the Lord, to play no more games?"

"Oh, I'm willing," she said. "What must I do to be saved?"

She got down on her knees and I began to give her a little guidance. I said, "First of all, I want you to confess your sins. Don't just tell God you're a sinner. You lay it out to God. Tell Him the condition of your life, the condition of your heart. Go back into your past. Tell Him the things that you have covered and don't want anybody ever to know."

Clear Conversion

She was so ripe and ready. She just broke her heart and began to clear her conscience, confessing one thing after another. She wept. She prayed and confessed, repenting and asking God to forgive her.

This dear lady went on like this for awhile, and then it got quiet. I said, "Is everything clear in your heart?" With a sigh of relief, she acknowledged that she felt clear at last.

As she was there on her face before God, I told her, "Now with your eyes shut, I want you to picture the Lord Jesus right now, hanging on the cross. Do you see Him there on the cross?"

She just started weeping, praise God. She had such a tender heart. What a beautiful time to look at the cross! Amen?

I said, "Now you call upon the Lord. Cry out to the Lord Jesus and ask Him to save you. Ask Him to wash away all those sins in His precious blood."

I didn't have to tell her anything. She just took off and prayed out of her heart, calling upon the Lord to save her and cleanse her.

When she was finished, I asked her, "Well, did the Lord save you?"

Her answer flowed out with joy, "Oh, He did, yes He did!"

I encouraged her to thank God for what He had just done in her heart.

She overflowed, "Lord, oh Lord, thank you for saving my soul."

She cried some more and praised the Lord as the joy bells began to ring in her heart.

Then I said, "Oh, that's beautiful. But you are not done yet. I want you to stay on your face just a little bit longer." I told her to sell out her life to the Lord Jesus right now. "It is our reasonable service, isn't it?" I asked. I said, "Give Him everything. Don't hold back anything. Tell Him you will go wherever He wants you to go, and do anything He wants you to do. Just lay it all on the altar." That's all I said, and she went back to prayer. This dear lady laid it all on the altar, playing no games. And then it got quiet again.

Then I said, "Alright, I want you to pray one more prayer." We went to Luke 11:13 where Jesus taught His disciples to pray. He said this to them, *"If ye then being evil, know how to give good gifts unto your children, how much more shall your heavenly Father give the*

Holy Spirit to them that ask him." I gave her this verse and said, "Now, I want you to ask your new Father for the Holy Spirit, because you can't do this thing on your own."

Oh, she was a very willing student, and quickly began to plead with God. It was not hard to get her to pray this prayer from her heart because she had been trying to do it on her own for a long time.

She prayed, "Lord, I can't do this. Please Lord, fill me with Your Spirit and give me a power other than what I have in myself." She prayed a sweet prayer like this for a few moments; then I laid my hands on her head, prayed the same prayer for her, and we were done.

I wish you could have seen her when we got up off of our knees. She was glowing. There was a radiance on her face and a joy that could not be hid. It was so sweet! Now, not every conversion is like this one, so don't get under condemnation if you did not have an experience like this sister. I chose this one so all can see just how salvation is supposed to work. It was beautiful. Her heart was full of joy. Her face expressed the reality of a clean new heart.

The prophet Ezekiel describes what happened to this dear lady in very graphic terms. In his description, God is promising future days of blessings for captive Israel. However, the prophecy also defines the promises of a changed life through the gospel. This is the nature of the prophetic word. Consider the prophet's descriptive words.

> *Then will I sprinkle clean water upon you, and ye shall be clean: from all your filthiness, and from all your idols, will I cleanse you. A new heart also will I give you, and a new spirit will I put within you: and I will take away the stony heart out of your flesh, and I will give you a heart of flesh. And I will put My Spirit within you, and cause you to walk in My statutes, and ye shall keep My judgments, and do them.*
>
> *Ezekiel 36:25-28*

God's word is very clear here. Salvation is a new heart, not just a reformation of the old. It is a regeneration, which literally means, a re-genesis. To try to live the Christian life without a new heart, is despairing. That is what this dear sister was trying to do.

As we stood there rejoicing together, I suddenly remembered her husband, and I looked over at him. He was not very happy. I gave him the opportunity to speak, and do you know what he said?

He said, "Brother Denny, I want to do that." He looked indignant as he continued. "They cheated me. Nobody ever told me these things. Nobody ever showed me how to do that. I want to do what my wife did." He wanted the opportunity to get thoroughly right with God.

I told him he should wait and spend the day pondering what he should do before the Lord. I encouraged him to respond at the altar call the next night if he still felt he needed to get right with God. We had a prayer for him and sent them home.

The next night, he was the first one down at the altar and he came through just like his dear wife did. Praise the Lord for His goodness unto the children of men. This is the testimony they gave on Sunday morning, "We came to these meetings because we wanted to put our home together. But now, we realize we had never been born again. How could we ever put our home back together if we were not born again? Now, we are ready to go home and bring order to our family."

Brothers and sisters, this is where your godly home must begin, with a clear conversion. You may say, "I didn't have a conversion like that." Well, many have not had a conversion like I have just described. I didn't. I wish someone had worked with me in this manner 30 years ago. It would have saved me from many struggles in my Christian life. Yet, God has been faithful to bring me to the same place as this sister: a total abandonment to God, holding nothing back.

Let us reason together for a moment. You may not have had an experience like this one to look back on. However, it is imperative that you have a clearing and a surrender like this in your own life. This is what you need if you want to embark on this journey of raising godly children. You need what this dear sister had when she got up off her knees. You need that beautiful, joyful, clearing and yielding of the heart to God. You do need that. You must have it. You need the blessing that comes on a life when that happens. It is not going to go well with you if you don't put first things first. This is the place where we must begin: either with a clear conversion in which you are born again by the Spirit of God, or with an old fashioned revival in your cold heart whereby heaven is open over you again.

As we conclude this chapter, let us reason together a bit more. God says, *"Except the Lord build the house, they labor in vain that build it"* (Ps. 127:1a). God is not talking about a literal building. He is talking about our households, our families. If we are not going to get right with God and stay right, yielding to Him continually, then He will not be able to help us build our families. We are destined for failure. This way will only lead to frustration and discouragement. There are many things in the following chapters that could change your home forever. However, if you do not come to grips with the truths in this chapter, you will find it hard to implement them. God has us in the corner. We want a godly family, and this is good. But we must do it God's way. He wrote the manual, and He doesn't budge, nor should He. He is the Lord, the Lord God Almighty.

Meditate on the life of Noah. He is a perfect example of what I am saying in this chapter. The Bible says some amazing things about this man and his household in Hebrews 11:7 *"By faith, Noah...prepared an ark to the saving of his house."* But how did he save his house? Did he force his family into the ark, or use some other means to convince them to get in? We know it was not that way. They willingly walked into that ark with the same desire Noah and his wife had. God's word is clear how this happened. *"Noah found grace in the eyes of the Lord"* (Gen. 6:8). Also, *"Noah was a just man and perfect in his generations, and Noah walked with God"* (Gen. 6:9). Because Noah was in the faith, he was able to bring his family into the faith. The blessings of his faith fell on the next generation, and they chose to walk into the ark on the day of judgment. God was able to say to Noah, *"Come thou and all thy house into the ark, for thee have I seen righteous before me in this generation"* (Gen. 7:1). It will be the same for each one of us parents.

Have you been born again by the Spirit of God? Do you have the witness of the Spirit in your heart, which says you are a child of God, adopted into His family? Is there victory in your personal life? Is God a living reality to you? These are the marks of a true Christian. You may think I am getting a bit too personal with these pointed questions. However, I must be frank. These issues are even more important than your family. If you are feeling uneasy as you read these words, let me give you some good counsel. Set the book down and fall upon your knees. Call upon the Lord with a sincere heart and ask Him, "Have I been born again, transformed by the power of Christ?" Pray the prayer that I have written below with an earnest open heart. Then wait before Him in silence for a few minutes and listen. The Father in Heaven loves you, and He will faithfully show you how you stand with Him. If you are not born again, all you need to do is cry out to God in the same manner as the couple mentioned in this chapter. God will save you. He promised that He would, *"Whosoever shall call upon the name of the Lord shall be saved"* (Rom. 10:13).

Prayer

Dear Heavenly Father, we come to You in Jesus Christ's name. Please open our eyes, and help us settle this very important matter. We want to be in the place where we can truly love You with all of our heart. We live in a very mixed up, gray Christianity. Clear away the fog upon our hearts. How do we stand with You? Send conviction, Lord, where it is needed right now, for the sake of our children who suffer for our lack of reality. In the worthy name of the Son of God. Amen.

Meditations

The Eternal Value of a Child

*Empires fall, houses crumble.
Cattle die, and machinery rusts away.
But a **Child** lives on and on*

*In the lives of its descendants
And in the lives of those he influences.
All the way into eternity*

3

The Eternal Value of a Child

*Lo, children are an heritage of the Lord:
and the fruit of the womb is his reward.
As arrows are in the hand of a mighty man;
so are children of the youth.
Happy is the man that hath his quiver full of them.*
Psalm 127:3,4,5a

What is the value of a child? Surely this is a major foundation stone in the house we want to build. The structure will rise or fall, stand firm or crumble, according to our answer to this question. As we move out of the introductory chapters, and into the main body of our subject, I want to spend some time on our vision. A vision is that which we see with the eyes of our heart.

The opening text above states that children are a heritage from the Lord. They are an inheritance from God, something left behind to bless us, to remind us of His love. As an heirloom reminds us of the one who gave it, so also God causes us to think about Him every time we look at our child. God made man in His own image, after His very likeness, so each gift of a child is a deposit of Himself, entrusted to us. How we view our children will affect every area of their lives, yea, and every area of our lives. God must enlighten the eyes of our hearts to see the awesome value of these eternal beings.

The Pursuit of Godly Seed

Some years ago, I was in a home having some fellowship and a meal, and I noticed a plaque on the wall that arrested my attention. The words on the plaque spoke deeply to my heart. I wrote them down so I could remember them. I have placed them opposite the title page for this chapter, so you can meditate on them.

A child lives on and on and on and on in the lives of his descendants, and in those he influences. What awesome words we have here! Stop for a moment and let them sink in a bit. Speak them out loud to yourself, slowly, and meditatively. I have been so challenged by these words. Where would you place your children if you were to write a priority list? Are they at the top of the list, or are they in the middle somewhere with some other things up at the top?

Fearfully and Wonderfully Made

What is the value of a child --just one-- just one precious little one? Who can measure it? I cannot, for I know not what God will do with this child. I cannot see into God's heart to know what His plan and purpose is for the child. One thing I can do. I can look into the pages of the Word of God, and find God's heart breathing in it. If we meditate on the value of a child from God's perspective, we see that He has placed a very high value on each one of them. My mind moves toward the verses in Psalm 139:13-18.

> *For thou hast possessed my reins: thou hast covered me in my mother's womb. I will praise thee; for I am fearfully and wonderfully made: marvellous are thy works; and that my soul knoweth right well. My substance was not hid from thee, when I was made in secret, and curiously wrought in the lowest parts of the earth. Thine eyes did see my substance, yet being unperfect; and in thy book, all my members were written, which in continuance were fashioned, when yet there was none of them. How precious also are thy thoughts unto me, Oh God, how great is the sum of them!*

These verses take us into the throne room of heaven, where plans and purposes burst forth from the mind of God. Picture the living

The Eternal Value of a Child

God, the God of the whole Universe who rules all things from His throne, forming your child in detail while he is yet in the womb, and planning it all before the foundation of the world. If my child is, in fact, fearfully and wonderfully made by Elohim (God Creator), then He surely has a purpose for him, a holy purpose, one that demands my utmost care and attention.

If we could get a glimpse, prophetically, of what God wants to do through our children, we would begin to see their value and act accordingly. Only God can help us see all this.

Susanna Wesley is an example to us. She was inflamed with a vision of the value of her children. God inspired her to raise a different kind of child. She was moved by the precepts she saw in the Bible, and by faith, she raised them for the glory of God.

What was the value of Abraham and Sarah's little baby boy? They had a prophetic word, and a promise from God, concerning him. Imagine the awesome joy at his miraculous birth. Yet even then, they had no idea about the magnitude of his influence.

Our levels of value vary. When a baby is born from a womb that has been barren a long time, you can see the value of that precious baby in the eyes of the parents as they hold their little one for the first time. They have waited a long time. They behold their gift, their reward from the Lord, with reverence and wonder. It seems that God often withholds a child to raise the level of value in the parents. I have meditated on the examples of barren parents in the Bible. Consider my musings:

- ❖ Abraham and Sarah waited 40 years for Isaac.
- ❖ Isaac and Rebekah waited 20 years for Jacob.
- ❖ Jacob and Rachel waited 20 years for Joseph.
- ❖ Manoah and his wife waited years for Samson.
- ❖ Ruth waited for 12 years before Obed was born.
- ❖ Hannah waited for years before Samuel was born.
- ❖ Zacharias and Elisabeth waited 50 years for John the Baptist.

Look at the beauty and wisdom of God in each of these examples. The withholding of children became days of preparation in the hearts of the parents. As the years went by, the value of a child rose higher and higher. In all this, we can see God training the parents to receive a child with reverence. With this high and holy view, the parents train the child for a special purpose in God's kingdom. It is beautiful to behold the wisdom of God working in these parents.

When we consider the New Testament context of God's work, the preaching of the Gospel, the white harvest fields, and the shortage of laborers, surely there is a work to do for every one of our children. If God had ten thousand John Wesleys, He would lay His hand upon each one of them and use them to shake a people for His name. However, before He can find all these usable servants, He needs ten thousand parents who will live by faith and raise their children with holy purposes in mind. How we view our children will affect what we do with the rest of this book.

We can see this concept of high value even in the natural order of human life. When a king has a son who is going to be the heir of the throne, that king puts a high priority on the training of his son. He is the son of the king, and everyone assumes that he will get special care in his rearing. What about our children? They are the sons and daughters of the King of kings.

Your First Love

Let me take you on a journey back into your past for a few moments. Remember how it was when your first child was born. Pause for a few moments and let your mind drift back there. Think about those first few days with your first child. You were in awe. It staggered your emotions as you held that little image of you in your arms or nursed it at your side. Remember how you felt.

I can quickly recall the memories of our first child, and all the rest of them for that matter. Jackie and I said to each other with joy, "This is our baby. She looks like us, bone of our bones and flesh of our flesh, a gift from God." We sat there overwhelmed with the responsibility of caring for this child entrusted to us. We were in our "first love" experience, as parents, and emotions ran high. I am sure you had a similar experience.

Let me explain what I mean when I use the phrase "first love." We all understand the principle of first love, taught in the Bible.

God uses the phrase as He pleads with the church at Ephesus in Revelation 2:4-7. He said to them, *"Thou hast left thy first love."* God was reminding them of the sweet love they had for Him in the early days of their church. You can read about it in Acts 19. The first love is the foundation stone on which a lifetime of love for God is built. It grows, deepens, and matures through the years.

This principle also applies to the commitment of marriage. We all remember our wedding day, and the glorious days of courtship before the wedding. That first love experience wrought lifelong vows that flowed from our hearts. We are supposed to build on top of that foundation all our days of marriage.

It is the same with the birth of each one of our children. Have we lost our first love for the children? Many times we start out right, but then other things distract us. Six of our eight children were born at home, which is a wonderful, deeply moving experience. With each birth, the Spirit of God drew near when the child came forth. Many midwives would agree with me that God is there in a special way when a child is born. I believe God sanctifies that sweet time of birth to bond parents and child together into a lifelong relationship of love. He does this so the parents will be moved to raise the children for Him. This relationship is the foundation stone upon which a powerful God-honoring life is built.

Revelations of Reality

Years ago I was sitting in the home of a dear brother and sister who had one little boy about three years old. They had invited me to their home so they could ask me a few questions about the training of their son. While we were sitting there making small talk, this little boy was all over the place. Some would say he was hyperactive. The dear mother would stop every few moments and try to get him to do better. You know how that is. "You have to behave now. Brother Denny is here."

Finally, the mother and the father broke down in frustration and said, "What do we do with our little boy? He is like this most of the time, and we are at our wits' end."

Well, I had already been studying the little fellow, and was praying about what I should say to them. God must have given me a word of wisdom, because I did not know what to ask them. I said to the mother, "How did you feel about your son when you were carrying him in the womb, and when he was born?" She looked at me with a stunned look on her face and said, "How did you know to ask that question." Then she began to cry.

Well it all came out. She was a spoiled child, and when she found out they were going to have a baby, in selfishness, she hated the child in her womb. All she could think of were the hardships that accompany the birth and growth of a child.

God changed a mother's heart that day through repentance, and the dear little boy's behavior started to change immediately. It is easy to see how this mother's view of the child was affecting her ability to train him. It also was affecting his response to his mother. The silent message was coming through loud and clear. His selfish heart was saying, "You will give me attention, even if I have to bounce off the walls to get it." I tremble to think what might have happened to this child if his mother had not found a place of clearing. Many children grow up with parental attitudes of rejection. These attitudes create confusion in the heart of a child. For some, these attitudes affect them way into their adult lives.

What Kind of Treasures

How do we value our children? On what line would they appear if we honestly wrote out a list of priorities? Perhaps we have swallowed some of the spirit of the age in which we live, and do not even know it. We all know that the world does not value their children very highly. They have many ways to "get them out of their hair," the worst being abortion.

I was meditating in the Sermon on the Mount about two years ago, reading it out loud, slowly, every day for six months (very convicting).

One day, as I came to the verses on our treasures, the Spirit quickened my heart about my treasures. I thought aloud, "My children are my treasures." Rebekah was now married to Daryl, and they were serving in Africa. I found myself thinking more and more about the work in Africa, and many more prayers were going up to God. It all flowed together during my meditations that morning. I thought, "My children are my treasures; that is why I am thinking and praying more about Africa. *"Where your treasure is, there will your heart be also"* (Matt. 6:21). I have deposited some of my treasures in Africa, and my heart has gone there in a new and refreshing way."

I shared my thoughts with Jackie, and the light went on in her heart. She said, "It is true. My heart is there continually since Daryl and Rebekah left."

Four years have passed, and we have deposited some more of our treasures in other parts of the world. Daniel and his wife Christy are serving in Ghana, West Africa among the Konkomba tribe, and Andrew and Elisabeth are serving in Guyana, South America. We find our hearts running there continually. The grandchildren are starting to come, and so the treasures are becoming a large pile. Hallelujah! I know that this is an application, and not an interpretation of the Scriptures, because Jesus was clearly speaking of material possessions. However, He was also admonishing us to focus our time and attention on spiritual treasures, and the eternal souls of our children qualify.

We Americans have many treasures that we have laid up here on earth. I am afraid that our neglect of the children is the result of our wrong focus. Somehow, we think that we can serve God and materialism, but we have deceived ourselves. The fruit of our deception screams at us from every corner of American society.

Would you allow me to be a prophet with a little "p" for a few moments? Would you allow me to turn the searchlight on to our hearts and priorities? When I say allow, I mean, would you stop a moment and open up your heart to the Lord and listen?

Consider another application of Scripture found in Matthew 16:26. *"What shall it profit a man if he gains the whole world and loses the souls of his children, or what will a man give in exchange for the souls of his children?"* Dear brother and sister, this is happening throughout all the churches in our land. Christian parents are selling the souls of their children for "stuff." The stories of brokenhearted parents go on and on, as they see their children go out into the world, or settle down in some half-hearted profession of Christianity. I think it is time we examine our values.

The Pursuit of Godly Seed

Open Rebuke Is Better Than Secret Love

I will never forget the time I sat in a ministers' seminar hosted by Brother Bill Gothard. Two thousand pastors and servants gathered to hear the Word shared and applied on a ministerial level. Bill stood up in his typical way and began to ask us how many children we had. He said, "Raise your hand if you have one child." Then he went on up the scale until he found one man who had nine children. Most of the pastors in the room had two, and a few had three. We all clapped and cheered for the man who had nine, and it was a great time.

Then Bill turned the attention to the rest of us in the meeting. He made the point that most of the pastors had limited the size of their families for the sake of the ministry. It was very quiet. He then proceeded to tell us in his gentle way that we had the spirit of abortion. It was very very quiet. Then he went on to explain that we were part of the reason why abortion has taken such a toll in America. You could have heard a pin drop. As the Church goes, so goes the world was one of the principles he brought out.

He said, "You do not value children. You do not want any more children. You feel you have better things to do with your time than raise more children."

Many surgeries had taken place to stop the conception of children. Bill reproved us for this and challenged us to repent, to have a reversal surgery, and to ask God to open the womb again.

I do not know what all those pastors did with that session. I'm sure some of them wrote him off as a fanatic and maybe a legalist. I'm also sure that some of them did indeed repent, making changes in their homes and in their preaching. My heart unites with the burden of the Lord that Bill Gothard shared with us that day. There is a small movement of couples whose eyes have opened to see the priceless value of children. They are repenting, and going back to the doctor for reversal surgery. Oh how the joy bells ring when a child comes forth after the surgery. They call them reversal babies.

How we value our children will affect what we do with them, how we train them, and how much time we spend with them. Somehow, our great God needs to open the eyes of our understanding, so that we may comprehend the value of the treasures He has deposited into our care. A child is an eternal being, made in the image of God, after His likeness, and God wants to dwell in that wonderful child someday.

I remember when little David was born. He is eight now, our youngest. Our hearts were full of awe, joy, gratitude, and responsibility as we found ourselves in that holy atmosphere described earlier. I picked up my son and held him before the Lord, dedicating his life to God. As I was praying a prayer of consecration, and asking for the wisdom and grace to fulfill my promise, it dawned on me, "I will be sixty-six years old when I am finished with my commitment to God for this son": twenty more years of training another precious soul for the Lord, praise God. You may think that is a long time, but that is all right, for He (the Lord Jesus) is worthy of such a sacrifice. You see, we are raising a soldier for the King. Someday, the King will come to him and take possession of him, and work through him to do damage to Satan's kingdom.

Prayer

Our Father, which art in heaven, hallowed be Thy name. Yes, Lord, may Your name be hallowed by the children which Thou hast given us. Let Thy Kingdom come and Thy will be done in the lives of each of our children. Help us to direct their hearts toward Thee and Thy Kingdom. Forgive us, Lord, for we have failed to see their value. Finally, open the eyes of our hearts to see our children as You see them, as vessels in Your hand. Amen.

Meditations

The Soul of a Child

The soul of a child is the lovliest flower
That grows in the garden of God.
It climbs from weakness to knowledge and power
To the sky, from the clay and the clod.

To beauty and sweetness, it grows under care
Neglected tis ragged and wild.
Tis a plant that is tender and wonderously rare
The sweet wistful soul of a child.

Be tender, O gardener and give it its share
Of moisture, of warmth, and of light.
And let it not lack for painstaking care
To protect it from frost and the blight.

For the day could soon come when the bud will be bloom
To the ways of the world beguiled
Let us win him to Christ, while yet there is room
In the sensitive soul of a child.

Author unkown

4

A Vision That Motivates

*Where there is no vision, the people perish:
but he that keepeth the law, happy is he.*
Proverbs 29:18

There was, in the days of Samuel the prophet, a sad state of affairs in Israel. The ministers of the day had lost their relationship with God, and compromise was creeping in on every hand. God used a few revealing words, which clearly describe the condition of the nation at that time. *"There was no open vision"* (I Sam. 3:1). Although we have several chapters of sad commentary to read after this statement, these words say it all, in a nutshell. There was no open vision, and the people were perishing. We seem to be suffering from some of the same in modern America.

What is a vision? It is important to give some definition to this powerful little word because I will be using it many times. In fact, the hope and future of your family lies hidden in this one word. When I use the word "vision," I am referring to a mental image imprinted upon the heart by the Spirit of God. A vision is that which you see with the eyes of your heart. The Apostle Paul described it as something *"written . . . with the Spirit of the living God . . . in fleshy tables of the heart"* (II Cor. 3:3). A vision is a spiritual revelation of the mind and will of God. That revelation usually comes through the avenue of the Scriptures. When we read the Word of

The Pursuit of Godly Seed

God in the Spirit, dreams and visions flame up in our hearts.

I was surprised and blessed one day as I was studying the Hebrew word "dream." It means "to make healthy," or "to be strengthened." A dream is an ideal or aspiration that makes us healthy and strong. Isn't that beautiful? We know that dreams work like that in man. When a man has a dream, he comes alive, he is filled with energy, and his whole being is consumed with what he sees and wants. This is what I mean when I use the word "vision."

Probably the most famous verse in the Bible on this subject is the one listed at the beginning of this chapter: "Where there is no vision, the people perish." A study of this verse is very revealing to our present day American problems. The people as a whole do not see what God sees or wants. There is a lack of open vision in our land. That spiritual seeing of the heart is missing in too many churches.

The word "perish" is even more descriptive. It means "to cast off restraint." It does not mean to go to hell. It is much more practical than that. Allow me to paraphrase my study of this verse. "Where there is no spiritual seeing of God's will in the heart, the people will cast off restraint, go naked, and live like savages." Wow! What a picture of the degenerated condition of America. In addition, of course, the end of that process is that they will go to hell. We must get a captivating view of God's will today and hold the eyes of our heart upon it until it motivates and activates us to keep His laws again. We know that this whole process of degeneration begins when a people who know God cease to walk closely with Him. The seeing grows dim because it is God's presence in the heart that stimulates vision. As the vision grows dim, the people begin to cast off restraint. We know the rest of the story. This explains the confusion of much of American Christianity.

God-Breathed Visions

All these thoughts preface my burden for our homes. We must get a motivating vision for our homes. Only God can give us such a vision. However, we have our part to play also. When we begin to sigh and cry unto God with a longing aspiration, He is obligated

A Vision that Motivates

to impart to us a revelation of His will, as well as a revelation of our need. It is my personal conviction that because we lack this spiritual seeing of the heart, our homes lack substance and direction. My constant prayer as I write these chapters is that God will graciously grant us this seeing experience again and again. This seeing brings a transformation of the heart, and of course, a transformation of the home will follow.

Having a vision is so important I cannot emphasize it enough. Your journey through this book must be more than a time of gathering information. New information usually lasts a few weeks, and then falls to the back of our memory. However, a vision is life changing, and it will last for many years. By the time Jackie and I finish the task of raising our children, we will have invested about forty years in the project (not to mention the years of grandparenting that follow the parenting). It takes a vision to last that long. My desire, *"by grace, through faith,"* is to impart to you a vision for your children that will burn in you and consume you for many years to come.

Let us ponder some of the inner dynamics of a God-breathed vision. God moves and motivates His people by giving them a vision. The Bible is filled with examples of this inner working of God's Spirit. When God is about to do something, He begins with a vision in the heart of a man or a people. When God spoke to Abraham, He gave him a promise, but that promise had a vision of His will in it as well. God began to call *"those things which be not as though they were"* (Rom. 4:17b). Abraham saw them with the eyes of his heart and began to act accordingly. This is how a vision works in the heart of man.

God spoke to the children of Israel in Deuteronomy 28. He painted a beautiful picture of a people baptized in and overflowing with blessings. This was meant to be a vision for all who would see it, believe it, and obey the conditions that He gave them. As we study the history of this people, there are times when they were literally blessed in everything they did. Those who walked in the vision that they saw received the reality of a life blessed on every side.

Now all these inner dynamics apply to our homes as well. The Bible is pregnant with God's heart for our homes. His promises,

His will, and His visions are waiting there to be birthed in our hearts. Visions are born when the Spirit of God takes the Word of God and makes it alive in our hearts. The New Testament word for this inner dynamic is the Greek word "rhema." It literally means God speaking His Word to me. We all know the joy of this experience, when a verse just jumps off the page and into our hearts. We know it is God speaking to us personally through His Word. As parents, we should be earnestly seeking God for these "rhema's" for our families. God will give them to us. We must have faith. He will do it!

The prophet Joel spoke of a day to come when the Spirit of God would be poured out upon God's people. He described the results of this anointing in some thrilling pictures. One of those pictures was a people filled with dreams and visions. This happened on the day of Pentecost, fifty days after Christ's resurrection. On that day, 3,120 people were filled with the promise of the Father. That anointing and the visions that came from it caused those disciples to fill Jerusalem with the doctrine of Christ and His resurrection. We still live in the age of this prophecy. We are to be a people filled with visions born by that same Spirit. God wants to fill our hearts with dreams and visions of a godly home. It is His will, and He is waiting to give us more than we ask.

A Disease in the Eyes

In the last days of the apostle John, Christ sent a message to the church at Laodicea, through him. Laodicea was a lukewarm church that had been hot and full of the reality of Christ at one time. Among other things, they had a disease in their eyes, and had lost their vision. Spiritually, they could not see anymore. They were beginning to cast off restraints, and Christ even told them they were naked, wretched, and blind. What a perfect description of the definition I gave earlier! They were perishing. His counsel to them concerning their blindness was to *"anoint thine eyes with eyesalve, that thou mayest see"* (Rev. 3:18c). We all know that God is referring to the eyes of the heart in these verses. He finished by pleading with them, calling them back to Him, speaking words of true reality. Let us read them out loud and slowly here:

A Vision that Motivates

*Behold, I stand at the door, and knock: if any man hear my **voice**, and open the door, I will come in to him, and will sup with him, and he with me.*
Revelation 3:20

Christ's words to the brothers and sisters at Laodicea were strong, yet true. He was outside their lives looking in. The reality of fellowship was gone. His voice was knocking, knocking, but they did not hear. They did not want to hear. Their ears were dull, and the eyes of their hearts were blind. He pleads with them to let Him in, through repentance. He promised them beautiful restored communion, and assured them of His love.

Beloved, where is your vision? What do you see with the eyes of your heart? As you sit and read these words, how do they find you personally? When was the last time you heard from God, and you knew it? Do you have eye disease like the Laodicean's did? They were thinking they had everything together, when in reality, they were falling apart. Maybe you feel these words are not proper to write in a book. However, let us reason together. I would be a very unkind friend to stir your heart about having a vision, and then not tell you how you can get one.

Visions come from God. He is the Author of every one of them. If there is no reality in your life, you will find it hard to get a vision and hold on to it. I want the instructions that will follow to be more than the "how to's" of raising children for God. What we see is very important. God always precedes the reality of what He is going to do with a vision. That is exciting if you know where you are going, because, according to the testimony of Abraham, what you see, you will have. However, if you do not see, that is very troubling because if you do not see, you will not have. What you see with the eyes of your heart now probably will determine where your family will be in five years.

I close this chapter with some of the most encouraging words in the Bible. Paul, writing to the church at Ephesus, admonished them with an overflowing proclamation about God. He said that God was able (full of power): *"Able to do exceeding abundantly above all that we ask or think, according to the power that worketh in us"* (Eph.

3:20). If I understand this verse, that covers our dreams and visions completely. Let us get ourselves to the place where this *"power that worketh in us,"* is working in us personally, and then the sky is the limit.

Prayer
Father, we bow before You, who sees. We know You see us even as we sit here pondering what we have read. Give us a vision for our homes, dear Lord. Open the eyes of our hearts to see. We desperately need You to work in our hearts this very moment. Help us to move into the rest of this book with an open face before You. Soften our hearts to receive Your imprint of a godly home. In Jesus Christ's name. Amen.

5

The Heritage of the Generation to Come

*But my servant Caleb, because
he had another spirit with him, and hath followed Me fully,
him will I bring into the land whereinto he went;
And his seed shall possess it.*

Numbers 14:24

We all are familiar with the principle of inheritance. It is practiced by most in our culture. Its roots are found in the precepts of God's Word. An inheritance is that which is passed on to the next generation. It is a sad but true reality that this word has lost its powerful meaning. We live in a departing culture, in a society that is slowly departing from *"the faith which was once delivered unto the saints"* (Jude 3b). Today, most people think of a piece of property, money, or a business when they hear the word inheritance. This is not entirely wrong. As we see in the Law, God did give specific instructions concerning the inheritance of properties. Yet, He says far more about the inheritance of spiritual benefits. We Americans have managed to retain these precepts on a material level, but have sadly lost sight of them on a spiritual level, even though God says ten times more about passing on a spiritual inheritance to the next generation.

In the text at the beginning of this chapter, we have one of my favorite Bible characters and a precious verse to inspire us. Canaan was a real place with real property and wealth, and God promised it all to the children of Israel. However, Canaan also represents spiritual realities that abound in blessings for the people of God who walk in the New Covenant. It is the will of God, yea, the command of God, that our children (our seed) possess all those spiritual blessings. This is "The Heritage of the Generation to Come." God wants each one of us to enter into the beautiful land of Canaan (the abundant life that is in Christ Jesus), and then to pass those treasured possessions on to our children. This, dear parents, is an inheritance that cannot be measured in dollars.

Two Ways To Build the Kingdom
In the Bible, God reveals two different ways to build the church of Jesus Christ. I believe that a balanced Christian parent will be active in both of them. In fact, if we do not follow both paths, the church will never come to the fullness of stature (or maturity) that Paul mentions in Ephesians 4. Both of these paths are found in Proverbs 11:30: *"The fruit of the righteous is a tree of life; and he that winneth souls is wise."* In the first part of the verse, we can see the influence of a godly person's life. It is as a tree that keeps on producing life and blessings to others. We know that generations of trees come forth from one tree. So also, in the kingdom of God, a righteous tree produces seed that will become a righteous tree. The church is built in this way. As parents possess spiritual realities, they pass them on to the next generation, and a strong church rises up from them.

The second path mentioned in this verse is to obey the Great Commission that Jesus gave to His disciples before He ascended back to the Father. *"Go ye into all the world, and preach the gospel to every creature"* (Mark 16:15). A healthy New Testament church will win souls. They will go out into the highways and hedges and compel people to come to the Savior, to be salvaged from their sin, and to unite with a fellowship of believers. If this path is not followed, the church will not mature. A church that does not win souls is standing on dangerous ground. Church history is full of examples in which sincere people focused on themselves and their families, neglecting evangelism. The results were many different expressions of religion. Christ's name was there, but He was not there.

The Heritage of the Generation to Come

Why am I saying these things? I want you to know that I believe in winning souls. You may wonder at times if I do because of the strong emphasis I place on the raising of your children. In fact, one of the reasons I want you to raise a godly family is so they can rise up by God's grace, go out, and win souls. Therefore, the church must follow both of these methods of growth if she is to increase in numbers and mature in stature. Let us win our children to a wholehearted love for Jesus Christ, and let us win a lost world to the same.

God's Plan for the Children

All through the Scriptures we find a revelation of God's loving concern for the next generation. In many places we are commanded to pass on the lively torch of the faith to our children. The Bible is full of verses in which God promises miraculous aid to those parents who set themselves to follow this plan. One of the clearest portions of Scripture that deals with God's far-reaching plan for the generations is found in Psalm 78:1-7. Read it aloud, with meaning, slowly and meditatively. I encourage you to read all portions of Scripture this way. You will get more out of them if you do. We tend to read the Bible the same way we take the rest of life here in America--in a rush.

> *Give ear, O my people, to my law: incline your ears to the words of my mouth. I will open my mouth in a parable: I will utter dark sayings of old: which we have heard and known, and our fathers have told us. We will not hide them from their children, shewing to the generation to come the praises of the Lord, and his strength, and his wonderful works that he hath done. For he established a testimony in Jacob, and appointed a law in Israel, which he commanded our fathers, that they should make them known to their children: that the generation to come might know them, even the children which should be born; who should arise and declare them to their children: that they might set their hope in God, and not forget the works of God, but keep his commandments.*
>
> *Psalm 78:1-7*

The Pursuit of Godly Seed

Before we study God's plan to propagate the faith to the next generation, I want to state the biblical position on salvation for all of our children. God has no grandchildren, only children, born into His family by adoption. Salvation for each of our children is *"by grace, through faith in the Lord Jesus Christ."* Every child who grows up in a Christian home must come to the age of accountability and acknowledge his own sinfulness and his own need of a Savior. Each child must repent of his sins and be born again, receiving a new nature.

However, I feel it is very foolish for us as parents to start resting on the hope of salvation for our children, while neglecting the propagation of the faith, as we have read here in these verses. I think we act foolishly, if we have the mentality that says, "Someday salvation will take care of my children." We are talking about preserving a godly seed upon the earth. Yes, it is true; the transformation of salvation will do a mighty work in them, and we pray for that day and work toward it. However, we will save them so much pain and heartache if we follow the directives laid out in these verses from the time they are very young.

God Commands Fathers

God's plan to propagate the faith focuses heavily on the fathers. They are to teach the mighty works of God to their children. This is clearly spelled out in the text. Then their children will rise up and teach the mighty works of God to the next generation, and on and on it goes. I am not talking about passing on religion to the next generation but rather a living, breathing, vibrant Christian faith. That generation then can rise up in their faith and pass the same living, breathing, vibrant Christian faith to the next generation. This is God's plan for propagating the faith, and the responsibility to do this is given to the fathers. Praise the Lord! You may get a little weary of me stating this, but it is the father's responsibility. Yes, God has given you a helpmeet. You wives do need to learn how to be a helpmeet to your husbands in this task. But what saith the Scripture? As I study Church history, I have noticed that the church has gone back and forth on this issue. We will see clearly, as we proceed through many scriptures, that God addresses the fathers. I pray for you fathers. You need big shoulders to bear the load of teaching that will come your way. The father is the head of the home. God has placed him there and designed him to carry the load. The responsibility lies heaviest upon him, and God looks to him when there is a failure.

A Four-Generation Vision

Now let's look more specifically at these verses. In verses five and six, we see a beautiful picture of four generations. It says, *"He commanded our fathers,"* That's one generation. *"That they should make them known to their children,"* That's the second generation. *"That the generation to come might know them, even the children that should be born,"* That's the third generation. *"Who should arise and declare them to their children."* That's the fourth generation. Oh, what a beautiful picture! The wording is a little difficult to follow, and it may be referring to only three generations. Either way, we can see the extending nature of God's vision and command.

These verses, as well as others we will study place the focus of the father on at least two generations. He is to turn his attention primarily on his own children. However, as he is training them, his sights also are looking ahead to the children that will be born to his children, and even to their children's children. His heart must be seeing and saying, "I need to so train my children that they will rise up and train the ones to come." The dedicated fathers in Israel followed these precepts, and those who did received the reward of godly generations, just as God said. When God gives a command, He has in mind that it will bring results. The Bible has examples of families who had this kind of results. Let's look at some these examples.

Seven Godly Generations

The genealogies listed in the book of Matthew describe an amazing line of godly men. I don't know if we can grasp the depth of this lineage, but as we study these men, we can begin to understand why David was a man after God's own heart. The seeds were being planted for two hundred years. I want to take a short look at each of these seven men.

Naasson

The Bible says that he was a Prince in Israel, a man of renown in the congregation. He was the head of the tribe of Judah, and all the tents were set around his in the wilderness. Naasson was the captain over 74,000 fighting men in Judah. He was a godly man chosen by God and Moses to fill this place. He had a son named Salmon, whom he raised according to the plan presented to Israel.

Salmon

There is not a lot of information recorded about this man's life. We know that he married Rahab, the harlot who aided Israel in the overthrow of Jericho, and who obviously converted to the worship of Jehovah. Through their union, a son was born whose name was Boaz. The testimony of this son speaks loudly for his father, and converted mother.

Boaz

With this godly man, there is more to write than I have room for. His name was and is famous in Israel. The Bible calls him a mighty man. There are many insights into the character of this man in the book of Ruth. He married virtuous Ruth, the Moabitess. It is beautiful to see how God leads to provide care for those who love Him. Boaz had a high esteem for Ruth's commitment because his mother also was a convert. Many prophetic words surround their marriage. Through their union, God opened the barren womb and gave them a son. His name was Obed.

Obed

Obed grew up in a godly home. There is nothing recorded about him. We know, however, what kind of a man he was by the fruit of his son's home. I think it also is safe to say that he received the kind of intructions listed in Psalm 78. Godly fathers and godly mothers usually bring up children after their kind. Obed also was blessed with the love and attention of a holy grandmother named Naomi. When Obed married, God gave him a son whose name was Jesse.

The Heritage of the Generation to Come

Jesse

Jesse had eight sons and two daughters. He was a devout man, and the testimony of his home comes through in several places in the Bible. Samuel was impressed with each of his sons, and they were mighty men of valour in Israel. This blessing of sons who are mighty men comes upon the fathers who fear the Lord and delight greatly in His commandments. Jesse had a son whose name was David. It is true that David made Jesse famous in Israel. However, it is also true that Jesse made David famous by all that he put in him.

David

David was the shepherd boy, the sweet psalmist of Israel, the giant killer, the Prophet, and the King. As you know, there are more beautiful thoughts to share about David than three books could hold. David was anointed with the Spirit of God in his youth. He learned to know God and walk with God, sitting at the feet of his father, and sitting out under the stars at night watching his father's sheep. I want to focus on David's obedience to the precepts listed in Psalm 78. In Proverbs 4:1-13, we have a clear picture of David teaching his children, motivating them, instructing them, and even pleading with them to seek the wisdom that comes from God. David married Bathsheba, and from their union, God gave four sons. Two of them, Solomon and Nathan, are very significant people. We will look at Solomon in some detail. But what about Nathan? It was through his future generations that Mary, the mother of Jesus, came forth (Luke 3:23-31).

Solomon

Solomon sat at the feet of his father David. He is the one who wrote the testimony of his father in the proverb I listed earlier. He is remembering how his father taught him when he was a boy. Wisest man in all the earth, he led Israel to its highest level of testimony among the nations. He built the temple in Jerusalem and led all the people to love God and keep His statutes. He wrote Proverbs, Ecclesaistes, and the Song of

Solomon. The end of his life is a sad story. The Bible says that he took many strange wives, who, when he was old, turned his heart after other gods, and he died with a curse from God upon his kingdom. His kingdom was divided during the reign of his son.

Only God's Spirit can help us to grasp the depth and meaning of this example. As I look back in a brief overview of these men, one message shouts out to me. God's principles work. His promises are true, and you can put your trust in them. Obey them, expecting the blessed results that these men enjoyed. God is no respecter of persons. He will honor those who honor Him and His Word. Down through the generations, men have found this to be true without fail. Can we believe it for our families and rise up in faith and build, God helping us? Let's look at two more examples.

Five Generations

Abraham: called the friend of God, the father of all who live by faith. He walked before God, and was perfect. He had a son named Isaac, who was the son of promise.
Isaac: the promised seed. He trusted God by yielding up his life to his father. He spoke prophetic blessings upon Jacob his son, which most assuredly came to pass.
Jacob: the suplanter who wrestled with God all night and became Israel, the father of the twelve patriarchs. God called him a prince who had power with God and men. He was given a son named Joseph, who preserved Israel.
Joseph: dreamer of godly dreams, and preserver of life for all Israel. This pure, godly servant became a king in Eygpt. He had a son named Ephraim.
Ephraim: He walked in the prophetic blessings of his grandfather Israel. His name was famous in Israel, and he prospered.

God said of Abraham in Genesis 18:18: *"Abraham shall surely become a great and mighty nation, and all the nations of the earth shall be blessed in him."* How could God make such a far-reaching statement about a man? He did not say these words simply because He is God and knows all things. The answer is found in the next verse. The Lord went on to say, *"For I know him* [Abraham], *that he will command his children and his household after him, and they shall keep the way of the Lord, to do justice and judgement; that the Lord may bring upon Abraham that which He hath spoken of him."* Beloved, this account took place before the laws and statutes were given. Abraham loved God, and God knew it, and was assured of what His servant would do with his children. What else would be expected of one who so loved his God? Let us do the same, brethren, for the love of God. Let's look at another example.

Four Generations

> **Amram:** One of the sons of Levi, Amram was the father of Moses, Aaron, and Miriam. By faith he discerned God's call on his son Moses. He and his wife prayed and saw God preserve their son with a miracle.
> **Aaron:** The second son of Amram, Aaron was chosen by God to be the high priest in Israel. He had two godly sons, Eleazar and Ithamar.
> **Eleazar:** This son took his father's place as high priest. The record of his life shows the impact that his father had on him. God gave him a son whose name was Phinehas.
> **Phinehas:** This man put away evil in Israel and received a blessing from God for his generations to come. He also followed his father as the next high priest. The record of his life shows that he was a faithful servant of God, serving his generation.

All these accounts are Biblical examples of how God's Word works. *"The statutes of the Lord are right* [they work], *rejoicing the heart"* (Ps. 19:8a). We need to take fast hold on these words for our own lives, and for our families. Let the words preached be mixed with faith and bring much profit to us who hear them. How would you like to receive a vision, a rhema from God that would enable you to claim generations of godly children? I believe with all my heart, that you can do that. I believe that it is within your grasp. God, who is no respecter of persons, is able to make all grace abound toward you, and bring it to pass. I will show you as we go along, that it is possible for you, even you, to so labor together with God that generations are affected.

Some may say, "The Lord may come before we get all that done." This is true. We never know when He may split the eastern sky, but, should we neglect our children because the time is short? God forbid! Surely the bride will bring her children along to the wedding. Even though the time may be short, God wants us to have a vision! God wants us to see the generations to come! God wants us to live in light of those generations to come! Remember, a heritage is that which is passed down from one generation to the next. We are talking about passing down a spiritual heritage of godliness from one generation to the next, and on to the next. This is a godly heritage.

Prayer

Holy Father, we thank Thee for the inspired records of ancient days. Our hearts are stirred by what the men of old did and what they received. Grant to us what they had. Yea, give us more, for we know we live under the blessing of the New Covenant. Increase our vision and expand our horizons to see the generations that will surely come from us. O Father, let responsibility settle down upon us as we gaze into the future. We want our seed and our seed's seed to possess a glorious inheritance with eternal value and impact. Wash us in the blood of Jesus Christ right now. Cleanse us from our sins, and fill us with Your most Holy Spirit, that we may see our children marching toward Thee all their days. In Jesus Christ's name. Amen.

6

A Godly Heritage Today

Thou shalt raise up the foundations of many generations.
Isaiah 58:12
They shall repair... the desolations of many generations.
Isaiah 61:4b

My heart thrills as I ponder the implications and the potential of the ancient promises and commandments that we considered in the last chapter. Although these words were written three thousand years ago, they are full of life, vision, and hope to them *"which are in Christ Jesus, who walk not after the flesh, but after the Spirit"* (Rom. 8:1b, 4b). It is a blessing to see how God honored the faith of these men who lived long ago. But what about us? Is there hope for the coming generations of our descendants?

Sometimes I feel we are so modernized that we can hardly think in terms of many generations. Families are splintered and scattered all over the country, and this hinders the vision. Even the basics of a unified family are fast eroding in our society. Yet in spite of all these negative influences, God's Word comes back, clearly speaking words of promise that cover many generations. Yes, there is hope for our generations. By grace through faith we can take our homes far beyond what is called "normal" today.

The Pursuit of Godly Seed

A Living Inheritance

There was no godliness passed down to Jackie and I from the generations before us. We had none! We are first-generation Christians. A good portion of our past is not lawful to think about. *"Whatsoever things are true, whatsoever things are honest... just... pure... lovely... of good report... of virtue, and... praise, think on these things"* (Phil 4:8). Much of our heritage we have had to forget. In fact, we have had to ask God to help us forget it at times.

However, although we look back with regret at our wasted lives, we look ahead with faith and confidence to a better way for our children. Our testimony and vision is this: by the grace of God, our children will have a godly heritage. My heart is fixed, and Jackie's heart is fixed. Our children will have a godly heritage. We want them to have something to remember, something that will stay with them and influence them all their lives, and for all eternity. We want to put some holy foundation stones under them, that hold them and guide them long after we are gone.

What do I mean when I say a godly heritage? Let me give some brief definitions that are expanded throughout the remainder of this book.

- ❖ Thousands of family devotions in which singing, teaching and prayers prevailed.
- ❖ Hundreds of verses from the Bible stored away in their hearts by many different methods.
- ❖ Sweet times of doing God's work together, building the kingdom.
- ❖ Memories of growing up in a home where there was a Spirit-filled atmosphere most of the time.
- ❖ Volumes of memories of godly living, holy activities, and heartfelt love for one another.
- ❖ A multitude of prayers stored up in vials in heaven, waiting to be poured out in later days when we are gone.
- ❖ A deep assurance that Grandpa and Grandma Kenaston loved God with all their hearts, and that they went to heaven, where we also are going some day.
- ❖ A clear record before God of love and obedience to Him.

A Godly Heritage Today

I am sure we would all agree that an inheritance like this cannot be measured in money. Leave your children this rather than ten million dollars. As we scan over the preceding list, it is easy to see how many generations will be affected by this kind of heritage. I want this for my children. The very failures of our past can be a motivation to press on to higher ground for the next generations.

I have seen families whose memories of their godly grandparents sanctified them for generations. Maybe you have a heritage like the one listed. Praise God if you do. You are very rich. For you who have this treasure, there is a danger of taking it for granted and becoming complacent. It is not wise to hitchhike on your heritage. Rather, pick up the torch, stoke up the fire, and pass it on to your children. Let us all rise up and say, "By the grace of God, we are going to leave this in our will when we die."

We can do it. We can change the entire direction of our family simply by submitting ourselves to God and obeying His Word. Remember, our God is the God of Abraham. He "calleth those homes which be not as though they were." Let us "against hope for our family, believe in hope, and not consider how it looks today." Let us "stagger not at the generational promises of God through unbelief, but be strong in faith, giving glory to God." Let us "be fully persuaded, that what He has promised, concerning my family, He is able also to perform." This is the nature of faith. Follow Abraham. Can you envision yourself, seventy years old, sitting in a chair with all of your grandchildren gathered around you listening to godly stories of old? We shall have it if we faint not.

The Test of a Man's Christianity

It is said that the test of a man's Christianity is his children, and this is a right statement. Paul tells us the same thing as he gives the qualifications for a church leader in I Timothy 3. Many of the qualifications are given in one word, but not so when he writes about a man's home. He focuses on the home much longer. The reason is very clear: the test of a man's true character will show in his children. Although this is true, there also are verses in the Bible that carry the test one step further.

Children's children are the crown of old men.
Proverbs 17:6a

The mercy of the Lord is from everlasting to everlasting upon them that fear him, and his righteousness unto children's children.
Psalm 103:17

These verses as well as others we will study bring the third generation into view. When a man's Christianity is deeply ingrained in his heart, he will propagate it so thoroughly into the hearts of the children, that they will be stirred and motivated to do the same with their children. His life will reach out into the lives of his grandchildren through his children. Therefore, it is also right to say that the test of a man's Christianity is his children's children.

Let's study a few examples of this parental influence in Christian history. My heart has been challenged many times as I have seen reality fleshed out in the lives of godly men and women, and the effect this had on their children.

William and Catherine Booth

The children of thy servants shall continue, and their seed shall be established before thee.
Psalm 102:28

This verse is one precious and powerful promise in the Scriptures, and the Booth family is a beautiful example of its fulfillment. William and Catherine were dedicated servants of the most high God. Both of these choice servants had a godly heritage that would be worthy of some study. However, they are such a good example of the parental generation in this promise that I have chosen to focus on them as the first generation.

William Booth was the founder of the Salvation Army. It was, for decades, a mighty force for the salvation of multitudes. He was all out for God and all out for lost souls. O God, give us more

A Godly Heritage Today

men like him! His dear wife was the same. She gave herself continually as a sacrifice for the Kingdom. God blessed their union with eight children.

It seems they had the proper balance of the two methods for building God's kingdom I mentioned earlier. They were: to pursue the lost and to pursue a godly seed. There was no question in the hearts of the children about their parent's dedication to the Lord. The atmosphere of the home was contagious. The example in the home was clear, and the training was filled with the purposes of God. The children grew up and chose to walk in the steps of their father and mother—all eight of them. The Lord scattered them around the world as missionaries preaching in some of the largest cities of the world. They went for the down-and-out part of society, just as their parents had done.

Well, from those eight children came over forty grandchildren, and what do you think those grandchildren did with their lives? They watched their parents wholly follow the Lord. They saw that Mom and Dad loved God. The children saw a real Christian life in their parents, and those grandchildren chose the Lord. Every single one of them rose up and said, "I'm going to follow the faith of my father and mother!" They all went out and scattered themselves across the world on mission fields to do the work of God.

I visited with a born-again Salvation Army lady on a flight to Kenya some years ago. I began to share with her my appreciation of William and Catherine Booth. Our conversation progressed to their home, and she told me that she went to Bible school with some of the great-grandchildren, who are out on the mission field this very day.

This is what God wants us to do: pass on a vibrant, living Christianity to our children, a Christianity that will cause them to rise up and go out and do the work of God. Then, as their children see and hear that their parents are serious about God, they will rise up and do the same thing. This should just keep going on and on from generation to generation. The only thing that breaks the chain is lukewarmness and sin in the lives of God's people. Let's look at another home.

The Pursuit of Godly Seed

Hudson Taylor

Here we have another example of a godly heritage today. Hudson Taylor was the founder of the China Inland Mission. Much of what is happening in China today can be traced back to this man's pioneering labors. There are tens of millions of Christians in China today because of one godly family that passed the torch on to their children.

Three generations of fiery Methodists preceded him. As I study the heritage of this famous missionary, I again see the promises of God being fulfilled. Great-grandfather James Taylor laid a many-generation foundation as he established his home. He was converted on the day of his wedding after hearing John Wesley preach a sermon on godly homes. The text was *"As for me and my house, we will serve the Lord"* (Josh. 24:15). There in his barn on the day of his wedding, he got on his knees and yielded his life to Jesus Christ. He was late for his own wedding because he was on his knees praying that God would bless his home. I don't recommend that you be late for your wedding. However, I can't think of a better reason to be late.

In time, great-grandfather James became a Methodist lay preacher. He had several sons, and they all rose up after the zeal of their father and became Methodist lay preachers. Then those sons had several sons who rose up and became Methodist lay preachers. Do you see the pattern? Isn't it a beautiful picture and example to follow? Out of those sons, one was the father of Hudson Taylor.

The home in which Hudson Taylor was raised would take a whole chapter to describe. It is one of the most Biblical examples of a Christian home that I know of. (I hope to publish the testimony of this home in a book on "Home Histories" some day.) When Hudson was a little boy, his father used to pray with zeal, every day, "O God, would you send missionaries to China?" There were very few missionaries in China then. The little boy heard those prayers day by day, and they fell like mercy drops upon his tender heart. When he was six years old, he got alone with God and said, "God, I'll go to China." From the day of that prayer, his heart was set, and his life was set apart for the Lord's work among the heathen in China.

A Godly Heritage Today

The "His-story" doesn't stop there. The generations of preachers keep right on going, up to this generation. There are now nine generations of preachers in the Taylor heritage. One is a missionary in Thailand today. Nine generations of preachers! This is a staggering example of a godly heritage. May the Lord inflame us with the same kind of vision and impower us to raise up generations of soldiers for Christ. We need to see the potential at our doorstep. God is no respecter of persons. These men were not special men that God chose to bless above all others. No, they were ordinary men who obeyed God, believed His promises, and received the fruit of their obedience.

O God ... Give us a Vision

One that consumes us
One that drives us to action
One that changes our priorities
One that draws us back when too busy
One that cannot be dimmed by this world

Jonathan Edwards

Let us focus on one more historical account of a godly heritage. God used Jonathan Edwards for revival in the eastern part of the United States 250 years ago. He is one of the most prominent men in revival history. Jonathan and his wife Sarah were dedicated to the Lord. Their Christian heritage can be traced back three generations. They began their life together with a solid foundation and a vision for a house full of godly children. God gave them eleven children and they gave them all to the Lord.

Jonathan and Sarah were anointed with the Holy Spirit. This fact is evident as you study their lives. The fruit of that anointing was manifested in their home, as well as in other areas of life. The order of the home and character of the children were examples followed by many. When George Whitefield came to their home on one of his American preaching tours, he changed his mind about marriage. David Brainerd, the famous missionary and prayer warrior for the Indians, was planning to marry one of their daughters, before he died of pneumonia. The posterity of the Edward's home is astounding. It is a powerful example of a many-generation household.

Five Generations of Light

Some time ago, the state of New York did a study on five generations of the Edward's family. I have read differing reports on the number of influential family members, so I will generalize it a bit. In those five generations that were studied, the researchers were able to trace 729 male descendants. Out of these 729, a couple hundred became preachers, sixty-five became Bible college teachers, 13 were university presidents, and 60 were authors. Scores of them held public office, and more than one hundred were lawyers and judges. Three score were doctors. A few were senators and governors, and one was a vice president. All this issued from one man and woman who loved God and set themselves to raise their children for God. We can see from these statistics how many sanctifying seeds were sown from that determined couple.

Five Generations of Darkness

At the same time, the state of New York did a similar study of an ungodly posterity. This study is worthy of our focus because it is a good example of what happens if we neglect our responsibilities. Max Juke and his brother married sisters. They were not Christians and rejected the teachings of the Bible. They believed in living their lives for themselves and going their own way. Five generations of their descendants also were calculated. They had 1,026 descendants, both male and female. Of those, three hundred died an early death because of a hard life. One hundred forty spent an average of 13 years each in the penitentiary. One hundred ninety of their descendants became public prostitutes and one hundred were alcoholics. It was calculated, back in 1900, that it cost the state of New York $1.2 million to take care of all these wayward people. What a different group of people this is! Truly, truly, *"Righteousness exalteth a nation: but sin is a reproach to any people"* (Pro. 14:34).

6 x 6 x 6 x 6 x 6 = More Than 10,000

Allow me to give you one more exercise with statistics? Some time ago in our homeschool, we were discussing the blessing of having many children. Someone had the bright idea of investigating the potential number of descendants, from those who believe in having large families. It was very interesting, and the children had a ball calculating it all out.

We put two marks on the board, to represent a father and a mother. Then underneath those two marks, we put six marks, and said, "Now the father and mother have six children." We chose the number six, which is a little low, so that we could be more realistic. Then we went to the next generation and said, "All right, now if each one of these children will have six children, that would be thirty-six." We followed this pattern out for five generations, and we added them all up, counting their spouses also, and came up with more than 10,000 descendants. The children sat speechless for a moment, and so did I, as I realized the possibilities revealed in our little project.

Now, maybe that doesn't do anything to you. I know that these are only statistics, and that there can be a lot of breakdown between the imaginative and the real. Even though this is true, I still am greatly moved by these numbers.

I'll tell you somebody else who is moved by these numbers. His name is Satan. He knows that there is some truth in these statistics. He knows if he gets the father and mother at the top of the chart, he will get most of the rest of the generations that follow, with very little added work. I think the surveys cited earlier in this chapter prove the reality of the potential.

Our Heavenly Father also knows these statistics, and the tremendous affect five godly generations could have on the world around us. God knows that if He can get a hold on some parents' hearts and set them in the right direction, it could influence many generations for His kingdom. I give this hypothetical illustration only to help you see the potential you as a father and you as a mother have with your children. Cut the figures in half if you want to. Make it 5,000. Still that is a tremendous amount of godly influence for one couple to have.

The Work of the Ministry

Can you see the potential ministry we have before us? Many are looking for ministry opportunities when right here is one of the most far-reaching ministries you will ever find. God is calling you as parents to your responsibilities, but you have to be willing to be real Christians, full-time. You have to be the real thing at home. You must be one who walks with God when the doors are shut and no one is watching but your children, one who will live a godly example, with a fire in your bosom, at home. If you will get consumed with raising your children and living out the principles of the Word at home, God can do something just as I have described. He is no respecter of persons. You could have a ministry that reaches much farther than you ever imagined possible. You do not have to be a preacher to do it. It is a great burden to me when I see preachers sacrificing their children and the time it takes to raise them right to be famous preachers. A godly home has a much more powerful effect than good sermons do. Some of you may have a hard time believing that God would work in this way with you. Without a vision, the people perish, but with a vision, God's work prospers unto the third and fourth generations.

Prayer

Father in heaven, we have heard with our ears, the fathers have told us and showed us what great things Thou hast done in days gone by. Now, make good Your promises Lord. Truth has fallen in the streets, and truth has fallen in our families. Have mercy on us. Amen.

7

The Influence of a Godly Home

*Ye are our epistle written in our hearts,
known and read of all men...:
manifestly declared to be the epistle of Christ.*
II Corinthians 3:2,3a

I have been relating to you about passing on a godly heritage to the next generation. Well, now let me share a little story with you about a family God used to implant some things in my heart that have changed the destiny of my children and inflamed me with a vision for a godly home. It all started when I met this family twenty-two years ago in Fort Frances, Ontario, Canada. This is a small town of about 6,000 people, a twin city to International Falls, Minnesota.

I was in International Falls working with a revival team and serving Lou and Ralph Sutera with the Canadian Revival Fellowship. They were there having meetings and seeking God for revival. These twin brothers have been my dear friends and mentors for revival for twenty-five years.

Well, much to the delight of my own heart, the meetings for revival lasted three weeks. Every night, there was this family that kept coming to the meetings, and I noticed them. They were a little bit different. The men wore lapel suits, but they didn't wear

The Pursuit of Godly Seed

ties. The women dressed more modestly than the other women who came to the meetings and wore this black veiling on the back of their head. I had never seen Christians like them in my life, and I was intrigued with the testimony of the family. They came every night, never missed, and always sat up front. I remember one evening when Ralph Sutera asked them to sing. Dad, Mom, and seven children sang in four-part harmony, without instruments. Wow, was that ever sweet!

One evening, the father of this family walked up to me after the service and said, "I would like you to come to my house for breakfast. Can you come?"

I said, "Yes, I can," wondering why I got an invitation.

We set a day and time, and he gave me some general directions on how to get there, I said goodbye, and he went his way.
Well, I started fellowshipping with other people, and I told them, "I have been invited for breakfast on Tuesday morning," and I gave the name of the family. When I said these words, their faces lit up with a great big smile, and they said, "Oh, you will really enjoy that home." I had no idea what they meant by that, but I remembered the family's unique testimony in the meetings. My vision was sadly lacking in those days, but God was about to change that.

Tuesday morning came, and I headed out for Fort Frances with a friend. We had to cross over the border into Canada. As I was driving through the city of Fort Frances, I made a turn or two that must have been wrong and got myself lost. I thought, "Now what am I going to do, and how am I going to find this brother's house?" I pulled into a little minute market there in the town to ask for help. I started to ask rather reluctantly because I didn't know whether anybody would know them.

I said, "I have gotten myself lost." I gave the name of the family to him and asked, "Do you know where they live?"

The man behind the counter got a big smile on his face and said, "Sure! I know where they live! Go down this highway, make a left-hand turn, make another right-hand turn and another left and you'll be there."

I looked at him, a little puzzled, got back in the car, and headed down the highway, pondering these things in my heart.

As I was driving down the highway, somehow I missed the turn that I was supposed to make. You know how it is when you miss a turn. You keep driving and looking, thinking it will be the next road. Well, I went on like this for some time before I decided that I must have missed the turn.

I stopped at an old gas station out in the country and said to the old man sitting there, "I'm looking for a special family." Again, I gave him the name and asked, "Would you have any idea who that is and where they live?"

The old man in the gas station got a big smile on his face, and he said, "Sure! I know where they live! Go back up the highway, make a right hand turn,"

He gave me directions from there, and I went on my way again, pondering.

This is not a fictitious story: it really did happen, and I usually can follow directions pretty well. Sometimes I think God put a fog over my mind so I would get lost again and again.

I went down the highway, made the turn, and somehow (let's blame it on providence), ended up lost again in a residential area. I thought, "Now what am I going to do?" The answer came quickly as the Lord reminded me of the many residential doors I had knocked on while out winning souls. So, I knocked on a door, and someone answered. I proceeded with my usual questions (I was getting pretty good at it), and I found the same response. They got a big smile on their face, and said, "Sure! We know where they live!" Well, they gladly gave me the final directions, and I arrived at the farm.

As I pulled up to the farmstead, I found the typical farm scene. The boys were still outside finishing the chores, and the girls were in the kitchen with Mama, helping her prepare breakfast. There were seven children at home at the time. Five had already left home. After the boys finished the chores, they all came into the house, and after the proper introductions, we all sat down at the table together for a nice country breakfast. All the conversations at the table were about spiritual subjects, and I was just taking all of this ordered experience into my heart. It was a lively table, with much rejoicing, and everyone was very active in the discussions. My head turned back and forth as I listen to the family table talk.

The Pursuit of Godly Seed

When the meal was over, the Papa, who was a short German man with a gruff voice, took his Bible and handed it to me. I was sitting at his right hand, and he put the Bible down and said, "Here, you will have devotions this morning." Now, I was a young Baptist preacher, and used to having some time to prepare, so I was on the spot. I opened up the Bible to Ephesians and started reading, as I whispered a prayer to God. While I was reading, feeling insecure in the situation, I looked up to see what everyone's responses were to my reading. I was taken aback, to say the least. All the children had their hands folded, and their eyes were shut. They looked as though they were squeezing everything they could out of the verses I was reading. That was very unusual to me, as I had never seen such earnestness in a family before.

All entered into the discussion we had out of Ephesians chapter 1, and when we were finished, I closed the Bible. Then the father passed out songbooks and said, "We're going to sing a while." Well, was I ever in for a treat and a lesson. When that family started singing, the heavens just opened up. The glory of God came down into that little dining room. I trust you know what I mean by that. The Spirit of God was there. It wasn't a dead devotion. It was alive with God. I was just sitting back, taking all this in and wondering, "What have I found here in this family?" When we were finished with the singing, we had prayer together, and then were dismissed for more casual fellowship.

As soon as I got up from the table and started toward the end of the room, the boys were right on me. They had tracts in their pockets--gospel tracts, tracts on the verbal inspiration of the Bible, and others that they wanted to give me. They were "throwing" tracts at me left and right, asking me questions. I was so impressed with these zealous young men.

When I finished talking to the boys, the mother of the house pulled on my coattail and led me into the living room. As I looked at her, she started crying. Then she said, "Please, pray with us for Fort Frances. We are praying that revival will break out in our town!" I had never seen anything like this before, and I was just taking it all in.

The Influence of a Godly Home

After I visited with the ladies in the house, the boys took me on a tour of the farm. They showed me the different facets of their farm. All during the tour, we were talking about the Lord. I was impressed, to say the least.

As we were heading toward the milk house, the milk truck pulled in to pick up the milk. One of the boys stopped right in the middle of his conversation with me, jumped up on the milk truck, stuck a track through the window and said to the man, "Hey, have you been born again?" I was just watching it all, taking it in, and wondering about this family. We finished our tour, with many more questions about the Lord and the Bible, and I could tell that each one of them loved God. This was how my whole visit went, so refreshing and inspiring.

I said goodbye to the men, but as I was getting into my car to leave, the dear mother of the house came out to say goodbye. She had a loaf of German bread and a dozen eggs that she put in the back seat of my car. I thanked her, waved goodbye, and drove away, just pondering this whole visit, wondering, "God, what are You saying to me? This is an unusual visit that I have had."

With these thoughts on my mind, I made my way back down the roads, and came to the gate to go across from Canada into the United States. It seems that God was not finished getting my attention, but had one more smile to impress upon my heart. As I pulled up to the customs booth, a big tall Canadian in uniform walked up to the door of the car. You know how officials are. They always seem to have a real gruff voice and frown on their face, ready to catch anybody who is being dishonest.

He spoke with a gruff voice, "Where are you going?"

I told him, "I'm going back to the United States. I have been visiting friends."

Then he asked me, "Do you have anything in the car?"

My first thought was "no," but then I remembered the bread and eggs that were given to me, and I said, "Yes—yes, I do. I have a loaf of German bread and a dozen eggs in the back seat."

When I said that, his frown turned into a big smile, and he said, "I know where you have been." He then gave me the name of the home where I had just visited, with a smile on his face and joy in his voice.

The Pursuit of Godly Seed

I looked up at that man with a look of bewilderment, and he said, "All right go ahead, on your way." I pulled away from the gate, pondering this whole thing, and wondering what God was trying to say to me.

God did something very special in my heart that day. He gave me a vision. We have stated already, "Without a vision, the people perish," but the opposite is also true. With a vision the people prosper, and I don't mean materially. That visit has affected me and our home for more than 22 years now. At the time, we only had three children: Rebekah, Daniel, and Elisabeth. Rebekah was about four years old; Daniel was two; and Elisabeth was a little nursing baby.

Our home has never been the same, from that day forward. God took His finger that day and drew a picture on the table of my heart, a picture of a godly home, a picture of the influence of one family on a community. Oh, the power of one dedicated Christ-centered home! God, please give us many more, all over this land of ours! The memory, the inspiration, and the revelation of that visit are still upon my heart as I sit here writing these words. It is so sweet to me! My heart rises up to God in worship and thanksgiving as I reflect upon His visitation to my poor blinded heart.

God gave me a vision that day as I saw the power of a godly home. It took a few days to settle and form in my heart, but as it did, my heart began to cry, "God, I want a home like that! I have got to have a home like that! Lord, if you can do it for that father, you can do it for me!"

Jackie and I were just a couple of converted "hippies" out of the late sixties and early seventies. We were not very old in the Lord at that time. We didn't have much vision for our home, but a fire began to burn in my soul.

I spent another week helping Lou and Ralph, and all the days were spent pondering this new vision. My prayers deepened as the purpose of God became clearer. A longing, a craving settled down upon me, and I began to pray, "Lord, I want a home that glorifies You. I want to have a family that is a testimony in the community where we live. I want to have a family that loves God, and everybody else knows it. I want to have a family that can preach the gospel and win souls when people come into the home. That's the kind of family I want!" My heart said, "And I shall have it, by Thy grace."

By the time I went home to my dear wife and children, my heart was fixed. My will had engaged itself with the grace that came through that revelation. I was full of zeal, and Jackie wasn't sure what had happened to me. God bless her. She has had to fasten her seat belt several times in our Christian journey, and this was one of those times. I shared my visit to this godly home with her, and how it had affected me. It tickles me now as I look back on those days. I know I made a lot of mistakes in my zeal, but my heart was sincere, and God blesses sincere desires. I got out the Bible, and I said to the family, "We are going to have devotions." We didn't have them before that, or very little. Maybe we read the Bible a little bit, but with very little purpose. You know how it can be. I had no purpose! I had no vision! I had no goals! But now, I had a dream, a holy dream, written on my heart.

We started in the children's bedroom. Mama was in a chair nursing the baby, Rebekah was in her little chair, and Daniel was sitting in his crib sucking his thumb (sorry, Daniel!). We started with three songs. I said, "We're going to sing in devotions! Someday my family is going to sing like that family in Canada, and we're starting now." So we took three songs, and we learned them. I'm sure that Mama got a little bored with the same three songs, but we sang those songs day in and day out until we had learned them well. I wanted the children to know the songs. We made a lot of mistakes back in those early days, but our hearts were right. I wanted my family to be a testimony to the glory of God, and that's what God wants for every Christian family. The vision has expanded through the years, but my heart still sings for joy when I remember the whole-hearted passion we had for our children in those early days.

There is a dearth in the land of families like the one I met up in Canada. It is not God's will that they be hard to find. You have to go a long ways to find one, and this is not right! God is no respecter of persons, remember! God wants to do a work in every single home represented in the reading of this book. He *wants* to do it again; He is *able* to do it again; and He *will* do it again! If we allow God to give us a vision of what He can do, He will do it again! But brothers and sisters, I'm sure we would all agree, it doesn't happen by accident. That godly home I saw was not an accident. There were many holy activities that took place in this home on purpose.

So, what is God saying to us as we sit and ponder these things today? He is saying, "My people! I want you to leave a godly heritage for your children!" He is saying, "My people! My Spirit is moving on the hearts of fathers and turning their hearts to their children. Open your hearts and hear My voice."

God wants us to raise our children to be a reflection of His glory, and of His work in these last days upon the earth. That is what He is saying to all of us. It is not right that there be just one or two godly homes here and there that get the attention of a searching heart like mine. There ought to be so many dedicated families in the church that we have many examples to follow. May God work by His Spirit in such a way that the church of Jesus Christ be filled with godly families. The church should be filled with godly fathers and mothers with a zeal, with a vision, and with a vibrant Christianity that they can pass it on to their children. Then those children will take those hot coals and pass them on to their children, and on down the line it will go.

I will never forget the visit I had at this godly man's home. He died ten years ago. His widow is still living. The church where the family went in those days had about forty people on Sunday morning. But at his funeral, there were 750 people out of a town of 6,000 who came to his funeral, out of every walk of life. They came to that man's funeral and honored him at his death. Why? Because one man and one woman, when they were first married, set themselves to raise their children in such a way that it would be a testimony to the glory of God. Let us be the same way, setting ourselves to be a testimony to the glory of God.

Prayer
Our Heavenly Father, Oh God, we thank You for Your gracious work in one family. But now it's our turn, Lord. Father, raise up more families

who have a clear testimony. I pray that You will raise up more Jonathan Edward families. God, I know that You want to. I pray for each family reading this book. Stir each one of our hearts Lord. Make us hungry, and make us thirsty, Father. Give us a vision that will not be put out no matter what comes our way. Oh Father, I pray You will turn the Spirit of the Living God loose upon each and every one of us, and may we not resist the grace of God that is turning our hearts toward our children. Father, we thank You for the sweet blessings of these testimonies, and we simply pray, do it again Lord, do it again. Oh God, if we truly have revival, it will touch our homes, or it's no revival at all. Father, we ask these things in the name of the Lord Jesus, with thanksgiving. Amen.

Meditations

The Worth of a Soul

*How inestimable does the worth of the human soul appear.
How clearly is it seen to exceed that of the whole world.
When we view it as endowed with the capacity
Of being made equal to the angels.*

*How momentous an event occurs when such a soul is born.
When an immortal being commences a flight through endless duration.
A flight which will raise him high to an equality with angels,
Or plunge him low among malignant fiends!*

*Think of this, ye parents! Ye to whom is committed
The care of giving to this flight its earliest direction.
On whom largely depends, under God,
What its termination shall be.*

Edward Payson

8

Bring the Fathers Home

> *That our sons may be as plants grown up in their youth;*
> *that our daughters may be as cornerstones,*
> *polished after the similitude of a palace.*
>
> Psalm 144:12

Our beloved father David was a prophet, one who moved in the prophetic realm by the inspiration of the Holy Ghost. As prophets often do, he saw deeply into things and bore many burdens that did not even occur to others. In Psalm 144 we find an expression of one of those deep burdens that God had pressed upon his heart. We find in this psalm some insights into the needs of the American family, as well as the rest of the fast-developing world.

Allow me to guide your thoughts a bit as we read a portion of this psalm. The context of this psalm is war. David is speaking about the Lord's blessings in the midst of war. Amid his reflections and praise, a prayer arises in his heart. This prayer, coming from the deep longings of his heart, is for the end of wars, a peaceful society, and the fruit that comes from that peace. Let's read the psalm with these longings in mind.

> 7. Send Thine hand from above; rid me and deliver me out of great waters, from the hand of strange children;
> 8. Whose mouth speaketh vanity, and their right hand is a right hand of falsehood.

9. I will sing a new song unto Thee, O God: upon a psaltry and an instrument of ten strings will I sing praises unto Thee.
10. It is He that giveth salvation unto kings: who delivereth David his servant from the hurtful sword.
11. Rid me, and deliver me from the hand of strange children, whose mouth speaketh vanity, and their right hand is a right hand of falsehood:
12. That our sons may be as plants grown up in their youth, that our daughters may be as cornerstones, polished after the similitude of a palace:
13. That our garners may be full, affording all manner of store: that our sheep may bring forth thousands and ten thousands in our streets.
14. That our oxen may be strong to labor; that there be no breaking in, nor going out; that there be no complaining in our streets.
15. Happy is that people, that is in such a case: yea, happy is that people, whose God is the Lord."
Psalm 144:7-15

A Prayer of David

In the first part of this psalm, David is reflecting, praising, and praying about the subject of war. He prays for God's help, and that God will deliver him from his enemies. We see here a righteous king's burden to be free from the influence of ungodly nations. In the last part of the psalm, (vs. 11-15), his focus turns away from war, and onto what life is like in Israel when there is no war. In verse 11, we find the prayer that I mentioned earlier repeated for the second time in this chapter. It is a prayer for Israel to be free from war. He says again: *"Rid me, and deliver me, from the hand of strange children, whose mouth speaketh vanity, and their right hand is a right hand of falsehood."*

Now, we all know that David was a man of war. In all the days of David, there was war in Israel. There was fighting in Israel. This means that the men of Israel had to rise up many times and go forth to battle. When Israel went to war, they could be gone from home for six months at a time. They lived out in the fields. They traveled long distances, and they were away from their families, their cities, their farms, and whatever their work was. They left all of that when they went forth to battle.

Now that we know a little of the cost involved when Israel went to war, we can see why David's longing prayer was for a peaceful society. David is crying for deliverance from war, to "bring the men home." Why? Well, there are seven things in this psalm that David is crying for, and all of them happen when the men come home. These seven aspects of a peaceful society all are prefaced by the word "that." David's prayer was simply "Lord deliver us from war and bring the men home so that:

- ❖ Our sons will be nurtured into mature men.
- ❖ Our daughters will be polished and molded into lovely ladies.
- ❖ Our fields will produce abundantly by the work of our hands.
- ❖ Our sheep will have shepherds and bring forth ten thousands more.
- ❖ Our oxen can increase strength and labor more because of our care.
- ❖ Our land can have all the blessings of peace upon it.
- ❖ Our people will be full of courage, and all murmuring will be gone."

When there was wartime in Israel, the men left their homes, their children, and their wives. They left their farms, their businesses, and their cities, and they went out to war. What happened to the wives, the children, the farms, the cattle, and all those things while the men were out to war? Well, what happens to our families, when the men are gone too much? We all know the answer to this question. We know the answer by personal experience. When the family is neglected, things do not go so well. We kind of put them on the back burner, and they suffer from the men's absence. Here in America, we do this one day at a time. Often, we say, "I will do better for the family tomorrow."

But that tomorrow never comes. There is always another voice calling us to something else.

Can you grasp the depth of wisdom and vision that David had in this inspired prayer for Israel? Here was godly David with a vision of what God had put in his heart through constant meditation in the Word. He knew what Israel was supposed to be. He knew what the children were supposed to be like. He knew what kind of a blessing God wanted to put on the nation of Israel if they followed the precepts I have already described. But, here was Israel going out to battle again.

David knew what would happen to the children while the fathers were away. We also know what happens to our children when we are away too much. David knew that it takes more than men going to war to make Israel a strong nation. There were foundations of righteousness that needed to be laid in the next generation, or the nation would not be what Jehovah intended it to be. With all this knowledge, David cried, *"O Lord, rid me and deliver me from the hand of strange children."* He prayed *"Lord deliver Israel from war,"* so that the men of God, the men of war, could go back home and guide their families, and take care of their farms.

How the Prayer Was Answered

Now the Lord *did not* answer David's prayer in his own lifetime, but the Lord *did* answer his prayer. His son Solomon had very little war during his reign. Consider the difference twenty or thirty years with no war would make. Twenty or thirty years with fathers home every day guiding the children and teaching them. Twenty or thirty years with men watching over the sheep and the farms, and in the streets taking care of things. All the leaders of all the homes in the nation of Israel are home! What happened to Israel in Solomon's day? Israel became the most powerful nation on the face of the earth during Solomon's reign.

Did you ever consider the how's and why's of Israel's testimony? It wasn't because Israel was a mighty nation of war, not in Solomon's reign! In David's reign, the enemies and the nations that lived near Israel trembled in fear. Yes they did! Israel was a mighty force of war and power. David ruled many nations with a rod of iron.

But we come to Solomon's reign of rest from war. It was during this period that many of the nations reverenced Israel. She became a testimony to all the nations far and wide around her. Israel stood out as a nation that was very different from all the other nations. Many of the nations looked on at Israel and said, *"Surely this great nation is a wise and understanding people"* (Deut. 4:6b). Israel was healthy, wealthy, and wise, more than all the nations round about them. Many of the nations of the world looked on Israel and said, "There's something special about that nation!"

One of the major reasons for their world-renowned testimony is that during Solomon's reign, the men of war came home! The godly fathers came home! Those men of God who stood out on the battlefield and fought the enemy in the power of the Holy Spirit came home. All the spiritual energy that they were directing toward the battle came home and was directed toward their families!

Israel became a mighty nation by the teaching and the preaching of the fathers in every one of the homes, and that is the only way any nation will become a mighty nation! When the fathers of the nation turn their hearts toward home, then that nation will begin to change. When they rise up with a burden and a vision of what God can do through them in their own homes, then the tide will begin to turn. Oh, listen! God could shake this country for Himself through godly families.

There is a lot of talk about revival these days and I praise God for revival! I believe in revival, that is, an outpouring of God's Spirit. I pray for and long for revival. I hear of many praying, "God save our nation through revival," but if all we see when we think about revival is preaching and souls coming down the aisle, we see only half of the picture. The other half of revival is a nation of godly fathers and mothers training their children. One of the clear biblical fruits of revival is a family that loves God with all their heart. Revival is more than a puff of emotions. If it is genuine, it will affect our closest relationships, which is the family, for years to come. If our revival doesn't touch our homes, there is something wrong with it.

So, how does this psalm apply to us? We live in America, and we are not being distracted from our duties by a war. Consider what is taking our fathers away from their homes. We live in an unusual society. We are a nation of men that *"will be rich"* (I Tim. 6:9a). We live in a nation where it is easy to make money. This is encouraging more and more men to "become successful," and the wives and the children are the ones who are paying for the success. The price being paid is very evident when you look at our overflowing prisons, and at the rising rate of divorce in our land, even among Christians. Let's face it men, prosperity is destroying our precious families one day at a time. Yet, everyone is talking about revival. Then why is this mighty move of the Spirit not turning the hearts of the fathers to their children? I know these are strong words, but the present distress is urgent. My heart unites with the prayer of David. Lord, bring the fathers home,

That our sons may be as plants grown up in their youth,
That our daughters may be as cornerstones,
Polished after the similitude of a palace.

Prayer

O Lord God, our Father, open our prosperous eyes to the reality of the true condition of our families. Bring the fathers home before it is too late, even if it means that we lose everything and find ourselves in poverty, even if we have to draw together just to survive. Plant us fathers back into the center of our homes, like the patriarchs of old. In Jesus Christ's name. Amen.

9

Bible Pictures of a Godly Home

*Thy wife shall be as a fruitful vine by the sides of thine house:
thy children like olive plants round about thy table...
...thus shall the man be blessed that feareth the Lord.*
                                                    Psalm 128:3-4

What a rich and full picture we have in these verses! They are pregnant with meaning, and deeply spiritual, as God's Word always is. Jehovah promised the men of Israel an abundant family life with lots of children if they would walk before Him and be perfect. How much more are these promises sure to us who now live in New Covenant relationship with God! There are several pictures just like this one found in the Old Testament Scriptures. They are waiting for us to glean a wealth of wisdom, vision, and insights from them. Shall we go digging for hidden treasure? In this chapter and the next, I draw out some jewels from several of these pictures of a godly home in the Old Testament.

Let me remind you before we start that the warriors we mentioned in the last chapter knew the verses we are going to consider. Those godly men--those men of war who came home from the battle to care for their families meditated on these Bible pictures. The verses we are going to peruse were their scriptures. This is what they heard preached at the temple and in the synagogues.

The Pursuit of Godly Seed

God has used these pictures to challenge and inspire His people for three thousand years. I pray for another burst of inspiration for us as we gaze into them.

Mature, Nurtured Plants

David cried from his heart to the Lord to end the wars, and bring the men of Israel home, *"That our sons may be as plants, grown up in their youth"* (Ps. 144:12a). The prophet David was making an analogy between our dear sons and plants. He was praying that God would bring the men home to their sons. As I studied this phrase, the picture became clear. David was talking about a plant that had been nurtured to the point of fruitbearing maturity. He was talking about a plant that had been nurtured carefully through the whole process of growth, and was now ready to bear fruit. The ground had been cultivated, and the seed had been planted. The shoot had pushed up through the ground and had been cared for all along the way.

Can you picture the farmer caring for his plant with a dream and a vision in his mind? The plant has been watered; the weeds have been pulled; and fertilizer has been applied. He is now looking at a mature plant, healthy, strong, and ready to bear fruit.

There is nothing more beautiful to a farmer than a plant that is just ready to bear fruit. You know, once the plant starts producing fruit and gets a little age on it, it starts losing some of its beauty. But right before it's ready to start bearing fruit, that plant is in its prime. It is beautiful! It is strong! The farmer looks at his plant, and he knows that the stage is set. The fruit is coming, and he rejoices. Some of you gardeners and farmers can relate to what I am saying. Plants grown up, still in their youth, but ready to bear fruit, this is the picture Israel had to inspire them.

Now let us relate this analogy to our dear sons. What is our goal? What do we see? God is giving us very clear direction through this picture. I see a young man, maybe eighteen years old. He is upright in his heart, with a clear countenance, because he has a clear conscience. He loves the Lord Jesus with all of his heart, and his testimony is sound among those who know him. He is a virgin, saving his purity for the wife of his youth. He is filled with the Spirit, filled with the Word, and busy about the Master's business. He loves his parents and finds great delight under their authority. He is ready for a life of bearing fruit to the glory of his God.

I'm not sure how this picture sets with you. Maybe you feel the standard is a bit too high or unrealistic. But this is exactly the picture that the analogy portrays. This is what spiritual Israel was working toward with their sons, and many of them obtained what they sought, prayed, and labored to achieve.

Three solid examples come to my mind immediately. Remember David the shepherd boy, who was anointed to be king at about eighteen years of age. Remember Daniel, the young man carried away to Babylon, who stood for right in a test that many would have failed. Finally, remember Joseph, the young seer of visions, who was placed in very difficult circumstances and passed the test.

Each of these youth was probably about eighteen years old. Ponder their young lives. They are "plants grown up in their youth." The Lord wants to lift our sights higher by these testimonies of godly young men. There they stand, each one of them clear, mature, and ready for a life of fruitfulness. This is what God wants of our young men. It can be done by the grace of God and our willing hearts. We can have youth that are mature, stable, and ready to face real life in righteousness. But we must see it with the eyes of our heart, as I have said earlier in this book.

Let's go back to the farmer and the plant for a moment, and look deeper into this analogy. The nurturing of this plant is a process. We all know enough about gardens to realize that many things need to be done to produce a healthy plant. It is the same with our sons. There is a vision, and there is work to be done. Every farmer knows that when he plants the seed, he already "sees" the plants growing tall with fruit on them. If he didn't have a vision, he wouldn't go to planting. It works the same way with our sons. Oh, may God give us a vision of a plant, a son who is standing tall, ready to bear fruit. Then may He give us the grit, the holy grit, the character, and the discipline it takes to carry out all the nurturing, the planting, the cultivating, the weeding, and fertilizing. May He move us to spend all the hours of time it takes to raise a mature plant, one that we can send out into a real world to bear fruit.

Polished Cornerstones

As David gazed longingly into the prophetic realm, he also saw some lovely daughters of Zion. This vision was part of his prayer. Lord, deliver us from our enemies, *"that our daughters may be as cornerstones, polished after the similitude of a palace"* (Ps. 144:12b). He is praying that God will bring the men home to their daughters. Many Christians feel that a father doesn't have much influence in his daughter's life and training. God's Word says nothing like this. What a dangerous teaching this is, and one that has already given us two generations of mothers who have lost their way! This is changing, and I praise God for this change in theology.

Cornerstones are very important stones in a palace. They are the stones that give stability to the walls of the building. They are the stones that connect the whole building together in strength. They are the stones that the builders use to plumb the rest of the stones into the walls. Therefore, they must be right. Because of this, they were carefully carved by hand.

Finally, the cornerstones of a palace must be beautiful, to give some ornamentation to a stark stone building. The palace must have strong flat walls, or it will not stand, so they use the corners for ornamentation, which makes the palace beautiful. Because of this, special care and lots of time is given to carving and polishing these stones. The prophet David is drawing an analogy between these special stones and our precious daughters. There is a wealth of inspiration and instruction in this illustration that guided the life of spiritual Israel.

Now, let us also relate this analogy to our daughters, as we did with our sons. What do we want our daughters to be like? What do we see, and where are we going with them? I see a lovely young lady about eighteen years old. Her face is shining because her heart is clear. She is one of the King's daughters, all glorious within, waiting to be placed in a building somewhere in God's Kingdom. God's grace is upon her, and everyone around her knows it. She is a virgin, saving her purity of heart and body for her husband. She stands prepared, ready to guide her home and care for a family. She is beautiful, like beauty used to be: no outward show, but an inward clothing of quietness and meekness. Can you picture her? She is truly beautiful.

Doesn't this picture stir something inside of you that says, "This is the way it should be?" She is a *"cornerstone, polished after the similitude of a palace."* Brothers and sisters, I want this kind of daughter and the kind of son described earlier in this chapter. What must I give for precious sons and daughters who have this kind of testimony? God has clearly revealed in His Word the price I must pay. In a sense, that is what the content of this book is all about, the price we must pay, and the precious jewels we will receive.

Let us turn back to our analogy and draw some practical applications from it. Again there is vision in this Old Testament picture. When the craftsman, that special carver of cornerstones, steps up to a stone to carve and polish, he has a vision of the finished stone.

He has a vision in his mind of what the stone is going to look like when he gets finished. He sees that cornerstone already shaped out, exactly the way he wants it. He sees that cornerstone already sitting in that building, beautifying it, and making it look like a palace. He sees all of that. But, oh, a lot of work must be done before that cornerstone fits into the building.

The man who does the carving has tools. He has a hammer, chisels, and some scraping instruments to carve and mold the stone. When he goes to work on that stone, he is going to make some noise, and there will be some pain involved as the parts of that stone are chipped away by the hammer and the chisel. Do you see the meaning and the methods hidden in this inspiring picture? This is what David prayed for. It was a prophetic burden to him.

We must see, dear parents, where God wants us to go with our families. A haphazard approach does not fit this analogy. God has plans for each of our daughters. They are to be strength and beauty to a household someday. They are going to be an example by which to plumb the building, and the vital connection to other stones in the house. Do we see the eternal implications in this? It is true, the mothers of a nation are one of the strongest influences to a people. But godly mothers don't just happen. They are molded day after day in the hands of parents who see a place where their little girl will stand someday.

Olive Plants

Isn't it amazing how the Lord teaches us humans the lessons He want us to learn? Nurtured plants, polished stones, and olive plants are used to help us understand what His will is for our children. There are some sweet promises found in Psalm 128, which have been a source of encouragement and instruction to many throughout the history of Israel and the church.

> *Blessed is every one that feareth the Lord: that walketh in his ways. Thy children [shall be] like olive plants round about thy table.*
> *Psalm 128:1,3b.*

I remember when I was a young man with only two children around my table, and one in Jackie's arms. I would meditate on this Scripture and dream of a day when I would have many children sitting around my table. If you are a young couple reading this, this is a good vision to ponder. The Lord eventually placed eight olive plants around my table, and my dream was fulfilled.

Olive plants for a man in Israel were a very meaningful illustration. An olive tree was a valuable piece of property. Olive oil was a symbol of peace, health, and wealth in Israel. It was used for many different things in Bible days. The oil was used to make a fire, which illuminated the house at night. It was used to make special anointing oils for health and healing. It was used to make the holy anointing oil which was used to consecrate certain prophets, priests, and kings. It was used to make soap for cleansing, and it was sold for cash to buy many other necessities. If you had eight or nine olive trees, you were a blessed man. An olive tree lived a long time; it seems, in fact, it lived almost forever. Let me explain.

An olive tree could live for two or three generations just by itself. However, when the old gnarled tree was ready to die, its roots would send forth several new shoots, and the tree would continue to produce through them. Can you see how this picture of promise would light up a man's countenance when he thought upon it?

How do these thoughts relate to our children? What can we learn from Israel's picture of promise? Once again, there are many beautiful correlations that we can glean for our modern-day families. Consider a few of them:

1. **We see the treasure we have when God gives us children.** The Lord could have used many other blessings to describe the man who is blessed by God. He chose to inspire us with the picture of a wife bearing many children and the picture of many children gathered around a man's table. God is using two of the most valuable assets in Israel to show us how highly He esteems children.
2. **We see tremendous usefulness in the olive tree.** Just as olive oil is used to benefit others in many ways, so also our children are to be great assets to us as parents, and to the society in which they live. They are to be lights to illuminate a lost and dying world, and a healing balm for the broken and wounded. We know that God called His two witnesses olive trees in Revelation 11. Wow, what a picture from which we can draw inspiration, a table full of witnesses for the Lord Jesus Christ! Lord, make our children olive trees from which the oil of the Holy Ghost flows.

    I want to say something about the financial blessing that children are also. I realize that many of you see your children as a financial burden, but that is because our society has drastically changed. The family farm and family business setting are almost gone. Consider the help that children are to their families when all work together to meet the needs of the home. That is the way it used to be everywhere. Oh, how far we have fallen!
3. **Let us remember, these are olive plants, not olive trees.** It takes about fifteen years to nurture an olive plant into its fruit bearing stage. These are years of tender care.

There were many wild olive trees in the land, but they had absolutely no value. A wild olive tree was an olive plant that was left to itself, to grow however it chose, without being cared for. Such a tree looked more like an ugly bush, than a tree, and the fruit was small with almost no oil in it. When a man had several olive plants, he had no problem spending his time caring for these promising plants. He knew that they would bless him and his generations with many years of valuable oil. What a perfect picture of child training. Does it get any clearer than that? A man had to water these plants because of the type of soil in which they grew. He had to loosen the soil several times each year for the same reason and apply fertilizer to the roots. He needed to do this faithfully for many years because he wanted to have a fruitful tree. We must do the same thing if we expect to see an olive tree that will bless the world some day.

4. **Consider the generational aspect of olive plants.** I mentioned how the old olive tree would put forth several branches from its roots before the trunk of the old tree died. This is a beautiful picture of our heritage going on and on through our children. Because the men of Israel knew the nature of the olive tree, their vision for the next generation was greatly enhanced. This is how we should be looking at our children, even when they are young. As fathers, we need to see way beyond the life of our child. As we nurture our "olive plants," we need to see the influence of our children reaching out for generations. If we see our children in this light, in a sense, we do not die. Our children are sprouts that eventually become trees right out of our root. Let us carefully nurture these plants. They will extend our life and influence after we are gone.

Do you see your children as olive trees, with oil flowing out of them to a dark and troubled world? This is the picture that God is giving us in this psalm. It is a picture packed with powerful visions. The most influential blessings on this earth are godly children who have been raised with purpose to be useful witnesses because the oil is on them. Let us believe God for olive plants that are growing up into olive trees, that are a fruitful and influential force in the world. This was God's vision for Israel, and it is His vision for the church today also.

Building a House

In Psalm 127:1 we have the next picture from which I would like to glean treasures. It is just across the page in your Bible from the last one. I would like to consider the building of a house: *"Except the Lord build the house they labor in vain that build it."* As I studied the word "house" in the Hebrew language, I found that it is used two ways: to refer to an actual physical house, and also to refer to a household. Because of this, the context must be considered in deciding which meaning is being used.

In this psalm, the word "house" is being used both ways. God uses the analogy of building a physical house to challenge us about building our households, our homes. This picture is not a promise, but a challenge and a warning to the men. The double use of this word is powerful if you understand life in Israel.

In Bible days, when a young man was ready to begin his household, he was the builder of the house for his wife and family. It is like that to this day in parts of Africa; every man builds his own house. Now, let's picture a young Jewish man for a moment. He has his espoused wife and he has gone to prepare a place for her so he can come again to receive his bride and begin his home. If he is a spiritual man, what do you think he is going to be meditating on while he builds his house? I think we would all agree that he will be dreaming dreams and seeing visions of his future family. In that context, these words come to his mind again and again, *"Except the Lord build the house, they labor in vain that build it."* God in His wisdom gave this verse to Israel, and especially to the young men, who build their own houses.

Now let's go on to the actual building of the house. When someone is going to build a house, he has a clear idea of what the house will look like before he starts. He has a blueprint, a builder's layout of the details of the house. He has materials and tools, and he must put much labor into it. All of this is involved in the building of a house. Again, we see how the illustration is perfectly tailored to relate to the building of a home for the glory of God.

As we seek to apply this ancient snapshot, we can draw from two different comparisons. First and foremost, we see a striking portrait of the Lord building a house. He is the Master Builder who oversees the whole project. I have often envisioned the Lord working behind the scenes, blessing, watching over, and protecting our homes. At other times I have envisioned a much more intimate and co-operational scene. I have seen the Lord with His hands on my hands carefully building the house through me. The first vision requires a great deal of trust and confidence in God. The second requires a continuous yielding of my heart to God, so I can be an instrument in His hands. My heart thrills at the potential of this kind of house building. O the depth of the wisdom of Almighty God. If the whole project is to be done right, it must be done His way, and His way is the way of utter abandonment.

The second comparison refers simply to the building of a house. As we have already stated, there are many different aspects involved in construction: the plans, the tools, the materials, the foundation, and the construction itself. I know that we are all in different stages of building our households, and some of us have awakened in the middle of the building. But for the sake of a pure model, I am going to give the ideal. Don't be condemned or discouraged if you started late: Jackie and I also began late. Rather, I challenge you to dream for your children.

The laying of the foundation begins in the hearts of godly youth who set themselves by their own choice to serve the living God with a pure heart fervently. As these youth are drawn together by the Lord, they enter into a courtship relationship, with marriage as their goal. Their hearts continue to unite around like-minded dreams and visions. Can you see the foundation being laid? It is powerful.

From here, they enter into holy matrimony or marriage, and a new household is begun. As they continue to walk with God together in unity of heart and purpose, a beautiful structure of peace, love, and holiness begins to rise. When God gives children, they receive them with reverence and joy, and begin to raise them according to the pattern given in the Book.

These little olive plants are planted in a powerful, fertile atmosphere of love, and they begin to grow and prosper. Do you see the house going up? Isn't it beautiful? Praise the Lord. This holy structure continues to rise as the parents pray, nurture, and discipline. The house takes thirty or more years to build, but oh what a beautiful house it is. Dear fathers and mothers, I want this mountain. I know that many of you do also. The Lord has given it to us. Let us rise up and possess it. Let us, with the vision before us, reach for our tools and build.

I Can't Do It

This is a statement that I hear often when I speak about the home and the raising of children. Parents say, "I don't see how I can do it! I don't have the abilities to handle the task. Please pray for me."

I understand what they mean when they say these words. Parents sincerely feel overwhelmed when they hear all the sermons, and many times they don't have the personal gifts to carry them out. However, let us reason together from some Old Testament stories.

Consider the building of the Temple in Solomon's day, and the building of the Tabernacle in the days of Moses. Did you know that when God wanted to build the Tabernacle, He put the Spirit of God and of wisdom upon the craftsmen so that they would be able to build that Tabernacle exactly the way He wanted it built (Exodus 31)? When it was time to build the Temple, the Spirit of God and of wisdom lighted upon its craftsmen also. God gave them special abilities to build according to the pattern given to David.

Let us reason together again. If God was concerned enough about an earthly tabernacle and temple to give extra grace to the builders, *how much more is God concerned about our little temples,* our children in whom He will dwell one day? How much more will God pour the Spirit of wisdom and love and power upon the hearts of every Christian father and mother. He will surely give grace to those who will, with all their hearts, cry unto Him daily.

You are right. You can't do it. But God wants to enable you to do it, and then He will get the glory. I think we have not because we ask not! And many times, we don't ask because we don't have a vision! We don't have a vision of what God can do through us! Beloved, let us wait at the gate of wisdom morning by morning. God will give you the deep desires of your heart. Only believe.

Prayer

Dear Father in heaven, hear our cry. You are the builder of the house. We acknowledge this before You. Many of us are overwhelmed at this very moment because of the needs in our homes. Have mercy on us and teach us where we lack. We see the pattern very clearly, but how to make it all work seems very far away. Give us faith to move forward and build the temples in which You will dwell one day. In Jesus' name. Amen.

10

More Pictures of Promise

Lo, children are an heritage of the Lord:
and the fruit of the womb is His reward.
As arrows are in the hand of a mighty man:
so are children of the youth.
Happy is the man that hath his quiver full of them.
Psalm 127:3-5

Before we move into another chapter on Old Testament pictures of the home, let us consider some of God's possible design in giving these illustrations. There is very little instruction in them unless one meditates deeply on the picture. So, what is the purpose?

God's purpose is to give vision, that is, Spirit-inspired pictures of His will for our families. Also, God uses these illustrations to motivate us to move toward that goal. We see something, and a desire is created in our hearts. With that desire, our heart is opened up to receive instruction and correction.

Sometimes the instruction can be painful, but our new desire helps us to move beyond the pain and gain new insights. This is precisely the intent of the first portion of this book. There will be much detailed direction given in the chapters that follow. Some of it may overwhelm you at times, so I am preparing you for that. If the teaching gets too heavy, maybe you can come back to some of these chapters and rekindle the vision and the desires.

The Pursuit of Godly Seed

Carefully Prepared Arrows

God has placed some powerful, motivating comparisons in the verses at the beginning of this chapter. I again encourage you to read these verses out loud, slowly and with meaning. My desire is to engraft in your hearts the many verses on the home so they will change you. If you plant the seeds of truth on the home deep into your heart, they will grow into life-changing results.

In the first verse, the Lord places His divine stamp of value and approval on each one of our children. Children of the womb are His special gifts to us. From these lofty statements, the Lord moves into several analogies worthy of our meditation. Allow me to make the spiritual comparisons as I draw our focus to these powerful pictures.

- ❖ A physical war — a spiritual war
- ❖ An enemy in war — our spiritual enemies
- ❖ A man of war — a spiritual father
- ❖ A weapon of war — spiritual youth

To understand what this picture meant to the men of Israel when they meditated upon these verses, we must consider the historical context. War was a very normal part of life. Every man was expected to train and prepare for battle. Every able man was expected to go forth to battle for the nation of Israel.

In the New Testament context, spiritual war should be a normal part of life. Therefore, these comparisons take on even more significance.

Arrows in the hand of a mighty man were very effective weapons against the enemy. In those days they didn't have factories in which arrows were made. If you were a man of war and skillful with the bow and the arrow, you made your own arrows. In the days of David and Solomon, the men were prepared for war. They had practiced from their early youth with many weapons of war. When they shot an arrow, it went where they wanted it to go. They didn't have a problem with missing when they pulled that bow back and shot the arrow. So the greatest need for the mighty man was to have an arrow that would go straight and hit the mark.

Arrow making was a very serious craft for the mighty man of war. It was done with precision and care. He knew if he had a straight arrow with a sharp point and feathers placed just right, it would hit the mark when he sent it forth. What was the vision in his mind while he carved away on those arrows? Where do you think his mind was? Yes, he was out on the battlefield, standing before the enemy. As he was carving away by the side of his house, his mind was elsewhere. He would shave off a little more here and a little more there, holding up the straight stick with a discerning eye. He was preparing an arrow so that when he pulled that arrow out of the quiver and put it in his bow, it would hit the mark. He had a vision of how that arrow was going to go when he sent it forth.

Can we see the patterns in these Old Testament pictures of a godly home? Every one of them is packed full of insights and motivating promises. Making arrows is very active work, and so is raising children. Remember the four comparisons that we listed earlier. Let me apply them with a bit more detail. I see a godly father who walks with God. He sees into the eternal, a spiritual war for righteousness and precious souls. To him it is a real war with very high stakes. There is an enemy and a wicked kingdom that are active in this war. Finally, he sees his children. They are to be weapons in his hands, sent forth by God toward a mark in the enemy's territory. These weapons are spiritual youth, prepared with care for the battle that lies before them. Joy fills his heart as he dreams of the day when he has a quiver full of these prepared arrows.

With all of this in his heart, the father sets to work, his wife joining him, and together they shape a quiver full of godly children to the glory of God. This is no small endeavor. This is a task that will take them forty years to complete. They will take special care that each one of the children will hit the mark that God has planned for them.

Is there anything more valuable than an arrow that will hit the mark? Oh, happy is the man that has his quiver full of them!

I don't know about you, but I am making arrows. And by God's grace, I plan to shoot them. And I plan for them to hit the mark. I'm holding the stick up, and I'm shaving it off, holding the stick up and shaving it off. It gets painful at times during the process, but I'm making arrows, and I want my arrows to count. *"As arrows are in the hand of a mighty man, so are children of the youth."* Happy is the man that has his quiver full of "arrows that have been made to hit the mark." Brethren, let's make them count.

I often hear people make a statement that grieves my heart. They say, "Well, I think my children will turn out all right." I know what they mean when they say that, but it is a statement that lacks purpose. I'm sorry, but I've got my sights set higher than "all right." Jesus said, *"The harvest truly is plenteous, but the labourers are few; Pray ye therefore the Lord of the harvest, that he will send forth labourers [arrows] into his harvest"* (Matt. 9:37,38). Let us make some arrows that will hit the mark of the enemy, where it hurts. It is in our hands to do it, and God will help us.

A Many-Generation Foundation

In Isaiah 58 we have an Old Testament example of a New Testament Spirit-filled life. In this passage, the Lord also defines what a Biblical fast is. We see God's purpose for fasting: to draw near to Him with a broken, repentant heart. There are several conditional promises in this chapter, that beautifully describe a life of overflowing grace. You can identify these conditional promises by the words "if" and "then" in the verses. I have put them in bold letters so you can see them easily. The Lord is a covenant-keeping God. He is Jehovah, the God who keeps His promises. The whole chapter is worthy of a long meditation, but for the sake of space, I have drawn out only enough of the content to make my point.

> ***If*** *thou take away the yoke, the putting forth of the finger, and speaking vanity;* ***if*** *thou draw out thy soul to the hungry, and satisfy the afflicted soul;* ***then*** *shall thy light rise in obscurity, and thy darkness be as the noonday:* ***then*** *the Lord shall guide thee continually and satisfy thy soul in drought;* ***then*** *the Lord shall make fat thy bones;* ***then*** *thou shalt be like a watered garden, like a spring of water, whose waters fail not.*

More Pictures of Promise

> ***Then*** *they that shall be of thee shall build the old waste places: thou shalt raise up the foundations of many generations.*
>
> Isaiah 58:9-12, adapted

I want to focus on three major truths from these verses. The first is our relationship to God. We must be clear with the Lord. Sins of commission and sins of omission must be repented of. This is one purpose of the fast. James 4:8 says, *"Draw nigh to God, and He will draw nigh to you."* The upward look must be right.

Second, as we come with an open face to the Lord and seek Him, grace begins to flow from God to our hearts. This experience is described in clear words in our text: God's light shining forth in our lives, God's voice leading us, health in our bodies, and water, overflowing spiritual water. Glory! Let's go for it with all of our heart, soul, mind, and strength.

The next thing that happens is an outflow of the grace flowing into our lives. This is where ministry comes in. We actually have no ministry if we do not have this dual flow of God's grace. Verse twelve describes this outflow of the inflow of the grace of God in our lives. One of the fruits of this powerful, Spirit-filled life is a many-generation foundation in our homes.

This brings us to our next Old Testament portrait of a godly home. Earlier, we were building a house. Now we are building a foundation. Everybody knows that the foundation is the true strength of the house. If you want the building to last a long time and stand tall, you must begin with a strong foundation.

Some of the skyscrapers in the big cities are a good example of this. The builders go way down into the ground when they lay the foundation, so they can build that skyscraper way up into the sky. The men of Israel knew this principle. They had to dig down past the sand and lay the foundation of their house on solid rock. It took a lot of time and effort to build a house with a good foundation under it, but it was worth the investment. Also, if you look at the context of this chapter in Isaiah, you will see that it was a time when the houses of Israel were falling down because of apostasy. This makes the analogy even more meaningful.

We can learn several lessons from this comparison. First of all, what kind of house do you want, and second, what kind of foundation are you laying for that house? If you are going to make a one-story slab house, all you need to do is pour a few inches of concrete on the ground and up you can go with your little house.

But the foundation referred to in this analogy is one that will hold a godly household extending into many generations. My question to you is this: how many generations do you want your foundation to hold?

Dear parents, have you ever considered that you are the foundation of the next generation?! Your household is growing up on you, who you really are personally in the Lord. Each generation is the foundation for the next generation, or generations. What kind of foundation are you laying with the life you are living? It is in your hands.

When Israel was in her glory, when Israel lived in power, when Israel lived in strength, she laid the foundation of many generations. Remember the examples cited in chapter six. These saints laid a far-reaching foundation by the love they had for God and the way they lived for Him. Do you see the picture? How strong, how sure, how deep is your foundation?

Let me give a little of our testimony to illustrate my point. It is time to stop and examine the foundation we are laying. Twenty some years ago, it began to dawn on Jackie and I that something was wrong in many of the Christian homes in our land. We noticed that the best evangelical churches were losing a lot of their children to the world. This evaluation covered several different denominations: Baptist, Christian Missionary Alliance, Charismatic, and Bible churches. These were the ones with which we had some experience. They were losing their children. By that I mean the children were not rising up to serve the Lord with all of their hearts. Many of them stayed in the church, but they were full of the world and complacent about spiritual things. Many others simply went out into the world and lived lives like other heathen do. The young ladies wore sensual attire, and the dating game was in full swing in most places. The result of these dangerous practices was fornication, not in all, but enough to alert any discerning father.

We began to realize that the foundation wasn't very deep. This was obvious. It could not hold even one generation. At first, one might bemoan, saying, "O well, this is just the way it is today." But after careful study of the many Bible texts on the family, we came to the conviction that God had something better. We began to see that this loss in the family is not normal. According to the Bible, normal is a generation of young people who rise up in purity and dedicate themselves and their future to the Lord.

Dear parents, it is not normal to lose your precious young people to the world. Something is drastically wrong with the foundation of the home when this happens. Let's get honest. Most of these parents who loose their children to the world are half-hearted Christians at best. The chickens do come home to roost. This half-hearted foundation produces the same kind of youth.

Way back then, Jackie and I said in our hearts, "Wait a minute. We are not going to lose our children to the world. No way!" It was with this cry on our hearts that we began to seek God for answers and for examples to follow. This probably is why I was so captivated by the family in Canada. There I found a whole house full of children on fire for God. Believe me, I was ready to take notes.

Dear fathers and mothers, the standard is high. Nothing short of a powerful Spirit-filled life will do. God is calling us to deep commitments today. Let us be honest with ourselves. What kind of foundation have we laid? How many generations do we want to have follow the Lord with all their hearts: no generations, one generation, or many generations? We are the foundation for the next generation. If we will live a consistent Spirit filled life at home, this is a solid foundation. The Lord says, "If you will love Me with all your heart, and walk in My ways, I will pour out My Spirit upon you," and "Thou shalt raise up the foundations of many generations!"

America 200 Years Ago

Many years ago, I read an article in a homeschool paper about the goals and dreams of education in our land 200 years ago. It was very revealing to my modern mind. Oh, how far we have fallen! I am sure that most of us have no idea how far. Let us consider several of the main points in that article in the light of laying foundations that support many godly generations. Two hundred years ago in America:

- Children began to learn Greek and Hebrew, at the age of six years, so they could study the Bible when they were older.
- By age ten, the children had put off silly-mindedness, and were preparing for real life.
- Young men entered the Bible colleges of Yale and others to study and prepare for ministry at the age of twelve.
- These young men had to be able to diagram a paragraph (e.g.r., noun, verb, adverb, adjective, preposition) in Greek, Hebrew, and Latin. This was part of the entrance examination for these colleges.
- It was normal for a twelve-year-old boy to be able to operate his father's business while he slipped away for a day.
- Our land was full of young ladies who could guide the home in every area while Mom was away for the day.
- America had three books to read: *the Bible, Pilgrim's Progress,* and *Foxe's Book of Martyrs.*

It would be very easy to exclaim how far American education has fallen after reading this list. And it truly has changed drastically. But we don't need to look just at the educational system to find fault. What about our own ideals of training? We Christian parents have fallen into the same trap. It may not be to the degree that the world has fallen, but nevertheless, we are far away from these kinds of dreams and visions. Do we believe it is right for the children to shake off the silly-mindedness of the fun life by the time they are ten years old? I know that our society has changed, and most people now live in the city where there is very little for youth to do. The serious things of life were very natural on the family farm. All had to help. I wonder though if we realize what we have thrown away.

What about some of the mental disciplines of those days? Greek, Hebrew, and Latin are not mastered without rigor, and many hours of hard work in memorization. Are we open to such discipline? What about all those twelve-year-old boys and girls who could handle the home and the business when their parents were away? Do we feel it would be cruel to train them like that? I see these realities all the time in Lancaster County, Pennsylvania, where I live. The children grow up with responsibilities, and because of that, they can take over for Mom or Dad when needed.

Have we given in to the philosophies of the world concerning our children? I tremble when I think of the silly reading material that the children of America are feeding on instead of the Bible. We think that childhood is a time of fun and play, and want to extend it as long as we can for them.

This was not so with our forefathers. They produced serious-minded children, filled with maturity by the age of twelve. The goal is adulthood, mature young adults. **I'm raising adults, not children.** I agree with Eve's statement when she bore Cain: *"I have gotten a man from the Lord"* (Gen. 4:1b). What did she mean by these words? She was saying, "I have gotten a child who will become a man."

Again, I think we have lost our vision. The goal is adults, responsible adults when the task is finished. We have enough children in our land, who are 21 years old, but still filled with play and frolic and jokes and silly-mindedness. I was a good example of this. I never decided to grow up until I was 23 years old. When I got converted, all of a sudden it dawned on me, "There's a real life to live." Many times, I feel as though I'm about ten years behind. We have set our hearts on higher goals for our children. The Lord is working with us. We shall have these goals, although many will probably think we are extreme.

Psalm 11:3 says, *"If the foundations be destroyed, what can the righteous do?"* We live in a land where the foundations of many homes have been destroyed. What can we do? One thing we can do to right this desolation is to turn our sights back to our homes. I don't know how to turn a nation back to its foundations. Only a revival will accomplish that. But in the meantime, I am not going to lose my children to its fallen influences. Again, let us so love God, and so live for Him, that our children will see and sense a better way. We parents are one of the foundations that have been destroyed, and there is something we can do about this one.

Prayer
Dear Father God, we cry out to You again in Jesus name. Send revival to this our land before it is too late. Open our own eyes, Lord, for we have been infected, and don't even know it. Send a revival Lord, and let it start with each one of us personally. We are the foundation for the next generation. Our children are going to be just like us. Have mercy, and wake us up from our apathy. Let us see the war that really is there. Pull back the veil and shake us before it is too late for this next generation. In Jesus Christ name. Amen.

11

Wholehearted Households

Choose you this day whom ye will serve;...
but as for me and my house, we will serve the Lord.
Joshua 24:15

These famous words were spoken by Joshua the son of Nun, the servant of Moses. If you read the words all by themselves, not knowing the context in which they were given, it would seem they are being spoken by a young man full of dreams and vision. But it was not so with Joshua. He actually spoke these words at the end of his long life. He was 110 years old and ready to die when these words flowed out of his heart and mouth in a sermon. It had been seventy years since God had said of Caleb and Joshua, *"They have wholly followed the Lord"* (Num. 32:12b).

As we glance over the recorded years of Joshua's service for God, we all agree: he lived wholeheartedly all his days. I am glad for his example, because true Christianity is a wholehearted religion. The Bible abounds with verses that atest to this definition. It seems fitting to me that our homes and the way we seek to raise our children should follow the same pattern. Many of us have Joshua's confession on the wall in our houses, and many of us men have quoted the verse as an expression of our own choice and direction for our homes.

Joshua was speaking prophetically as he proclaimed his intent and the intent of his family. He knew his days would be few on the earth. So how could he say these words? I believe he could say them because he had passed on his zeal and love for God to his seed. At the time of his confession, there were four generations of his children living. That is what he meant by his "house." He was a true patriarch, looking out over his descendants and prophesying, *"my house will serve the Lord."* The house of Joshua is a beautiful example of a wholehearted household.

A Jewish Home

Some years ago I was preparing a message on the home. It was Saturday, and I was planning to preach the next day. As I was preparing, the Lord directed me to study the Jewish home. It was one of the most revealing studies I ever pursued. I was so excited by the time I had finished the sermon that I could hardly wait until it was time to preach.

I was astounded when I saw how the Jews ordered their homes and raised their children. It confirmed the testimony and vision of my own heart. It became very clear that the wholehearted household was the standard that God had given to Israel. Spiritual Israel was totally consumed with raising their children for Jehovah.

In the middle of my investigations, it dawned upon me that this was the kind of home in which Jesus and John the Baptist grew up. I am convinced that when God's people get consumed with raising their children, when it becomes top priority, they will raise up godly children!

Spiritual Israel was consumed with the rearing of their children. It affected the way they built their houses. They built a house with small rooms, where everyone slept, and one large room in the center, where the family spent most of their time. They cooked in this room, ate there, had devotions there, and used it to extend hospitality to others. This room was the central part of the home. In Israel's day, they only had one light, which they carried around the house. Now we have a light in every room. The parents would put the light in the main room of the house, and all the children would gather together. What a beautiful picture. I'm not against electricity, but I am for gathering the family. They built their homes with raising children in mind.

I have noticed similar patterns among the Mennonite people where I live. So many decisions are made with a godly family in mind. Large houses are built for the possibility of twelve children. Father plans a family business with training children in his mind. All other plans are made accordingly.

The Sabbath

As I studied the Jewish home, it was a blessing to see the way they conducted the Sabbath evening. Every Friday evening they had a ritual that they went through at home. When father had finished his work for the day, he arose, changed his clothes, and went to the synagogue. Only the fathers went to the synagogues. The rest of the family stayed home to prepare for the Sabbath.

While the fathers went to the synagogue for prayer and preaching, the whole house was being changed. The whole family was busy getting out the best dishes they had and preparing the best food available in the house. The children all took baths and put on clean clothes in preparation for the Sabbath. The table was set; the Sabbath light was lit; and Mama and the children were waiting for father to come home.

When the father arrived, the children were all lined up, one after another, waiting for the father's Sabbath blessing. As he entered his house, he walked up to each one, put his hand upon each head, and spoke the blessing of Israel upon them. Can you visualize the picture in your mind: those children all lined up, looking up to their father with reverence and respect?

God's Law

The Jewish father taught his children the Word of God. Day in and day out, the fathers were consumed with teaching their children the Law of God: *"Precept upon precept; line upon line, here a little, and there a little,"* as Isaiah 28:10 says. This sounds like an all-inclusive training program to me. They believed Deuteronomy 6:1-7 was to be obeyed. These verses instruct the father to be teaching his children continually.

When a young man was deciding on his lifetime occupation, he measured his choices up against these verses. He asked himself,

"Will this occupation allow me to teach my children the Law of my God?" Many times a young man would choose a lesser profession, so he could be active with his children during the day. I know that our modern society is making choices like this more and more difficult, but even so, if you go to a strong Jewish community today, you will see this principle being lived out. I think we New Covenant Christians have a few things to learn from these Old Covenant Jews.

The father was constantly connecting the actions of his family's life with a command in the Law. Everything they did had a reason. "This is why we pray; here is the verse for it." In this way, the father methodically catechized the children. "This is why we keep the Passover, and here are the scriptures for it." The children learned from little on up. I mean from the time they were suckling children, they learned why they did what they did and what the verses were behind everything they did. Their father taught them God's Word.

Ancient Homeschooling

The father taught the children how to read in the Jewish home long before they were involved in a systematic education. Do you know how he did it? They all used the same learning-to-read curriculum. They used the Word of God. That was their textbook. Do you know what the father's motive was? He would have said, "I want my children to be able to read the Law as soon as they can." He wasn't planning out the children's formal education when he started to teach them to read. He wanted his children's hearts to be full of the Word of God. So the father would sit the children down in the evening and teach them, beginning with the Hebrew alphabet. After the children had mastered the alphabet, he would move on to simple words out of the Bible, and then on to simple sentences. Slowly but surely, day after day, the father would teach them until the children could read out of the Law by the age of five. As I ponder early American life, I imagine some of the same scenes in the homes, with many of the same motivations.

The fathers taught the children to memorize Scripture long before they could read. As soon as the children could talk, they were learning to quote Scriptures by memory. As soon as the children could understand words, they were taught by rote and repetition, Scriptures, proverbs, and songs to sing. One of the first psalms that the children memorized was Psalm 119, because it follows the Hebrew alphabet and flows more like a song.

Dear brethren, have we lost the vision? I think we have. We are too soft and too busy. I don't think we realize the mental abilities of these little minds. Our children can memorize Scripture much sooner and much faster than we think they can. If we would begin, and be consistent in helping them, our children could have chapters of God's word hidden in their hearts by the time they reach seven or eight years of age. In these ways, the father catechized the children. God's ways and God's words were the center of conversation and the center of life in a spiritual Jewish home.

They pursued the next generation with their whole heart. It is time we do the same. Many of us get uneasy when we hear talk about rules and standards in the church, but we ourselves are not willing to make the sacrifices needed to put the standards in the hearts of our children. We need to take the Bible and break it down to a child's level, and teach them why we do what we do. We need to teach them why the sisters wear a covering, why we dress modestly, why we kneel for prayer or raise our hands when we sing. This is the responsibility of every father in every home. That is what catechism is, and the fathers are supposed to do it, not the pastor.

When the sons reached the age of eight, they went away to a more formal school. It was different for the daughters in a Jewish home. They had school at home with their mothers. They received an education, but the emphasis was placed more on learning how to take care of the home. They stayed home with Mama and learned to cook, sew, garden, and care for children. I know this may get a rise out of some ladies reading this. I think our daughters should be educated. However, we see a clear division of responsibilities here that is being lost in our land.

Let's go on to the boys. When the boys were of age, whom do you suppose they hired to train their sons? (I mean no reflection on any teachers reading this. God bless every one of you for your sacrificial labors.) They didn't just hire a young person who needed a job. No. They sought out the most spiritual, mature rabbi that they could find, and put him in the school to train those boys. Now why did they do that? Because they were raising up leaders for the nation of Israel, and that is a very serious task. They put the most spiritual men to the task.

What am I saying in all this? Am I saying we should all go to Jewish practices? No, I am not saying that at all. What I am saying is this. Spiritual Israel raised their children with a purpose. They had many verses to direct them and a vision to inspire them, and they did it with their whole heart. I believe we need to follow the example of spiritual Israel, and reap some powerful results.

Did you ever consider, as I mentioned already, that this is the kind of home in which our Lord Jesus was raised? You can be sure that when the Father in heaven was searching to find the right family setting for His Son, He made sure that all these things were in place. This would also apply to the home in which John the Baptist was raised. The Bible says of John's parents, *"They were both righteous before God, walking in all the commandments and ordinances of the Lord blameless"* (Lk. 1:6). This is quite a powerful statement. What do you think their home was like?

Remember the Bible pictures we looked at: polished cornerstones, nurtured plants, olive plants, the house, making the arrows, and laying a foundation. These visions are the fuel that made the fire, that produced the Jewish home we just viewed. Each illustration is full of vision, method, and action. Acting on these visions and methods, Israel raised up godly children for Yahweh. Their lives were filled with raising their children.

The question that comes to my mind is this: are we willing to pay the price? There is a price tag on a beautiful home like this. What is the price, and who is ready to pay it? When I am preaching about the home, it often happens that older folks stand to testify at the end of the message. They testify with tears, " Oh, if only I had heard these things thirty years ago!" They always admonish the young parents to pay the price at all cost because they have lost their children to the world. Their perspective is worthy of our consideration. When those who have lost their children look back, having lived with that loss every day, it puts an urgency in their plea.

Who then are willing to consecrate themselves to the Lord, so that grace may flow through them, so that they change their priorities and train up their children in the ways of the Lord? Up until now, there have not been many who are willing. This is changing, and I praise God for this change, but there have not been many. If this statement seems too strong, stop and look around you. How many homes do you know in which the children are all-out for God? We have very few examples to follow. The churches should be full of gray heads who have successfully reared a generation of soldiers, out on the fields fighting the war. In reality, they are but a very few. Dear fathers and mothers, we owe the next generation of parents an example that they can study and follow. Pay the price; pay it all. Don't hold back, and don't let up one bit! Give your whole heart to it, you will never be sorry.

The House of Stephanas

Ye know the house of Stephanas...that they have addicted themselves to the ministry of the saints.
I Corinthians 16:15

Here is the testimony of a wholehearted household in one simple sentence. As in the previous text about Joshua, this word "house" is referring to the whole household of Stephanas: father, mother, children, and even servants. When Paul went to Corinth to preach the gospel, this family became his first converts. There is not much written about them. However, as you can see from the verse, what is written speaks volumes about them. It seems that when they heard the Good News, they all entered in from the beginning with joy and enthusiasm. They are a special family to me because of the word "addicted" in the verse. I was addicted to drugs and alcohol before I was born again, so I know the strength of the word "addicted." When Paul referred to this family in his letter to the Corinthian church, he used the word "know." This is an experiential word. Paul was saying, "You know how this family lives; you know their testimony among you."

Here is a godly family whose commitment to Christ is without question. Stephanas and his wife were so in love with Christ that the whole family was affected by it. The house of Stephanas addicted themselves to, or allowed themselves to get hooked on, serving the saints. Wow! What an example for us today!

For the past twenty years, I have taken this family as a model to pattern after. May God give us a vision like this today, that it may be said of our family ten years from now, "that the whole family is given over to the work of God!" This is my goal that from the youngest to the oldest, the whole family will be sold out to live for God. I believe if we live a life of zeal and joy before them, the little ones will want to serve God in their innocence, and the older ones will rise up and say, "I want to serve God with my life." They will do it, yes they will! They will want to pass out tracts, go out preaching, work on the streets of some major city in America, sing, pray, and so on. They will want to do all the godly things that you do.

I don't know what your response is to such an example, but my heart says, "Oh, God, I want that mountain, and I will have that mountain." May God give us the Spirit of Caleb, who believed God's promise to him and rose up in strength to possess it.

The House of the Elder

Consider the illustration of a bishop (elder) in the New Testament (I Tim. 3:1-7). One requirement of a bishop is to make sure he has a family that is in order. Many of the character requirements listed for church leaders were described with one word. But when the Holy Spirit came to the area of the leader's home, many words are used. A man's family is probably the greatest revelation of who he really is. Someone once said, " True character is who you are when no one is looking." I think this is what God is saying when He places so much emphasis on the home of a potential leader. The Bible uses terms such as "faithful children" and "one that ruleth well his own house." We know it is true: if you find a home that is in order, you have found a man who lives right, behind closed doors.

You see, our family gives us away. We cannot hide who we really are. We may think for a few years that nobody knows who we really are. But it's not true. Our children give us away every time. If father and mother are sober, the children are sober. If father and mother are critical, the children are critical. We cannot hide ourselves. A man's family speaks volumes about his private everyday life. A happy wife and faithful children give a silent message that the head of the house is walking with God when the doors are shut. My family is an expression, and an extension of me. That can be a very painful reality to face at times, but we men must get honest with ourselves on this point.

I realize I am saying some pretty heavy things in the last few pages. I am moving beyond the realm of inspiration and challenge on purpose. We need to make some changes. It is time to get serious about our homes. Many of them are going the way of most homes in America today--nowhere. Very few people are really willing to pay the price it will take to turn their homes around, very few.

Most people are too busy, too busy to raise up godly children who will hit the mark in the enemy's camp some day. This doesn't make any sense in my mind, but it's a matter of priority. We are too busy making money, building a business, or chasing the American dream, or maybe we are simply caught in the rat race of our society. Brethren, stop the wheel; I want to get off.

We say in business, "You get what you pay for," and this is true. However, if it is true in business, how much more is it true with our families. You will get what you pay for, although it may be 30 years before you see what you bought. II Corinthians 9:6 is a powerful verse when applied to the time we invest in our families. Hearken to these words. "But this I say, He which soweth sparingly shall reap also sparingly; and he which soweth bountifully shall reap also bountifully." For some of us, applying this verse to our homes calls for a major change in our priorities. True repentance is a change of mind that brings about a change of action. This is what is needed in many of our hearts. Old-fashioned repentance says, "Lord, I'm going the wrong way, and I turn." This is the kind repentance that Paul describes in II Corinthians 7, an absolute change of heart and action.

Now It Is Our Turn

It is God's will that we have wholehearted households. You may not have much of this to look back to when you consider the home in which you grew up, but it is God's will that your children have it. Yes, maybe our parents have failed, but now it is our turn. There are two things we can do with our parent's failures in the home. We can let the memory of it make us bitter, as we complain about how bad it was. Or we can let the memory provoke us on to higher ground, and thus make us better. The choice is ours. Let us rise above their failures and march to the beat of a different drum. Let us chart a new course for the sake of our children, so that we can give them a different kind of heritage, a godly heritage.

Dear parents, now it is our turn. Raising children is no sideline issue with God. It is a major part of the Christian life. This is evident from all we have considered thus far. Besides the work of the ministry, rearing my children for God is the most challenging, maturing, self-denying, time-consuming thing I do. It must be so for all of us. In fact, the longer I ponder the responsibilities of raising a family, the more I realize that they prepare a man for ministry like nothing else can do. We need to follow the words of Paul in Philippians 3:13b,14, *"Forgetting those thing which are behind, and reaching forth unto those things which are before, I press toward the mark..."* Surely, the raising of our children is part of the *"high calling of God in Christ Jesus."*

Prayer

God our Father, what shall we do Lord? We live in America, and we have lost sight of Your vision for our children. Please come and help us to regain the desires we once had. How do we do these wholehearted things in our fast-moving society? We open our hearts and homes to You right now. Redirect our hearts and our homes. In Jesus' name. Amen.

12

Garden Rules for Raising Children

Ye fathers, provoke not your children to wrath: but bring them up in the nurture and admonition of the Lord.
Ephesians 6:4

The title of this chapter seems fitting in the light of some of the Bible pictures we have been considering. We have pictured our sons as plants, nurtured to fruit-bearing maturity. We have also pictured our children as olive plants, waiting for parents to bring them up to mature olive trees flowing with oil. "O God, grant us the wisdom and the grace to do it."

The verse I have selected to begin this chapter is one of those all-inclusive verses in the Bible. It has a volume of admonitions hidden in it. I say this because of all the instructions we find in God's word preceding it. God does not say a lot in the New Testament about raising children because He has already said it in dozens of verses in the Old Testament. If we spent 30 minutes a day for an entire year meditating on and applying this simple little verse, we would not exhaust its wealth. That is the way God's Word is: it has many applications tucked away inside it. But we must meditate in order to draw them out for our lives.

The opening verse begins with a clarion call out of heaven to us men: *"Ye Fathers."* I am gripped again and again by the persistent call to the fathers to shoulder the burden and responsibility of the home. It is clear from the whole of Scripture that God has commanded patriarchy in the home and society. This word "patriarchy" is an older word, which simply means that the fathers are to be the heads of families.

Paul then presents us fathers with two contrasting ways that we can go: we can make our children angry or we can lead them in the ways of righteousness. Allow me to share my personal observations on how this verse shakes out in real-life situations. I have noticed that wherever the parents are neglecting to lead the children down the paths of righteousness, there is a very natural, continual provoking to wrath. Let me explain.

Where there is a neglect of caring, positive direction, there usually is disorder, disobedience, and chaos. When these three sisters dwell in any household, the parents begin to rule in frustration, anxiety, and anger. A child left to himself will quickly bring the parent to the place where they have "had enough." This causes parents to scream at the children, spank in anger, and many other abusive actions. Obviously, the smart approach to family life is a well-thought-out plan of positive direction: *"Bring them up in the nurture and admonition of the Lord."* I say more about anger later, but let's go on to the better way.

A couple of human examples illustrate the far-reaching scope of this verse. If I were to say to you gardeners, "Go and raise up a garden," or if I were to say to a builder, "Go and build a house," this is not a simple one-step command. There is a whole volume of lesser commands in each statement. This is exactly the kind of command that God is giving us here in His Word.

To the builder, dozens of activities come to mind. To the gardener also, dozens of subpoints immediately fall in line under the one all-inclusive command. In the same way, when God says, *"Bring them up in the nurture and admonition of the Lord,"* dozens of principles should come to mind. When we hear this command, if our mind is relatively empty, we have a big problem. Just like the gardener does who cannot think of much to do when he hears the command to raise a crop. The gardener needs to get the books out and study. I think that is where many of God's people are. Their minds are rather blank when it comes to raising children. As I am writing the pages of this book, one of my goals is to help fill the blank mind with dozens of inspiring ideas on how to raise your children for Christ. This will not happen unless there comes up in you a strong desire to become a student in Child Training 101. Your response to what you read is the key to the future of your family.

I have had a tape set on the home in circulation for many years now. I have noticed the different ways people respond to those sermons when they hear them. Some people listen to them once and put them on the shelf. Some people listen, fall on their faces, repent, and are changed. But then, there is a smaller group of people who carefully listen to them a dozen times. Which group do you think gets the most mileage out of the tapes? We all know the answer. When I am in the home of one of those couples who became students of the Godly Home tapes, I immediately know something is different.

Back To The Garden

I want to consider another aspect of the garden illustration for a moment and stir some faith in our hearts for our homes. Our God is the creator of all things, both in heaven and on earth. As the Creator, He also established laws, or principles, by which all of His creation functions. There are natural laws as well as spiritual laws, and we as human beings must learn to function within both sets of laws. The natural laws of raising a crop in the garden are well known by all gardeners. They know them well because the laws always operate in the same way. For example:

- ❖ If you don't plow and loosen the soil, the plants won't grow well.
- ❖ No water, no crop--plain and simple: This law never changes.
- ❖ If you don't enrich the soil, the crop will be poor.
- ❖ If you don't keep the weeds pulled out around the plants, you will have very small fruit.
- ❖ Corn seeds grow corn; bean seeds grow beans; and so forth.
- ❖ You must learn to plant at the right time of the year, or the seeds won't germinate.

THE PURSUIT OF GODLY SEED

I think I have listed enough examples to bring the point home to our hearts. God's laws of gardening are unchangable. I am a city boy. I grew up in Omaha, Nebraska. When I moved to the country twenty years ago, I jumped into gardening with enthusiasm and a teachable heart. I have learned firsthand that these principles do not budge. They work every time. God has set them in order just as He has the law of gravity. You follow them, and you can expect a harvest, without fail.

Receive and Believe

I would like to convince you that the principles of raising children work as surely as the laws for raising a garden. The question is, do you believe that? *Many of God's people do not believe.* In fact, they live in fear, doubt, and unbelief in the area of their children. The enemy has blinded God's people in this realm, and they can hardly believe that God will save and sanctify their children.

Our heavenly Father has established spiritual promises and principles, that apply to the raising of children, and they work. We could call them "The Laws of the Harvest for Godly Children." I believe if we follow the principles God gives in His Word, we will see results, lasting results. If we go out into our garden and plant seeds in the ground, we know something is going to grow. We believe in, or have faith in, the laws of the harvest and confidently sow our seeds in the ground. My prayer for each of you is that God would infuse into your heart a believing faith for your home. We cannot be full of doubt as we endeavor to nurture our children. We must be like Caleb of old who said, with a heart full of faith in God's promises, *"I want that mountain."*

My testimony is this: I believe, and I do not faint in my heart as I raise my children. I do not listen to the lies of Satan who comes along and says, "It's not going to work out." I have faith in the promises and the principles of God's Word. I believe if I do what the Bible says, then God will do what He said He will do, and I am confident about it! Raising my children is not a giant to me. It is a blessed opportunity.

May God give us a vision of faith, faith in what God will do if we will just simply follow His Word in raising our children. The promise is a harvest of godly children who love the Lord fervently and obey Him willingly. The elements of faith and a promised harvest will change our whole perspective. Instead of a new list of things we have to do, our hearts rise up with joy, and we say, "These principles work! Let's do them and get the harvest!"

The element of faith also changes how we receive instruction and correction. We can approach them with joyful anticipation. Most people get rather touchy when you try to talk to them about their children. They are easily offended when you try to give them an admonition. Maybe you have tried before and have sensed that coolness of spirit, that quietness, that wall going up. I have noticed it many times as a pastor. I believe it happens because our children are a part of us, an expression of who we really are. I would like to encourage you as you read this book to open up your hearts to learn. If we really have our sights set on a godly home, we will welcome the admonitions that come our way.

Jackie and I receive much criticism concerning our home, and our children. I often wonder about the motives behind some of the criticism, but nonetheless, we receive it with an open, learning heart. We are students of training our children, and we have much to learn. When somebody comes to me with some criticism about my home, I welcome it and receive it very seriously. I go home and think about it. I bring it to Jackie, and we sit down and take a look at it. We discuss the concern that has come and pray about it. Why do we respond this way? Because we don't want to make a mistake. We don't want to find out ten years from now that we made a big mistake. We want to know now.

We humans do a lot of things that do not make much sense, and the area of the home is no exception. We readily take advice in many lesser things, yet ruffle at the advice given about the most important things. If a sister has found a way to clean spots out of a garment in half the time, or a way to get rid of potato bugs in the garden, we listen with attentive ears. If a brother has discovered a way to save three miles to the gallon on fuel, we men perk up our ears and tune in. No one would even think a negative thought about it. We rise up in faith, quickly make the change, and eagerly await the added benefit. But somehow, when someone comes with a helpful admonition about having peaceful children, we take it so personally, get offended, and pass it off as nothing. I encourage each one of you to have the humble attitude of a learner. Come to each chapter with a teachable spirit, and with an open heart, willing to examine your home. Shall we give our gardens more openness and care than our children receive? God forbid.

Lessons From the Persecuted
The life and testimony of the persecuted church has been a rich blessing to me throughout my Christian life. I cannot begin to explain how much persecuted believers have influenced me and my theology. I read books about them whenever I have opportunity. They have been humbled and purified through suffering, and the beautiful life of Christ flows out of this. We have much to learn from these simple saints. I have been challenged by their diligent pursuit of godly children. Because of the elements of persecution, they must attend to their little olive plants with careful zeal. Oh, what diligence they exercise in the training of their children.

Let's take Russia as an example. I know that persecution has eased there for a while, but it was intense for many years. In Russia, the children went to the Communist schools. At these schools, the Christian children were laughed at and openly mocked. They were beaten and had their Bibles torn up in front of the class. Things were very hard for them at school. Imagine what it would be like. The teachers were determined to tear Christianity out of the hearts and minds of these children and openly preached against it in the classroom.

The parents knew their children would have to go through these kinds of experiences when they sent them away to the Communist schools. What could they do? They didn't have the opportunities we have to send them to a Christian school or teach them at home. These hard circumstances wrought something in the hearts of the parents that we need here in free America. It made those fathers and mothers very earnest. They had to do right. They had to train those children. They had to pray for their children. They had to live out a Christian example before them because they had to send those children out into an ugly, mean

Garden Rules for Raising Children

world that was set to destroy them. With brokenness and determination, they earnestly applied the garden rules for raising children.

I tremble at times when I think about our children facing persecution. Millions of them are not prepared for even a small amount of it. I am convinced that it will come to America. We must prepare. It would do us good to meditate upon the example of the persecuted church as we examine how much time we are giving to the training of our children. And by the way, the Communists didn't get very many of those children. God's promises and principles prevailed even in the midst of Communism.

There is, however, a sad ending to the story of some of these Russian Christians. Many of them have now fled to America to escape future persecution. They haven't done so well here with all the freedom and worldliness of the "Christians" in this land. Many parents have let up, and even given up their responsibility to raise their children, and the results are tragic. They are losing them to the world by the hundreds. They have joined in with the "Christians" in America and have allowed their children to drift slowly into the world. How sad this is to me, after being so inspired by their fervent approach to child training.

I spoke to a sincere Russian Christian some time ago about the differences between Russia and America. He made this staggering statement. He said, "I have learned that the devil has put on different clothes. In Russia, he had a stick in his hand. But in America, he has a smile on his face." Maybe some of us Americans should learn the same thing.

It's Just the Grace of God

Many years ago we had the opportunity to spend some time in the home of a dear Mennonite couple who had twelve children. They had invited us over for a meal and a time of fellowship. We were so excited about the visit because of the opportunity to learn from them about their home. We had three small children at the time, and we were like sponges looking for water. We sat down at a long extension table prepared for twenty people. It was an inspiring scene to say the least. There sat father and mother and twelve olive plants around the table, all in lovely order. We had a nice visit at the table while we shared a meal together. Then came the words that I had been waiting for. When the meal was finished, the father spoke to me and said, "Let's go sit in the living room and visit awhile."

You can imagine how I felt inside. This man has what I want, what I want with all my heart--a godly family. The ages of his twelve children ranged from three to twenty-five. I was thinking, "I am sitting on a gold mine, and now it is time to ask questions." We went into the living room and sat down, and I proceeded to glean all I could. I began, "Please tell me, sir, what principles did you follow to produce these lovely, obedient children?"

I'll never forget what he said. He said, "Well, I didn't do anything. *It's just the grace of God.*" I thought to myself, "What? Is it just the grace of God? I know there is more to it than that."

Now I know it is a good and humble thing to say, but it's not true. It's *not* just the grace of God. If you leave it all to the grace of God, you will be sadly disappointed. Could this be one of the reasons why things have not turned out very well, because we have left it all to the "grace of God" when God gave us principles to follow? It's *not* just the grace of God. I agree, when we get all finished, and we are old, and all our children are raised, yes, we will say, "If it wasn't for the grace of God, we never could have done it." But we also will have to acknowledge that there were many things that we did, according to the Word of God, in order for the children to turn out right. In reality, God's mysterious grace has no platform on which to work if we do not pick up our tools and go to work.

Imagine going out into the garden, planting the seeds, and then sitting down on a lawn chair and trusting the grace of God to take care of the rest: no hoeing, no weeding, no fertilizing, no cultivating or watering. Imagine how foolish that would be. If you plant a garden like that, and just trust the grace of God, you will have a weed patch, with a little bit of fruit on some very small plants.

So let me encourage you. There are many things that we must do. It takes a proper balance of faith and works to produce a healthy garden, and it is the same with our families. The truth is, true faith fills the heart and moves the will to get up and do something, with joyful expectation. Israel trusted in God, but they also went out to battle. Abraham believed God, but he still commanded his household after him. We need to trust in God, believe His promises, and *"bring them up in the nurture and admonition of the Lord "* (Eph. 6:4b).

Prayer
Our God and Father, hallowed be Thy name. We see so clearly that You have not left us here without good instruction about the children. Make us students of child training. Give us the openess and brokeness we need to be teachable. Put a fervent spirit in us and help us to see the urgency that is reality. We are so often asleep. Please wake us up to the promises and the provisions You have made. In Jesus Christ's name. Amen.

Meditations

A Parent's Love

Love does not lose patience with the children.
Love looks for ways to be kind to the children.
Love is not envious of the children.
Love is not eager to impress the children.
Love is not boastful to the children.
Love has good manners with the children.
Love doesn't pursue selfish advantage over the children.
Love is not easily provoked by the children.
Love does not rejoice over evil that the children do.
Love rejoices when truth prevails in the children.
Love bears all things for the children.
Love believes the best in the children.
Love hopes for gain in the children.
Love endures all that opposes it for the children.
Love never fails for the children.

...based on I Corinthians 13

Brother Denny

13

Blessings: the Key to Obedience

We love him, because he first loved us.

I John 4:19

I have spent many chapters looking at the visionary aspect of our homes. I feel this is very necessary if we are going to consistently carry out the practical side of child training. As our hearts are inflamed with God's vision for the family, we will be moved with desire, and infused with the daily power to obtain that desire. Now that the vision has been well covered, we are going to turn the corner and move into the practical "how to raise children" aspects of this book.

The title of this chapter holds the most profound wisdom you will ever glean for child training. In a sense, this is the fountain from which everything else flows. I have chosen the word "blessings." I could have easily used the word "love," but it is so overused, I hesitate to do so. We all feel as though we love our children.

As we move into some of the more practical issues of training children, it is important to have these issues in the proper order of priority. Love and blessings come first. There is a danger of passing over the aspects of love, blessings, and relationships, and quickly going on to corrections, spanking, and standards of holiness. I don't want you to do this. It is a grave mistake made by many.

Years ago, I was intrigued by the pattern I saw in many people as they listened to my set of tapes on the home. They would draw out the tape on discipline and listen to it first. They had a whole set of twelve tapes in their hands, but they would reach into the center of the set and take the one on discipline. I thought to myself, "Why do they choose that one above the others?" I know the answer to my question now, and it saddens me to know it. They think that spanking their children will be a cure-all for their family woes. It will not solve them. The needs in our homes go much deeper than spanking and obedience.

The Law Is Love
Our Lord Jesus Christ had a way of saying deep, far-reaching things in a very simple statements. Because of this, his words often went over the heads of the Pharisees. They were always after him about laws and traditions because that is how they viewed God. Jesus summed up the whole of the Christian life for them in two statements. They missed the depth of what He was saying, but we do not have to miss it. He told them that all the law and all the prophets hang on just two commandments: "Thou shalt love the Lord thy God with all thy heart," and "thou shalt love thy neighbor as thyself" (Matt. 22:37a, 39b). You can trace every precept back to these two basic commandments.

This applies to all that I say about the home also. It all can be traced back to love and should all flow out of love. Paul made it even stronger when he said, "Though I give my body to be burned, and have not charity, it profiteth me nothing" (I Cor. 13:3b). This is what was wrong with the Pharisees. They did all kinds of right things, but not out of love for God and love for their neighbor. Beloved, we can do the same thing with our children. We can neglect the "weightier matters of the Law" as they did and pass on a religion to our children but not "the faith." I assure you, it doesn't come out right. The law is love. The motivation is love. It is very important to keep this in mind as we look at many practical issues.

Years ago, when my tapes on the home first started to circulate among God's people, I received many troubling phone calls. Parents called me to tell me that my teachings did not work. They were referring to the tape on discipline, and many times they were one of those parents who listened to that tape first. They said to me, "My child doesn't respond the way you said he would on your tape. We are not friends when I am done spanking."

At first, I wasn't sure where the problem was. I spent much time in prayer and personal meditation, with a question mark before the Lord. One day the answer came to me. The difference is love. That is the key. We spanked our children in the midst of a loving relationship and had beautiful results. Many parents are not close to their children. If a parent begins to use the rod without a relationship, the results can be negative.

I wanted to test my answer with some of these parents who were calling to make sure I had the right revelation. As the calls came, I began to ask the question, "How is your relationship with your child? Is it a close one?" The answer was the same every time. They admitted that the child was not close to them. I realized then that there was a hole in my teaching. Jackie and I love our children deeply, and I didn't realize that others might spank theirs without that deep love. The law is love and blessings. We cannot get away from this. This is the key that opens a great big door of many opportunities in child training.

God's Burden for Relationships

And he shall turn the heart of the fathers to the children, and the heart of the children to their fathers.
Malachi 4:6

We look at this verse in detail later, but I want to draw out the burden of the Lord for a moment. In this verse we have a revelation of God's concern about the flow of love between fathers and children. This flow of love and blessing is the foundation of all your child training. Remember the first love I mentioned in Chapter three. In the first days after they are born, love flows from your heart to theirs. This first-love relationship should be the foundation stone of a lifelong flow of love between parents and child. Hearts connects and grow closer together as the days go by. If this connection of heart is lost through ignorance or neglect, problems arise very early in the development of the child. Many parents then try to use the rod to cure the problems. It won't work. Blessings is the key to obedience.

This closeness is understood by many mothers. It is part of a mother's love, something God gives her instinctively. A mother builds on this as she cares for her baby. She talks to the baby while she is nursing, even though the baby cannot understand words. A mother knows that communication is taking place. I have always enjoyed watching Jackie nurse the children. She is an excellent communicator, and the words of love and affirmation flowed while she nursed. She was building a bond with the child, and I knew it.

But God is concerned about the fathers. I meet many fathers who are not close to their children. They complain to me that there is very little heart connection with them. They are confounded over the lack of respect and obedience they receive from their children, not realizing that the one breeds the other.

Brethren, this is part of the desolation of past generations. It must be repaired, as Isaiah prophesied in 61:4b. We need to join our wives and build a bond of love with our children when they are very small. I know that many of us are crippled in this area because our fathers were also. They did not bond with us, and now we do not have a clue how to bond with our children. This must be broken! We can learn how to build relationships with our children. God will help us if we cry out to Him. I can testify to God's enabling in this area. I didn't know what I was doing, but God and my wife taught me how to build.

Many fathers live under a false assumption that we have no responsibility until the child gets older. This is a lie. We must build a foundation of love with our children from the beginning, and then we can build a structure on top of it all their days.

My children heard the gentle voice of their father continually from the moment of birth. When Jackie needed me to hold the baby while she attended to other household duties, I held the baby with purpose. It was an opportunity to communicate. I gave words of kindness, and the baby gave me back a smile and kicked its feet. Some undiscerning parents might think this is folly, but I disagree. I talked to the child about all kinds of things.

I got baby toys and dangled them before the child in play, talking all the while.

You see, there is more to words than sound. In words, heart talks to heart, and the spirit of love or rejection is transferred to the child. Many of us do not understand the unseen dynamics of communicating with a child. We see a small baby's body, and forget that it is an eternal being with a never-dying soul. I am using this big word, "communicate," on purpose because of its meaning. The root word of communicate, is "commune," which means to have a two-way interchange, a two-way flow of conversation, and a two-way flow of hearts. This is what a parent should be doing with a small child.

As parents, we are the initiators of love to our children. This is very obvious, but often missed. It is the same way with our heavenly Father: *"We love him, because he first loved us"* (I Jn. 4:19). This verse can be applied to our homes. The children could easily say, "We love our parents, because they first loved us." How sad it is for a child to grow up with a disinterested father, or even a disinterested mother, for that matter. This is a plague in our land. We are reaping the fruit of two or three generations of disconnected fathers. Again, I say, God is greatly concerned about the relationships of fathers and their children.

I made it a priority to play with my children as they were growing up. I got down on the floor like a little boy, grabbed my son's toy tractor, and away we would go, vro--om, vro--om, vro--om. We plowed the fields and loaded the hay. We drove the truck over to the barn as I lived in his imaginary play world. What was I doing? I get no thrill out of playing tractor on the floor, besides the fact that it thrills the little boy. What was I doing? Building a bond of love with my son. His face would light up when he saw me come into the house, and my face did too. We were buddies.

Have you ever gone into your little girl's make shift playhouse and played dolls with her? Try it some time. Pick up her favorite doll, hold and rock it for awhile and see what happens. You will notice a look of endearment on your little girl's face as she watches you love her baby. Dear fathers, this is not simply child's play. We are laying the foundation stones of a lifelong love and respect for each other. Your child will think you are "the best daddy in the whole wide world."

Someone said to me, " How do you get your twelve-year-old to talk to you?" This is a good question. Let me tell you how I did it. You let him talk your ear off when he is five, and you talk his ear off while he is five. Be his buddy! Be her sweet daddy friend.

I will never forget the first time Elisabeth gave me this name. I think she was about four years old. I was carrying her up the stairs, and she stopped me halfway up, put her little hands on my face, and said, "Papa, do you know what? You are my sweet daddy friend." I was smitten by love from that day forward. As I reflected on those words, I thought, "there is a lot of meaning in these words. You're sweet, you're my daddy, and you're my friend." Amen? Build a relationship with your children. Get close to them, give them "horseyback" rides and wrestle around with them in the yard. Have fun with them, work with them, and hold their hand. Enjoy your children, and they will sense it and draw close to you. The closer your relationship is with your children, the more they will receive all the things you want to put into them.

The Power of Love
As parents manifest sincere love to a small child, the child begins to reciprocate the same back to them, and a mutual bond of respect and honor is formed. This bond is very important when it is time to teach, to train, to spank, and to correct them. This close relationship will encourage a natural flow of obedience and a desire to please in the child. If you try to raise your sons and daughters without it, you will have many more problems with practical training and obedience.

Let us reason together for a moment. In your own experience with God, what motivates you to serve and obey Him? Is it the fear of chastisement or the love and blessings that God pours on you daily? For me, I feel so willing and free after a sweet time in His presence, as I am assured of His love. I believe it is the same with our children. They will prosper under the shining faces of their parents. This is the theology of the New Covenant and the foundation of our service to God. God loves us and accepts us as his beloved children. Because of this, we are motivated to obedience.

Love is Spelled "T-I-M-E"

Some time ago, when Esther was a little girl, we started having a problem with her that concerned me. I felt as though she was not responding well when asked to do something. Her obedience was slow and half-hearted. This went on for a couple of weeks, and we started thinking that maybe we had a strong-willed child on our hands. Our natural response was to increase the discipline and bring her will into subjection. As I was praying over her one morning, the Lord spoke to me in the quiet of my heart. He seemed to say to me, "Maybe Esther just needs more loving attention from her Papa." I received this word with a willing heart and set out to work on our relationship in many small ways.

For about three weeks, I took her along when I went to the store. I spent more time reading books to her and just talking about things she wanted to talk about. I turned my attention on my sweet little daughter, and many good things began to happen. The obedience problems disappeared in about two weeks. I noticed a new light in her eyes when she saw me come into the house, and she just wanted to be with me all the time.

I was preaching at a church in northern Pennsylvania a few years ago, and a friend of mine brought me his "hard" child-training questions. He said, "Brother Denny, what do I do with my strong-willed child?" He had a small boy about two years old. He asked me if I had any special secrets for the strong-willed child. I didn't answer quickly, although I already knew what I was going to say. Then I said to him, "Yes, I do. I have a great secret for you, but I'm not sure you are ready to hear it." I was leading him a bit, in hopes that I would really get his attention. It worked well because he was soon begging me for the advice. I said to him, "The secret is, t-i-m-e," spelling out the word. Then I gave him a short explanation of the principle of building a relationship with his child.

T-i-m-e is something that we Americans don't have a very great quanity of. This is ironic, to say the least, because we have more time-saving devices than anyone else in the world. We also have more time freedom than any nation in the world. I'm sure my friend was expecting me to say something about spanking the child, but that is not always what is needed. We think that spanking is the answer to all our woes, but it is not. We American Christians want a quick fix for obedience, so we go for the rod. This will not come out right. A sweet flow of love and respect is more powerful than the rod. Take the t-i-m-e and draw close to your child.

The New Covenant Law of Blessing

All through the Old Testament, we see the principle of blessings being practiced. I have already described to you how a Jewish father blessed his children every Sabbath evening. The Lord God is the One who started the practice when He gave a blessing to Adam and Eve. Fathers blessed their children. Leaders blessed the men who were taking their place, and old men blessed their sons as they were preparing to die. I love the picture of a string of children all lined up waiting their turn to receive a spoken blessing from their father.

Some time ago, our family was standing in a line waiting to ride the elevator in the Washington Monument in Washington, D.C. As we were waiting our turn, a Jewish man walked up and cut into the line where I was standing. I believe he thought I was a Jew. We had a nice conversation about many things, including the Messiah. During our visit, I asked him about his family. His face lit up with joy, and he told me all about his children. While I was listening, I thought to myself, "I'm going to see if he gives the Sabbath evening blessing to his children." I asked him, and sure enough, he said he does it every Friday evening.

One day, as I was meditating on this principle, it dawned on me that this is an Old Testament ritual, a law, something that often was done out of duty. I have learned in my study of the word that what God commands as a duty in the Old Testament becomes a beautiful way of life in the New Testament because of the power of the Holy Ghost. For example, they gave the tenth part of their increase in the Old, but we joyfully give everything in the New. We give our money, our time, our plans, yea, all of our life to God, with joy.

If "the blessing" was a ritual and a duty under the Old Covenant, then it should be a way of life in the New Covenant. What does this mean in practical everyday living? Your children need your blessing all day long. It is the will of God that they grow up in an atmosphere of affirming love. As much as I like the ritual of blessing the children, it is not enough. They need to be surrounded with a life of blessings that they receive from their parents. Oh, the power of such a life! The effect this has on your children cannot be measured.

Consider the example of the Jewish father blessing his son. Picture the sincere father, standing in his house, ready to bless his son . As the son approaches his father, the father's face shines out at his boy with a smile of love and affirmation. He reaches out to touch him, as he speaks words of value and love over his life. Any child would prosper under this kind of weekly blessing, but what if it happened in spirit many times in a day? What would the results be? Words of this nature spoken with true love behind them will influence a child into eternity. This should be happening many times in a day from your heart in your home.

Let's plant this picture into some everyday life experiences and see how it fits. It is much easier for us to grasp the principle if we have some real-life situations to ponder. By the way, this is for mothers also. However, there is something about a father's blessing that seems to have more effect. Maybe it is because he represents God to the children. Although this is true, with many dads away working, the mothers have more practical opportunities to bless the children. Here are some instances in which your children ought to hear words of affirming love.

Children ought to see and hear words of blessing...

- ❖ When you see them first thing in the morning
- ❖ When you check up on some of their schoolwork
- ❖ When they have done a good job with the chores
- ❖ As you sit down to have a meal together

- ❖ When the child comes to confess something he or she did that displeases you
- ❖ When they come into the house after their playtime
- ❖ After you have given them a spanking for a wrong they have done
- ❖ When you come home from work or from running an errand
- ❖ When your child comes out to see you while you are working in the shop
- ❖ After prayers at bedtime
- ❖ On the child's birthday or during other special events in his or her life
- ❖ When they are leaving home for a longer period of time.

Can you see how the principle and spirit of blessings can be incorporated into all of these situations? Wow, that could change the atmosphere of your home! If you had any idea how much influence this could have on your home, you would start today. Children thrive under this kind of care. This is the oil that lubricates all the rest of the aspects of training. By the way, this kind of stuff is contagious. It spreads to everyone in the family. In time, you will have everyone blessing each other, and this is good training for the future.

Some time ago, when our youngest son David was two, the whole family was sitting together having our traditional Sunday evening snack. We were all enjoying little David as we talked and laughed. You know how a two-year-old is. His sweet young life was blessing all of us, and everyone was loving him and affirming him as we laughed together. As I sat there and watched, I thought to myself, "David, you have it made; you have no idea how blessed you are." There he was, surrounded with love and affection, not just from Mom and Dad, but from seven of his brothers and sisters also. What a life he has! What an influence we are having on him! He will never grow up thinking that he is of no value. This is the way God planned it to be. You see, the children are very valuable to Him. We are to communicate that value by our love.

BLESSINGS: THE KEY TO OBEDIENCE

There are so many hurting, rejected people everywhere. The wounds run very deep at times, and they often come by the neglect and rejection of parents in the home. This is a tragic situation. These hurts are often carried into adulthood and on into marriage. Our homes are turning out dysfunctional adults who have a hard time in a real world of cares and responsibilities. Marriages are on the rocks. Prisons are filling up, and even the health of many is affected by the confusion that this neglect brings.

I was in a meeting a few months ago in which a sermon was preached about fatherhood, and the destructive curse that has come by absentee fathers. The preacher asked the question, "How many of you in this meeting have never heard your father say, 'I love you?' " Because of my burden for the homes in our land, my eyes perked up to see the hands that were raised. I was shocked, hurt, and frankly devastated at what I saw. Ninety percent of the people raised their hands. Then the preacher went on to say that he had been asking that question all over America, with the same results. I weep for the children who grow up in this environment of rejection. We are suffering from two generations of absentee fathers, and about a half generation of absentee mothers. The results are devastating. When will it all end? We are missing the mark with our precious children, and many of us do not even know how we are hurting them.

A Natural Desire to Please

God has placed in the heart of every child a natural desire to please his parents. All parents acknowledge this God-given desire. The children just love us and overlook many of our faults. We all have seen it in their faces when they have done something for us and they want us to know what they have done. They look expectantly at us for approval. They want to please. If this is so, we ought to take advantage of this desire and increase it by showering them with love and acceptance. If we will go after the heart of our child and be his friend, we will reap the results of "much more obedience" from our labors. A close relationship is the key to obedience, not spanking. Many parents squelch this desire by neglect and nagging because they are too busy. I call them "not now parents."

The child comes again and again looking for affirmation from his parents, and all he hears is, "Not now …I'm too busy. Later."

I often hurt deeply for the children of busy parents. The zeal to please is slowly put out, yet the "Christian" parents demand obedience and respect from them. This is a gross perversion of truth. The Bible calls it iniquity. It is truth out of balance. I am not saying that we should not require them to obey. We must. I am saying that we as parents need to do our homework. If there is a strained relationship with any of your children, I urge you to do whatever you need to do to clear the air. Sometimes parents need to get right with their children. If you are one of those "not now parents," I encourage you to have a family revival meeting where everyone gets everything out on the table and makes things right. Be the example in this, and be the first one to bow your heart in humility and say, "I have sinned." You will see. The children will quickly forgive and give you a chance to change. Go after the hearts of your children with zeal and purpose. This is a "must do" before we get into the practical issues that follow in this book.

Prayer

Father in heaven, have mercy on me. I have sinned against You and my children. Please forgive me in Jesus Christ's name. I am too busy. I see it clearly, and my priorities are not right. I repent before You right now. I will make a change, I will get things right with the children, and I will turn this curse into a blessing. Give me Your grace. I cannot do this on my own. I will only fail again if You don't help me. Open my eyes in the days to come, that I might see my need more clearly, and never go back to my folly. I pray for my children. Renew their desire to want to please me, and give me their hearts. I pray in Jesus Christ's name. Amen.

Papa blessing David on his third birthday. We always give the children breakfast in bed on their special day. Sometimes we follow a theme. David chose to be a shepherd boy, and Jackie had fun doing everything in the form of sheep.

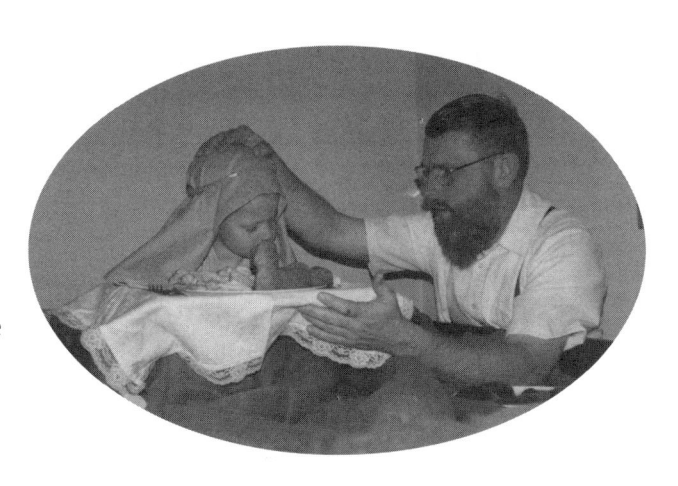

Rebekah is getting a blessing from Papa when she came home from Africa for a visit. His name of endearment has always been "the general's daughter," and she loves it.

Daniel gets a blessing on his wedding day as Papa walks with him down the aisle. This was a sweet tender moment for father and son.

We took a break from an intense preaching schedual and rented a simple pontoon boat for a couple of hours.

A family baseball game at Akron Park during the day when no one was there. We had great fun, and nobody felt pressure to win the game.

One week before Rebekah got married, we planned one last family fun night. We knew our times of being all together would be limited after this. We had a pillow "fight," and finished with this pyramid for the final backbreaker.

14

The Hearts of the Fathers Must Turn

*Behold, I will send you Elijah the prophet
before the coming of the great and dreadful day of the Lord:
And he shall turn the heart of the fathers to the children,
and the heart of the children to their fathers,
lest I come and smite the earth with a curse.*
                                                Malachi 4:5-6

In this chapter we come to a subject that is very dear to my heart: the hearts of fathers. I want to look at verse six almost word for word. There are some awesome truths in this verse for us American men that should make us tremble. Let me encourage you to read the whole of Malachi four as preparation for our meditation. As you are reading, notice the prophetic nature of these verses.

There is a miracle taking place in this land of America among many Christian fathers. God is at work in His usual mysterious ways, working behind the scenes and bringing about change. It is not because of tapes or the result of seminars. It is the Spirit of God working by many different means to fulfill verse six in the hearts of men. Nobody can explain it, except that it is God. He is hovering over the hearts and lives of men in a mysterious way, and doing a work in them, in a way I have never seen. It is amazing to behold.

The Pursuit of Godly Seed

As I travel around the country, I meet doctors, lawyers, business executives, technicians, engineers--all kinds of professional men --who are making major changes. Men are laying aside their professions and finding a little farm for their familes in the country somewhere. If you ask them why they are doing it, they say, "I want to spend more time raising my children." I don't mean to lift up doctors and lawyers, but I use their example because they have invested a lot of money and many years to prepare for their life's work. And now they are laying all that down and moving to a little farm out in the country where they can work with their children. This is a miracle!

One business executive shared with me how God dealt with him concerning his children. He was a computer engineer making seventy thousand dollars a year. God began to minister to him and burden him for his children. At first, he couldn't see clearly what God was saying. But the still small voice got louder as time went on. He would sit at his desk in front of a computer on the thirty-fourth floor of one of those high-rise office buildings and wrestle with God. The Spirit of God kept saying to him, "What about your children? How are they going to make it? They need you."

This went on for many days until finally he had to have it out with God. We men know how it went. Real issues were coming up in his mind. How could he walk away from this career and all it's security? Finally, the Spirit of God prevailed, and he surrendered to the leading of God for his life. Now that father joyfully works with his boys building things out of wood. He is not making big money anymore, but he is making something more precious than gold.

The Nature of the Prophetic Word

As we move into a study of the actual text, I would like to say a few things about how the prophetic Scriptures affect us as readers. God had used the prophetic Word in many ways. First of all, He used these utterances to speak to the people who heard them the first time. They were given by the prophet in the context of present day circumstances. Second, a prophetic utterance projects out into the future, thus putting a bit of mystery around it. I have noticed that many times the future fulfillment comes in more than one age. The second chapter of Joel is an example of this. It has not been completely fulfilled. Again, this keeps God's people looking out ahead, wondering, and preparing.

Our text in Malachi is another one of these utterances. I believe that the complete fulfillment has not yet come. This is very important because it helps us to understand what is happening in our day. Because we have read the New Testament, we know that the spirit of Elijah was upon John the Baptist, fulfilling at least part of this prophecy (see Lk. 1:11-17). Yet Jesus also said that Elijah will come and fulfill all things (see Mk. 9:11-13).

These things are a mystery to us. God wants it to be that way. Many Christian leaders around the world agree that God is stirring men about their children in these last days. It is important to acknowledge this so we can yield to His stirrings. God is fulfilling His word; He always does. We need to see what He is doing and get in line with it. This will bring blessings into our lives and to our families. Let's look into the depths of what God is doing, as we search for understanding in this verse.

Repentance

It is the Spirit of God who is brooding over fathers in these days. He is jealous: jealous for the children, jealous for a godly seed. He uses different men, as He did in the past, to try to get the attention of us fathers. We need to understand this. If we can assent to this fact, we may be able to understand some of the quiet thoughts of our hearts. Dear father, that stirring deep within you, those thoughts about the children, it is the Lord. He is pursuing your heart, with a jealous love for your children. He is after one thing. He wants to turn your heart.

This word "turn" in our text is a life changing word, a radical word, demanding radical actions. It means *repent*. God's grace is prevailing on the hearts of men to repent. Some who read this may have a vague understanding of this word. But this is a foundational word with far-reaching effects for those who allow the deeper dealings of God in their lives.

Repent means a complete change of mind that in turn brings a change of action. We truly believe only that which moves us to action. It is in the will that repentance takes place. Repent is a one hundred eighty degree turnaround. We understand in salvation, that except we repent, we cannot be saved. We must repent of our sins and of going our own way. Then we must believe on the Lord Jesus Christ, and we will be saved. This is what happened to the man and his wife described in Chapter 2.

This is what the word "turn" means. In this verse, however, God is not dealing with salvation. He is dealing with our heart priorities about our children. The word is no less radical in this verse than when related to salvation. An utter change of heart is what God is calling for. As always, God has His part, and man has his part. For us, God says, "Repent." As we men sit in the quiet of the morning and muse with our own hearts, it is good to know where God is drawing us: to utter change. In these last days, God is using men who come in the Spirit and power of Elijah with a burden to restore and recover the hearts of fathers to their children. That is what this text is saying. My, that is powerful! Are you listening, dear father?

The Heart: The Most Powerful Part of Our Being
The next word I want to study, is the word "heart." This little word is the most important word in this text. All the other words get their meaning from this word "heart." We must understand the depth of what God is saying in His use of this word. The heart is the seat of our affections. It is the place where we love, the place where we desire. It is the most powerful part of our being. The heart is the place where we dream dreams and see visions. This is also the place where we set goals and determine what direction we are going to go. All these things take place in the heart, as a choice of our will.

The heart is the place where our affections lie, the place where we covet--and it is all right to covet right things. Truly, it is the center of man's being. God, who made us, knows this. That is why He said, *"Thou shalt love the Lord thy God with all thine heart."* He wants the seat of our affections, our desires, to be upon Him, because He is God.

Think with me for a moment. If a man gets a desire in his heart to do something, he can do just about anything. The advance of technology in the past fifty years is an example of this to us all. What is next in the accomplishments of man? God knew the power of man's heart when He confounded the languages at the tower of Babel. He slowed down the process of "progress" by creating language barriers. Man can do amazing things if he sets his heart on it, because the heart is the motivational center of his being.

Think about the Olympics for a moment. If a man gets a desire in his heart to have a gold medal hanging around his neck, nothing can stop him. He will not rest until he runs for the gold. It all seems rather absurd to me, in light of eternity, and God's purposes, but that is the way man is. He will run as he never ran before. He will change his eating habits, his social habits, his sleeping habits, yea, he will change his very life to see that gold medal hanging about his neck. Why? Because he has set his heart on it.

This powerful heart is the issue God is addressing in this verse. God wants to turn the seat of our affections to Him first of all, and then to our children, who are our closest neighbors. I wonder what would happen if we fathers would get a strong desire in our hearts to nurture our children, desire that consumes us like that of the Olympians who pursue their goal with all their heart. This explains the miraculous changes made by fathers mentioned earlier. They had to change because their hearts were filled with a new desire that had to be fulfilled. If the heart desires something, no sacrifice is too great.

God knows the heart is the deepest need we have concerning our children. The need is not for more consistent devotions, a different home setting, or the like. The need goes deeper than that.

Think about it. We live in America. There is more teaching on the home in this land then in all the rest of the world. There are more seminars, more tapes, more books, and more ministries focusing on the home in America than in all other places put together. What is wrong then? Why are the homes of this nation falling apart in spite of all this good teaching? I think I know why. Because it is a matter of the heart. When God's people get extravagant about their love for Him and for His little lambs, then things will begin to change. Many honor the Lords teachings on the home with their lips, saying "amen," but their heart is far from them. The bottom line is the heart, and until the Lord is allowed to deal with our hearts in a radical way, nothing is going to change.

When your heart focus is turned toward the family, then all the "how to's" come following after. You won't need any more sermons or books. When I preach on the home, I am continually grieved over the response of many of the men. I hear them stand and confess that they have lost sight of the needs of their family, and they are glad to be reminded again. I groan when I hear this. I believe when we fathers turn the focus of our affections upon the children, we will not need to be reminded repeatedly.

Fathers: The Buck Stops Here
This brings us to the next important word in our text, "fathers." We all know the cliché, "the buck stops here." We understand that it means the responsibility lies on us men. It may not seem fair sometimes, but this is the way God has ordained it. The text addresses the fathers, not the mothers. God knows that if the heart of the father gets turned, the heart of the mother will follow after. I have seen this many times. The fathers are the cure for many of our woes in the feminist movement. All these dear ladies are wanting to take their place among the men as leaders in our society. These are woes. It will not come out right. It goes against God's revealed plan. But, it is not all their fault. Our fathers have sinned by turning away from the home, and pursuing other things. The women are just following their husbands.

Many Christian leaders bemoan the fact that the mothers are turning away from the home to seek "higher goals." But this is not the root of the problem. The fathers left home a long time ago. They turned their emotional focus to other priorities, and finally, I think the mothers said, "We are going too." The fathers are the answer. They are the ones who can break this curse that has come upon us. The fact that many mothers have joined in with this perversion of affections is shocking. How can a mother forget her child? Yet multitudes have turned away from their children's cries for nurturing. They quickly turn away at the daycare while the child pleads after them. They silence the voice of conscience, trusting that it will be okay. Oh fathers, hear the word of the Lord. He is calling you back to the basics, back to the things that really matter.

Repent From What?

Will you fathers allow me to get very practical for a few moments? We will not get very far toward recovery if we stay in the realm of vague general principles. If I don't make any applications, then you may all say, "Yes, he is right. I need to love my children more" and be done with it. But remember, God is calling us men to radical repentance.

If God is wanting to turn the hearts of the fathers to their children, then I think it is safe for us to assume that the hearts of the fathers are on something else. This is where the problem lies. The fathers have turned away from the needs of their families, and set their affections on "better things." The heart, that powerful heart that loves, is loving lesser things. That heart that has dreams and visions is dreaming other dreams. This is where the problem lies.

Dear fathers, if we are neglecting our families, then there are real everyday issues to face. What are your issues? Let me challenge you right this moment. Stop for a moment, bow your head, and ask the Holy Spirit to convict you in your areas of need. Ask the Lord, "Where is my heart?" Allow me to give you some radical challenges. Consider these issues.

Materialism

American men have lost their way seeking wealth and all that money can buy. They are serving mammon. Fathers, what shall it profit you if you gain the whole world and lose the souls of your children? Many are doing just that. At the end of your life, you may have a big pile of possessions to leave behind, but what is that? You may leave your children behind also, not to mention your own soul.

The American Dream

Some of us fathers are ignorantly going the way everyone else is going. We are just following the rest of the sheep, out into the wilderness. We think, "This is what you do as an

American." A new house, two new cars, a boat, and many other things are the norm. This dream doesn't come cheap, so we even send our wives to work to help pay for it all. Then the family suffers even more.

Loans and credit cards

This is a trap that has slain many a happy home. You want it now. The loan officer says, "No problem. Let me help you reach your dreams. Just sign on the dotted line." He never tells you that there is a ball and chain at the other end of the whole friendly procedure. Many are in this prison for years. If they do wake up every now and then and try to change their priorities, the friendly banker, who is now the scowling prison warden, tells them, "You can't do that." Dear father, get out of debt.

My career

There is nothing wrong with having a profession or a promising job. However, most companies today are not concerned about your wife and children. If you want to keep progressing up the ladder, you have to be "a company man." What that really means is the company comes ahead of everything else. If you tell the company you must have time for the family, you will not get the next raise.

My hobbies

This has become the norm in America. Every man has his hobbies. He may give himself to watching sports or playing them himself. He may spend his free time going hunting with the boys. There are too many for me to list here. The point is that he has very little time left over for the little souls that live at his house.

The entertainment world

I have no problem with family- friendly fun. However, most of the options that people take today are not family friendly, encouraging communication and relationships. Think about a few of them: television, videos, computer games, and amusement parks. In all these, you just sit and watch something, or laugh and scream at each other. This does not build meaningful relationships. I wonder how many hours of precious family time have been wasted by fathers as they bow before the TV, the movies, and the computer.

My ministry
This is a subtle one because it is sanctified and often encouraged by many well-meaning people. Please don't misunderstand me. We need to be about the Master's business, but not at the expense of our children. The church programs can run you and your family ragged, and then there is no time to build relationships or have a family altar.

Okay, maybe you are growling at me by now, but let us reason together. These are the issues that have taken men away from the priorities of the home. The hearts of American men are pursuing all the things in the preceding list and more.

Let me give personal confession of my own sins in this area. When God began to deal with me about my children, my heart was set on the ministry. My affections had completely turned toward God's work. Soon after my radical conversion, I went away to Bible School, and there I set my heart to become a man of God and a well-known preacher. I am sure the motivations were mixed, because I did want to serve God with all of my heart. My focus got off-balance. I served from early morning till late at night most of the time. Jackie and I were newly married and just beginning to have children.

I gave the children some "quality" time, but my heart was far from them. It's not that I despised them. I felt love for them, but my time was full. There was no time left for them. I was totally blind to the true condition of my heart. Somehow, I had the idea that you don't have to spend a lot of time with your children. You just need to make sure it is quality time. So I put in my 15 minutes of quality time each day. Oh, the remorse of the whole thing, when I think about it.

The Lord had to wake me up to reality. He allowed a string of circumstances to happen in my life that put me at home all day with my children for about a year. When I was faced with my children all day, I found out that they were more of a bother than a blessing to me. They were in my way, and their distractions annoyed me. When my true heart was exposed, I couldn't believe how I viewed them. I knew this was not right. I fell on my face and repented.

As soon as I had repented, my heart began to change toward my children. I wanted to be with them, I wanted to talk, and walk, and tussle around with them. I am so grateful to God for this overhaul in my heart before the children could get bitter. Many children who have fathers who minister resent their absentee father. God spared me of this. As time went on, I realized that many of my dreams and aspirations were motivated by my pride — pride of position.

Dear father, how is it with you? What issues rose up before you as you read and pondered these words? This is where God wants to go to work. Will you let Him in? Will you let the Holy Spirit go into the secret places of your heart and turn on the searchlight?

The Children

The next word that I would like to look at is the word "children." This is a beautiful, meaningful word that appears twice in this verse. Let's personalize it: "my children." He shall turn my heart away from many things, and turn it to "my children," bone of my bone and flesh of my flesh. Do you remember how you felt when they were born? Do you remember how you joyfully received them? Think about your children for a moment. I have been drawing your minds back to your children all through these chapters. Remember, the Spirit of God is calling your father heart back to your children. Stop a moment and allow your heart to go there.

I love to visit young couples who have just had their first child. They are in awe and filled with a sober joy. Do you remember how it was? How can it be that parents can go from this holy scene to a place of neglect and even considering their children as a bother?

They walk away from the flames of their first love, filled with dreams and responsibility, and pursue the American dream.

The Spirit of God is brooding over fathers throughout the land and saying to them, "What about your children?" His goal is to turn their hearts back to the children. Are you listening? Allow me to ask you a deep question. What will you give in exchange for the precious souls of your children, a farm, a big business, a pile of money, a career? This is a good question. Maybe it is a habit or a secret sin that you are enjoying. Will you exchange the souls of your children for that? I hope not.

This turning of the heart is more than a father agreeing to have family devotions. It is much deeper than that. That is just a law, a duty to be done, an obligation to fulfill. God is after more than that. The text says *"the children."* It doesn't say "the statutes about the children." It is heart turning to heart. Then, many practical, loving things will follow. God still is working, just like He promised right here in Malachi. He is pleading with the hearts of fathers, convincing them to turn their hearts, the seat of their affections, away from whatever else they have it on and back to the children. God is very jealous over our children. He made each one of them for His purposes.

The Powerful Heart of a Child

Look with me at the heart again, the most powerful part of our being. Only now, we are moving away from the heart of a father to the heart of a child. However, I want to remind you that it is the same heart. It is the seat of their affections, and the place where they make their decisions. All that we have seen about the power of the heart with fathers applies all over again with the children. Oh, the blessing when the powerful heart of a child is guided from childhood! Oh, the curse when it is not.

God needs to teach us some things about the heart of our child. We live in a land where the hearts of the children are set on everything else but their fathers. This is a curse on our nation. We live in a land where multitudes of things draw the hearts of children away from their fathers. These things have very little power over our children if their hearts are turned toward Dad. It is time we start doing our homework. If we don't, we are going to weep for it later.

This mysterious miracle of God's grace is happening not only with fathers. It also is happening with children. God is drawing your children, father, so rejoice! There is hope for your home, even if you have made some mistakes. I think it is good for us to look deeply into what is happening inside the hearts of our children, so we know what we are up against.

The children's hearts are set on other things. They saw that dad was too busy and didn't have time for them, so they ran after other loves. This did not happen suddenly, but was a gradual process of departure. The natural desire to please father was quenched by neglect. The child wanted a relationship with Dad. They came many times in their little child ways and sought for his smile of approval, but he was too busy. Dad was too busy and gave them that infamous answer, "Not now, child, not now."

The child's heart slowly turned away, and now the peers are more important than the parents. The children are more concerned with what their friends think than what Dad thinks. But God wants to change that if we will repent.

My heart hurts at times as I hear what fathers demand of their children while their own hearts are far away on other things. It is not right for fathers to have their heart affection on other things, and with a broken relationship tell the children, "Honor your father." It is not right!

It is the will of God that every father be highly esteemed in his home, highly honored by his children. Although it is a grief to look at the negative side of this principle, it is good to remember that God has a positive side also. Let's consider the positive side for a moment.

If relationships are healed and heart turns to heart, there are some beautful things that can flow from a child's heart. The heart also is the place where the children honor and give respect. It is the place where they desire to please their parents again like they used to. The heart is the place where the children choose to obey and yield everything to their parents. These are precious attitudes for parents to find coming forth from the heart of a child, and they will come as relationships begin to heal.

The Hearts of the Fathers Must Turn

Let me give you fathers a word of encouragement here. God also is working by His Spirit to turn your child's heart toward you. You are not alone in your pursuit of a fresh open relationship with your child. We can co-labor with the Lord on this one. Your child has all the potential abilities to give you this kind of reverence, but you must get your heart right toward him. Then beautiful things will follow.

A Mysterious Blessing

As we meditate on this verse, maybe it has already dawned on you that the turning of the one heart brings the turning of the other. Have you seen this? As the father turns, or repents, the heart of the child is affected and turns also. There is a mysterious blessing hidden away in this principle, just as with every principle in the Bible. It is tucked away in there, but you will never find it or experience it until you live out the reality of the verse. Maybe you are a father or a mother who realizes as you read, "I have lost the heart of my child." You know there is no honor coming from them. You have to admit, "There is no desire to please in my child." Perhaps you have even wondered at times what is wrong. Well, God is giving you the answer. But don't despair. There is a way to change everything.

There is something mysterious that takes place in the heart of a child when that child senses deep down in his soul, "My father loves me, and his heart is turned toward me." There is a powerful draw upon a child's heart when they can see that their father cares, and that he would do anything for them. Something takes place in the heart of a child when he senses these things, and attitudes begin to change. All of a sudden, the child's heart begins to turn as well. The child's heart turns away from all those other loves that were drawing him. The heart of the child begins to turn toward his father. Suddenly, there is a desire for a relationship again, a desire that was not there for a long time.

Let me use the example of homeschooling to illustrate this principle. Jackie and I have been schooling the children for more than twenty years. Homeschooling requires a tremendous amout of time and attention. Over the years, we have seen dozens of parents follow the same path with their children. I have noticed something beautiful happening with every one of them. After they have been teaching awhile, as those parents turn their attention onto their children, I see it happen. As they start pouring their lives, their time, their emotions, and their prayers into them, the children turn their hearts toward their parents. I have heard the testimony countless times. "My children love me like they have never loved me before."

The children can see and sense that their parents are different. It is quite a labor of love to teach your own children. The children see this, and up from within their heart rise feelings of love and respect. When the heart of the parent turns, the heart of the child begins to turn also. Rejoice fathers and mothers. There is hope for you. If the heart of your child does not respond immediately, don't despair. This principle is at work. Keep on sowing the good seeds of time and attention. They will bear fruit in due time.

God is jealous over the relationship between fathers and children. It is not a little thing to him. He knows that the whole issue of pursuing a godly seed will not happen unless this is in place. From the father flows love, care, discipline, and teaching. And, in a reciprocating fashion, from the heart of the child flows love, honor, respect, and a desire to please. When the two of these are put together, they produce a godly seed on the earth. And this is what God is after, that He might be glorified.

A Painful Lesson

Let me share another failure with you. Aren't these failures encouraging. They help you to have hope for your situation. I share them so you can see that cause and affect is working here.

Some years ago now, we had some hard lessons to learn with our older children. Rebekah, Daniel, and Elisabeth were not little children anymore. We were moving into a new stage of parenting, and we were not very alert to the changes. Jackie and I noticed that the respect level with these three youth was not where we wanted it. They would obey, yet we could sense that their hearts were not in it. We were tempted to think, "Here come the terrible teens."

After much prayer, we sat down with our young people to have a long family talk. I could have taken this meeting down the authoritative road, reproved them, and told them to straighten up. But I heard the Lord saying, "Take the low road."

Jackie and I began the meeting by asking the children, "What are we doing wrong? We really want to know." They looked a bit unsure at first, wondering if it was really safe to share, and then they opened up their hearts to us. They shared with reverence and respect, and we listened with an open heart. Relationship was the heart of the problem. Mama and I were very busy. The church had grown very fast, and the needs were many. TIME was the issue with them. No time to talk, no time to share, and no time to ask questions. We knew that the deeper issue was our hearts. The focus of our hearts had been drawn away by the many voices of need.

We bowed our hearts in that meeting, repented, and asked for forgiveness. Everything was clear, but we didn't stop there. The Lord led me to take a six-month sabbatical from the ministry. Everything stopped for six months. This radical change was interpreted by the children as a great sacrifice for them. Guess what happened? You know already. The hearts of the children turned to their father, and all the attitudes were changed.

I have thought about those days many times in the past seven years. We could easily have taken the other road, demanding respect and obedience. We could have forced things to go our way, and sometimes parents need to do that. But if we had in that situation, things could have gone very differently. Many youth get bitter and rebel when parents force things without facing their own failures. This is a grave mistake. Sometimes we are the ones who are wrong, and we need to repent.

Smitten with a Curse

There is one last word we should look at before we finish here. That is the word "curse." God promises a curse if we do not yield to the Spirit's pleadings. I believe that the curse is in the disobedience, just as the blessing is in the obedience. Dear fathers and mothers, we live in a land that is under this very curse. We are suffering the results of two or three generations of absentee fathers.

When will America wake up to the cause of all its woes? It's so bad now that you can't even walk safely down the street at night.

The Pursuit of Godly Seed

You can't send a virgin daughter to the grocery store for fear of rape. You have to lock your doors while you are driving down the street and watch for someone who might shoot at you. This is the land in which we live. Who is doing all this? Two or three generations of neglected children—sweet, pliable, moldable, innocent children—that is who is doing it.

I read an article years ago written by a longtime prison evangelist. After ministering to scores of thousands of inmates, he made a shocking statement. He said, "They all hate their dads." What a staggering word this is! What has happened? How can it be that they all hate their fathers? Do you know the answer by now? I hope so, or I have failed in the writing of this chapter. Think about it: the boys are in the prisons, but who should be there right alongside them? The fathers. They destroyed their sons through neglect and lost their hearts. The sons turned to other loves and lost their way. Now they are in prison.

Brethren, we have sinned, and our fathers have sinned. Are we on the same road that all these traveled? If we are, it is time for radical measures. If the cancer is there, let us do everything we can to cut it out and let the wounds be healed. Let us free ourselves of this curse through radical change. Every curse can be broken in the name of the Lord Jesus Christ through the power of His might when we repent.

Prayer

Father in heaven, have mercy on us. We have sinned, and our fathers have sinned. We have sinned against You and against the children that You have given us. Grant us a broken heart and the good gift of biblical repentance. Help us fathers to see where things are with our children. We don't want to wake up someday and be shocked at what has happened. We are under the curse of generations before us. Free us in Jesus Christ's name. Amen.

15

The Rod Is Love

He that spareth his rod hateth his son: but he that loveth him chasteneth him betimes.
Proverbs 13:24

In the two preceding chapters, I laid the foundation for the use of the rod in the Christian home. We are dealing with some balancing principles that are powerful if kept together, but devastating if you let either stand alone. If you heed the message of the previous chapters, yet neglect those to follow, you will raise a silly, uncontrolled child who will not serve God and will bring you to shame. However, as already stated, if you neglect a relationship of love and pick up the rod, you will produce children who despise you and obey out of fear and law (somewhat like robots).

Having said these things, let me express my goal for this chapter. My goal is to convince you that using the rod is one of the most loving things that you can do for your children. This holy exercise falls in the category of "most loving activities." A trip to McDonalds, a special time of loving affirmation, and a sweet time of chastisement all fit into the same category. I also want to convince you that it is a sin if you don't use the rod in the rearing of your children. The Word of God is very clear on this subject. It is not just an option for some to choose and some not to choose. It is a sin of omission, with serious consequences. *"If ye be without chastisement, whereof all are partakers, then are ye bastards and not sons"* (Heb. 12:8).

Many years ago, we had a dear family visiting in our home whose parents did not believe in spanking their children. It was very interesting for me to observe the interaction between these parents and their children. This was the first time that I had experienced any personal contact with people who believed this way. The children were very active and kept getting into things. I kept watching the parents as they gently pleaded with the children to be good, and to sit still. The children would sit for a moment, then quickly get up and move again. Then the parents would go over to the child and say, "Please Susie, would you please calm down and sit still." It was very clear to me who was in charge of the evening. I felt sorry for the parents and said a prayer for them in my heart, because they had no rest throughout our visit. Earlier in the evening, they had boldly stated, "We don't believe in spanking our children. There are other ways to motivate the children to be good." I knew they were living in ignorance, and I longed for the parents and the children to be set free to enjoy each other.

About three years after that little meeting in our home, somebody else gave them a set of The Godly Home tapes. The Lord had given them a precious son since their visit, and he was taxing their theology on child training to the limits. They listened to the tapes with new interest, and when they came to the tape on spanking, they listened with an open heart and realized their mistake. The father added the use of the rod to his tender loving approach, and testified, "My home will never be the same."

When I am preaching on the subject of discipline, I usually bring a paddle along to the service. I hold it up in my hand from time to time during the sermon. I have been intrigued with the different responses to the paddle. Some people don't even like to look at it, they kind of turn their head a bit. The children sit on the edge of their seat in rapt attention. They want to hear what this preacher has to say about the paddle. Somehow they instinctively know it is going to affect their future.

One mother shared a testimony with me of her son's response to spanking. She had listened to the tape on discipline and was convinced that she must begin to spank her children. Well, the fateful day came when her son needed to be spanked. She had the

The Rod Is Love

little fellow over her knee and was ready to commence. He stopped her by crying out, "Wait mom!! I'm not sure about this Brother Denny. He might be a false prophet." What a clever little boy he was, but it didn't work. He received the spanking anyway.

I realize that many of the different feelings about the rod come from bad experiences. Maybe your father or your mother used it in a wrong way on you, and because of that, you don't have very good ideas about it. Well, I hope, by God's grace, to change your mind. I want God to show you that using the rod is not some "mean" thing to do, but rather, it is one of the loving ways that God has ordained for you to train your children up to be a godly testimony upon this earth.

We use the rod at our house. It gets used more often on the younger ones than on the older ones. We spank the children, and the children still love us. In fact, they honor me and love me more than I deserve. I find myself at times sitting in my house and weeping over the honor and the love they give to me. I believe that one of the reasons why my children love me and honor me so much is because I discipline them when they need it.

This may surprise some of you, but many times after we have given a spanking, the children have come to say, "Papa, thank you. Thank you for spanking me. I needed that." When Samuel was just a little tike, I remember hearing these words often: "I don't enjoy the spankings, but I sure do like the feeling that I get in my heart after one." In this chapter, we are going to learn why the children come and say thank you after they have received a spanking. This may seem hard to believe as you read it right now. However, by the time we come to the end of this subject, I believe you will feel different.

The Devil's Lie

The devil has lied to us, and we have swallowed his subtle lie. We have believed the lie that spanking is a negative form of discipline, when in fact, it is one of the most positive forms you can use. There are other forms of discipline, and we address them later, but for now, how do you feel about using the rod? If you are feeling uncomfortable, even as you sit and read about discipline, you probably have swallowed more of the philosophies of the world than you realize. Acknowledge it in your heart and pray, "God, maybe I haven't looked at this subject right. Would you just teach me and show me where my thinking is wrong?" I encourage you to open up your heart and let the devil's lies be exposed.

Oh, what a mysterious power is the rod of discipline. Its wonders are many. It will bring order where there is chaos, peace where there is turmoil, freedom where there is bondage, and zeal where there is apathy. It is easy to see why the enemy is working hard to convince many people against spanking their children. In fact, it's getting more and more that way in America.

If God doesn't send revival to our land and change the direction that we are going, we will see the day when it will be against the law to spank our children. There are countries in the world today where it is already against the law, where Christians are afraid to spank their children because they could be thrown in jail and lose their children if anybody finds out about it.

Many people react to the teaching and practice of biblical chastisement. The world says, "It is cruelty. It is oppression. The children will hate you. It will cause rebellion in their hearts." Even many of God's people are flirting with these statements and wondering if maybe spanking is too harsh. But nothing could be further from the truth. The correct use of the rod makes bright, happy children who love and respect you. Many times, it is those parents who have withheld the rod whose children have put them into the rest homes. Have you ever considered making a connection between untrained neglected children and rest homes? The rest homes are full and running over today. Why? Who puts their fathers and mothers into the rest homes? I wonder how many dear old folks in the rest homes would say, "I didn't spank and train my children." It would be a very painful survey if you conducted one, but I wonder what they would say. The rest homes are full of lonely people who rarely get a visit from their children. Did you know that? Someone asked me recently what I am doing to prepare for retirement. I don't believe in retirement, but I knew what he was implying. My face welled up with a big smile, and I said, "I am pouring my life into my eight children. I know they will take care of me."

Natural Love and Spiritual Love

There is a natural love, and there is a spiritual love. We need to look at them and give them some definition before we get into the meat of some of these verses on spanking. We need to have both kinds of love for our children. By "natural love," I mean, the emotional feelings of love and compassion that we have for our children. This is beautiful. We must have this, and our children must sense these feelings flowing from us. However, many times the use of the rod goes against our natural love for the child.

If your poor heart says, "Oh, I could never spank my children! I can't bear to give them pain, or see them cry out, " you are being motivated by natural love. I also feel you are a bit shortsighted, not realizing the long range effect of using or not using the rod. If our natural love stops us from disciplining the children with a rod, then that natural love needs to be crucified and replaced with spiritual love. "Spiritual love" is agape love. It is Godlike love, which is love that loves by principle, and not by feelings only.

The Holy Spirit has inspired some very powerful words that encourage us to practice this very spiritual love. The question is, "What do you want for your children?" The Bible says, if you lovingly use the rod to correct your children, these things will happen:

- ❖ It will give wisdom to your children. (Pro. 29:15)
- ❖ It will cleanse evil from their heart. (Pro. 20:30)
- ❖ It expresses love to them. (Pro. 13:24)
- ❖ It will give them a clear conscience. (Pro. 20:30)
- ❖ It will keep them from going to hell. (Pro. 23:14)
- ❖ It will bring quiet order to your home. (Pro. 29:17)
- ❖ It will drive out foolishness from them. (Pro. 22:15)

A Silent Message of Love or Hate

He that spareth his rod hateth his son: but he that loveth him chasteneth him betimes.
Proverbs 13:24

What kind of message do you want to leave with your children: " I love you," or "I hate you?" According to the preceding verse we have a choice which message we give them. Also, please note, there are only two options from which to choose. They will receive one or the other. I circled four key words in this verse when I studied it in my Bible. Let me begin with a definition for each of these four words.

- ❖ Spareth: "to hold back, to use sparingly"
- ❖ Hateth: "to stand and face an enemy"
- ❖ Loveth: "to stand with outstretched arms to receive"
- ❖ Betimes: "early in life, and repeatedly"

Let's look at the word "spareth" first. According to this verse, if we hold back the rod, that is, if we use it sparingly, we hate our children. I know that sounds pretty strong, but that is what God says. We should also note that if it is hateful to hold back, how much more hatred is expressed if we spank not at all. God, who made us and knows our weaknesses, is giving us a warning here. He knows that it is our tendency to slack off on this task. We have many reasons for this neglect. Some parents are too busy. Some don't want to be bothered, whereas others simply avoid the unpleasant task. Whatever the reason, God says it is hatred to spare the rod. He that spareth, hateth.

The next word to consider is the word hateth. In the Hebrew language, words often are defined as word pictures. This picture is rather troubling. The spirit of this picture is very clear: a man standing with hatred before his enemy. The man in this picture hasn't said a word, but he doesn't need to say anything. The message is clear, and his enemy knows it. This is the silent message that we give to our precious children when we hold back in this area. You may say, "I have no such feeling in my heart toward my child" I'm sure you are right, but God says that you hate them. The point being made here is a point of neglect. Our neglect sends the unspoken message of hatred to them, or, they hear "I am not loved."

Earlier I mentioned the neglect of proper training, and the confusion that it will work in our relationships with the children. Well, here is an application of how that works. No spanking, or very little spanking, brings a multitude of frustrated corrections (nagging) from the parent, and the child never gets a clearing of the heart. This produces a barrier in their relationship. I have never seen nagging produce a good relationship. Have you?

On the other hand, a spirit of love is manifested to the child when the parent gives the proper correction and clearing. This Hebrew word "loveth," is also a word picture. It is the picture of a person standing with outstretched arms. When Hannah and Esther were little girls, they used to run and greet me when I came home from a preaching trip. I would get down on my knee, so I could be on their level, and stretch out my hands and arms to receive them with a big hug. That is the picture of this word.

Many people have a hard time understanding how chastisement could be such an expression of love. This usually comes from their bad experiences during their childhood. It is so sad to realize that for many of us, we are the third generation of children who were not spanked properly. I believe this is one of the reasons why so many are pushing for laws against spanking. So what do we do? Do we listen to the spirit of the age, or do we listen to the timeless principles of the Word of God? God says it is an expression of love. We are saying, "I love you," when we spank properly. In the next chapter, I give a detailed explanation of how we spank our children. After you read this, I think you will then agree that biblical chastisement is an overflowing expression of love, and a key to building a sweet relationship.

The last word I want to emphasize in this verse is the word "betimes." It means "early," or "at the dawn of life." Many parents ask me questions about this word. They want to know how soon they should start to spank their child? Well I believe we need to begin training them early in life. However, we need to adjust the spanking down to the young age of the child. I have more to say about this later. The plural form of the word also seems to infer that it is something a parent should do again and again. Now let's put a paraphrase of this verse together: "He who holds back the use of the rod manifests a spirit of hatred, but he who wants to manifest a spirit of love will use the rod early in life, again and again."

Children Without a Father

There are many promises that God makes to His people in the New Covenant. We rejoice in them all. But the sweetest and most important promise that He makes to us is the promise to be our Father. *"I will be a Father unto you, and ye shall be My sons and daughters, saith the Lord Almighty"* (II Cor. 6:18). This fatherly promise is the all-inclusive promise from our God. It contains all of the other promises in it.

We rejoice in the overreaching blanket of our Father's love. However, part of this blanket of love is chastisement. Hebrews 12:5-13 reminds us that our Heavenly Father is going to spank us from time to time, or betimes. These verses are very clear to us as Christians. Spanking, is a tender expression of our Father's love, and if we don't have it, we are sons and daughters without a father, or bastards.

Dear fathers and mothers, come let us reason together on this most vital point. We fathers represent God to our children. Their perception of God is greatly affected by the experiences they have with us. If we will not spank our children, or if we hold back in spanking them, or if we do it in a harsh, angry way, what will this do to their concept of God? Consider this also: if we neglect our children in this area, they are like children without a father, although one lives in their home. Or they are children, with a father who doesn't love them. They are like bastards, "illegitimate children."

> *For whom the Lord loveth he chasteneth, and scourgeth every son whom he receiveth.*
> *Hebrews 12:6*

Surely we can apply this verse to our homes. The son or daughter who lives under his or her father's loving care and blessing will be chastened by that father. The children who do not receive correction from their fathers are not loved by their fathers, for whom the father loves, he will chasten. I am not stretching the interpretation or application of these verses by making such strong statements. Dear parents, we need to wake up to our responsibilities as parents. We need to wake up to the far-reaching effects of our disobedience. We will be held accountable for our neglect when we stand before the God who gave us our precious children.

What about the children? Look what they are missing. If your children are without the proper chastisement, they are missing some of the sweetest experiences of their lives, and so are you parents. You don't know what you are missing.

Think about the present dilemma in this land. We now have millions of children growing up in homes where there is no father or where they have an absentee father. This is tragic. Where did this curse originate? Could it be that our present situation is the fruit of two or three generations of children who grew up without the loving discipline of a father? I think so, but who will break this chain of irresponsibility? The devil has blinded us oh so very subtly because he knows what a powerful effect this could have on the next generation. "Rise up O men of God, have done with lesser things," as the song says. We must turn our hearts toward our children before we lose another generation.

A Paradox

Biblical discipline brings a rich fullness of love between father, mother, and child. That may be a little hard for some to grasp who haven't experienced it, but it is the truth, and nothing but the truth. This is one of the many paradoxes in the Bible. It doesn't make sense to the natural man. Every fall, we at Charity Fellowship have a one-week-long Bible school for youth. I have the privilege of counseling with a lot of young people during that week. There are statements that I hear often while counseling struggling youth. They say, "I was never close to my father. We just don't communicate well, and I feel estranged from him." Have you ever heard words like this? Many parents are shocked when they find out their children feel this way. What would your youth say if they were asked about how close they feel to you?

I'm sure there are many reasons why a child feels estranged from his parents, but I know that our subject at hand is one of the reasons. Loving discipline brings a close relationship between those involved. My children are close to me. We are buddies, and it is easy to talk about everything. When we have a spanking, it just takes their heart and my heart and knits them closer together. I know that might seem strange to you as you first consider it, but it is a paradox. God's ways are not like our ways They are very different. I am giving you an awesome paradox that doesn't make any sense to the natural mind. Just as the Bible says in so many words, "the way up is down," the Bible says that the way to a close relationship with your children is to make loving use of the rod. Let's look at another verse.

> *Chasten thy son while there is hope, and let not thy soul spare for his crying.*
> *Proverbs 19:18*

God begins this verse with a command to us: "Chasten thy son." Oh that we would keep His commandments. We would surely reap His blessings too. I want to focus on two points in this verse. First of all, the little phrase *"while there is hope."* This very phrase signifies to us that there will come a time when there will be no more hope. There will come a day when it won't work anymore. There will come a day when you will not be able to have an influence upon your child with the rod. So God is using this verse as a motivational verse for us. He is encouraging us to spank our children while they are pliable, while they are bendable, like a young sapling.

It is easy to train a young tree to grow up straight. But if you let it grow a few years and then try to bend it back and make it straight, it becomes almost impossible. There is no more hope. You have to live with a crooked tree. Spank them while they are moldable. It is a motivational verse to us. There will come a day when you will not be able to mold your children with the rod anymore.

This brings us to the last part of the verse. We have a loving, all-wise God who knows us all very well, so He placed this admonition in the Bible for us. God knows we are made of flesh, and that we have natural love for our children. It is not wrong to have natural love, but it must be balanced and strengthened with agape love. So God finishes the verse with a gentle reminder to our hearts: *"Let not thy soul spare for his crying."* We all know what that feeling is like, don't we? We know the thoughts that go on inside us. We don't want to keep going. We hear the child crying, and we want to hold back. I believe God breathed this little part of the verse out for every one of us. God is saying, "Keep going." Just a couple of swats will not do. The child needs a thorough spanking, and I will define what that means in the next chapter.

Children are pretty smart also, and God addresses their needs in this phrase. The little ones know if they let out a wail that sounds like they are about to die, you will let up before you're supposed to. But God is smarter, and He knows what their flesh is like. So he gives a warning to the parents: "Don't fall for their deceptive wailings." When I preach on this subject to a crowd of families, I usually ask the children if they do in fact "put on the dog" to make it easier. They raise their hands in the affirmative, and we all laugh together. Some of the parents look on in shock as the hands go up. Just because the child starts to cry does not mean the job is done. I know it sounds pretty mean, but it is not. This is what God reveals to us in His Word.

Give Your Child a Revival

The blueness of a wound cleanseth away evil: do stripes the inward parts of the belly.
Proverbs 20:30

The proper use of the rod of discipline is one of God's methods for clearing the conscience of your children. I want to draw our minds to this very important aspect of discipline. It may be an entirely new perspective for the exercise of spanking, but bear with me. I think you will agree.

Have you ever had a revival in your own personal life with the Lord? I think many of us know the sweet experience of responding at a revival meeting, or falling on our faces at home and breaking our hearts before God. He shows us our needs. Then we mourn over them, and confess them to Him. With a heart of repentance we call upon God to forgive us and to wash our hearts clean by the blood of Jesus. Oh what clearing comes from this. Oh what brokenness, what sweetness is upon our hearts after we have had a revival like this. We all know the joy, the blessing, the yieldedness, and the obedience that is wrought in our lives when we break before the Lord (II Cor. 7:11).

Brothers and sisters, the rod of discipline is God's method for producing the same thing in your children. You see, your children don't understand all that is involved with getting right with God. They don't understand the power of the blood of Christ yet. There is much they do not know about God. But God has provided a way to produce in them the same kind of heart that we receive when we get our hearts right with God. They also need to get clear from time to time. Some of your children need a revival—and God wants to use you to help them experience it.

This beautiful state of freedom, joy, and clearing is exactly what the quoted verse is describing. When our child does wrong, or transgresses our laws, his conscience becomes guilty. God has designed the conscience to function in this way. When a child's conscience is not clear, a cloud of unclearness comes over him. If you are a discerning parent, you can see it on his face. Sometimes a good honest talk with Mom or Dad can clear the air, and the child is free again. However, there are times when children choose to keep silent about their wrongs. If so, the cloud prevails over them, and usually they will get into more trouble.

God in His wisdom has given us the principle of chastisement for these very times. The child who is in such a state needs a good old-fashioned spanking. Some parents will let this cloud hover over their child for days and days. This is a grievous mistake for all involved because the child's spirit and conduct torment the whole household. There is no rest in the home or in the child (see Pro. 29:17). We must do the child a favor and administer some loving discipline into his life. This is part of the government of a home.

Look at the clear, strong words that God uses in our verse. God says that a spanking *"cleanseth away evil"* and that it cleanses our *"inward parts."* This verse is describing a deep work in the conscience of one's being. The spanking cleanses away the evil, the desire for evil, and the guilt that the evil brought upon the child's being. This is awesome. Parents, do you see the power of this principle for good in a child's life? He or she can grow up with freedom, joy, and blessings, which is what God intended for the child. We are the governors of that blessed life, if we will do our part.

Children who have a clear conscience also have a clear countenance. This is true in our lives as parents, and it is the same for them. They will have a bright, happy countenance, and that is what a child *should* look like. Many people have said to me, "Your children have such a bright countenance." It is true, they do. But this should not be anything special. This is the way all of our children should look. I can tell by a child's countenance whether that child is being disciplined properly or not. A child who is being disciplined properly has a clear conscience. His heart is broken, and his will is yielded to his parents. As a result, his countenance is clear. It is that simple.

You may say, "Now wait a minute. How can you be so sure about the face of my child?" Remember the illustration of the builder and the gardener. Because they know their work, they can spot a need in the house or the garden very quickly. None of us would be surprised at their quick discernment because we know that they know what they are doing. This is where God wants to take us in the area of training our children. He wants us to become students and then masters of training our children. As we learn the principles, they will become a natural part of our understanding, and we will know, just as the gardener knows.

We have a generation of children that is being destroyed because of our lack of knowledge. Dear parents, it is just that simple. I know there are hard cases that require special help, but most of the needs in our families can be met by parents who know the Word, and who have chosen to obey it.

Other Forms of Discipline

Now, I want to hasten to say that there are other forms of discipline besides the rod, and we use them. I will list some here, and explain how we use them.

- ❖ Standing in the corner: We will put them in the corner, as a gentle reproof and a warning, "Correct your ways here and you'll be alright. Don't and you're going to find yourself with stronger discipline."

- ❖ Take away privileges: If a child has a certain activity, that they really enjoy, losing it can be a very effective warning and reproof.
- ❖ Take away the toy: Sometimes when a child is being selfish about their possessions, taking them away will get their attention.
- ❖ Save the food: When we are in the process of teaching our children to eat their food till all of it is gone, we will take the food they don't want to eat, and save it for the next meal. This can work better than a spanking. To sit and face that same plate of green beans at the next meal is very convincing.
- ❖ Spank the hand: Sometimes if it's a smaller child we will spank the hand. With a real little child you can break their will by spanking their hand, just one time. One or two swats on the hand, smartly applied, and that child will just break and cry, and everything is taken care of.

So, there are other forms of discipline, and you can use your own creativity to come up with others. These are a few of the ones that we have used. The idea is that we are in a process of training.

God's Principles Work

Many years ago (I guess it is twenty-six years ago now) when Jackie and I were working on a church bus route in Chicago, God gave us an experience we will never forget. I was in charge of a bus route that picked up ghetto children and brought them to Sunday school in Hammond, Indiana. There was a single mom on my bus route who had four children. She was not a good mother. She had never been married, and she was an alcoholic. She was a neglectful mother, and her children were very wild. I pitied the children when I visited the house on Saturdays. She had twin boys, four years old, and they were wild little boys.

One Saturday when I was visiting families on the bus route, the mother came to the door in total frustration. The twins had really misbehaved that week, and she was ready to ship them out for good. This tugged on my heart, as I was very close to them. I was the closest thing to a father the children had ever had. She gave me one option: "If you want to take them home and try to straighten them out, go ahead."

It was during the holidays at Bible school, and I knew I would be home all week, so I told her I would come back and pick them up when I finished visiting the rest of the children. I picked up those little twin boys and brought them home to my house (was Jackie ever surprised!).

For two days, Jackie and I followed them everywhere they went around the house. We gave them instruction and guidance about what we expected of them, and warned them that they would get a spanking if they didn't obey. When they got out of order (and they did, because they had never been trained), I took them into a room and lovingly spanked them. They had never been spanked like that, only beaten in anger and rage. These little fellows were my buddies, and they loved Mr. Denny.

After two days of this kind of consistent, loving training, those two little fellows had figured it all out in their minds. Things started falling right into place, and by the end of the week, they were well-behaved little boys. Those little fellows would sit up at the supper table and eat with a spoon instead of with their hands. They would say "please" and "thank you" when they wanted something. They ate all their food when we sat them down at the table. They were good little boys.

When the week was over, I brought them back to their mother and went on my way visiting other children. The whole next week went by, and I again came by, knocking at the door of their ghetto apartment. When the mother came to the door, she just looked at me at first, and then she said, "What did you do to my boys? I can't believe it! They are nice little boys! What did you do to them?" She was totally taken aback by the change in her boys. Because they were very small, she had been beating them, slapping them in the face, chasing them out of the house, and yelling at them in anger. They only got worse by the day. She didn't realize that she was compounding the problem. But after one week of loving discipline with the rod, those boys were well behaved. I wish I could have adopted them and made them my own. What a difference it would have made in their destiny.

I have received other testimonies just like this one that I have shared with you, examples of similar experiences in which problem children were brought into a godly home as a last effort. The stand-in parents simply applied the good old garden rules of raising children, and they got the good old garden results.

Dear parents, it works! If God's principles work for the hard cases, they also will work for you. Your children are not different then everybody else's children. There may be a very few who do have a special problem, but for the most part, it is a matter of learning how to train, and then obeying what you have learned.

A child that is disciplined is at rest in his soul. There is a peace about him that affects every area of his daily life. The clear and happy heart that he has is truly a gift. That gift is given to him by responsible parents. It is a gift of love.

Prayer

Open our eyes Lord, the eyes of our hearts. We have been infected by the spirit of this age. Forgive us, for we have not obeyed You. We have known, but we have not obeyed. Sanctify and purify our hearts until we are moved by spiritual love to care for our children in these holy ways. Dear Father, we have reacted to the failures of our parents. Forgive us. Change us and heal us so we can go on. In Jesus Christ's name. Amen.

16

A Sacred Exercise

*Now no chastening for the present seemeth to be joyous,
but grievous: nevertheless afterward
it yieldeth the peaceable fruit of righteousness
unto them which are exercised thereby.*

Heb. 12:11

I have a very sensitive and tender subject to cover in this chapter. As I begin to write, the tears are starting to flow. I am going to attempt to explain how we spank our children. I have many sweet memories to draw from, but they are also tear-filled memories. Do you remember that in Chapter 9 we pictured the Lord putting His hands on our hands and helping us build our house? Well, this is one of those sacred times when it seems as though God puts His hands on mine, and together we are correcting one of my children. I searched my heart for a verse that explains the joyful sadness that has come over me as I sit and ponder the correction of my child. The one at the beginning of the chapter came to my mind, and it fits my heart perfectly. I love my children, and it is not easy to bring pain upon them through chastisement. There is the sweet flow of a loving relationship between my children and me. This is the context of the spanking when it is given.

I have taught this principle earlier, but I want to point it out here again briefly. I guess that is what makes the tears flow as I begin to write. It is not easy to spank your best buddy or that sweet little girl who makes your heart sing. I have prayed much about the right or wrong of sharing these sacred experiences. It makes my children very vulnerable. I have discussed it with them, and they have given me the freedom to share for the sake of the many homes that could be affected by this testimony.

The discipline I am going to explain is given in the context of all the other principles shared in this book. This is very important to remember. The principle of spanking does not stand by itself in the Bible. There are many other holy methods that stand with this one. Let me share some of the issues of the heart before we look at the actual details of spanking a child.

NEVER Spank the Children in Anger NEVER

We never spank the children in anger. This may surprise you, but that is not allowed. Just as we never drink whisky, or never smoke cigarettes, we never spank in anger. As I am writing these words, my burden and prayer is that God would change your heart on this point. I pray that God will put a holy barrier in your hearts that will never allow you to spank a child in anger again. I am sure this seems a bit strong to some of you. However, the sin of it is worse than that of drinking whisky. Many parents come to me confessing a problem with anger, and they often speak of it as a small issue they are working on. I see it as one of the largest issues in child training. It has devastating effects.

If you have a problem with anger, you need a deliverance from that anger through repentance. If that doesn't help you, then get some personal counseling. Do whatever you must do, but get free of that anger. The laws of our land are quickly changing, and some of us are going to be forced to deal with our anger, or the government will take our children away from us. Many of the child abuse cases involve parents who beat their child in a rage, and beat them too hard or in the wrong places.

Many times the anger is there from your own bad experiences with abusive spanking when you were young. For the sake of God, who is being terribly misrepresented, and for the sake of your child, who is being warped by it, get help for your anger. Please forgive me if this is too strong for you, but I feel urgent about the abuses that happen even in Christian homes.

We fathers represent God in our homes and even mothers represent God's authority. When we spank in anger, we give our children a wrong picture of God. They get the impression that God is standing there in heaven with a big stick in His hand, waiting for us to do wrong so he can punish us for it. This is a perverse picture of God. Many of us adults have thought of Him that way. It often comes from the way we were beaten when we were young. God is not that way. Until you get free from this plague of anger, I suggest that you send your child to a room to wait for a few minutes while you pray and calm your heart. You actually can make the childs behavior worse than what it was before if you walk into that room in a spirit of anger and spank them.

Many parents are missing the whole concept of chastisement. Chastisement is not judgment meted out for wrongdoing. It is correction for wrongdoing with future conduct in mind. There is an element of punishment in biblical chastisement. However, it is not the primary motivation. Hebrews chapter twelve is clear on this. There is a big difference between the two views. If we are meting out punishment, then we feel justified in our anger.

Many of you parents feel it is all right to go into the room with fire in your eyes and a paddle in your hand, speaking strong words of condemnation and judgment. If you do it this way, I feel you are missing the whole concept of chastisement. Chastisement is correction for future conduct, not punishment for past deeds. It is true that the deed is an issue. However, the motivation is entirely different, and you will get entirely different results.

Maybe you are feeling overwhelmed even now by these words, thinking "How can I ever do this right?" This is why I say we need to be so yielded to God that He can put His hands on ours and lovingly spank our children. I cannot emphasize our need of God enough. If we will love Him and walk with Him, we will find grace to do what seems impossible.

The Pursuit of Godly Seed

Your Children Are Sinners

Your children are going to fail. Plan on it, expect it to happen. Then you won't be so disappointed with them when they do. God has placed them under your care because they need help. We need to change our mind about the failures or sins of our children. Somehow we have gotten the idea that they are supposed to be saints, and then we get frustrated or even angry with them when they fail. I am not implying that we should let them go and not be concerned with their conduct. But if we understand that this is all part of the process of their training, we can be peaceful and calculating in our discipline. Here's how I look at it. Every time my children fail and transgress my law, I just look at it as another opportunity to correct their future conduct. It is time to have a lesson. Only this lesson has some pain in it. They are going to fail; that is how they learn. Godly character and the peaceable fruit of righteousness will be the fruit of these lessons.

I think many times we parents get angry at our children when they fail because of issues of pride in our own lives. We think, "You're my child, and you ought to know better." Jackie and I have had to resist these temptations with our children, especially as I became known for preaching on the home. We resisted it, believing that our children needed to be allowed to fail and learn just like any others, no matter what others might be thinking.

Your children are going to fail. Plan on it. Plan on it so well that you know what you are going to do the next time they do fail. That way you can calmly administer the discipline when it is needed. Wouldn't that be nice?

There have been times when I could tell a child was in need of correction. The child hadn't done anything that I could specifically deal with him about, but I just knew: "This child is not right today." You know the feeling. He is not content; he is hesitant in his obedience; and you expect a failure will be here soon. You know that there is something not right in the heart, and you know it won't be long until he will do something wrong. Well, when I see a child like that, I pray about it, sit back and watch, and wait. Usually, before the day is out, I have an opportunity to take care

A Sacred Exersice

of the child. I don't consider that to be mean; that is loving my child. Remember, we are training, not punishing so we are always looking for opportunities to train.

Spank Your Children the Way That God Spanks You

If we could bring this concept into our heart and meditate upon it, we wouldn't need anybody to teach us how to spank our children. That sounds pretty simple, and it is, yet it is a most profound statement. How does God spank you? Does He grab you by the scruff of the neck, shout at you, and tell you how wrong you were? Does He spank you in His wrath with a scowl on His face? We all know the answer. God doesn't spank His children like that. Aren't you glad He doesn't?

When our heavenly Father spanks us, *"Mercy and truth are met together, righteousness and peace have kissed each other"* (Ps. 85:10). He very lovingly and calmly reveals to us a need in our life, picks us up in the comfort of His hands, and spanks us. When He is done, He continues to care for us and instruct us in the way He wants us to go. He loves us and affirms us in right paths wherein to walk with eternity in view. This is how God spanks us.

True godliness is Godlikeness. It is imperative that we become like our Father God in the area of chastisement. If you can just get that picture in your mind, then reproduce the same thing when it is time to spank your children, you've got it.

A Consecrated Ritual

We take between fifteen and twenty minutes to spank a child. You may say, "Twenty minutes! I don't have that much time to spank my child" I understand. Time is precious to us Americans. However, if you will practice this holy task with the right heart and care, you may not have to do it as much. There are times when a short discipline may be in order, such as when you have visitors. But usually, when a parent grabs his child and gives him a few frustrated swats as a correction, it only increases the need for more corrections, and often makes the child angry.

So, here's how we spank our children. When the child transgresses one of our laws, we very calmly inform him that he has done wrong, and that he is going to get a spanking. We do not raise our voice. Raising your voice sets the stage for an improper session of instruction. In modern terms, you must be "cool, calm, and collected." Many parents raise their voice in hopes of establishing their authority. It actually does the opposite. Usually a parent resorts to yelling because he has put off the correction too long, and now he (the parent) is upset. We never raise our voice. Oh, how well you can establish your authority if after you correct verbally one time, you follow it up by calmly informing the child, "You have done wrong. Go to your room. You're going to have a spanking."

(Note: please understand that when I refer to the child as "he" in this book, I really mean to include both sons and daughters.)

A Time of Weeping

After I send the child to his room (where he is to sit down and wait for me), I reach for the rod (to spank with) and the Bible (to instruct with). You need your Bible. It is a divinely inspired tool that will sanctify the very things you are about to do. I walk to the room with the rod and the Word. As I go, my heart is crying out to God for wisdom and grace. I realize that He knows my child better than I do, and I lean heavily on Him to guide me, just as I do when I enter into a counseling session with a seeking soul.

When I walk into the room, the child is already crying because he doesn't like spankings; they hurt. As I look upon my crying child, I begin to weep along with him. Can you do that? Can you so sanctify your own heart that the tears begin to flow out of a heart of compassion? Did you know it is scriptural to do that? *"Weep with them that weep"* (Ro. 12:15b). I put myself in my child's place for a moment to feel what he is feeling. It is all right if you cry with the child. You do not have to maintain this austere posture of a judge. You are a loving father.

At this point, I reach out my arms to my child and welcome him. The child quickly comes up into my lap, and we snuggle a moment. I look into his face and let him talk to me. The child almost always begin with, "I'm sorry Papa. I love you." Then I tell him with tears, "I know you are sorry. I love you too."

A Sacred Exercise

I've heard people say, "Don't give your children any comfort when they are supposed to get punished." That is so wrong, it is so punishment oriented.

I just hold them for a couple minutes giving them comfort. Then I say, "I'm sorry I have to give you a spanking, but you know you have done wrong." I tell them, "Papa loves you and is not mad at you. You are a dear son (or daughter) to me." It is good to say words like these to reassure them that you have their good in mind.

A Time of Instruction

Then we have a time of instruction. We talk about what they have done. I usually ask my child, "Do you know what you have done?" I do this to make sure they understand why they are being corrected. Sometimes a child really doesn't know why and he simply says, "I did wrong." It is important to make this clear. I talk about what my child has done, and walk through it with him. It is a time of instruction. The length of time for this varies, depending on the age of the child or the complications in the offence. It takes longer when they get a little bit older because they get a little wiser and they think that they can talk their way out of it.

I see this instruction time as a key to biblical chastisement. If a parent is correcting a child for the future, then the parent will take the time to talk about issues. If the parent's motivation is simply to punish the child, then it is easy to give them the pain quickly and be done. I take the Bible and share verses with them about spanking, and about their failure. It is very important to establish what you are doing on the sure foundation of God's Word.

I also take this time of instruction as an opportunity to teach the children the principles of Biblical chastisement. Read the verses on correction in Hebrews twelve. You will see that the attitude of the one receiving the spanking is very important. I teach them how to receive their correction with the most benefit. It is the teachable moment, and they are very open to learn. I teach them about yielding the heart and opening the heart. Sometimes I even let them pray a little prayer about their response to the correction. It might surprise you what a child will say at a time like that.

The Pursuit of Godly Seed

What is the purpose of this instruction? The more they give their heart over to the instruction and the spanking, the deeper the lesson will go. The deeper the lesson goes, the fewer times they will need to be spanked in the future. A child can understand this, and gain more character from each correction. Do you see what I am saying? Eventually, the child begins to work with you in the spanking, and you don't have to spank as hard or as much. This is also the way that you get your children to thank you afterward, as they begin to understand the blessing of getting a spanking. When Hannah was about three years of age, she couldn't figure out how Samuel could come back after a spanking and say, "Thank you Papa, for giving me that spanking. I feel so much better now."

A Time of Spanking

After we have a time of instruction, it is time for the spanking. I encourage you to take time to instruct your child on how to receive the spanking. He can learn to hold still, to keep his hands out of the way, and to take the correction submissively. The child must lie still and take the spanking. We do not allow the child to jump and wiggle all over the place. If you are chasing the child all over the room to give the spanking, he is not getting very much help from it. That is out of order. Have you ever had to do that?

Many parents have tried to give discipline without this order, and it is counterproductive, to say the least. It is very hard to swat in the right place (on the bottom) if the child is moving around. There are many creative ways that you can help the child to hold still. We have told our children that we will lessen the stripes if they hold still. We also have given another spanking because the child was totally out of order and not submissive.

Children can develop a determination to hold still while they receive discipline. We have the children lean over the couch with their face in the cushion. It is not easy to get a spanking. They hold still by determination.

With the child holding himself in place, we give him a thorough spanking. Chastisement is supposed to hurt. God designed it for that purpose. There are things that need to take place inside the heart that won't happen if you don't give a good spanking.

A Sacred Exercise

There are many questions that arise on this point. How hard, how long, when do you stop, how do you know when you are finished? All I can say is, God must lead you in these things. The law is compassion and a clear conscience on your part. If you walk with God as you spank, you will know the answers. The more you understand what needs to take place in the heart, the sooner you will feel sure about what you are doing. We give at least ten good swats on the bottom. A couple of swats will not do much in most situations, unless you have an angel. It fact, some children only get angry when they get a short spanking. During the spanking, we try to sense how the child is responding in his heart. As I have already shared, brokeness is what we are after.

As the child learns what God's purposes are for the spanking, he will yield and give in to what he is receiving. He will learn to let it do its work in him and get done sooner. There must be enough pain to drive evil out of the heart. However, this has been grossly abused by undiscerning parents. We use a different size rod depending on the age and size of the child. I am not for abuse in this area. Our hearts should be filled with compassion. This becomes a monitor to us as we give the spanking.

Some people laugh about children getting a spanking. This is not right. Such people need to let some adult give them about ten good swats with a paddle some time. I have heard parents laugh as they tell stories about the spankings their children receive. To make matters worse, they tell them while the child is listening. How unkind this is! When this happens, I think the parent needs the spanking.

A Time of Affirming

When we are finished with the correction, I fall on my knees next to the child. I put my arm around him and we cry together. It is not hard to cry because I have allowed my feelings to flow with the feelings of my child. There have been times when I was so overcome with weeping that the child was taken aback by it. At times like that, the child reaches over to comfort me. This often breaks his heart more than the spanking did.

The Pursuit of Godly Seed

Then we pray together. I encourage my children to talk to God about all that has happened. Those prayers are awfully sweet. They ask God to forgive them for what they did, and to help them to change in the area of the correction. Then I pray. This is a time of intercession for the child. I let my heart go out in fervent prayer. We pray about what has happened. We ask God to help him. We pray for love between the two of us, and we pray blessings down upon the child. This is very good for the child to hear. It affirms him tremendously. I claim the promise right there while we are on our knees together: "Lord, you said he will love me if I spank him. I'm believing you for this."

When we are finished with our prayer time, I usually hold the child on my knee again. I give him a big hug and tell him I love him. I get a tissue, help him to wipe his eyes, and blow his nose, and then we have a little instruction again. I go over the things we have already talked about, asking questions to discern how much the child understands. I usually spend some time affirming him with pleasant words. I tell him that he is a good son, and that most of the time he fills my life with joy. Then we often sing a little child's song to lighten his heart. Many a time we will sing "Everything's all right, in my Father's house." As we start to sing, the child often start to cry again because his heart is soft and tender.

Dear parents, discipline done in this way, when all the other aspects of training are in place, brings lasting results. A spanking becomes a positive life-changing experience. A little later in the day, the child usually comes back and says, "Papa, thank you. Thank you for spanking me." Then we are friends all the rest of the day. Good buddies.

I have also noticed that he wanted to be where I was throughout the day. I've never seen a spanking rightly done drive my child away. I've heard parents say, "When I finish spanking my child, he looks blankly at me and doesn't want to be around me." I've never seen that one time. They want to be close to me. They love me, and they know that I love them.

I remember when Hannah had her lesson on hitting. We do not hit in our house, but every child has a time when he or she is confronted with the evil of hitting. We consider it very wrong--like playing in the street or walking near a pond. You know how all little children are. They all will do it. They walk up to a sibling and hit him in the face, for various reasons. Maybe you snickered when they did it the first few times, but it soon looks pretty ugly. At our house, the first time we see it, we go after it.

Well, the time came when little Hannah lifted up her hand and hit Samuel. He was doing something she didn't like. She is a sinner, and sinners do things like that. We gave her some good seasons of instruction about not hitting, showing her what it is and acting it out so she knew what we wanted. These are very positive teaching times with some emphasis on the negative. We raised her hand and "almost" hit Samuel a few more times during the teaching process to make the "no-no" very clear.

Then, some days later, she hit Samuel again. I had been waiting for it, knowing it would come, and planning on the next phase of teaching. I thought to myself, "It is time to have the lesson on hitting with Hannah." I walked through all of what I explained to you in this chapter, and she was completely cured of hitting. We never saw it again. After our lesson, she would walk up to me three or four times a day and say, "Papa, Samuel did something that I didn't like, and I didn't hit him!" You know how it is. With big wide eyes, she would say, very authoritatively, "We don't hit with our hands." She was an expert on the subject now. This is how it should work, and it does work if we will be consistent. That lesson is done, and on to the next one we go. We go in love, with purpose and a plan, guiding the soul of our child in righteousness.

Prayer

Father in heaven, teach us how You discipline us. I know that we do not see it clearly. Please Lord, would You write this scene upon the table of our hearts, so we can see it when it is time to spank our children. Make us like You, O Lord, for our children's sake and Yours. Amen.

Meditations

Resolved

*At the birth of my children, I will resolve
To do all I can that they may be the Lord's*

*I will now actually give them up by faith to God
Entreating that each child may be*

*A child of God the Father
A subject of God the Son
A temple of God the Spirit*

*That each child be rescued from
The condition of a child of wrath
And be possessed and employed by the Lord
As an everlasting instrument of His glory*

adapted Cotton Mather

17

The Training of the Will

Withhold not correction from the child:
for if thou beatest him with the rod, he shall not die.
Thou shalt beat him with the rod,
and shalt deliver his soul from hell.

Proverbs 23:13-14

Have you ever noticed that God gives only two commandments in the entire Bible for the children to follow? What a simple carefree life they can have if they will follow them! He tells them to honor their parents and to obey them. If they will do these two things, then it will be well with them, and they will live long on the earth (Eph. 6:1-2). We will turn again and again to these two commandments as we study different aspects of training, but I want to tie them to the area of discipline. I have given you a clear example of how God wants you to spank your children. I think you will agree that it is easy to see how the child learns to reverence his parents through that sacred exercise. But let us look at the issue of obedience.

The ultimate goal in discipline is to bring children to the place where they cheerfully obey their parents, and eventually obey their God. Again, notice the corrective nature of the discipline. While there is some judgment involved with spanking, the primary goal is to correct, with future obedience in mind. We do our children a great disservice if we do not teach them to obey. All the blessings promised to them are conditional—if they obey their parents. We parents then have a large part to play in the lifelong blessings of our children.

We have seen in the previous chapter the power of a loving relationship. Its ability to stimulate a desire to please and obey cannot be measured. Although this tool is very effective for motivating the children to obey, it is not the only tool that God has given us. As the proper use of the rod teaches the child reverence, and honor, so it also can be used to guide them unto heart-felt obedience. The value of this precious jewel cannot be measured, considering the blessings, and fruitfulness it will bring as the child learns to walk with God.

Obedience is a matter of the will. God has wisely created man with a free will. It is clear to me that the will of the child is the focus of the two quoted verses. First of all, we see the Lord repeating what he has already stated earlier in Proverbs. God repeats what we need to hear over and over in the scriptures. Correcting our children is one of those areas. In this verse, He is reaffirming His word to us: *"Withhold not correction from the child."* Again, we have a tendency to hold back, so He tells us to deny that impulse and to correct. The second half of this verse has two interpretations. I will give them both because they are both worthy interpretations. The word says, *"If thou beatest him with the rod, he shall not die."* He may sound like he is going to die, the way he yells. He may act as if he is going to die, the way he carries on, but he will not die. If you spank the child good and proper, he won't die. That is one interpretation, and it is a good one that seems to flow along with other verses. Oh how the children can carry on when it is time for him to be spanked. We must rise above his pleadings, and do right. The other interpretation that I found is also worthy. *"He shall not die"* refers to an early death because of a foolish, reckless life. This also flows along with other verses. But look at the next verse. *"Thou shalt beat him with the rod, and shalt deliver his soul from hell."* Now that is a very sobering verse to me because of one sobering word that moves us into the realm of eternity. That word is "hell" *"shalt deliver his soul from hell."* This is an awesome command given to us. I have a part in the eternal destiny of the soul of my child, and God tells me to, "deliver his soul from hell." How? Thou shalt spank him. This means if I allow my sentimental love to keep me from my responsibility, I am playing with the destiny of my child. This is no small omission. You may say, "How can this be? A child that is not spanked will go to hell?" Let's put it this way, a child left to himself, has a very good chance of going to hell. That is what the Bible says.

We need to look a bit into the nature of saving faith to understand this fully. Remember the testimony of a clear conversion at the beginning of this book. That holy exercise had a lot to do with man's will: a willingness to confess sin, a willingness to repent, to turn away from those sins, and a willingness to yield the heart to God's full control. Then from that glorious change came also a responsibility to walk after the dictates of the Spirit of God. All of these must be carried out by a yielded will. When God's grace and man's will meet together on God's terms, salvation takes place, and man is transformed. Like Paul said in Romans 6:17b, he must *"obey from the heart, that form of doctrine that was delivered to him."* As I understand the doctrine of salvation, where there is no yielding of the heart to God, there is no salvation, only a spurious counterfeit that confesses, but never possesses.

Now let's go back to the training of the will through the use of the rod. I have already described in Chapter 15 how a child should receive a clearing of the heart through spanking. I also mentioned that they have a broken heart after the spanking. What is a broken heart? As I understand the Bible teaching on a broken heart, brokeness is yieldedness. God tells His people to rend their hearts, circumcise their hearts, and break their hearts. These all refer to giving up the will to God. This is where we are going with our children. The use of the rod breaks the will of the child and brings it into subjection, first of all to the parents, and then later to the Lord who made them. When I use the term, "breaking the will," I do not mean to destroy it, no never. The child's will must be very much alive, only yielded now to a different master.

The new master at first is the parent. Then someday when God calls and says, "My son, my daughter, follow Me," the child will say, "Yes Lord, I will follow You!" But a child who has been "left to himself," has a rebellious heart or an unyielded will. When God says to that child, "My child follow Me! Give Me everything! Yield it all up to Me!" they may say, "No, I'm going to do what I want to do," and go to hell because of it. That is the bottom line of it all.

This is also a good explanation for many of the "worldly Christians" in the churches today. There was no submitting to mom and dad, and there is no submitting to God, just a prayer that was prayed, a good feeling, and a baptism, but no *"new creature in Christ Jesus."* Do your children a favor. Spank them.

Saint Susanna

Susanna Wesley was the mother of John and Charles Wesley. John Wesley was the founder of the Methodist Church. Charles was the songwriter of the movement. Most of you reading this are not Methodists. However, these two men have impacted your lives in many ways. We quote their words and sing their songs. Mother Wesley had nineteen children. Nine of them lived to adulthood. Her words on this subject are not canon, but it is pretty close to that. I'm sure she is the most quoted writer on the training of the will. I want to look deeply into her words for a moment.

> I set out at an early age to conquer the will of each child.
> Then I continue to bring it under subjection
> until it is totally yielded to Christ.

These words paint a beautiful picture before the eyes of our hearts. This elect lady had clear direction for her heart and hands. It is easy to see that there was nothing haphazard in her child training methods. With vision and purpose, she moved from point A to point B. Maybe the use of the word conquer seems too strong to you, but remember, our children are sinners. They are "a few days and full of trouble." All of us parents know there is a battle of the wills at first until the child learns who will be in control. We must be careful to use all the child training principles to accomplish this, but it must be done. I don't see how you can effectively train children until the will is conquered. Let us follow the example of Mother Wesley, and set out to conquer the will of each child

The Training of the Will

at an early age, with the supreme goal in mind: their total surrender to Christ someday.

It is possible to bring your children to the place where they willingly and joyfully obey your first command without hesitation. I am not dreaming. This is God's heart for your children. We need to see it, believe that it is possible, and move toward it with confidence, knowing that God our Father is working with us to obtain it.

You are supposed to be the authority in your home. Establish that authority by the means that God has laid out to us in His Word. Your family will prosper under this biblical authority. It shall fall over them like a heavenly blanket of blessing and protection. My heart has been grieved so many times on airplanes and in grocery stores when I see a 3-year-old child ruling a father or a mother. I am sure you have noticed this also as you are out in the public. Sadly, it happens sometimes among God's people too.

I have sat for two hours on a plane and watched a small child control and disturb the lives of twenty people. This is a sad spectacle to observe. The whole scenario is made worse on an airplane. There, the child doesn't want to sit down, but the FAA says he must sit down. In the store, the parents can just give him what he wants and shut him up. But on the plane, the parent's creativity is stretched to the max. How can they convince Johnny to sit down. They shudder under the embarrassment. The chickens have come home to roost. Reality is being displayed in front of twenty staring people, and there is nothing the parents can do.

My heart goes out to the parents, and I at times have given them a number to call, where they can order tapes on child training. Does this story come close to your home experience at times? It reminds me of the curse mentioned in Isaiah three. *"I will give children to be their princes, and babes shall rule over them."* Also, *"the child shall behave himself proudly against the ancient."* This curse is the result of several generations of men who have turned away from God to pursue other interests. They have lost their authority. The children are out of control, and ruling through the ignorance of their parents.

Obedience 101

The term 101, is used in college courses to signify the beginning course, the introduction. We humans tend to get things all turned around, and the subject of obedience is no exception. We think we should wait until the child matures a bit before we start training them to obey. This is only partially true. There are deeper levels of obedience that a child must learn, and these lessons must wait until the child gets a little older. But we should always remember that if we have not taught the basics of obedience, they will have a much harder time with these deeper lessons.

The truth is, it is very easy to train a small child in areas of obedience with very simple lessons. Remember the principle of little and much. If they learn to faithful in the small lessons of early childhood, they will also be faithful in the deeper lessons to come.

By the time our children reach the age of one year, we have begun the training of the will. We have lessons on "coming" at our house. As soon as they can understand the word "come," as soon as those little legs can go across the floor, we start having lessons on "coming." These are very purposeful lessons, with the will in mind.

I remember when Hannah was very small. She would be across the room, and I call her, "Hannah, come to Papa." When she comes toddling over to me, I give her a blessing, "Oh, what a good girl you are!" Then I send her back to the other side of the room and call her again. I tell her, "We are having lessons on coming." Then I send her into another room, and she goes into the other room and waits in there until I call her again, "Hannah! Come to Papa!" Here she comes running from the other room. When she arrives, with a big smile on her face, because she knows she is pleasing Papa, again I say, "Oh, good girl! Good girl!" Then I pick her up, give her a hug, and send her back into the other room again. Do you see what I am doing? This little girl is having fun. She doesn't even know that she is being trained for life.

We do this from time to time until Hannah clearly knows what it means to "come" when Papa says "come." Then I make the lesson a little bit harder. Some people think I'm unkind in doing this, but that doesn't matter to me. I will wait until she's busy playing

The Training of the Will

with her favorite toy, on purpose. Then I call to her, "Hannah! Come to Papa!" We repeat the whole procedure again until she understands what is required of her. Finally, it will happen as it always happens, the toys are there, and it seems more important to play than obey. Then she will get a swat. You see, I know what is going to happen, and I already have plans to correct her when she fails. When the children are small, we just spank their hand or swat them on the behind once during this kind of training. The size of the rod changes as the child gets bigger.

I call these experiences training sessions. It is almost like dog training isn't it? It is kind of sad when you think about it, but many of us train our dog better and with more care than we do our children, who have a never-dying soul. Do you know what I mean? When you are going to train a dog, you do it with a purpose, don't you? You plan it out carefully. One half hour of training each week for the dog. You even plan the lessons with expectations of what you want the dog to accomplish. He must be able to sit, fetch, roll over, not jump on people, and hopefully not bite anyone. And guess what, you get the dogs to do those things you want them to do.

Oh parents, this may seem a little crude to some of us, but this is the mentality we ought to have about our children. We need to take special care, and plan out how we are going to train our child.

One time, while sitting at the dinner table, I look over at the smallest child, and notice, that she has found a food that she doesn't like. In my mind, I think, "Well, here we go! Now it's time to learn our lesson that we all must learn about eating our food until it is all gone." Do you understand what I am doing? I'm not angry at the child. I have been waiting for this opportunity to train the child's will in the area of eating. I am training her will for God so she can give it to Him someday.

With smaller children we have lessons on laying the head down when it's time to go to sleep at night. You lay them down in the crib and work with them, giving them the command to lay their head down, and then gently pushing it down. If you repeat this, they will learn what the words mean and what is expected.

Esther was learning this lesson at the same time Hannah was learning more complex lessons. As the class progressed, eventual-

The Pursuit of Godly Seed

ly, Esther didn't want to lay her head down, and she tried us out to see if she could get away with it. She put a big smile on her face and put her head up. At that age, we swat the children on the back of the leg with two fingers. Esther was eight months old at the time. As soon as the swat was given, the command was repeated, "You lay your head down." She then started crying, and down went the head, and she learned.

These are simple little lessons given during the early years of the children's development. Why wait until they are ten years old, when the lessons are much harder, on both them and you? It is so easy to teach them great big lessons on obedience while they are learning to eat their green beans, to come to Papa, or to share their toys.

When Esther had just started crawling about, it was time for the "no-no" lessons. We don't put everything away when the child learns how to crawl. No, this means it is time to start training them to understand what "no-no" means. I don't start with a real hard slap on the hand, but just a gentle tap on the hand, followed by "no-no," and then I pull the child's hand away. This is repeated often, and the child begins to learn what I mean.

Esther would go over to the book shelf. She always liked all the books on the shelf in the family room. She would go crawling over there with her eyes on those books, then reach up for them. At the same time she would reach, she would look over at mama because she knew it was a "no-no."

Once we had gotten Esther to that place where she knew she was not supposed to put her hand on that book, we slapped her hand when she touched it, and followed this by those famous words, "No-no, Esther, no-no!" Then she would cry big old crocodile tears, shudder a bit, and crawl away, a bit wiser.

The list of lessons can be endless. I am giving you some ideas for your gleaning, but you must come up with your own lessons for your children. I want you to get the idea that these training exercises are done on purpose, not haphazardly.

Let me give you one more example, which is classic. Very young children can learn very big lessons about obeying from this one. I always carried a pen and my checkbook in the pocket of my shirt. Well, you know how it is with small children. They want whatever is in your pocket. Not only do they want it. They have to put it in their mouth. That's okay with a pen, but unhandy with a checkbook.

Well, one day it dawned on me that I had a good training tool at my fingertips. I decided, the pen is okay, but the checkbook is a no-no. Honestly, it's such a simple little thing, but it works. I trained Hannah this way, and then the others who came after her. It is a more casual training time because you can do it when ever you have the child in your arms. They will immediately see the objects in your pocket, and the training begins as I have already described.

Hannah learned quickly: she could play with the pen, but she could not play with the checkbook. Long after the lesson was learned, Hannah would sit on my lap, point to the checkbook, and say, "That is a no-no, Papa."

> *The rod and reproof give wisdom: but a child left to himself bringeth his mother to shame.*
> *Proverbs 29:15*

We are learning about bringing the will of the children into subjection to the will of their parents. We do them such a big favor if we train them in these ways. We fill their hearts with wisdom, practical wisdom. Cheerful obedience at the first command, should be a law in your house, one that you should take the time to enforce. To give commands and then let them go unfulfilled is to teach the child to disobey. A child left to himself is not loved, no matter how many fuzzy feelings the parents have when they think of their child. You know, there are hundreds of illustrations like those ones that have been given. When we become students of training our children, we will think of our own simple little methods. If we start when they are young, start working through these kinds of things, we will give them a ten-year head start on life.

The context of the verses in Proverbs 29:15-18 is staggering. When you align them next to our present American desolations, it is more staggering. We are now gazing at *"the desolations of many generations"* I don't need to go down the same list that many others have already made. I am convinced that the homes are a major problem. It seems that everything is overflowing except revival.

The prisons are full and running over, as well as the hospital. The rest homes are the same, and mental problems are so widespread we can't count them all. Could our neglected homes be the problem? Look at these verses. God says that when we discipline our children, they will learn how to live. If we don't, they will not learn how to live, and bring us shame. The next verse carries the neglect further yet. When there is no correction of our children, the wicked multiply, and sin is on the increase. Does this sound close to home? The next verse again mentions correction, and the blessed fruit of it for us, and to our nation. Rest and delight shall be our portion. Look at the last two verses as a unit. It seems that they flow together.

> *Correct thy son, and he shall give thee rest; yea, he shall give delight unto thy soul. Where there is no vision, the people perish: but he that keepeth the law, happy is he.*
> *Proverbs 29:17-18*

I have explained this word "perish" before. It is very significant in light of the context of these verses. It means "naked, unrestrained, wild, and scattered." What a revelation for us Americans! That is exactly where we have arrived. How did we get here? The verses tell us. Look at the context. God is pleading with us to have a vision of order and righteousness. This vision must have substance to it. It must be more than illusive dreams. The actions that flow from our vision are the training of the next generation. The rod of correction and reproof will give wisdom to the next generation, and wisdom will produce right living. Right living will produce a righteous people, and all will be at rest. Let me attempt to give a very broad paraphrase of these two verses, with the child training applications in them:

> Chasten and train your son with a vision of righteous order, and his ordered life will give you rest, and fill your heart with joy. When this vision of righteous order is neglected, the result is a

wild, unrestrained society, heading for destruction. If you keep this law, and teach your son to keep it, you will be happy.

I have been in some homes that were absolutely the opposite of rest. The children were wild and unrestrained, and the parents were frustrated. Listen, children are one of the greatest joys this side of heaven, but some parents are so frustrated with children that they don't want any more than one or two. In some situations, the way the children behave, I don't blame them for not wanting any more. Do we realize that we have not followed God's laws, and that is why everything is in confusion.

My children are such a joy to my house and to my soul. There are times when I sit as a king in my house with a heart overflowing with joy because of my children. This is your portion. If you will just follow God's laws, you will have rest in your home.

Here is a prayer that I want you to pray with a fervent heart before the Lord every day. "Oh God, make me a student of training my children." That is all. If you have that desire, everything else will take care of itself, because God is a teacher to those who are willing to be students. No one has discipled me in training children. There have been many times when I longed for a teacher. I have simply prayed, "God, I don't know how to train children. Please teach me how to do it?" God is no respecter of persons. What He does for one, He will do for all.

Prayer
Our Heavenly Father, we come to You in Jesus' name. God, we come with thanksgiving. Oh Lord, my heart is full. It's so simple, it's so clear. Will You not put a hunger in our hearts that will make us rise up and learn how to raise our children? Oh Father, there is such a dearth in the land. There is so much wickedness everywhere. Let us be known as a people who train our children. Raise up thousands of godly families. Amen

Meditations

Spiritual Leadership

*When a man rules his family
righteously in the fear of God.
He is anointed with spiritual authority.
His influence shines on them
like the morning sun on a clear blue day.
They grow like fresh grass
in the sunlight after a rain.
His effectual life comes down on them
like showers that water the earth.
His righteous family will flourish,
and peace shall prevail in his house.*

adapted 2 Samuel 23:3,4
Psalm 72:6,7

Brother Denny

18

The Bondage of Foolishness

*Foolishness is bound in the heart of a child,
but the rod of correction shall drive it far from him.*
Proverbs 22:15

The next verse we shall study is one of the key verses on child training in the Bible. I say that because it has a word in it that reveals some of the heart issues of a child, one who is devoid of wisdom. That word is "foolishness." I pray that God will open the eyes of your understanding concerning this word, so you can go deeper than actions with your child, to discern his needs much sooner.

We shall look at several words that will help us define this word "foolishness," but first let me state a word that we understand better in our modern English. That word is "silliness." Foolishness and silliness are synonyms, which means they have the same meaning. Thus, we could read the verse, "Silliness, is bound in the heart of a child." All parents can relate to this word and have seen silliness in their children many times. Our children can act very silly at times.

I will give you a word picture that I found somewhere in my studies of this word. The picture is that of an uncontrolled spiral, like a spring that you turn loose. You never know which way it is going to go. On the basis of this explanation, we could say, a disposition out of control is bound in the heart of your child.

When I am preaching on this subject, I often ask the parents if they know what I am talking about. They always raise their hands in agreement. It is very important that we learn to identify this foolishness, and then to realize that God wants us to deal with it. If we deal with foolishness while the child is young, we will never have to deal with much greater transgressions later on. Consider some of the following definitions.

Foolishness

- <u>Foolishness</u>: The Hebrew word is defined as "stupid, silly, no sense." The picture is a fat, jolly man. Have you ever seen any of these?
- <u>Foolishness</u>: The Greek word is defined as "silly talk, joker, and buffoonery." The Greek word is "moro," from which we get our word, "moron."
- <u>Folly</u>: The Hebrew word is the same as foolishness.
- <u>Folly</u>: Webster, 1828. "Not a high criminal act, but actions of nonsense. Silly, vain, and trifling."
- <u>Silly</u>: Webster, 1828. "Want of common wisdom, simple, witless, silly or stupid. Harmless folly."
- <u>Fool</u>: Webster, 1828. "To trifle, to toy, to spend time in idleness, sport, or mirth."
- <u>Stupid</u>: Webster, 1828. "Dull and senseless, no senses, nonsense. No control over the senses."
- <u>Joker</u>: Webster, 1828. "Buffoon, a jester, one who speaks to excite laughter. Words that are not real, to no purpose."
- <u>Buffoon</u>: Webster, 1828. "To be funny, to trifle, to joke and play the fool."

This is quite a list of words to ponder, but let me encourage you to ponder them meditatively. There is a gold mine of discernment in these definitions. These two words, "foolishness" and "folly" do not describe evil and wickedness. This is an important distinction.

The Bondage of Foolishness

There are other words in Proverbs, also translated "fool" and "foolish," that do describe evil, but these words do not. As stated earlier, these words do not imply a criminal act, but actions and attitudes of nonsense. The distinction is there because of the nature of the Proverbs. They were written so that parents can instruct their children in the right way. In a child, it is simply silliness, nonsense, and a lack of control. But if the child is " left to himself," the child grows up, and the silliness grows up also. When folly grows to maturity in adults, the Hebrew words change to evil, wickedness, and perversity. These are very different words.

Let's go back to our children now and apply some of these definitions. We all know that this silliness is in our children. We see it all the time. They can be quite "out of control" at times. We have observed their nonsense and their witless behavior. Many of us are guilty of doing the same things and stimulating it in our children. Their lack of common wisdom is very evident. So what are we supposed to do with what we see? We need to use the spiritual means that God has provided and train these attitudes and actions out of them.

Maybe you react in your heart and say, "Can't a child be happy?" The answer is a resounding "Yes!!" However, there is a difference between a silly child, one filled with nonsense, and a child who is happy, joyful, and in control. Here is the importance of this teaching. If we will use some of the discernment given in these words, we can begin to work at a new level with our children. When we learn to deal with this folly and get rid of it, then we begin to see other qualities take its place. Godly character will replace the folly. A calm controlled spirit is a beautiful exchange for the unrest that was there.

We have been influenced by our society more than we realize. Let's face the raw facts: America is laughing her way down the broad road that leads to destruction. Everything has to be funny and full of fun. The people who make movies, print books, and design toys know about this foolishness in children. They have developed a whole new way to reach the next generation. It is called "Foolishness 101." Even Christians have succumbed to these new methods. Now Moses is a funny little man with a big nose and a funny beard instead of a mighty, anointed prophet with a stern face.

I want to encourage you to meditate upon the definitions of this word and this whole principle of foolishness in a child's heart. This revelation changes our perspective on a child's silly antics. They are no longer cute. When we begin to understand what silliness is, we also gain insight into what causes it. Sometimes it is we parents who draw it out of the child. Sometimes it can be a brother or sister, or maybe a foolish-minded playmate. It can be stimulated by silly activities, certain books, or certain toys. The blessing in all this insight is that it can help you begin to eliminate the things that cause it. This is love, very practical love.

Loose Him and Let Him Go Free
The next word that I would like to study in our text puts an air of urgency in our child training. The verse says that this folly is "bound" in the heart. This is the same word used to describe Samson when they bound him up so he would not get away. They did a thorough job on him. He was a prize that they did not want to lose. So you get the picture of someone being wrapped in rope and tied securely. Well, the Bible says that foolishness is bound in the same way in the hearts of your children! The desire to do wrong, this silly nonsense, this out-of-control attitude is bound in the heart of your children. Let us also remember that the heart is the most powerful part of their being.

You are probably thinking, "Yes brother, I know it is bound there." Maybe you have tried different methods to deal with it, to no avail. Some parents simply live with it. They call it the "terrible two's" and wait for it to pass away. I do not believe in the terrible two's. It is not biblically correct. I assure you, there is a way that you can set your child free. The "terrible two's" can become the sweetest stage in a child's life, the "tremendous two's!" We often say at our house, "Every house ought to have a two-year-old!" We say this because of the pleasant joy that our two-year-olds have always brought us.

So what do we do with this foolishness bound in our child's heart? Parents have tried many methods over the years. You can yell at it, or stand it in the corner, but foolishness will not leave. You can talk nicely to it, or give foolishness a reward, but it will not leave. You can slap foolishness on the hand, or shake it thoroughly, and give it a good ol' talking to, but foolishness will not leave. **Foolishness is bound in your child!** Only the Bible gives us a clear way to get rid of it.

God's answer is given in the last part of the verse: "The rod of correction shall drive it far from him!" Very far away from him. The rod of correction is God's ordained way to drive foolishness out of your children. Many of us know by our own experiences that this works. We know those times when a child was manifesting the conduct mentioned earlier. We gave him a good spanking and found peaceable fruit in the child when we were finished. He was peaceful, contented, kind, and willing to share his toys--just a well-behaved little boy or girl the rest of the day. The child was set free. Why? Because you drove that foolishness far away from him. Do your children a favor, and drive that foolishness out of their hearts. It's not right for you to leave it there. God never intended for your children to live with all those things on them.

Some children live in the midst of all the silliness and nonsense described earlier. It breeds more of the same, and even worse things. This foolishness builds up day by day. The child's conscience gets defiled, selfishness takes the lead, and things go from bad to worse. This is what happens, and it is not right to leave him like that. As I see it, it is a terrible injustice, and an unloving thing to let your child go around for days in this condition needing a spanking. He is frustrated and discontented, and not happy with anything. You know it, and he knows it too.

Parents, we need the discernment to understand what is happening with our child, so we can sense the need much sooner. Remember what I said earlier. When I sense that something is just not quite right with the child, I watch and wait. It won't be long until I have a reason to take care of the need that is down inside the heart. Please notice again, I'm not just spanking for the thing he did wrong; I see the need down inside that heart.

When a child is full of foolishness and guilt, he is in need of a revival. He seems to be out of order in everything. When he is in this state, it doesn't take long until he does something that is worthy of a spanking. Parents who understand these heart issues of silliness can start watching for it, out of love, because they want to deliver the child from his bondage.

Dear parents, do you see what a help this can be? It is all part of a training process. There is no anger on your part. You are in control. You are molding the soul of your child. You become a parent who has discernment into the needs of your children even before they do something wrong. This eliminates most of those frustrated, angry corrections. You are a parent who is in control. When a child commits a trespass, you have been expecting it. You take him into the room where you give discipline, spank him in the manner I described in the previous chapter, and set him at rest. Let him have a happy day. God's plan for the children is that they live a life that is clear, bright, cheerful, and content. This is how you maintain that clarity for them.

Some time ago, when Joshua was about six years old, I noticed in the beginning of the day that he was out of sorts. This foolishness was manifesting itself in lots of little attitudes of nonsense. I lifted up my heart to God for a moment and prayed, "Father, Joshua needs a spanking. Please bring something out in the open so I can set him free again."

After that prayer, I went out to the shop to build picnic tables. I was cutting boards for about an hour, when God prompted me, "Go to the house." I was not thinking of the prayer I had prayed, but simply walked up to the house. As I opened the door, Joshua was throwing himself on the floor because he didn't get the toy he wanted. Imagine how he felt, "Oh no, caught in the act!" It was beautiful. Because the Lord and I work together on these things, I knew exactly how to respond.

I calmly told my son to go up to our room and wait for me there. We went through the spanking exercise as usual, and had a sweet time. Because I had prayed about his heart that morning, I was able to show him how the Lord was working with me to train him. We also talked about his silly attitudes, and I was able to help him see that the silliness led to the actions which brought the correction.

The Bondage of Foolishness

There are times like this when you can see the foolishness bound up in the heart and discern that the conscience needs to be clear. The use of the rod is the only way that you can drive foolishness away. Do it right, and do it now. It is not right to put it off; it is unloving. You are giving them a silent message that says, "I don't love you." Do you know how the old saying goes, "Spare the rod and spoil the child?" This is exactly what we are doing when we neglect discipline. Do you know what that word "spoil" means? It means to make them rotten, ineffective, and of no use anymore. When we neglect our responsibility and don't set our children free, we make them so they are like garbage and have no value. It could also mean that we allow the enemy to come and spoil our child, like an enemy plunders the treasures of a city. Either way, this is a tragedy that must be stopped.

Prayer
Father in heaven, we pray right now, help us to see what is so close to our grasp. We want happy children, Lord, and we need Your grace to make them that way. Open our eyes to this key principle in child training. Make us much more aware of all the nonsense that bombards our children in modern America. Plant this new insight deep within us, so we can see into the hearts of our children. Give us the knowledge to act out of love, instead of reacting out of frustration. In Jesus name, Amen.

Meditations

Eternal Builders

A builder builded a temple;
He wrought it with grace and skill.
Pillars and doors and arches,
All fashioned to work his will.

Men said, as they saw its beauty,
"It shall never know decay;
Great is thy skill O builder!
Thy fame shall endure for aye."

A father builded a temple
With loving and infinite care,
Planning each arch with patience,
Laying each stone with prayer

None praised his unceasing efforts,
None knew of his wondrous plan,
For the temple the father builded
Was unseen by the eyes of man.

Gone is the builder's temple
Crumbled into the dust;
Low lies each stately piller
Food for consuming rust

But the temple the father builded
Will last while the ages roll
For that beautiful unseen temple
Was a child's immortal soul

adapted, author unknown

19

Father: An Anointed Teacher

*And these words, which I command thee this day, shall be in thine heart. Thou shalt teach them diligently unto thy children,
And shalt talk of them
When thou sittest in thine house, when thou walkest by the way,
When thou liest down, and when thou risest up*
Deuteronomy 6:6-7, adapted

Father, you are a teacher. You are the head of your home, the leader, and that makes you a teacher. Teacher and leader are so closely connected that it is hard to say a man is a leader if he is not a teacher. In the same way that God called Abraham the *"father of many nations"* (Gen. 17:5), He calls you a teacher. The Lord has called each of you fathers to preach and teach in your home. The ability to fulfill the task is in the call; the Lord He is God. When God said, *"Thou shalt teach,"* He meant to give you everything you need to do it. Do you believe this? Dear brothers, we are dealing with God. *"God who quickeneth the dead, and calleth those things which be not as though they were"* (Rom. 4:17b). I wonder if we understand this life of faith to which we all are called to walk. According to the Bible, without this kind of faith, *"it is impossible to please Him"* (Heb. 11:6a).

The Pursuit of Godly Seed

Why am I speaking so firmly and confidently? I will explain. Most men whom I meet, who are coming to grips with the needs in their homes, say they can't teach. They are reluctant to begin because they say they don't have the ability. That is absolutely not true. That is like looking at an acorn and saying it doesn't have the ability to become an oak tree. Those who believe that it does will put it into the ground and watch it grow. Faith works in the same way. I have seen dozens of men who "could not teach" become effective preachers and teachers in their homes, and in the pulpit. By faith, we look at an acorn, and say, "You are an oak tree." This is exactly how faith works with you men. You are a teacher.

When God called Jeremiah to be a prophet, He said to him, *"Before I formed thee... I ordained thee a prophet unto the nations"* (Jer. 1:5). That is how God works. Jeremiah said, *"I cannot speak, for I am a child"* (1:6b). God would not hear that excuse. And brothers, God will not hear our excuses either. God said to Jeremiah, *"You are a prophet,"* but Jeremiah said, *"I am a child."* Which one was more right, God or Jeremiah? Brethren, we need to rise up, believe God, and step into the water of teaching our children. Most men who "can't teach" grew up without being taught; it was not passed on to them by their fathers. We must break the chain of disobedience and pass on a legacy of teaching to the next generation. I believe God will meet you at your point of need as you trust Him and obey His precept to teach. The Bible is filled with men who felt inadequate, yet moved ahead trusting God. That is why they are described in the Bible, because they trusted in God.

When God wanted Moses to build Him a tabernacle in the wilderness, He put His Spirit upon certain men to build it. He called Bezaleel to lead out in the work. Look what God did for him. God said, *"I have filled him with the Spirit of God, in wisdom, and in understanding, and in knowledge, and in all manner of workmanship"* (Ex. 31:3). In this manner, a place was built where God could dwell.

God still works the same today. He is building Himself a habitation by the Spirit. It is not a physical tabernacle, but a spiritual building. For *"the most High dwelleth not in temples made with hands"*

Father: An Anointed Teacher

(Acts 7:48), but in the hearts of men and women who are set apart for Him. We, as fathers, are called into this eternal work. God will give us abilities for the task, just as He did the men of old.

If your children are going to turn out the way God wants them to, you have to become a teacher. It is not an option; it is imperative. My burden in the beginning of this chapter is to create a desire. You do not have to be an apt teacher to teach, or to learn to teach. All you need to have is a desire to communicate the Word of God into the hearts of your children. If you truly have the burden, God will teach you how to be a teacher.

Let's reflect again about the family I met in Canada. When I visited that family, I received a vision that changed my life. God placed in me a desire and a burden to go home and train my children. That father did not sit me down and teach me anything that I needed to do when I went home. I saw a godly family that was having a godly influence, and I said, "Lord, I want it. I've got to have it. I will have it by the grace of God."

I went home with that desire, and I started. I was not a good teacher, but I started. I made a lot of mistakes, but I started. And because I had a desire and moved forward with purpose, God taught me how to teach the children.

Allow me to reflect a moment on who should do the teaching. This is a very important question in our modern American society. I believe the father is to be the primary teacher of the Word in the home. This is very clear as we stay close to the Word in our studies. At first, as I began to write, I thought to myself, "Does the father do it all?" No, he does not do all the instruction of the family. Mother is also to be active in teaching the children. We can see allusion to this in Proverbs. She is to come alongside her husband's primary teaching with more of the same as she walks in her house. She is in the supportive role, a helpmeet for her husband.

There are a lot of strong feelings today that the woman is more suited to relate to the children on a teaching level. This is very wrong, and as always, it has dangerous repercussions. God, who made man and woman, knows who is best suited to carry out this most important task.

A God-Given Door of Opportunity

In the preceding two chapters, I several times mentioned the natural desire of children to please Mom and Dad. This desire is placed there by God, who had special training purposes in mind. While we fan the flames of these desires by building close relationships, God wants us to be busy teaching them how they can please us. We have been given an open door of opportunity. This special period of grace is given to us and our children by Almighty God. It is His design. Consider some clear signs of this special grace period:

A desire to please their parents

There is a natural desire in the heart of children to please their father and mother. They feed on our approval and live to see us smile at what they are doing. I have already covered this blessed desire. Since they want to please us, why not teach them how they can do it?

A desire to learn

There is a natural desire to learn. Children come into life knowing nothing, but longing to gain information and skills. This is the teachable moment stage of life for them. If they are crawling, they want to walk. If they are talking, they want to learn to read. We need to seize the moment, teaching and training them with all we have.

They do not see our needs

During the first years of their lives, because they are ignorant, they don't see our needs. The needs are there, but the children are ignorant of them. This adds to their admiration of us, and they are very open to receive all we teach them. I remember when Elisabeth was about ten years old. I felt the need to make a confession to the family during our devotion time.

Elisabeth came to me later and said, "Papa, you don't need to do that. You never do anything wrong. You're the best Papa in the whole world!"

I just smiled at her and said, "Well Elizabeth, when you get a little bit older, you will feel differently about this."

Father: An Anointed Teacher

This is even true in the ghettos of Chicago. Dad is a drunk, and has left them. Mom drinks, and beats them in anger. Yet the children are still proud of them. Proverbs says *"and the glory of children are their fathers"*(Prov. 17:6b).

They have quick sharp minds
When children are young, they have the ability to learn very quickly. Their minds are sharp, fresh, and impressionable. They can memorize with ease.

They have a mind free of clutter
Their minds are not loaded down with cares, distractions, and many things they want to do. A mind that is pure from all of these can learn very easily. The process of meditation and application comes naturally to them.

They are masters at imitation
This is where the little cliché "monkey see, monkey do" originates. Because of their admiration of you and their ability to mimic and learn by example, they want to be just like you. Let us give them something to copy.

They are gullible
They will swallow anything you give them. They believe in you, and they believe you. You can teach them anything you want, and they will believe it. The nonsense of Santa Claus and the Easter Bunny are good examples of this. Why not take advantage of this and put what is true in them?

I think I have listed enough examples to make my point. We have been given a special door of opportunity. We dare not pass by this door and do other things. It is open only for a short time. I am not a child psychologist, and I have no formal education about how all this works. I have, however, studied by observation. By my observations, it seems that a child is in this stage of openness for about ten years. If parents do their homework during these crucial years, the heart stays open, and the training process continues. Even if you have missed these years, don't despair. God is for you and for your child. Press on. I am giving the ideal for the sake of teaching and for the sake of those parents who are just starting.

When you pull all of these natural, God-given desires together, it is awesome. What an opportunity God has given to us parents! Think with me. You have a child who wants to please you, so you teach and train him in the ways of God. You have a child who admires you, believes in you, and can see no wrong in you, so you fill his hearts full of truth and righteousness. You have a child whose mind is a blank piece of paper, so you spend your days writing on the tables of his heart *"all the words of this life"* (Acts 5:20b). You have a child whose quick mind can memorize dozens of things, so you teach him to memorize the Word of God, and it makes him prosper. Finally, you have a child who loves to imitate you, so you live an example before him that he can follow, and you back it up with the teachings of the Bible.

Dear parents, we can't go wrong on this one. All we need to do is do it, just do it. Many fathers have this opportunity confused in their minds. They think the children need them most when they become youth, until then they think it is mother's job to care for the children. I have heard many fathers confess this false idea. These fathers miss the formative years, and then are puzzled when their children won't listen to them.

What is a Teacher

Websters 1828 dictionary says that to *teach* is "to instruct or communicate knowledge to one who is ignorant; to impress truth upon the mind; to admonish or counsel by words and example." These are good definitions. We all have the ability to communicate something that excites us. In a sense, we all are teachers when we find something that we feel others would like to know about. If a man finds a way to get five miles per gallon more from his auto, he will find a way to tell it to others. Even the stuttering man can get his point across if it is important to him. A true teacher is one who is convinced of his subject and wants others to be persuaded also. He will find a way to get it into his hearers.

FATHER: AN ANOINTED TEACHER

To broaden our defintion a bit more, let's look at Isaiah chapter twenty-eight. In this chapter, God is pleading with apostate Israel to learn her lessons and come back to Him. Israel was learning the hard way through judgment. In the midst of His pleadings, God mentions the easy way to teach and learn lessons. As an example to them, He refers to the teaching of children, and how it is done. It is a beautiful insight for us, as we consider what it means to be a teacher.

> *Whom shall he teach knowledge? and whom shall he make to understand doctrine? Them that are weaned from the milk, and drawn from the breasts. For precept must be upon precept, precept upon precept; Line upon line, line upon line; here a little, and there a little.*
> Isaiah 28:9-10

These verses give us a good biblical definition of a teacher. The Bible interprets itself. One of the definitions of the word *train* is to "catechize," and that is what we see in these verses: line-upon-line teaching, with questions, answers, and open discussion. I get the picture of an instructor engaging his students in meaningful dialogue, with learning in mind. The students are interested asking questions and giving thoughts about the subject at hand.

This is teaching. It is much more than sitting with the family and reading the Bible to them. Praise God if you do this, but I want to stretch you on to higher ground. God requires more of us. It is not enough to put the children in a good church and send them to a Christian school. We must develop the spirit of a teacher.

Father, God's Anointed Teacher

In Deuteronomy 6:4-7, we find more insights into being a teacher. This is the most powerful outline defining a teacher you will find in the Bible, and guess what, it is written to fathers, not to preachers.

> *Hear O Israel, the LORD our God is one LORD: And thou shalt love the LORD thy God with all thine heart,*

> *and with all thy soul and with all thy might. And these words which I command thee this day, shall be in thine heart, and thou shall teach them diligently unto thy children, and shalt talk of them when thou sittest in thine house, and when thou walkest by the way, and when thou liest down, and when thou risest up.*
> Deuteronomy 6:4-7

This portion of Scripture is rich with revelation from God's heart about our dear children. I would encourage you to read from the beginning of the chapter. We are going to plumb the depths what a teacher is. Allow me to go down below the surface here. I want to give you the fullness of God's heart, although it may be way beyond you at this point in your life. I want you to get a glimpse of who you can be if you sincerely, in brokeness, step into the water and begin to teach.

In this most famous text, we have a lovely picture of an anointed father teaching the next generation to love his God. You will not find the word "anointed" in these verses. However, when we look at this man with New Covenant eyes, we see he is an anointed teacher. As we look at this inspired snapshot, please, don't be discouraged. Let us dream together. There are five holy qualities about this man to which I want to draw our attention.

He loves God

He loves the Lord with all his heart, and God has the first place in his life. This dear father has a single eye. The eye of his heart is fixed continually on God, to love Him, to worship Him, and to walk with Him. There is nothing half-hearted about this man. His heart is yielded to God, and to His ways. Nothing shall turn him aside for very long. Here is the inner foundation that supports this teacher. This first point is, without question, the most important of all. The lack of love for God is the prime reason for most of the devastation we see in our homes in this land. Our fathers have not loved God with all their hearts, and many of us have followed their half-hearted ways. Although this is a book on raising godly children, I feel an urgency to permeate its contents with this, our greatest need.

He loves God's Word
In a sense, this point is synonymous with the preceding one. *"These words, shall be in thine heart"* is a basic principle for any teacher. A teacher must love his subject and be excited about the textbook he is using. Have you ever sat under a teacher who had these two qualities? He can inspire you to love English, or even math. This is an important factor in making true disciples, and that is what we are endeavoring to do. We need to understand the depth of what "in thine heart" really means. It is way, way, more than reading the Bible or memorizing verses. I wrote earlier about the power of the human heart. That is what is implicated here. The Apostle John said it this way: *"The word of God abideth in you"* (I John 2:14b). Jesus said, *"Out of the abundance of the heart the mouth speaketh"* (Matt. 12:34). This applies on the positive side as well as on the negative side. Therefore, this is a strong requirement for a teacher of the word. These two words, "heart" and "mouth" are so closely linked together that God refers to the mouth at times when He means the heart. The natural outflow of a heart that is full is teaching, whatever the subject may be.

He loves to obey the Word
This anointed teacher is not merely passing on information. It is so much more than that to him. He has obeyed what he is teaching. He has *"observe[d] to do it"* (Deut. 6:3a). He knows it works. Therefore, he teaches. This is the most powerful tool that a teacher can have to influence his students. He lives his subject, and they know it by his life. It is not a "have to" thing with the true teacher, but rather, "he gets to obey." He has tasted of the fruit, and therefore he is excited.

He loves to teach the Word
Here we have the picture of a wholehearted teacher. *"Thou shalt teach them diligently."* Teaching is not done in a haphaz-

ard way. It is purposeful, enthusiastic, and he loves to teach. A person who loves his subject and loves to communicate it will be a teacher, one way or the other. The methods will flow out of his desire to motivate his children. These words give us insight into this teacher's heart, but we can also learn much about his methods from the word "teach." This father is not merely reading the Word to his children. He is finding ways to put it into their hearts. The word *teach*, means "to sharpen or to whet" like sharpening a sword or a stick. This father will find a way to simplify the precious Word of God so he can put it into the heart of his child. The picture is of one who is whetting his sword and sticking it into the heart of the child. Isn't that beautiful? The second definition in Websters 1828 dictionary is also worthy to consider. It says to whet is "to provoke; to excite; to stimulate; as to whet an appetite." I see another clear aspect of teaching demonstrated in this word "whet." Either way these are beautiful pictures of a father's responsibilities.

He loves to talk the Word
We have here a second method of teaching the Word to our children. As I see it, the previous method is planned, prepared for, and carried out with purpose at specific times of the day, as in family devotions. But to *"talk of them"* is more of a casual instruction that takes place as you walk through life, day by day. That is why four different settings are mentioned here. In this example, I see a father sharing and applying the Word while he is working in the field with his son, or while the family is traveling somewhere. This is not difficult because the Word is in his heart, deeply in his heart. It is a very natural thing for the Word to flow out as he *"walks by the way"* with his family.

This is God's inspired revelation of what He wants us fathers to be. Don't be discouraged. Let's dream a bit more as we expand on this picture. Let's consider these two methods and how they work together to produce a godly seed in the next generation.

Father: An Anointed Teacher

We have a father who loves God and His Word with all his heart. Because of this, he wants to pass both on to his children.

He says, "I want my children to love my God, and I want them to love and obey His Word."

He is like Ezra, who wanted others to taste what he was enjoying from the Lord. Ezra's testimony is recorded in Ezra 7:10: *"For Ezra had prepared his heart to seek the law of the LORD, and to do it, and to teach in Israel statutes and judgments."* In this example we have a true teacher, one whom every father can follow. He was a student of the Word, and sought to learn for himself. He became a doer of the Word thus tasting the blessings that come from obeying. Then, having tasted this good fruit himself, he rose up with joy to teach others also.

With these motivations, a wise father then will seek to sharpen the Word so it will enter into the hearts of his family. Early in the morning, he is alone with God with his Bible open. He finds a verse that he can teach to his family. As he continues to seek, God gives him wisdom to sharpen the verse, to break it down, and to simplify it so his children can grasp it. With that Word, he sits the family down at devotion time and teaches it to them. What a beautiful picture! This is teaching the Bible to your family. According to Jewish history, this was done morning and evening. I understand that the Puritan fathers gathered their families twice in a day also. I wonder what impact it would have on our families, if we started gathering them twice each day. This is catechism at its best, *"precept upon precept; line upon line,"* as it says in Isaiah. Fathers, we need to come to God in the morning and ask Him, "How can I break this verse down, and make it easy to understand?"

I use all kinds of object lessons to open up a verse to the children. Once I got up right in the middle of family worship and disappeared out into the shop. The children didn't have a clue what was coming. I came back with a rope, grabbed little David, and tied him up on the floor. I had everyone's attention, including Jackie's! David loved it, and Joshua longed to be the one on the floor. I taught on the subject of sin binding you up so you can't move spiritually.

Another time I jumped up and went into the kitchen, returning with a butcher knife. All eyes were on me when I returned. We had a lesson about using our tongue wrongly, and how destructive the tongue can be. These are simple ways to illustrate divine truth to the heart of a child. This is sharpening the Word, so you can stick it into their little hearts.

Maybe your heart is saying, "Brother Denny, I can't do that. I'm not you; I'm different." Listen, when I got converted, I was not a teacher. Speaking was very hard for me. I remember the first time I was asked to share my testimony in a youth meeting. It was a disaster. I was given thirty minutes to share with the youth. It was terrible. I stood up there behind that pulpit, and they just stared at me. I spoke for three painful minutes and then sat down in utter humiliation. Jackie stood up to finish the half hour and saved the day. My issues were fear and insecurity. By God's grace--and I mean that deeply--I overcame my obstacles, and today I am a teacher. God will help you. Just step into the water. Trust Him to lead you and help you each day, and soon you will find things going much better. If you transfer only 20% at first, who cares? It is better than nothing, isn't it? That 20% will become 50%, sooner than you think.

Jesus Christ is our clearest example of One who made disciples. As we look into His methods of teaching, we notice that He used both of these methods to train His disciples. We see Him sitting them down, and preaching a sermon to them. He used stories, objects, and parables to get His point across to them. At the same time, we see Him teaching as they *"walked by the way"*

As they passed by the widow casting her two mites into the treasury, He taught them the deeper meaning and motivation behind giving. He taught about humility by using a little child. He could do this because the word was abiding in Him. When we are filled with the Word and filled with the Spirit, the whole world becomes a giant classroom with endless illustrations to draw from. This is teaching at its best, with high learning levels as well.

Father: An Anointed Teacher

A Motivating Teacher

Hear, ye children, the instruction of a father, and attend to know understanding. For I give you good doctrine, forsake ye not my law. For I was my father's son, tender and only beloved in the sight of my mother. He taught me also, and he said unto me, Let thine heart retain my words: Keep my commandments, and live. Get wisdom, get understanding. Forget it not; neither decline from the words of my mouth. Forsake her not, and she shall preserve thee: Love her, and she shall keep thee. Wisdom is the principal thing; therefore, get wisdom:
Proverbs 4:1-7a

In these verses, we have another glimpse of a father who is a teacher. I see a father setting his son down and instructing him about wisdom. He is stirring him and motivating him to be hungry for wisdom and to obey the instructions and the authority of his father. I believe the father here is David, and the son is Solomon. Solomon is now writing to his sons, giving them a testimony about how his father taught him when he was a boy.

The main thing I want to draw out of this text is the element of inspiration in teaching. It is clear by the words used in this passage that David wanted to move his son to action. He used motivating words and urgency in his words to do this. We know that in this case, it worked very well. Solomon became the wisest man in all the earth.

God woke Solomon in the middle of the night to talk to him. Solomon received quite an offer that night. I wonder what we would say if God came to us and said we could have anything we asked. Solomon passed the test. Maybe his father's words came ringing back to him: *"Wisdom is the principle thing; therefore get wisdom."* He asked for wisdom that night, and God gave it to him. The point here is this: the father passed the desire on to the son through teaching, and the son received the desires of his heart.

The Pursuit of Godly Seed

Family Devotions

I want to take a few minutes and share with you a little about devotions at our house. Many different terms are used to describe this special time of the day in the life of a godly family:

- ❖ Family devotions because we seek God together.
- ❖ Family worship because we all enter into the worship of our God.
- ❖ Family altar because there the family fires are kindled, and sacrifices are made.
- ❖ Wisdom search because we are searching for wisdom in the word.

These all describe different aspects of the activities that take place during the family devotional time. All of the above should be taking place as the family gathers to seek God together.

Devotions are very important at our house. It is not something that we "get out of the way" so we can go on with our day. It is very high on the priority list, up there with eating and sleeping. We do not read a chapter in the Bible, have a little prayer, and go our way. No, devotions have a very high priority at the Kenaston household. If this is what you do, thank God; keep going, but I want to lift your sights much higher than this.

I want to encourage you fathers here. Be a bulldog about family devotions. Let me explain. When a bulldog gets his teeth into something, you can hardly get him lose. Do you get the picture? We live in America. There are so many activities to pull you away from this most important task. Many of them are good things. They become the enemy of the best. These distractions pull the priorities down to "every now and then."

When I travel, I often ask questions about family devotions. Most of the people I ask admit that they rarely have a time of the day when they gather to seek God. They usually answer that they have devotions "every now and then." When it drops to this level, you have lost the battle, it is time to press the reset button. These are not half hearted Christians who answer this way. These are the ones who really want to do right. Fathers, be a bulldog about devotions.

Father: An Anointed Teacher

We have our family devotions in the morning and in the evening. Sometimes we miss them in the evening, but rarely in the morning. I have learned that other things tend to bump it out of the way, so we aim for twice each day. The most important thing is that you give it a specific time in your day.

Our devotions last about forty-five minutes. They often go beyond that because the time just gets away. Devotions at our house are not boring. They are enjoyable and very interesting. It is always a nice family time. We talk; we share things about the day. Somebody will ask a question, it is a relaxed time with the family. If a younger child says something cute, we all laugh about it and have a good time. It is not a time where we all sit very firmly and soberly and read the Bible. Sometimes it is a revival meeting with brokeness and confessions. Sometimes I have to steer it a bit, but most of the time it flows right along, and I am able to cover the main goal that I have for the time. It is a spiritual time, but it is an interesting time, with all kinds of different things in it. Let me share some of the specific things we do.

1. We have a good time of **singing**. We will sing three or four songs, and sometimes we will sing for twenty minutes if we sense an unusual spirit of worship. We teach the children to sing with the whole heart, and we always have a good time singing. When we had younger ones, we sang a few of the songs for younger children, adding some actions to the words. Each time we have a three-year-old coming along, I select about twenty-five hymns to sing. We sing the same ones for quite a while until the child can sing them by memory. This doesn't take as long as you would think. We want them to have these solid hymns filled with doctrine hidden away in their memory from an early age.

2. Sometimes we have an **open sharing** time, when each one is called on to share something out of his or her life. If we have had some special meetings at the church, I open it up for all to share how God dealt with them or inspired them during the meetings.

3. **I have the children share** from the Word at times. I give them all an assignment at the end of devotions for the next day. They are given a portion of Scripture to meditate on, and then we all share what God is saying to us from these verses.

4. We always have a time where **the Word is opened** and taught in the manner already mentioned. I believe the father is to be the interpreter of the Bible in the context of the day in which the family lives. The world in which we live is changing all the time. There is no verse in the Bible that says, "Thou shalt not watch television," but there are principles there that must be taught and then applied. I do this all the time during family devotions. The children grow up knowing Bible verses for everything we do, and they should. If we don't do this, then we pass on only traditions instead of living principles. Our church sisters wear a veiling to cover their heads. We explain this with the verses from the Bible. However you define *"the faith,"* it must be interpreted to the next generation. We must take the Bible and make it practical, applying it to the world in which the children are living. And every generation lives in a different world.

5. We have a time of **family prayer**. Sometimes I am the only one who prays, and at other times, we have an old-fashioned family prayer meeting. It depends on what is happening in our world at the time. If the children in Africa are facing some real battles with sickness or evil attacks, we have a longer prayer time. If the church is having one of their fasting and prayer weekends, then we might spend the whole time in prayer.

This gives you some idea how we conduct that special time each day at our house. I vary it even more at times, as God leads. Brothers, imagine. If you do this every day except Sundays, for twenty years, what kind of children will you have? That is more

Father: An Anointed Teacher

than six thousand sessions in the Word with your children. They will know the Bible. It will be in their hearts. Not only will it be in their hearts, it will be in their lives. They will live it.

People ask me at times how we could send our son to Africa to be a missionary, when he didn't go to Bible School.

I answer them, "He did go to Bible school—for twenty-one years!"

This is home schooling at its best, isn't it? He has been discipled by his father for twenty-one years.

Well fathers, I need to draw this chapter to a close, although my heart is still full of more to say on this subject. I want to encourage you to "step into the water" and move ahead. God will meet you. I didn't know how to be a teacher, but I wanted to be one. I came back from a godly family's house, with a desire, and nothing else. I stepped into the water and just kept on going, crying and praying as I went. I turned around a couple years later and realized, "Hey! I'm teaching! These children are learning! They are grasping eternal truths, powerful truths, out of the Word of God. I am a teacher!" And so are you.

The same thing will happen to you if you will just step into the water, brother. You know, the Jordan River doesn't part until you step into the water (Josh. 3:13). How long are you going to wait for the water to part? God is saying to us, "Step into the water! You just move ahead by faith, and I will meet you and help you. I will make you a teacher!"

Prayer

Dear heavenly Father, I pray for each of the parents reading this chapter. I pray that You will baptize them with the Spirit of a teacher. Fill them with confidence. Strengthen them with might, and make them teachers. I pray for all the trembling fathers. Give them courage, and boldness, to do what you are commanding them to do. I pray for their wives, that they will get under their husbands and support them. In the name of Jesus Christ our Lord. Amen.

Bible story time in the evenings make the Bible come alive with a little added emphasis by Papa

Special class for the younger ones, given on a more simple level, before we all gather for Family devotions

Family devotions in the motor home while we were on a five week family preaching tour. Lots of talk time.

20

Train Up a Child

Bring them up in the nurture and admonition of the Lord.
Ephesians 6:4b
Train up a child in the way he should go
and when he is old, he will not depart from it.
Proverbs 22:6

In chapter twelve I likened the whole training process to raising a fruitful garden. By now, as you can see, the list of things to do is growing. It makes my heart sing as once again I look at all the wisdom God has revealed to us about our children. He has not left us in the dark not knowing what to do or which way to go. You may have felt as though you were in the dark, but now you can see; God is very clear. Jackie and I felt the same way in the early days of our family. But as we cried to the Lord for wisdom, He made many things clear to us. Hallelujah!

The opening verses draw all that we have been learning into a nice blend of several child training principles. As I studied the word "*nurture*," I found its meaning to be full of this blend. When we think of raising a plant for production, we use the word "*nurture*." The very word "*nursery*," means a place to nurture. We use it when referring to plants, but we also call the new baby's room the nursery. The meaning of this word is a beautiful blend of teaching, discipline, and the actual guiding of the life into the right paths of the Lord.

The Pursuit of Godly Seed

The Greek word for *"nurture,"* is found in some very interesting passages in the New Testament. It is found several times in Hebrews 12:5-13, where God teaches us about chastisement. We could easily read verse five this way, "Despise not the nurturing of the Lord." God uses this blend of principles to mold us into the holy image of His Son. Look at all the different aspects of child training found in this text.

Our heavenly Father teaches us His Word by the Spirit of God, thus showing us the way that will please Him. He surrounds us with His love, as He moves in on an areas of our lives that He wants to change. He admonishes us, warns us, and eventually spanks us, to get us to change a habit pattern in our lives. As we are receiving discipline, He is admonishing us about what we should change. And when the peaceable fruit is there, He smiles upon us, to encourage us in the future. Like our Father in heaven, we are seeking *"the peaceable fruit of righteousness"* in the lives of our children. This is child training, in all its beautiful balance. There is so much that we could learn about child training from our heavenly Father, if only we would meditate on His ways. All the teaching that has been given thus far comes together in the words *"train"* and *"nurture."* To change and direct a life is the goal.

Training children is a very active, hands-on affair. I do not mean spanking by this statement. That is a part of the training process, but only one part. I am fully convinced that the use of the rod diminishes as the other aspects of training are given their proper priorities. If we are going to train our children, we must be actively and daily engaged in their lives. This is full-time work, not a sideline job that we fit in here and there.

We as parents must pick up the tools that God has given us in His Word and begin to mold the nature of our children into godliness. The Bible likens us to clay in the hands of a potter. The potter picks up the clay and begins to mold it and shape it into a desired vessel. This is the relationship we parents have with our children.

There is an urgency in this illustration. The clay is soft now and easy to form and mold. But the day will come when the clay will get hard and difficult to form. I have heard the analogy of the small tree and the large one. When a tree is small, it is very easily trained into place. But when the tree gets big, it is extremely hard to train it. The point is to bend the tree while it is young. That is the basic message of our verse in Proverbs. Do the work while they are young.

In Proverbs 22:6 we have another one of God's *"exceeding great and precious promises"* (2 Pet. 1:4). This promise, which was available to the Old Testament saint, is much more effectual to us parents who choose to live under the blessings of the New Covenant. Again, this promise is conditional. God desires to enter into covenant with His people.

Many grieving parents have wondered over this verse as they watched a child go out into the world. They wonder what went wrong. They question whether they understand the verse as they look back over their sincere attempt to raise the child for the Lord. I have heard them say, "We don't understand what went wrong. We put them in a good school and church. We showed them the right way. What went wrong?" Some have even said that the verse doesn't work because it didn't work for them. We must be careful how we evaluate these setbacks in life. God does not change; His promises are always sure. I have learned that if a promise is not fulfilled, it is not God's fault. Either we have done something wrong, or we don't understand the promise. It is important that we understand the conditions of this promise.

What It Means to Train

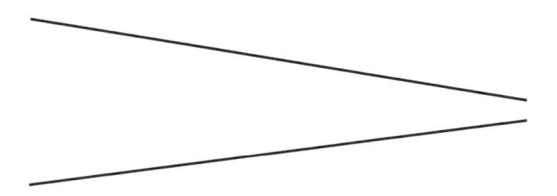

We need to understand what God means when He says, *"train up a child."* The word *"train"* means "to narrow." We could read the verse this way: "Narrow up a child in the way that he should go." I have drawn these two lines to show what the word is picturing.

We are starting at a wide place and moving toward a narrow place, like the "broad" way and the "narrow" way. What a beautiful way to describe the way it is with our children. God gives us little children who are innocent, yet they are sinners, and we know it. It doesn't take long for us to realize that our children are sinners. They are made of the same kind of flesh we are. Nobody has to set them down and give them any lessons on how to be evil. Nobody taught little Hannah to lift her hand up and hit her brother when he did something she didn't like. She got that from her father Adam.

So, we start in a wide place, but God says, "I want you to end up in a narrow place." Day by day we slowly teach and train the child into this narrow place. We start with a child who is in a wide place, and we start moving toward the goal. The goal is much more than a good moral person when we are finished. The goal is a disciple of Jesus Christ completely dedicated to God, a young adult who joyfully walks on the narrow way that "leads to life."

This little phrase *"train up a child"* also means to "catechize." I have covered this word already, but I want you to be aware that teaching and instruction is part of this process of bringing a child from where he is to where God wants him to be.

The last definition on which I would like to focus is very enlightening. I like this one the best because it gives the positive side of training up a child. *"Train up a child"* means to stimulate the palate. Here we have a picture of a Hebrew mother who is beginning to wean her child. She takes the food, and chews it up in her mouth. Then, when it is well chewed, she takes it back out and puts it into the mouth of her child. This is how she stimulates the mouth of the child to like the right foods. Isn't that beautiful?

This gets very exciting. Just picture this in the spiritual sense for a moment. Except for the chewing, we did this with each of our children when it was time to wean them. Jackie was very wise in this. We didn't introduce desserts to the children, but the foods that would be good for them. To this day David loves carrot juice because Jackie introduced it in a positive manner.

The child training implications are powerful. We could read the verse this way, "Stimulate the palate of your child, in the right ways that he should go, and he will still love them when he is old." What a picture of how a parent trains the children! Day by day we introduce the good and the holy. This is done in a positive way, with joy, by a motivated parent. We want them to love this new habit, discipline, or activity that we are introducing because we know that it will be a blessing to them in the future.

I want my child to love family devotions, so I introduce it with enthusiasm. Day by day we go through this exercise until the child is saying from the heart, "Papa, I love family devotions. When I grow up, I will have them for my children."

As this exercise is repeated over and over, the children develop a taste for that which is good and right. This is augmented with some discipline if needed, and, of course, we teach them what the Bible says about this new activity. It is good to mention the negative side of this also. If we allow the children to develop a taste for that which is not good, we are also setting lifelong patterns. I will write more on this later

Enter Helpmate and Mother

A child left to himself, bringeth his mother to shame.
Proverbs 29:15b

A horse left to itself is wild, dangerous, and of very little value. A dog left to itself will embarrass you and trouble your neighbor. And a child left to himself will reflect upon the character of his mother. This is what God is implying in this opening verse.

There is much that we can learn from the dog trainer and the horse trainer. It is sad to me that we must go to them for instruction. I think it should be the other way around. Anyway, we can learn from them. Both of these trainers have a clear plan about what they want to do. And by the way, they use very little punishment to accomplish their goals They know what they want to instill in the animal they are training. It is done very purposefully and methodically, as I have already mentioned. They invest lots of time and patience. This is how we ought to approach the training of our children.

The Pursuit of Godly Seed

Father and mother should sit down together and plan out what they want to instill in their children, and then go for it. Here is where the powerful influence of a mother comes in. Obviously, Dad cannot be around all the time. Someone does have to work and provide for the needs of the household. The supportive wife steps in and begins to walk through these many training exercises with the children. These should be approached from a positive perspective, even though you may use the rod at some times during the process.

The Sports Nut

Let's see what we can learn from the sports enthusiast. If a father is a sports nut, he may want his son to be an outstanding baseball player (this seems odd to me, if we are suppose to train their palates in righteousness). But let's say that is what he wants for his son. This father will get very active in his son's life. He will approach his goal with much positive input. He will not pursue this goal in a haphazard way. Consider some of the things he will do for and with his son.

- ❖ He will begin to talk about baseball with his son to motivate and create desire.
- ❖ He may get a baseball magazine and spend time looking at it with his boy, interjecting comments as they go.
- ❖ He may plan a special trip to the store, for just the two of them, where they buy the baseball gear.
- ❖ Mom will join in the excitement when they come home from the store.
- ❖ Dad will spend much time with his son teaching him the rules of the game.
- ❖ He will get right down to the game with his son, training him to throw the ball, catch the ball, and hit the ball.
- ❖ He will praise the boy for every little bit of progress made in these skills.
- ❖ He will be firm with his son, pressing him to spend time in practice.
- ❖ He will even use disciplinary methods when the little fel-

low gets a bit tired of the whole thing and wants to go on to something new.
- ❖ He will get his son involved with a team so that he can play with others and increase his skills.
- ❖ He will go to the games and sit on the side lines, cheering his son on as he plays.

I have made the list long enough for you to get the point: this father is determined to develop his son's abilities in the area of baseball. This illustration comes closer to home than many of us are willing to admit. Also, this senario is lived out millions of times in our country for goals that have no eternal value. We can learn from this example. Fathers and mothers, what do you want? If you would approach godly character with this kind of purpose, you would be amazed at the results.

Positive Learning Experiences

Many years ago, it was time for Joshua to lay aside the diaper thing and become a "Big Boy" This was not a new thing for us; he was the seventh child. I am going to be a witness to Jackie's positive approach to this lesson.

I was sitting on the small couch in our bedroom at about six o'clock one morning. Jackie came into the room to wake up Joshua and go through his morning routine. The first words that little fellow heard were the sweet, loving words of his mother saying, "Joshua, it's six o'clock. Time to get up my son. I love you." What a way to wake up in the morning!

Then she reached down to pick him up and gave him a big hug. The next thing I heard was the enthusiastic words of Mama saying, " Joshua, let's go potty on the potty chair." Joshua marched in there to take care of business with a big smile on his face. I could hear Jackie praising him for keeping his diaper dry all night. She put his "big boy" underwear on, and asked him, "Are you going to keep them dry all day?" He nodded his head with an emphatic "yes, " and down the stairs they went.

I sat there and pondered what I had just heard, thinking to myself, "That lady is a master at this!"--and she is. The children learn very quickly with this kind of positive encouragement. Now Joshua did get a few spankings before he had mastered the goal of keeping things dry, but they were sandwiched in between all the other training. Once we knew that he clearly and willfully refused to stay dry, he was disciplined for it, in the manner I have already described.

Someone said to me when the children were younger, "Brother Denny, how do you get your children to sit through a long church service?"

I responded back with a question. I said, "How do you keep your children from playing in the street?"

They knew the answer, and all of us do. You make it a top priority, teach and train, take them near the road, and go through the big no-no scene. You watch them a while, test them, go over the lesson again, and praise them for staying out of the street. It doesn't take long until we are confident that they will stay out of the street.

This routine can be duplicated over and over with different issues in the children's lives. Consider a few suggestions.

- ❖ **You can** teach them to sit and listen during family devotions. By the way, that is how you get them to sit in church. You do your homework, then transfer the lesson to the church service.
- ❖ **You can** teach them to eat all the food on their plate every time they sit at the table.
- ❖ **You can** teach them to eat foods that they don't care for. Walk them through the whole exercise, instructing them about what you are expecting from them. After a good time of training, you give them some food that they don't like, and tell them, "This is the lesson that we have been talking about. I know you are going to do very well in this."
- ❖ **You can** teach them to put all the toys away when the day is over, or when you are going to have visitors. You can even teach them to put some of them away before they get others out.
- ❖ **You can** teach them to have good manners by routinely going over what is expected in different situations. Walk

them through it. Set up practice times of meeting new people or excusing themselves from the table.
- **You can** teach them to wake up cheerfully and get up promptly when called in the morning. This doesn't happen naturally; they need to be trained. Train them up in the way you want them to go. Some adults have yet to learn this basic lesson.
- **You can** teach them to lay their head down and take a nap without any fuss. Wouldn't that be nice, mothers? You can just lay them down in the crib with some sweet words of love and blessings, and they will submissively go off to sleep.
- **You can** train them in simple chores when they are still very young. Get excited about it and walk them through it with positive encouragement. You would be surprised what a five-year-old can do.
- **You can** train them to receive a spanking with a yielded heart and no extreme crying.
- **You can** root out all the complaining and whining that children often express when they don't like what is happening in their lives, and they know they can't pitch a fit.
- **You can** teach them to win souls, even as the sports nut taught his boy to play ball. That would be a good ten-year goal to have. That is about how long it takes that father to get a good baseball player.
- **You can** teach them to memorize Scripture at an early age. Start working with them and helping them do it when they are about six years old. Two verses a week. By the time they are seven or eight, they will do it on their own. Two verses a week for fifteen years is about fifty chapters in the Bible.

This is called stimulating the spiritual palate of your children, guiding their desires in the way they should go. The list is endless and probably a bit different with each family. Maybe I rang your bell on some of these points. Dear parents, we need to walk our children through these basic lessons. There are husbands who still don't clean up after themselves or pick up their clothes in the bedroom--to the shock of their wives. Some mother failed that man when he was a boy. There is no end to what you can do; use your imagination. The mothers in Africa train their small babies to tell them when they have to go. The mother then takes them into the bush; they do their job and go on their way. Hey, if you didn't have Pampers, you might go after it sooner too!

Developing Character by Responsibility

Character is defined as "virtues, qualities of moral right, and holy habits of the heart." This definitely falls under the category of *"the way he should go"* We are preparing our children to be servants of the Most High God. They are going to represent Him someday, so they must develop inner character. I have found that responsibility can be an effective tool to help mold these traits in a child.

We have a little farm that consists of fifteen acres of land. It doesn't make much money at that size, but it does some other things far more valuable than money. I often tell people, "It makes godly men and women out of boys and girls." We also have a family business that is designed to do the same thing. The boys and I build picnic tables for a living, and Hannah is the secretary. When things get busy, Mama and the girls get out in the shop and help too. We always have a ball on those days, and the girls love the change. I know that many fathers in our society don't have the blessing I have, and I want to be sensitive to that as I write. However, I want to share the treasures I found when I decided that a professional career would not be the best for my family.

Twenty-three years ago, Jackie and I lived in suburban America. We lived in a typical residential area. There was nothing for the children to do but play. As the principles that I have been sharing with you grew in our hearts, we became increasingly burdened about training the children. I started looking for chores that they could do. You can take out the trash only so often, and the garage doesn't take long to clean if you clean it once a week.

With this burden, I began to long for a country setting where we could provide more learning experiences. We had no television, and had taken a stand against the things in the world, but there was nothing to replace what we had separated from. There were beer parties at the swimming pool on one side of us, and drug parties with motorcycles on the other side. I told the children that these activities were bad, and we all agreed that we wanted nothing to do with them. The children would look out the window and listen to all the frolic. It seemed to them that the people were having fun. What does a father do, and how long do you continue in limbo? I felt like Lot at times, *"vexed with the filthy conversation of the wicked"* (2 Pet. 2:7,8). Although the evil around us was troubling, our main motivation was to provide training opportunities. With these things driving us, we moved to the country--not a little task for two city slickers.

To train a child in qualities of godly character, you must be willing to get involved, intimately involved. You must be willing to come alongside of your child and do it with him joyfully and diligently. You need the tools of daily responsibility to aid you in this task. These inner qualities of virtue are developed over the long haul. That is where responsibilities come in. Here we see the constraining power of a sense of duty carried out on a daily basis, over a long period. The end result is character. I well remember Daniel at age seven getting up at five in the morning to milk the goats. We approached the whole project in the same manner as I described with the father of the baseball player. After I worked through the learning stage of this project with him, he did it faithfully on his own for two years. Was I making money? No way, I was making a responsible man.

Old McKenaston had a Farm

The farm and the family business are tools in my hands--tools to be used to mold and shape children into respectful, responsible, God-fearing Christians. They provide a natural flow of demands with varied experiences. The cows get out of the pasture, and the little boys have to face that big cow and help chase it back in. The fence needs repair, so the boys and I spend three hours talking and fixing as we go. We need a loft in one of the barns, so we figure out how to build one and all learn together. And every day eleven-year-old Joshua and eight-year-old David have to face the rats in the barn when they feed the cows, morning and evening. They

Papa and the boys cutting fire wood to heat the house during the winter. They were always thrilled for work projects with their father.

Joshua (six)
David (three)

Little girls delight to "get to" help Moma run the house. Here they are doing the dishes. We should seize the opportunity to train them while they are still young, and work is considered fun.

Hannah (seven)
Esther (four)

A day of hard work in the shop for all the "men." We had a large order of twenty tables to build. The young boys count it a privilege when they get to be part of the crew.

David (five)

Joshua designed and made these benches to raise money for the missionaries. Who wouldn't buy one from a little fellow for such a good cause?

Joshua (eight)

After several trial runs, with Papa walking along side the tiller, Daniel was ready to do the big man stuff. He was beaming with joy at his accomplishment of doing it "all by himself."

Daniel (ten)

David felt like a real farmer as he milked this goat. His hands got tired by the time he got done, but he gained in character training.

David (seven)

Simple farm chores help make men out of boys.

must do it when it is hot; they must do it when it is cold and dark outside. They must do it when they are having fun riding their bikes, and even when visitors have arrived. All of this is a tool in my hand to build character.

We even get the girls out there from time to time for some good old down-on-the-farm experiences such as chasing a steer around the barnyard in slushy manure. You may ask, "Brother, where are you going with all this?" How about a mud hut in Africa with all the trimmings? It is time we raise up some gospel soldiers in our land.

There are lots of things for Mama and the girls also. They take care of the garden and put up the fruit thereof during blessed days of canning and freezing, when Mom and the girls can *"talk by the way."* There is bread to bake, meals to cook, and children to help care for. The girls help with the homeschooling, which is excellent training for their homes some day. Sewing their own dresses has been a real blessing, with skills increasing every time.

By the time the girls are twelve, they can easily manage the house with all its varied responsibilities. Many times I hear mothers say, "I don't have time for all the work that a large family brings." They are missing some of the hidden secrets. Make a disciple, share the load, and raise a responsible young lady, one prepared to guide her own home someday. All this works together. God has beautifully tempered all of these needs and responsibilities together, for the good of all, even for the good of society.

I view the family business the same way I view the little farm. It is packed full of learning experiences. We do have to make a living, and the boys help to carry the load of this. But even this becomes training for them. Someday they will be the providers. I look at the family business this way: I use the business to build my children; I do not use my children to build my business. I have a problem with some fathers who have their own businesses. They see children as moneymakers, and direct them accordingly. I feel they have it mixed up. The goal is a well-balanced, godly servant of God, not money.

We used to have a retail lawn furniture business before Daniel went to Africa. This was a hands-on experience for the boys in how to operate a business. When Daniel was twelve, he could run the sales lot for me when I was away. He answered the phone, dealt with the customers, solved problems, wrote up orders, and even faced an unhappy customer. He learned all these skills in an apprenticeship role. He stood beside me and listened. Then he started to do what he had heard. Again, the business was a tool in my hand to develop many aspects of godly character.

Samuel is now twenty years old. He is running the whole family business while I write for five months. Joshua and David both help him in the shop. They help in the assembly of picnic tables; using no big equipment, just carpenter tools, a hammer, a measuring tape, and a hand drill. This little business provides a multitude of learning experiences for the boys and the girls. Let me walk you through a couple of examples.

The Little Boys Become Men

The boys want to be with the men. They grow up playing at our feet in the woodworking shop. From the age of two, they are there watching us work, playing, and playing at working. It is very natural for them to get involved and help. One day we were all working together, and Joshua was really helping that day. He did the job of a man, working from morning till night building benches. Little David was five at the time, and he was with us playing. I noticed him crying softly in the corner and asked him what was wrong.

He said, "Papa, I want to help. It is not right for me to be playing while others are working."

The Lord prompted me, "Denny, don't miss this one!"

I told David I would have something for him to do the next day.

That evening, David and I went to the hardware store.

I told David, "We are here to buy your hammer and tape measure." His eyes lit up with excitement. As we picked out the tools, I told him he would have a job to do tomorrow. I told him how much we needed his help, and we did. This whole story was carried out very purposefully in the manner I have already described. I knew where I was going.

In the shop, we anchor the table tops together with screws placed in a wooden brace. I knew this was something David could do. Hundreds of screws needed to be tapped slightly into holes for assembly later.

As we finished family devotions that morning and headed to the shop, how do you think David was feeling? He walked down to the shop like a man, hammer in hand ready to join the work crew. At first, I set the screws with his hammer. Then I let him try. I put my hand on his hand, and we did a bunch of them together. Then I did some, and he worked at his beside me. Soon he was doing them all on his own.

We figured out how many screws he set by lunch--about three hundred. Guess what David talked about at the lunch table that day. He sat down at the table like one of the men, proclaiming how many hundreds of screws he had set that morning. Guess how Mama Jackie responded when she heard his proclamations.

She said, "Oh, David, Mama is so proud of you! You work just like the men do!"

It is now three years later, and David is a very valuable part of the shop operations.

Do you see how this all works? Last year I built Joshua his own special work bench. He can't reach the other ones. I set it up with a new hammer, a special wrench, a drill, and a tape measure. "Joshua," I said, "This is your very own work bench" His eyes lit up with joy.

Some time ago Joshua was busy working in the shop, and one of the workers was standing in the corner watching him. I walked up to the worker and whispered in his ear, "Shhhh, he thinks he is playing. Don't tell him any differently." That is exactly how it is. Many times the boys are anxious to go to work just as they are to play. There are hard times in this whole training process. The boys are still boys and want to play when it is time to work, but that is where the character is built.

Qualities of virtue are instilled in a child as parents set them up for learning experiences like these. They catch the spirit of diligence as they work alongside of us, whether in the shop, or scrubbing the floor next to Mom. If we love to work, they will pick up the same attitude. If we hate housework, so will they. We are making disciples either way, whether by neglect and laziness or by purposeful apprenticeship.

I know that many of you do not have the tools I am describing to you in this chapter. Some of you probably long for this kind of opportunity. I'm sorry, and my purpose is not to overwhelm you. But I wanted to show you what can be done. There are times when I weep for joy as I stand in my shop, and realize what God has given me. I get to work with my sons, Thank You Lord.

There was a day when I didn't have a shop or a farm to use. I found other means to make learning experiences happen. I chose to burn wood to heat the house, just so the boys and I could go out and cut the wood in the forest. This provided many manly exercises for both the boys and this city slicker.

In closing this chapter, I hasten to say I am not telling everyone to leave the city and find a place in the country. That is hardly possible in the society where we find ourselves. What I am saying is this. We must find ways to build character in our children. We must have some tools in our hands to aid us. I believe the sports world is a poor second choice for building character in our children. So much of it is motivated by the pride of life, money, and positions of fame. These are destructive motivations. Good old-fashioned hard work guided with the daily call of duty will instill humility and responsibility in our children.

Prayer

Father in heaven looking down upon us all, we cry unto You for our children. We want to train them in these kinds of ways. Please help us find our way. Keep us from extremes, but guide us down a clear path of godliness. I pray for all the parents who are feeling a bit overwhelmed right now. Draw near to them, and encourage them as they seek to walk the right way. Lead them in paths of righteousness for the sake of a godly seed and for Your name's sake.

Meditations

The Hand That Rocks The Cradle

Blessings on the hand of women!
Angels guard its strength and grace.
In the palace, cottage, hovel,
Oh, no matter where the place;
Would that never storms assailed it,
Rainbows ever gently curled;
For the hand that rocks the cradle
Is the hand that rules the world.

Infancy's the tender fountain
Power may with beauty flow,
Mother's first to guide the streamlets,
From them souls unresting grow...
Grow on for the good or evil,
Sunshine streamed or evil hurled;
For the hand that rocks the cradle
Is the hand that rules the world

Woman how divine your mission
Here upon our natal sod!
Keep, oh, keep the young heart open
Always to the breath of God!
All true trophies of the ages
Are from mother-love impearled
For the hand that rocks the cradle
Is the hand that rules the world

Blessings on the hand of women!
Fathers, sons, and daughters cry,
And the sacred song is mingled
With the worship in the sky...
Rainbows evermore are hurled;
For the hand that rocks the cradle
Is the hand that rules the world

William Wallace (1819-1881)

21

A Quiet Ordered Life

The work of righteousness shall be peace;
And the effect of righteousness quietness and assurance forever.
And my people shall dwell in a peaceable habitation,
And in sure dwellings, and in quiet resting places.
                                                        Isaiah 32: 17-18

There is a beautiful flow of thought in this portion of Scripture that probably expresses the goal of every sincere parent reading these words: a quiet orderly home. If you read the verses that precede these, you will find that this will not happen *"until the spirit be poured upon us from on high"* (Isaiah 32:15). This inviting picture painted for us by the Holy Ghost is the fruit of the Spirit. O, that God would pour out His Spirit upon our families and transform our homes into *"quiet resting places."* I see a motivating progression of truth in our text. The Spirit is poured out on us, and that produces the right ways of God in our lives. As we walk in these blessed ways, they produce peace in our lives. This peace is first of all an inner peace, and then a peace that works it's way out into our everyday life. This outworking of inner peace produces a quiet inner assurance, which in turn affects our homes. Our homes become stable and secure, havens of order and rest--yea, a little bit of heaven on earth. *"Thy Kingdom come, O Lord, even as it is in heaven."*

I know it is a little hard to imagine this state of quiet and order in our American homes. We tend to live at a very fast pace. Some have even cynically called it "the rat race," alluding to a rat endlessly running on a wheel. Have you ever felt that way? I have. Although the society goes on in an ever-increasing speed, there is a way that you can turn your home into a haven of rest and refreshment for all who enter there or live there, even if you live in a city. However, you must be willing to take over the control of your environment.

This chapter is not a teaching on destructive influences in the home, but I wonder what would happen if we got rid of all the noise makers--things such as the television, the radio, the boom box, the computer games, and even the telephone ringing all the time. Silence has to be more peaceful than noise, even in a secular home. That is not the point of this chapter, but I'm sure all these can affect the spirit of your home.

A little later I address a happy marriage void of conflict, and that will surely affect your "peaceful habitation." But we are meditating on child training in these present chapters, and I ask you to consider with me the benefits of an ordered life--benefits for your home and for your children.

Who Is in Charge?

The typical American home is far from common order. We hardly eat together any more. The members of the family get up at different times, eat at different times, and so on. Home has simply become a house, a place you pass through on the way to the next appointment, a place to lay your head at night to grab six hours of sleep before the next day's schedule. Truly the "rat race" is in charge of such homes.

We have chosen to order our home in a different way. If you want to eliminate the scattered family thing, it is best that you start when the children are young. I have learned that children do not prosper or feel secure if they do not know what will happen next. Also, they do not prosper if they are allowed to be in charge of their life. I have found this to be true from very small children all the way through to youth. An ordered life is the most productive.

A Quiet Ordered Life

This ordered life has been an issue of debate lately, and there are extremes on both sides of the spectrum. The debate centers around the little ones. How much order can you expect from them and how soon? I can see why it centers there, because of the young age. However, this order applies all through the child's life. We have always given good healthy structure to the children's lives, with good results.

The bottom line of the whole debate is: who is in charge? Is the baby or toddler in charge of the mother, with life revolving around its needs? Or is the mother in charge, and can she order this baby's life enough that she can continue on with other parts of life: the rest of the house, the rest of the children, and her husband?

I recognize that a small baby has some special needs to deal with, but at the same time, order is needed. I believe that the more you can direct the routine of a baby, the less training you will have later. It might surprise some of you, but a small baby can be trained to do much more than you think. It seems to me from my studies that Mother Wesley knew this and had a quiet home that caused others to marvel.

Calm, Quiet Authority

It is very clear that God has placed the children completely under the authority of the parents. This is a place of great prosperity for the child. It also is a place of abundant freedom. All the children have to do is obey their parents, and it will be well with them all their days. I have learned by my own parenting experiences that God works mysteriously behind the scenes to establish this authority. I, for one, don't believe parents have to push their weight around to gain this authority. They already have it and need to confidently exercise it. There are several ways this authority is established. Consider of few of them:

>First, because this authority is already given by God, you just need carry it out. Lead your family in the way that they should go. Let me use the example of the policeman. If you were given this responsibility, you would just start being a policeman. You wouldn't need to shout or wave a gun in the air. You would have a uni-

form on, and that would be it. You would just need to go do it. In the same manner, God has called each of you to be parents. Now just go do it confidently and calmly. This will establish your authority more than anything else you can do.

Second, you need to walk with God. As you walk with the One who has ordained you to be parents, He will establish your authority. He will do this in the same way He did with Joshua when Moses passed off the scene. Authority is a work of God. Trust Him to work in your home as you give direction.

Third, build a relationship with your children. In this sense, being a parent is different from being a policeman. As you draw close to your children, you will establish your authority. In a way, you earn the right to be obeyed. This does not apply on the children's side. They must obey because of your position. But we as God's representatives in the home must build confidence as we lead.

Fourth, you must be consistent in your directing and in your discipline. Children are very discerning. They discover your true lines very quickly. Be consistent with anything that you want to accomplish, and you will have success. This is where the will of the child comes in strongly. If you win here, you win in most other areas of child training.

All this is done in a cool, calm way. There is no need to push your weight around because everything you are doing is well established by God in His Eord. Many parents are slow to do this. Then through neglect, things get out of hand, and they rise up with emotional strength and attempt to set things in order. For some homes, this scenario is repeated over and over. The children slowly learn that this is what authority is, and this is how it operates. They quickly figure this out and live it up until Mom gets to that point where she "exercises authority."

This is all wrong, a total distortion of God's original intent. Moreover, the children are receiving a perverted view of God's authority through it. If you are caught in this emotional trap, and your children are "playing you" to their advantage, I strongly encourage you to establish godly authority in your home. This is done by taking charge of your home, staying ahead of the children with consistent discipline, and calmly directing them in the ways that you want them to go. God has given you a charge and He has promised you His help. Just start being the one in charge. The children will quickly evaluate the change in order and make the necessary adjustments.

Positive Order or Negative Correction
The clearest expression of this authority is seen when parents take the active, leading role in the home. They are the ones directing the children. Obviously, if God tells the children to obey their parents, then He had in mind that we shall tell them what to do. I know that sounds silly to say. We all know this. But the truth is, many parents are not active in leading the children in the home. Somehow, they think that being an authority is making corrections. They just let things go as they will, and then give corrections when the children get out of line.

Let me ask you a question to which you already know the answer. Which one of these approaches calls for more corrections? If you guide the children in your home, filling their days with good wholesome activity, you will give very little correction, and you will have a peaceful home. This is God's way: a calm quiet authority expressed in positive direction most of the time, with occasional correction for disobedience. This is an authority that is in control, guiding the child's activities in good and right paths. A child that grows up with this kind of authority learns to give up his will to many positive influences. Dear parents, and especially mothers, this is freedom, blessed freedom, for both child and the parent. This is a child walking through life guided by loving parents into activities that will profit him all his days.

Imagine trying to run a business the other way, with very little guidance and very little order. Imagine just sending all the workers out to the shop to do "something," then spending the rest of your day solving problems, correcting mistakes, and answering questions. No thank you. That business will not last long. It will never make a profit, and the workers will soon quit out of frustration. We wouldn't do that; we know better. We would order a schedule for the day, assigning different workers to different tasks. We would train the workers so they know what is expected of them, and so on we would go.

Some mothers allow their homes to function in somewhat the same dysfunctional way. Their lives are full of frustrations, and at times they they are tempted just to give up. I am sure it is not as extreme as I just gave it, but many of the traits are there. Children who are given too much "freedom" get into more trouble, tend to be more discontent, and require many more spankings.

Stop and think about your home for a moment. How is your home ordered? Maybe it would be helpful for you and your spouse to sit together at the end of a day and evaluate. Ask yourselves, "What was the order and atmosphere of the home like today?" I have developed four categories here to help you evaluate. Which one fits the order of your home?

> **Pro-active:** actions in advance to deal with expected difficulty. This is the home in which the parents are actively leading the children into the good and the right. Planning and forethought are involved.
>
> **Re-active:** responsive actions based on difficulties that arise. The parents in this home are very sincere, wanting the children to go the right way. However, they are more on the corrective nagging side of parenting. The children are allowed more "freedom," and then, out of concern, they are corrected when they do wrong.
>
> **Non-active:** a passive attitude toward difficulties. These parents, through ignorance or carelessness, leave the children to themselves. They say, "Children will be children" and other such statements showing their uninvolved mode. These parents need a wake-up call from the Lord before they reap the harvest of their apathy.
>
> **Explosive:** a frustrated, highly emotional reaction to difficulty. These parents have a mixed motivation. They

tend to be self-centered. They could be foolish, undisciplined Christians, or they could be totally lost. Either way, these parents neglect the children and allow them too much liberty. Then, as the children express their nature, the parents explode in frustration. High emotions, strong hateful words, and the like are used to bring order in their home.

I am pleading for pro-active parenting because it is the most Bible-centered way to raise a godly generation. It also will give the most peaceful parenting experience of the options listed. Obviously, you will have the best results if you begin your child's life with this kind of directed order. However, I want to say quickly, any time you move into the pro-active mode, your children will prosper under it. I will apply this pro-active approach to infants first, and then make some applications to children at any stage of development.

Start Young

For many parents, it is a totally new thought that one can order the life and schedule of a small child. This is because we are so used to meeting the "urgent needs of a helpless child." I have emphasized these words on purpose because that is how many think. It may be that what we consider urgent needs, actually are urgent demands of a self-centered child. If the needs are, in fact, urgent demands, then we are training a selfish, demanding child each time we cater to his cries.

A small child can be guided into an ordered life. He does not have to eat every time he cries. He does not have to be held or rocked whenever he cries out for attention. I encourage some of you parents to stop and meditate on what I have just written. It may be a foreign thought, therefore requiring some reflection. If it is a selfish demand, this is not a little thing.

The question is this: Is the child's life to be ordered by careful parent's love or by its own desires? This may surprise you, but a small child can be taught to wait thirty minutes before it is fed. There is nothing wrong with an empty stomach. Nothing will happen to the child if he doesn't eat right away. In some cases, the child is being trained to express frustration and even anger if he is not fed right away, at the first whimper of hunger. I feel this is wrong.

Mothers, think what it would be like if your baby could learn to sleep six or seven hours every night. What a difference this would make in your day! There is nothing wrong with an empty stomach. We all break fast in the morning after going about twelve hours without eating. It actually is good for our body functions to get a rest. It will not hurt the child. You will have to work the child into this, but it can be done more easily than you think. You actually can come up with a predictable routine for the child, which will bring much peace and blessing to your home. Let's look at a list of possible activities that mothers have ordered for their child.

> The child can learn to eat at given times throughout the day. They can learn to be patient, and wait until Mom is ready to feed him.
> The child can learn to take a nap in a peaceful way at certain times in the day. How pleasant to lay your baby down for a nap and have him curl up and go to sleep. And if sleep doesn't come right away, he will lie quietly in the crib.
> The child can learn to enjoy quiet time for thirty minutes during the day. We often have let our children listen to the Bible on cassette during this time.
> The child can learn to have playtime all by himself each day, and even learn to be content with three or four toys.
> The child can learn to sleep through the night. If he wakes up in the night, one word can send him back to sleep.
> The child can learn to relish special playtimes with mama, a time when relationships are built. A child thrives on this kind of focused time.

These are just a few examples of good helpful activities that will benefit everyone involved. A child guided in this manner will be content, secure, and very pleasant to have around. The home in which this child lives will be a peaceful habitation. I'm sure every mother reading this would agree, this would be nice. But how do you do it? It can be done; it must be done. This is guiding your child into the right, training him to give up his will to good things, things that he will learn to love and anticipate. Also, add a couple more children to this ordered home, and again, it is easy to see how helpful this would be. It's true that many children make a busy mother, but if some of this order is in place, life goes much better.

Blessed Order at Any Age

Perhaps it is too much for you to grasp to imagine a small baby fitting into this type of schedule. Okay, then wait until he is four months or six months old. The sooner you implement a life directed by the parents, the better it will be for the child. The longer you wait, the more selfish demands you will have to work through.

Even if you are in the midst of raising a family, it is not too late to implement this principle. Take charge, and begin to guide them into the right. Order their day for them. Plan out what you want them to do.

I remember sitting down and making a list of good activities for little ones. I think I had about fifteen different things for a toddler to do while Jackie directed the schooling. With a list, Jackie was never at a loss for direction.

I encourage you to try an ordered life for a week or two, and see if you are not pleased with the results. I do believe there will be less nagging, with fewer corrections and spankings, if you will move in this direction.

Consider also the results of the demand approach to early child care. By putting several examples together, it is easy to see how selfishness can be strengthened in the heart of a child.

> If you feed your child when he demands to be fed, by crying, then the child is learning, to get what he wants by crying. When a mother has this mentality, and can't get to the child quickly enough, then the child cries louder, and even more forcefully. This strengthens self-centeredness even more. Many times the child may not need to be fed, but we have patterned ourselves to feed him when he cries. I'm sure some colic comes from this

overfeeding.

If the child is picked up and held each time he cries for attention, this also teaches the child how to get attention. Every child would rather be held than made to play or just lie by himself for a time. So the child cries more and gets held more.

If you develop the pattern of rocking your child to sleep each time he is to take a nap, then the child will demand that you keep this up and will let you know by pitching a fit about it.

Once the pattern is established in the child's mind, the demands will increase as the child grows older. And guess what he will do to express his new demands? He will cry and sometimes even scream to get his way.

Many parents have innocently allowed this demanding nature to form. As the months go by, the child's will becomes stronger and more demanding. At about eight to ten months, the sincere parents realize there is a need in the child. Because they are not aware of what has happened, they usually think that as the child is getting older, this is normal behavior. So they begin to bring correction and training. I have seen parents start to spank their child over and over because they now see this willful self-centeredness and want to deal with it before it gets out of hand. Dear parents, there is a better way to do all this. A child this small cannot comprehend all these spankings. You need to get on the directing side of this whole issue quickly. Lead your child in the ways of righteousness instead of correcting him into them.

Prayer

Father in heaven we cry out to You for the wisdom to understand something new. Open our understanding that we may see into the real issues with our little ones. I pray for these parents. Give them wisdom. Let Your still small voice witness to them as they ponder the chaos of their homes. In Jesus' name. Amen.

22

Three Mysterious Influences

*Except the LORD build the house,
they labor in vain that build it.*

Psalm 127:1a

I would like to turn our attention to three of the most important areas of child training. These areas are the most exciting aspects of all because they cover the divine perspectives of child training. The word *mysterious* means "beyond human power to explain or understand." This is a good way to describe this chapter. We want to look behind the scenes and see the dynamics of a living God working in the lives of our children. I have used the word three, but in reality we want to look at three different ways in which God builds our houses. He in His own hidden ways prevails upon our sons and daughters to make for Himself holy generations.

These three ways still depend very much on us parents, although it is God who is doing the mysterious work. I have shared many things to do, in our pursuit of godly seed. This is right. However, if we do not have the element of a living God in our homes, the do's and don'ts will not have much affect. I have been alluding to this divine element all through our study. Now I want to center on the impact of God's presence in our homes. The lack of God in the home is the formost reason for failure and loss. I mentioned in Chapter 20 how parents are confused about a wayward child. Many parents have shown their children the things they should do. However, they have not shown them the person behind it all: Jesus Christ. Let's look at these three ways.

1. The Powerful Atmosphere of the Spirit

> *I will pour water upon him that is thirsty, and floods upon the dry ground: I will pour my Spirit upon thy seed, and my blessing upon thine offspring. And they shall spring up as among the grass, as willows by the water courses. One shall say, I am the LORD's; and another shall [call] himself by the name of Jacob.*
> *Isaiah 44:3-5a*

These verses are so dear and sweet to me that I can hardly write them without weeping. O what precious promises God gives to us fathers and mothers as we endeavor to raise up a godly seed!

Let me begin by asking you a question. What kind of water is mentioned in the first verse? Is God talking about giving us a drink of water as from a glass? Or is God promising us a deeper drink than that? We know the answer. God is talking about the water of His Spirit, the fountain of living waters. My heart cries out to God continually for more of this water in my own life.

We should also consider the word "thirsty," for this is a key word in this conditional promise. I'm not sure that we can understand the depth of this word thirsty. We live in a land where it is easy to get a drink of water. Consequently, we are hardly ever really thirsty.

I have been going to Africa for about sixteen years. Over there I have learned what it means to be thirsty. I have learned the hard way that I dare not drink just any water while I am there. I have been deathly sick because I unwisely drank when I was thirsty. So I have to wait sometimes for three hours before I can get water that is safe to drink. By then I am very thirsty. That is what God is saying to us.

Three Mysterious Influences

This verse is talking about the spirit of a beggar: *"Blessed are the poor in spirit"*(Matt. 5:3a). Ah, when we get really thirsty for God, for the living God, as David was in Psalm 42, then He will surely come and pour out His Spirit upon us from on high.

When this happens, something else happens also. God pours His Spirit upon our seed, that is, on our children. This is a very motivating verse to me. I have it on the wall of my large living room to remind me continually of this promise. I need to remember that God's blessing on my children is dependent on my thirst for God. We could say to the degree that I am thirsty for God, to that degree, will God pour out His spirit upon me, and to that degree will He put His blessing on my seed. What an exciting promise this is! I want God's Spirit upon my children; I want this desperately. This is a promise that I pray to the Lord concerning my children.

Let me explain how this promise is fulfilled. As God pours His Spirit out upon me and my wife, it runs over and falls on our sons and daughters. We are to be a cup that is full and running over in our house. The children are the recipients of that overflowing life.

I have used my two younger sons in meetings to illustrate what God is saying. I have the two of them sit down on the platform of the church. Then taking a glass in one hand and a pitcher of water in the other, I start pouring water into the glass. I hold the glass over the two boys, as they looked up expectantly waiting for the water. As the glass fills, I keep on pouring, and the water overflows the glass and pours down on the boys. This is a powerful picture. I have at times broken down and wept as the water has fallen on their heads.

This pictures the mysterious influence of the Spirit of God upon our children. God's plan for our families is that they grow up in an atmosphere of the Spirit, an atmosphere of the presence of God. The presence of God is present in my house. What better way to raise my family!

Think about a small child playing at his mother's feet while she is working in the kitchen. Little ones are so open to every influence around them, and they receive all day long. How powerful it is for this child to dwell in a house where mercy drops are

The Pursuit of Godly Seed

falling all around him day by day! This has an amazing effect on the development of the child. The influence of the Spirit is falling upon him through his parents every day. This is the picture we see in these verses.

Young Hudson Taylor grew up in a home such as this. The mercy drops were always falling on him from the time he was a small child. Those mercy drops fell in the form of godly parents and earnest prayers for China. It is no wonder that by the age of six, he said to his father, "Dad, when I grow up, I will go to China."

For the past two years, I have been studying the biographies of godly homes. I hope to publish them all in a book some day soon. In my studies, I have noticed that many of the choice servants God used in the past grew up in one of these Spirit-filled homes. An atmosphere of the Spirit prevailed over the home as they were growing up. I believe this is one of the greatest keys to securing the next generation. God has us in a corner, so to speak. We must be spiritual. This is not just an option, it is imperative.

In verse four, God gives us a lovely picture showing the result of such an atmosphere. He says that our children will be *"willows by the water courses."* This is the same analogy used in Psalm 1: *"a tree planted by the rivers of water."* A willow tree planted by the water courses is going to grow: It is going to prosper exceedingly. We should also consider the tree planted somewhere else. It gets water every now and then when it rains. It will grow. It will mature and eventually bear fruit, but not like the tree by the water. Some Christian homes are like this also. The children get some water every now and then, maybe through a belated family devotion or special meetings at church. This is surely better than nothing. Thank God for what they do get. But this is not what God planned for them.

When we as parents are wholly consecrated to the Lord, seeking Him with our whole heart, this creates an entirely different setting for the children. We become the water courses. We are the rivers of living water flowing continually through the house. The children are to be planted beside us, the spiritual parents. As we walk with our God day by day, He pours out living waters upon us. These waters overflow to the rest of the family, and all prosper.

Three Mysterious Influences

Do you see the vision, parents? Isn't it an inspiring perspective? Oh, what a difference this will make in our child training! This is so much more than simply having family devotions once a day. I don't want to discourage you if you are doing that. I want to stir you on to higher ground. In a sense, many of us have a more Old Testament view of training a child: teach them, train them, spank them, and so on. All this is good, and I do it all. However, we are New Covenant Christians who have received the Holy Ghost, the promise of the Father. We must move on into the realm of spiritual child training. All the practical things God has given must be graced by the Spirit of the living God.

The question arises here: What do we want to pass on to the next generation? We are to pass on *"the faith which was once delivered unto the saints"* (Jude 3b). What is "the faith"? Do you think it is a system of teachings and doctrines? We all know the answer. It is a vibrant faith, an abundant life in the spirit, with teachings and doctrines. God has provided the easiest way for us to do this: *"Be filled with the Spirit"* (Eph. 5:18b). The Greek tense beautifies and magnifies this verse exceedingly. It can be paraphrased this way: *"Be being continually filled and controlled by the Spirit."* If we parents follow this biblical command, our children will prosper in the atmosphere of the Spirit.

I don't want to shock you, but sooner or later we must come to grips with what God is saying about the Christian life, and about child training. Let's face it, most of the church is losing the next generation, something drastic is wrong. I know it is so because of all the letters I receive from parents crying over their children. They are looking around them and seeing the youth in the churches filled with the world, and they want help.

There is one more promise in these verses that we should observe before we move on to the second influence in this chapter. In the fifth verse, we find the fulfillment of every sincere Christian parent. Children who grow up under this blessed atmosphere will choose the Lord. The sense of the words denotes an enthusiastic choice: "I am the Lord's." This is what we are all working, praying, and longing for.

The Pursuit of Godly Seed

Herein is the longing of my heart. I want my children to rise up on their own and choose the God of their father. This is not simply a baptism or a confirmation class. This is a whole-hearted surrender to the Lord Jesus Christ, which brings a total regeneration of their inner man. Genuine salvation for my children—oh, what a joy when this happens!

Dear parents, we can have this most excellent joy. It is a promise that shall be fulfilled. If we are willing to walk with a clear heart under an open heaven, God shall bring it to pass.

2. The Power of an Enthusiastic Anointed Example

Praise ye the LORD. Blessed is the man that feareth the LORD, that delighteth greatly in his commandments. His seed shall be mighty upon earth: the generation of the upright shall be blessed.

Psalm 112:1-2

The Psalmist begins his presentation of these precious promises with praise. That seems fitting to me because God's promises fulfilled make the heart overflow with praise. These promises are conditional but they are not presented in a commanding way. Instead they present an endearing snapshot of a truly godly man and the resulting influence he will have on his children. The example of a godly father is the second way God mysteriously works in the lives of children. A little proverb expresses this truth: "More is caught than taught." This is no small statement. It can be a very encouraging or a devastating thought depending on where you are with the Lord and how you live before your children.

The Holy Spirit has painted us a portrait of a spiritual man who loves the Lord with all his heart just as commanded in Deuteronomy 6. He fears the Lord, which means he sees the Lord always before his face. This fear is a reverence for God, not a state of being afraid of Him. This godly man loves the Word, delights in it, and he joys in obeying it. He is a Psalm 1 kind of father, a nut, a fanatic. He is excited about living the Christian life. He has moved beyond the duty of the Law, and into the beauty of the Law. This

Three Mysterious Influences

is not a "have to" thing with him. This whole-hearted father has children living around him in his house all the day long. How do you think he will affect his children?

Some years ago, I spent my Saturday preparing a sermon to preach the following day. As I arrived home, little Esther met me with this question: "Papa, do you have to preach tomorrow?"

I thought for a moment before I answered. My heart was overflowing with the message I had prepared, and I love to preach. So I told her, "No, sweetheart, I don't have to preach. I *get* to preach!" Then we had a lesson on the joys of serving God.

This is the way it is with this man in the Psalm. It isn't a "have to" thing, but rather a "get to" thing that he does with all his heart. To put it in New Testament language, he loves to go to church; he loves to read the Bible; and he loves to tell others about Jesus. I picture a man full of enthusiasm. He is living out his Christian life with joy, and the commandments of God are not grievous to him. Again, this man has children that live in his house under his care. They will be affected by him. What kind of teacher do you think he will be when he is teaching his family: dry and dutiful or fresh and lively? We all know the answer. He may not have all the abilities he needs, but his excitement will make up for that.

The effect that this man will have on his children is a bit mysterious. Their hearts will be moved in his direction by an unseen hand. Enthusiasm is contagious. It has a way of getting hold of you and carrying you along. You find yourself wanting to do what the enthused person is doing. You just want to be like them because you admire them. Imitation is the highest form of admiration. We all know this. We can see this even in the world. Look at some of the crazy things youth will do because of some weird musician they admire.

What we love, our children also will love. We have seen it in our families. If a father is a sports fan (short for "fanatic"), usually the son also will love sports. That is just the way it is. My children all love to garden. Do you know why? I love to get out there, put my hands in the soil, and make something grow. When spring comes, garden fever settles in on all of us. It's my fault. I take the blame for it.

This principle works whether it is applied to good things or bad things. It is very powerful if used for the good and the right, but very destructive if it involves a love for the wrong things. I enjoy working hard, and so do my boys. That is just the way it is. Whatever we set our affections on our children will want to do. Because of this, we fathers need to be fanatics about the kingdom of God.

My mind goes to the testimony of William Booth. He was a fanatic for the kingdom of God. I studied his life in detail for a Home Histories article I wrote for the *Remnant* magazine.

He loved the Lord extravagantly every day. We have already looked at how this man affected the generations after him. This was one of his secrets. He lived a dedicated life before his family, and they all wanted to do the same. Coming home after a street meeting, he would tell all his children the beautiful things God had done. They anxiously waited for him to come home and share. Each of the eight children was allowed to go along with dad after they became twelve years of age. They could hardly wait, although they knew that people would throw rotten tomatoes at them. Now, how do you get a twelve-year-old to look forward to a rotten tomato in the face? That is easy. You enjoy it yourself and make it a privilege.

When I am teaching on the home, parents often come up to me and ask, "Brother Denny, how do you get the children to fast, to get up early, to read their Bible, and to do many other things? Are these laws in the house that they must obey?"

The answer is "no," we never force these kinds of things on the children. These are voluntary disciplines that must be embraced with a willing heart, or they don't come out right. The key to these issues is an enthusiastic example. These are precious disciplines at our house. If a father or mother joyfully turns his or her plate over at breakfast time, and then follows that with a joyful testimony of blessings in the fast, it is not hard to get a child to fast. We have always had a problem with them wanting to fast when they were a bit too young. David is eight years old right now, and he enters into a fast with the rest of the family. He has been doing this for about two years.

So where does all this enthusiasm originate? This is a good question. I am not referring to a fleshly generated excitement. There are men who are experts at being excited. They are paid thousands of dollars to give one enthusiastic speech. I am not implying this. But we must find a way to get from the "have-to-do-it" side of all this to the "I-get-to-do-it" side. The answer is that this change is by the Spirit of God. Here we are back to being spiritual again.

The Greek word for *enthusiasm* is "enthusiasmos." It literally means "God insidedness." This comes from the root word, *"entheos"* or "in God." We are talking about a God-inspired life that we live out as an example to our children. God is inside me, moving me, inspiring me, and empowering me to live my Christian life. And my children are watching this example every day. Look at some synonyms of the word. They are "whole-heartedness," "fervent," "spirited," "eager," and "zealous." We already know we are to live our lives *"heartily as to the Lord"* (Col. 3:23). God has us in a corner, and there is only one way out of all this. We must learn to walk in the grace that is in Christ Jesus.

Really, we are talking about basic principles of discipleship. Love them, live them, teach them, and the children will follow you. The question is, what kind of children do you want? The sky is the limit. You have a whole Bible packed full of principles to live by. Whatever you want your children to do, if you will love it with a joyful heart and live it out yourself, they also will want to do it.

Do you want your child to be a soul winner? Then go for it with all your heart. Show them and tell them what a blessing it is to win souls, and soon they will be out fishing with you. It is far more exciting to fish for men than it is to fish for fish isn't it? They will catch the fever if you have it. When all our child training is over, we will all have what we were willing to settle for. Let us pay the price of personal revival and watch what happens in the children.

3. Prevailing Intercessory Prayer

This last mysterious influence is also a very spiritual one. You can not work prayer up in the flesh. Nobody prays prevailing prayers but those who abide under an open heaven. But those who abide in this state can pray powerful, prevailing prayers that move the hand of God to change the lives of their families. This could be the most powerful of all the influences we have already described.

> *Arise, cry out in the night: in the beginning of the watches. Pour out thine heart like water before the face of the Lord: lift up thy hands toward Him, for the life of thy children.*
> *Lamentations 2:19*

The text that I have chosen flows from the heart of Jeremiah. He was a prophet who loved God's people deeply, but was misunderstood by them because he spoke of judgment. In Lamentations, judgment has fallen, and Jeremiah is pleading for the children. I am afraid America is in a similar state, but she doesn't know it. My heart has united with this man's heart many times when I was up in the night. I choose this verse to open the last part of the chapter because it clearly shows that this is not regular prayer.

Jackie and I pray for the children continually. It is a regular part of devotional life. When I send the children to bed at night, I always have a season of prayer with them and for them. We are always praying for the children. But I am talking about something deeper than this.

I am referring to those times when you are caught up in the Spirit, and the inspiration of prayer is upon you. This is intercession, when a man or woman lays hold on the horns of the altar and won't let go. This kind of praying must be done for your family. There must be those times when you are absolutely broken before God for the needs in the home.

There are times in the life of a child when he needs someone to pray him through on a certain issue. As young people mature, sometimes they lose their sight on what is right. This is when they need a father or a mother who will intercede for them and pray them through their difficulties. There is something sweet about the middle of the night. It is something needful to rise from your bed while others sleep and pray effectual, fervent prayers. Many parents have no vision for this. They often wait until there is a tragedy, and then they get earnest and pray.

I remember reading the story of James Stewart's mother. James was an evangelist from Scotland in the early 1900s. God used him mightily in Eastern Europe before Hitler and Communism. His mother was a devout woman of prayer. She had dedicated her son to God at birth, but in his early teens he was all wrapped up in soccer. He was a young man of fourteen years on the road to becoming a star player.

This dear "mother in Israel" was not about to let that happen. Day after day she arose in the night to intercede for her son. She resisted the devil in Jesus Christ's name. This continued for several days until she had prayed through. She got a witness from the Spirit that her son was going to come through. The night that James was converted, he was on the soccer field in the middle of the game. Heavy conviction seized him on the spot, and he surrendered by the end of the game. When he walked into the house that night, his mother was not even shocked, for she had heard from the Lord already.

This is the kind of prayer I am advocating. It is my conviction that we need to be praying this kind of prayer in the good times. We need to resist the devil in our children's lives while things are going well. We need to pray our children through to God's will when they are sincerely wanting it.

Some time ago an individual described to me the effectual, fervent prayers of his mother. He told how he had heard his mother pray fervent prayers when he was a little boy. He had heard her cry out to God as she dedicated her children to Him. She had asked God to use them and to bless the generations to come. What was the outcome of her prayers? Well, three of her sons and four of her grandsons became preachers, and we haven't seen the end of the story yet.

My heart is overwhelmed again to realize how much we can touch the generations even after we are dead and gone. Our prayers, hot intercessory prayers, can touch the lives of our children, our children's children, and our children's children's children. O that God would raise up mighty men and women of God who know how to get hold of God, who know how to touch heaven for the lives of their children.

Andrew Murray prayed this kind of prayer. Eight generations of Murray descendants have risen up to serve God since that godly man prayed for his generations. I discovered this in a recent study of his home and his father's home. I was amazed at this godly man's far-reaching influence as I studied for one of the Home Histories. Eight generations have come from his prayers. He believed in praying for the generations to come. I do too. I have spent much time in prayer for the generations that shall come from my children. Brothers and sisters, our prayers can chase after our descendants long after we are gone. Let us chase them with our prayers. God is on His throne.

Wailing Women

> *Thus saith the LORD of hosts, Consider ye, and call for the mourning women, that they may come; and send for cunning women, that they may come: and let them make haste, and take up a wailing **for us**, that our eyes may run down with tears, and our eyelids gush out with waters...Hear the word of the LORD O ye women, and let your ear receive the word of His mouth, and teach your daughters wailing, and, every one her neighbor lamentation.*
>
> Jeremiah 9:17,18,20

In this section on prayer, I feel this is an appropriate place to plead with you sisters to pray for the men. This is part of the mysterious way God works in a home. Mothers, the most powerful way for you to touch the lives of your children is to pray for your husband.

When things were looking pretty bad in Israel, God called the women to gather and wail for the men. I wonder what would happen if all the mothers in our land would begin to intercede for the men. I have laid a lot of responsibilities upon the shoulders of the men because God does. But the men need your prayers. Your prayers can be part of that mysterious influence of God in your home. You have no idea what God could do if you would pray. Sisters, take up a wailing *for us*. We know that we have missed it in many areas. We know that we have made a lot of mistakes. We have grown up in a generation without leaders, and most of us are not the leaders we ought to be. We readily acknowledge it. Take up a wailing for us. Go and get hold of God.

Another word to you mothers, don't complain to your daughters about their father. Teach them how to wail. Teach them how to sigh and cry and pray before God. Again, the kind of prayers we have in mind are deep ones. Sure, you pray for your husbands, but we men need some intercessors who will travail and prevail with God. These verses in Jeremiah present an awesome picture: a whole group of men, so broken that water gushes out of their eyes. Pray that God will make us thirsty with a deep longing in our hearts for more communion with Him.

Prayer

Father in heaven have mercy on us. We have seen Your standard clearly presented in these words. What can we say? We fall so short of Your plan and purposes. Make us spiritual men and women, whatever the cost. We now see how important it is to walk with God. Send us a personal revival that can be seen by the children. In Jesus Christ's name. Amen.

Meditations

Take My Child

Take my child and let him be
Consecrated Lord to Thee
May his moments and his days
Overflow with ceaseless praise

Help me guide his hands to move
At the impulse of Thy love
May his feet always be
Swift and beautiful for Thee

Take his voice, Oh let him sing
Always only for my King
Make his lips a burning fire
Filled with words of pure desire

Take his will Oh let him yield
First to me and then to Thee
Take his mind with all its powers
I have trained it for this hour

Take my love my Lord I pour
At Thy feet its treasure store
May this child I give to Thee
Be ever only all for Thee

adapted from Take My Life
Frances R Havergal

23

A Dwelling Place for the Living God

For ye are the temple of the living God: as God hath said, I will dwell in them, and walk in them: and I will be their God, and they shall be my people.
II Corinthians 6:16

What? know ye not that your body is the temple of the Holy Ghost which is in you, which ye have of God, and ye are not your own? For ye are bought with a price: therefore glorify God in your body, and in your spirit, which are God's.
I Corinthians 6:19-20

We are coming to the end of this section on practical child training. This chapter is intended to be both motivational and informative. It is a bit of a glimpse behind the reasons why training is so important. As we hold a newborn baby in our arms, it is hard at times to imagine that God desires to dwell in this child someday. God says of Himself that He is *"the high and lofty one that inhabiteth eternity"* (Isa. 57:15a). Again He says, *"Heaven is my throne, and the earth is my footstool"* (Isa. 66:1a). This awesome God wants to come and take possession of my child. This leaves me staggering with a task that is beyond my understanding. The everlasting God has given us a child, a vessel to prepare for His indwelling. When my task is finished, I want to say what Solomon said at the dedication of the earthly temple. "I have built an house of habitation for thee, and a place for thy dwelling for ever" (2 Chron. 6:2). May God deepen our understanding of this principle.

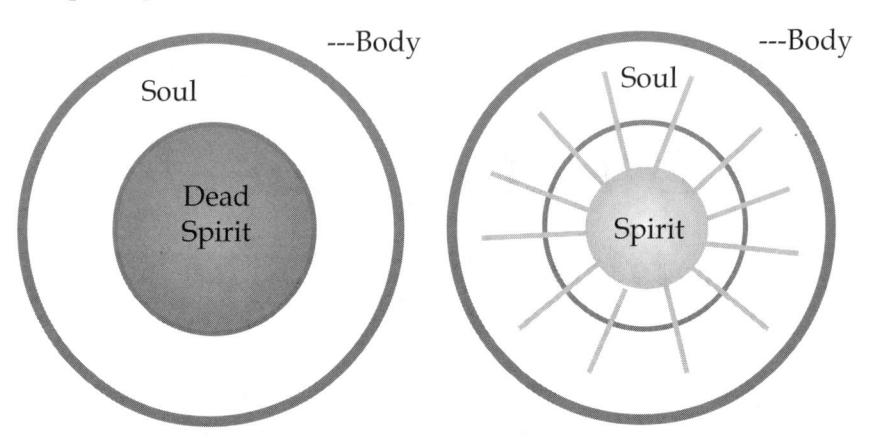

Diagram: Two circles representing man as a triune being. Left circle labeled Body (outer), Soul (middle), Dead Spirit (inner). Right circle labeled Body (outer), Soul (middle), Spirit (inner) with rays emanating outward.

I have chosen two simple diagrams to illustrate some very important truths in this chapter. I'm sure you have seen these circles before. They represent man as a triune being. When God created man, He made him a tripartite being: spirit, soul, and body. With his body, he can relate to the physical world around him. He can see, he can hear, he can eat food, and so on. This is man's body.

God also made man with a soul. Man's soul is made up of his mind, will, and emotions. We use our mind to think and reason. We use our will to choose right or wrong, and we use our emotions to love and set our affections on things.

The third part of man is his spirit. The spirit of man is the center of man's being. It is here that we have fellowship with God. It is here, in man's spirit, that God has chosen to dwell.

God made Adam in His own image, and placed him in the Garden of Eden. Adam was one beautiful creation of God. Everything was perfect. He was filled with God's presence and able to love God with his whole heart. He was able to fellowship with God and to hear His voice. Adam was a God centered being, and God was all he needed and wanted.

Consider how man functioned there in the beginning. His spirit was filled with and controlled by God. His mind, will, and emotions were in subjection to God, who ruled in his spirit, and his body was ruled by his spirit and his soul. Adam was a beautiful God-centered, God-controlled being. No patterns of sin had come and defiled him in any way. God looked at man and "behold it was very good" (Gen. 1:31).

But then came the fall of man. When man fell in the garden, something happened inside him, something that changed him completely. God had said, "Of the tree of the knowledge of good and evil, thou shalt not eat of it, for in the day that thou eatest thereof, thou shalt surely die" (Gen. 2:17). We know that Adam did not drop dead when he took a bite of that fruit. His body was still there. His mind was still thinking. He still had a will by which he could choose. But something was drastically different about Adam. In the center of Adam's being, in his spirit, he died. His ability to fellowship with God died. The place where God's spirit had dwelled had died. The Spirit of God was not there anymore. Man went from a God-centered being to a self-centered being, because of his rebellion. God was not in him anymore. The history of man has been a tragic one from that day until now. This change is illustrated in Figure 1, which depicts a body, a soul, and a spirit cut off from God. I know this is a bit theological, but we need to look at God's plan for man so we can see what God's plan is for our children.

A God-Centered Man

From the time of man's fall, God set His plan of salvation in motion, so He could bring man back to the place where God was again in the center of his being. This is the purpose of redemption. Regeneration, which means "regenesis," takes place in man's spirit. This is where we are born again by the Spirit of God. We receive a new heart, a new spirit, and God puts His Spirit in us and dwells in us again. This is illustrated in Figure 2, which depicts a body yielded to God, a soul that also has yielded to God, and a spirit made alive unto God again and filled with His presence. This is salvation, and it is glorious. Now man can have fellowship with God again through the blood shed on Calvary.

All this is explained in Ezekiel 36:25-27. I do not mean to be dogmatic in my explanation of these diagrams. I am using them only to

The Pursuit of Godly Seed

help us see that a major change takes place at conversion. God, through His plan of Salvation, is seeking His original, beautiful relationship with man back again. God is seeking and pursuing man, that He might save his soul and dwell in him again. God is pursuing man, that he might become a God-centered being again, one possessed and controlled by God. God then will have a man who is totally yielded to Him, filled with His Spirit, and led by that Spirit.

This might be a bit too deep for some of you. This is, however, what God is after for every one of us. He will not be satisfied until we are back in that beautiful place of fellowship with Him again. If God is seeking all this for me, then He is also desiring the same thing for each of my children. It is helpful to know where God is going with my children. That way, I can indeed be a laborer together with God for the full salvation of each of my children.

Consider Christ's Disciples

I was meditating on the disciples of Christ some time ago in the light of the diagram I have been describing It came to me in my meditations that God had not come to dwell in them yet. They were, as the diagram in Figure 1 explains, body and soul with a spirit dead and cut off from God. Jesus called the disciples and said, *"Follow me."* They were willing to follow, but God was not inside them yet. They were good Jews. They had been taught what was right. They had gone to the synagogue and learned the law for many years. Even so, God was not inside them yet.

For three and a half years, they followed the Lord Jesus around in their bodies. They followed Him with their mind, will, and emotions. They saw the miracles He did and listened to what He said. They saw the example of His righteous life, and their minds were taking it all in. Oh, what a beautiful example they had before them --God in human flesh walking around before their very eyes. What a training program those disciples had, but they had no change on the inside yet. They were still very self-centered individuals. We can get a bit frustrated with them as we study their lives: three and a half years with the Lord Jesus and *still* acting the way they did. But what can you expect from a self-centered being? Consider the many blunders these disciples made, even though they were with the Lord Jesus for three and a half years. Things didn't go very well, did they? Although God was with them, He was not in them.

However, when the day of Pentecost was fully come, everything changed. All those years training in the law and teaching about what is right really made a difference then. All those years of being taken to the synagogue and those beautiful years with the Lord Jesus Christ all made a big difference then. They had been trained on the ourside, but now, they were empowered on the inside. When the day of Pentecost was fully come, the Spirit of God came upon those disciples and filled them. They were totally changed from that day forward. Peter, the man who shook and trembled before a little woman, was changed into another man. He became Peter, the man who stood before a crowd of thousands and told them, *"You crucified the Lord."* He was fearless, even though they had the power to cut off his head. What a transformation took place when God came to dwell in them. What an awesome group of men they became.

Consider with me a moment. All those years of training at home and at the synagogue were not wasted. All those days of time spent with Jesus were not wasted, not at all. They were days of preparation for the day when God would come and give them a new heart and make them God-centered men again. Jesus trained them and disciplined them in the mind, the will, and the emotions, but the inner man could not be changed until Pentecost.

Do you understand that this is the very same training we need to give our children who have not been born again? It is important for us as parents to understand how this diagram relates to our children. As with those disciples, our children are in the midst of the training program that God has ordained and revealed in the Bible. But someday, God is going to come and give them a new heart and dwell inside them. It is good for us parents to understand where God is wanting to go with our children, so we can co-labor with Him.

What is God after? He wants a disciple filled with His presence, a disciple that He can possess and in whom He can dwell. He wants a disciple over whom He can rule in every part of his being, and whom He can use for His glory. There is so much that God wants to accomplish upon the earth, but He needs yielded vessels whom He can use. This is what God is after for our children. I want to go a bit deeper in our consideration of these diagrams and how they relate to the training of a child. I think it will motivate us to see the tremendous impact that we can have on the future usefulness of our children.

Two Innocent Babies

As I see it, when God gives us a newborn child, that child comes to us as pictured in Figure 1. Man is born after Adam. His spirit is dead to God, having no ability to commune with God. Our children come to us very self-centered beings, simply because God is not in them. However, they are not yet filled and controlled by their selfishness. In a sense, they come to us totally blank. The mind, the will, the emotions, and even the body come to us blank. The body has not been turned loose to defiled itself. The soul (the mind, the will, and the emotions) has not been left to itself yet.

O the beauty of a newborn child! Everyone agrees with this little statement. Did you ever consider what makes a newborn child so beautiful? It is more than the pink skin on its cheeks. When you hold a newborn child in your arms, you are holding a living soul with nothing written on it. There it is, innocent and open like a blank piece of paper. Nothing has been written on it yet, it is innocent. This is what makes a newborn child so beautiful.

Now, come reason with me awhile. What will happen if we take this beautiful innocent child and put it in the wrong environment for five years? If we leave the child to itself, with all its openness, in the midst of anger, lust, and gluttony, what will happen to the child? If we submit the heart of this child to all the world has to offer on television, (evil spirits, conflict, hatred, pornography, drugs, drinking, and stealing), what kind of a child will we have in five years? As we look into its face, will we see innocence, purity, and openness? We all know the answer. One trip to the inner city of any town will show all of us what happens. In some cases, you don't have to wait five years. Just two years, sometimes only one year, will show the change. In the evil environment of an inner city, the soul of the child is imprinted with all kinds of evil.

Now, come reason with me again on the more positive side of this illustration. If we put the child with its sweet open innocence into a righteous environment, what do you think we will have at the end of five years? If we place the child into the midst of love, kindness, purity, church life, the Bible, a spiritual atmosphere, and all that we have been saying, we will get a very different child. I think we all agree with this and understand how it happens. This is why we say a child is the mirror of its parents. The true life of the parents is etched out in the soul of their children by the things the child hears and the things it senses.

Both types of children are pictured in figure 1 at this point in their lives. They are both unregenerate, needing to be born again by the Spirit of God. However, consider how differently they come to the place of personal salvation, because of their environments.

The life of the parents is etched on the soul of the child. We all know this. O parents, I hope we are alert and can grasp the implications of all this. Can we see the impact of the positive and negative sides? The negative side makes things very urgent. But the positive side makes things very exciting. Both types of children are going to grow up and hopefully hear the same plan of salvation someday. They both will need to be saved. They both will have to deal with their own selfish, self-centered nature. But let me ask you a question. Which one has the better chance, and which one would you rather be? Again, we all know the answer, but remember, we are reasoning together. What a blessing and favor we give to our children when we recognize what God is after. We begin to co-labor with God to preserve their souls from many evil patterns. We give the children such an advantage when we watch over them and guide them along these lines.

Loose the Heavy Burdens

I know that all children are self-centered. They are each born after Adam with a sinful nature. I know we are not able to preserve them from everything, but we can preserve them from many things. What a tremendous disfavor to them, what a great burden we place on them if we neglect our responsibilities and just let them grow up.

Some will say, "Well, someday my children will get converted, and then they will be alright." This is only partially true. Yes, they will have an opportunity to give their lives to God, but they also will have more burdens to bear in their Christian lives. The process of sanctification will be much harder for those who were left to themselves. I think of some major things I had to deal with after I was converted. I was lazy and didn't like to work hard. After I was born again, I had to deal with this sin. I faced it many times until it was totally rooted out of my life.

If we neglect to train our children, we place a heavy burden on them that they have to drag along with them. Yes, God will help them. Yes, God will set them free. Yes, God can give them victory over every one of these sins. God can change every character flaw in their lives as the life of Jesus is manifested in their mortal flesh. But it is so much easier for a child coming to conversion who was trained according to the Bible pattern. Such a child gets converted and takes off running for the glory of God.

Some of the verses we have addressed take on new meaning when we look at them in the light of these diagrams. *"A child left to himself bringeth his mother to shame."* Again, *"Train up a child in the way he should go: and when he is old, he will not depart from it."* And one more, *"Thou shalt beat him with the rod, and shalt deliver his soul from hell."* Do you see it? They are not yet converted, but we are responsible to train their soul and their body, looking to the day when they will give their hearts to God and be converted.

May God renew our vision, and help us to see, "I have a child from the Lord." God Himself places them one by one into our hands. We must realize, "Here is a living soul given into our care. God wants to possess this vessel someday." For every one of our children, let's consider each of the four areas in the diagram: the mind, the will, the emotions, and the body. All the teaching given so far covers these four areas of a child's person.

The Mind

God gives us a baby, and this baby has a clean mind. It is empty. It has nothing in it yet. It is like a new computer. The new computer comes with sufficient data for it to function, but the memory is blank. What are we going to do with the clean fresh mind of our child? What kind of data will we put into his mind? What kind of impressions will we allow to flow freely into his mind? Will we protect our child's mind from the multitudes of media vying for the opportunity to fill his little fresh mind full. These are good questions for challenging our hearts. It is not right to allow this little child to be filled with useless data, foolish data, worldly data, and especially not filthy data. Will we, out of our neglect, allow his mind which is blank, to be filled with all that?

As we all know, the things that go into the mind do not go away. They are etched upon the memory. Many of us have hundreds of memories that we wish we could take out of our minds. Praise God, you can push such memories to the back and fill the mind with good things. You can renew your mind with beautiful things from the Bible.

All this helps, but unwholesome things you did, thought, or saw remain in the back of your mind. They sit there just waiting for the right input, such as a little phrase of a worldly song while walking through the grocery store. At this signal, those unwanted memories come marching like soldiers into the front of your mind. This is how the mind works.

We do our children such a service if we stand guard over all the data that goes inside their young minds. They are not old enough to do that on their own. It is our responsibility. We are responsible to make decisions for our children about the television, the radio, the books, the computers, and the magazines. The list is endless. The people behind all these media are vying for the opportunity to fill our children's minds with things that shouldn't be there.

What kind of words will enter into their minds at home? What will they hear? Will they sit at the feet of parents having an argument, again and again? Some parents think, "Oh, that child is only one year old. They don't understand anything." This is not how you should look at it. You are feeding data into their "computer" and all that data are going to bear fruit someday. All the hateful words, all the silly words, and all the harsh words will go into their minds and bear fruit. God is calling us parents to sanctification. We as Christian parents are not allowed to live in these realms anymore.

But what about the positive side? We have the opportunity to fill that computer with data that will bless their lives all the rest of their days. At our house, we have used the Bible on cassette to fill the minds of all our children. From the time they were one, they went to sleep listening to the Bible. Sometimes they went off to sleep, but other times, they just lay there listening.

Many chapters of the Bible can be hidden away in their minds. Bible stories, holy books, sermons, and theology discussions on Sunday afternoon, all these can be used to influence the mind of a child. The family table is an excellent place to fill their minds with the holy and the right. I approach each mealtime with purpose and vision, planning out things I want to talk about. There are times when the breakfast discussion gets so good and extended that we just sing a hymn and go to prayer. I tell the family, "We have been having devotions already."

Fanny Crosby is a beautiful illustration of this very point. Fanny Crosby got converted when she was about thirty-one years old. She had lost her eyesight when she was a very little girl. Her grandmother said, "I am going to be Fanny's eyes." She told Fanny how beautiful the sunsets and the sunrise were. She sat next to this little girl and went over verses, again and again. Fanny Crosby had literally scores of chapters of the Bible hidden away in her mind.

One day, at conversion, the Spirit of God came to dwell inside Fanny Crosby. When the Word of God and the Spirit of God met each other inside the being of Fanny Crosby, thousands of hymns rolled out. Hallelujah! What a hymn-making machine she was for the glory of God!

I'm not saying that if we do all these things the children will not need to be converted. They will be self-centered instead of God-centered until the Lord Jesus comes to sit on the throne of their hearts by His Spirit. But O, there is so much we can give them in preparation for that day. When the Word of God and the Spirit of God meet in the being of our children, beautiful things will start flowing out.

The Will

Let us go on to the will. The will of the child must be in subjection to the parents from an early age. I have given much instruction on this subject already. However, I want to pick it up again to make a point. The mind-set of the parents looking at their children should be, "Not your will, but my will be done." Why? Because someday God will require them to say, "Not my will but Thine be done." We must train our children to give up their will and yield it to us. Someday they will need to give it up to God. This will be so much easier if all their life they are taught to yield to their parents. I believe that is why God tells the children only one thing: "Obey your parents." If they do this with all of their heart, then when God knocks and says, "My son, give Me thy heart," it will be much easier.

Remember Susanna Wesley? This is what she was after. The will of the child was of utmost importance. I have said much on this subject already, but I am bringing it out again, so you can see how all these connect at conversion. We must know that our child's will is yielded to our will.

Many everyday activities can be used to bring the child's will into subjection and hold it there. They have foods they don't like, toys they want to play with, and chores they don't feel like doing. There are naps they don't want to take, and morning times when they don't want to get up. There are many opportunies to train the child's will. We should be asking ourselves the question, "Is my child's will yielded to me?"

The Emotions

The affections and feelings of children like the other parts of their being are totally blank. We have the blessed opportunity to train the palate of their soul from the time of birth. Just as a parent enjoys introducing new foods to a growing baby, we can enjoy training them to love what we love. Here is where example plays a very important part. What we set our affections to love our children will set their affections to love. Although God is not living inside a four-year-old child, that child can love to go to church because you love to go to church. He can learn to love singing the songs or going out on the streets to pass out tracts. Words and repetition do not teach this. It is taught only by the example of the parents affections. This example then is picked up by the emotions of the child and he finds his affections set on the right things even though God is not inside of him yet.

A little two-year-old boy will want his Bible in his hand. He can't read it, and he doesn't know what is in it, but there is something inside of him that he picked up from his father and mother that says, "There is something special about this book called a Bible." He is going to hold it in his little hand and carry it to church proudly. What is he doing? He is setting his affections on the things his parents have set their affections to love. Bless God, someday the Spirit of God is going to come inside the child and then he really is going to get excited about the Bible.

Until then, let us guide the affections of our children in the ways they should go by examples. We must guide them to love the right things and hate the wrong things. Watch the thrill level of your children. I say more about this in the next chapter. What thrills your children? That is, what they are setting their affections to love. Today it is called a rush, a rush of their emotions. I want my children's emotions to rush when they walk through the doors of the church on Sunday morning.

Our emotions cover more than just our affections. We express anger with our emotions. We express love through our emotions, and many other things. A child's emotions should be trained to express the proper emotions at the proper times. Wouldn't it be a blessing to them if they had never had an outburst of anger in their emotional experiences. It is possible. If they never see and hear one at home, and they are never allowed to view one on TV, they may not ever express one. Emotions are caught, as I explain in the next chapter.

The whole purpose of teaching and training is to fill the mind with the right things, to guide the will to choose the right, and to encourage the emotions to get excited about the right things. If you work these three things together, godly character will come into the heart and life of your children even though God is not inside them yet.

The Body

Let us go on to the body. We do our children a great favor if we help them gain control over their bodies. We do them a great favor if we protect them and help them stay pure in their bodies. They are going to have to live with that body and the patterns of that body all the rest of their days on the earth. If we with loving direction guide our children into proper habits, these will just be normal life to them.

For example, when you hear the alarm go off, you get out of bed, right? Or maybe it isn't that way with you, and if it isn't that way with you, I can almost guarantee it wasn't that way with you growing up. No one made you get up when you were called. So here you are, many years later. Even though you love God and want to do what is right, you don't get up when the alarm goes off. For your children, it can be as normal as 1-2-3. When the alarm goes off, you get out of bed. You tell your body, "Body, get up! I'm in charge, and it is time to get up. You are going to eat green beans body. I'm in charge. Not you." Some people think it is ridiculous to work with your children in this way, but the body is going to rule them if you don't teach them to rule their bodies. They can look at those green beans on their plate and say, "Praise God, they're not my favorite. But we are going to eat green beans today because that is what mother has put on the plate." They can even learn to thank God for those beans with a sincere heart.

Help your children bring their bodies under subjection. Watch over them, guide them, and keep them from defiling their bodies. Don't let them go play behind closed doors. Don't let them go play in the barns on Sunday afternoon while you're having such a good time talking about the Bible. They may defile their body by the suggestion of a playmate.

It is our urgent responsibility to watch over these things. Why? Because someday God is going to come and dwell inside them, and they will have to deal with their bodies. Praise God, He can deliver them and purify them of their passions, but what a blessed favor if we keep them from these things. Talk to your children and communicate with them about these things up to their level, God giving you wisdom. The purpose is to teach them to keep themselves pure.

The Pursuit of Godly Seed

I am not talking about making a robot out of your children. I'm talking about having a vision and understanding where God is going with them. I am going to guide my children in such a way that they will have a ten-step head start on me when I was born again. How beautiful it is for the child whose body and soul has been guided and disciplined in right paths. It's easy to see what will happen when they come to a saving knowledge of Jesus Christ. The battles will be short lived if we have helped them in these areas.

John Wesley did not get converted until he was thirty-five years of age. But the things his mother put in him gave him an advantage. All the things she kept from him and all the disciplines she ordered for his life helped him. He knew how to get up in the morning. He knew how to drink the castor oil that didn't taste good. He knew how to be content with lesser things. Then when he was thirty-five years old, he was listening to the introduction to the book of Romans by Martin Luther, and a light went on inside his soul. God came to dwell in that man named John Wesley. God, living within him, turned England upside down. He didn't have a lot of garbage in his life. He rose, went forth, and ran for the glory of God.

I have been doing a lot of research into godly homes of the past. I have observed that the men and women who were preserved and trained seemed to have more grace on them when they get converted. There was a special blessing upon them. When the Spirit of God comes to dwell inside the children who are guided through their days in Christian principles, they just take off running. The others, like me, stumble around quite a bit. O, we are there, and we love God. But we stumble around quite a bit. Let's give our children the edge that we didn't have. May God help us.

Prayer
O God, who dwells in man, hear us. We pray for wisdom to build temples for the living God to dwell in. Lord, we live in a difficult age. Media are everywhere calling to our little ones. Make us strong to protect them in Jesus' name. Amen.

A Dwelling Place For the Living God

Meditations

GOD NEEDS MEN

Men who will stand before Him and hear His voice daily.
Men who love righteousness and hate iniquity.
Men who are full of the Holy Ghost.
Men who are rooted and grounded in Calvary-type love.
Men whose hearts are clothed with humility.
GOD NEEDS MEN!
Men who are firm, diligent, and hardworking.
Men who are gentle enough to play with their children.
Men who know the joys of a disciplined life.
Men who are not afraid of trials and hardships.
Men who are not enslaved to the world's entertainments.
GOD NEEDS MEN!
Men who find their delight in God alone.
Men who are full of joy and the fruits of His Spirit.
Men who follow the promptings of the Holy Spirit.
Men who pray effectual, fervent prayers.
Men who tremble at God's Word.
GOD NEEDS MEN!
Men who are open to criticism and correction.
Men who will not cool off in their devotion to Christ.
Men who will not compromise their convictions.
Men who will train their children to the glory of God.
Men who discern all of life from heaven's point of view.
GOD NEEDS MEN!
God needs men who burn with passion.
God needs men with Spiritual Authority.
God needs men of Christ-like character.
O God, in this our day. Raise up men who walk this way.

24

Father: The Watchman

> *The wall of Jerusalem also is broken down,*
> *and the gates thereof are burned with fire. . . .*
> *When I heard these words, . . .*
> *I sat down and wept, and mourned certain days,*
> *and fasted and prayed before the God of heaven.*
> Nehemiah 1:3b,4b

As a father, I tremble at times as I ponder the responsibility I have to protect my children from the influence of evil. We live in a world that is coming up with new inventions almost daily. Because of "progress," this world is able quickly to inform us and our children of its latest pleasures. How does a godly family deal with all of this? In the preceding chapter, we saw the overwhelming blessing that results when parents train and preserve the body and soul of their children. This chapter deals with some practical ways by which we can protect our children's minds and bodies. I have some strong things to say here, and I pray that God will give you an open heart to reconsider some very important issues that affect your children.

Nehemiah was an overseer. He was the governor of Jerusalem during the time of rebuilding after the captivity. The opening verses reflect the deep burden he had when he heard that the wall of Jerusalem still was broken down and the gates had not been repaired. City walls were needed to stop the enemy from flooding in and overtaking the people. The gates were there so that with the help of a gatekeeper, no one could sneak in and destroy from within. God's people were living without any protection from their enemies. Nehemiah was greatly burdened about his people's vulnerable condition.

Let's use this illustration to focus on the protection of our homes. Father is Nehemiah, the overseer, and the one responsible for the welfare of the family. He builds a wall around his family by raising up basic Bible standards that the family should live by. He not only is concerned about the convictions of the home (the walls), but he also is responsible for the gate. We fathers are supposed to stand at the gate of our households and make sure nothing gets through the gate that could destroy the family from within.

John Bunyan wrote an allegory called *The Holy War*. It is a story about the devil's attempt to conquer and control Mansoul, or the soul of man. In this story, man's soul is likened to a city with five gates. The enemy makes his way into the city through these gates. The gates represent man's five senses. It is not just a story, for it represents the realities of how Satan does indeed take control of man through these very gates. We don't have to look very far to see how he still is using ways and means to enter the souls of men through the same gates.

That brings us again to the fathers. In this modern world, our families are in desperate need of a gatekeeper who will with loving scrutiny check out everything that tries to get into the home through the gates. The gates are five: the eyes, the ears, the nose, the mouth, and the touch. A discerning father will watch out for dangerous influences in these areas. Most of us agree that there is something drastically wrong with the Christian home and the church. I believe these five gates are at least part of the problem.

What Is the World?

This is a question that every evangelical needs to re-ask himself. We have lost a clear unquestionable definition of "the world." It seems that Bunyan's Vanity Fair now dwells in the church. It is time for an examination. Forty million American "Christians" profess to believe in the doctrine of separation from the world. Yet, recent polls indicate that there is no difference at all between the lifestyle of Christians, and the rest of the people in our land. In some aspects such as divorce, Christians are worse than they are. It is time to make an evaluation of where we are heading.

We all believe in separation, but very few are separated. That makes us hearers, but not doers of the Word. The world is under judgment. It is reserved unto fire. It is a sinking ship, and everyone is dancing while it is slowly going down. I like what Tozer said: "The world is not a battlefield anymore; it is a playground." I know this probably sounds pretty strong to some of you, but somebody needs to blow the trumpet in Zion. American Christians are losing their children to the world en masse. I just heard the testimony of the man who pastors of one of the largest churches in nation. This church is supposed to believe in separation from the world, yet it loses fifty percent of its young people to the world. But, they do play in the world all the time, and most of the youth activities center around fun. Again I ask, what is the world? Maybe we need to evaluate our definition.

This is not a teaching on the doctrine of nonconformity. I have simply raised the question so that I may address some destructive influences that are eroding sincere attempts to raise a family for the Lord.

I have observed over the past twenty years that when parents get serious about raising their children "in the nurture and admonition of the Lord," they suddenly take a fresh look at what is coming in at the gate of their home. I want to fan the flames of this new desire by taking a very frank look at what we have invited into our homes. Many have allowed a host of evil teachers to gather their children around them and teach them *"the way of the heathen"* (Jer. 10:2a). To some of you, I know I probably will sound as though I have come from another planet, but I am willing to be misunderstood. I cannot be silent. What I write, I write with a deep burden. At times, I hurt inside with a grief that overcomes me. Even while writing this chapter, I learned of the latest deceptive teacher who is allowed in the homes of millions of Christians. I just sat astonished and grief-stricken for a long time. Fathers, please consider your ways.

Who Dwells in your House?

Before reading Psalm 101 quoted after this paragraph, consider its emphasis. I call this Scripture the fathers' Psalm. David wrote it, and his dedicated heart expresses itself so beautifully. In reading the text, it is easy to discern who does not dwell in his house. My sincere challenge to each father is "Who dwells in your house?" O that every father reading this chapter would make this Psalm his prayer. Let us consider some of the evil teachers we have allowed into our houses.

> *I will behave myself wisely in a perfect way....I will walk within my house with a perfect heart. I will set no wicked thing before mine eyes: I hate the work of them that turn aside; it shall not cleave to me...Mine eyes shall be upon the faithful of the land, that they may dwell with me: He that walketh in a perfect way, he shall serve me. He that worketh deceit shall not dwell within my house: He that telleth lies shall not tarry in my sight.*
>
> Psalms 101:2-4,6-7

Television.

A whole chapter could be written about the evil character of this teacher. He has slain his ten thousands. No single influence has destroyed more lives than he. The "positive" advertisement proclaims the negative reality quite clearly: "We bring the world into your home."

The television is full of those who turn aside from the Lord. How can we set our children down before them? It is a wicked thing that we have set before their eyes. Through the eye gate, our children are inflamed with passions that plague them all their days. Most of those who stand before the cameras are filled with lies and deceit. If we place their opinions and values next to the Word of God, they are antichrist. We are warned to *"walk not in the counsel of the ungodly"* (Ps. 1:1).

The television is Satan's number one tool to train the next generation in his ways of evil. America is drunk on this thing. She stumbles on in silly ignorance, drinking at its fountain, laughing at its utter foolishness, not knowing that the serpent is there. God's people should not be there with them and our precious children should not be allowed to sit at its feet, and bow at its altar.

I once heard a sermon preached by Billy Graham in 1953. It was a powerful, prophetic message to the Christians in our land. He warned us in 1953 of the destruction the TV would work in our homes. This was back when television was "okay." He said it would be used by the devil to rob Christian's of their quiet times. Was he ever on target with that prophecy!

I personally believe this issue is urgent and calls for strong measures. Fathers, take that wicked thing and hew it in pieces before the Lord and your family. Throw that evil teacher out of your house and lock the gate afterward.

Movies and Drama

Hollywood is like the troubled sea that cannot rest. Its waters cast up mire and dirt continually. I have set this evil teacher by itself because I feel he reaches far beyond the television. The theaters, the videos, and now the DVDs all are shouting for the attention of our children. For the most part, they have gotten what they are crying for. This form of media is Deception with a capital *D*. It is all fake. It is all an unreality. Hurting people put on false faces, and act as though they are enjoying the blessings of life when in reality they are dying on the inside and contemplating suicide. Why would we want to sit our precious sons and daughters down before these hypocrites?

There also is the matter of desensitizing the conscience about sin. Watching people sin in the movies has a dulling effect on anyone. After you watch so many murders, the murder isn't so bad. My children have never watched movies. If I permitted them to view one of these bloody movies, they would be in utter shock. I would never do such a thing.

The thing that makes a movie interesting is drama. Drama is the use of extreme emotions to make a story grip the audience. Anger must become wrath, love must be manifested in deep lust, and disagreement must become a slugging fight, or it just isn't very good. The flesh is never satisfied with what it sees, so the movies move on to rape, murder, and witchcraft.

Where will this all end? When will America realize that she is training her own terrorists and purveyors of destruction by these means? We Christians must bail out of this sinking ship, and we must do it now. Have a burning in your back yard in Jesus' name.

Modern Toys

One courageous man (Phil Phillips) wrote a book some time ago called *Turmoil in the Toy Box*. It never hit the best-sellers' list, and it probably offended many, but the man was right on in his evaluations of toys. Toys are not tools for innocent child's play. The devil wants you to think that they are, but they are not. Play has always been practice and meditation for future living. We all know this if we stop and think for a minute. When hearts were right, the toys were baby dolls and tractors, and real life followed accordingly. It is not this way anymore. Times have changed. The function of toys still is the same. Children in America still are practicing and meditating for future conduct, but what kind of toys are they playing with these days? The baby doll has become a Barbie doll that wears miniskirts and paints her face. She has a figure that is impossible to match. But girls are trying with every means they can think of to match it, including anorexia and bulimia. The tractor has been replaced with a hot rod that peals down the street and is the pride of every young man's dreams. These are the firstfruits of destruction.

We have gone way beyond these to utterly evil, demonic toys. You can now practice witchcraft and prepare for deep satanic rituals by purchasing Dungeons and Dragons. The stuffed toys have been replaced with these gruesome-looking creatures from the underworld of the damned. Brothers and sisters, Satan is behind all this. My heart hurts when I think how many of our children are ignorantly playing with these evil teachers. I have listed a few. There are many more. Parents, I beg you to meditate on this principle of play, and then start evaluating your toy box. Play is practice for future living. What are your children practicing to be and do?

The World of Thrills
Have you looked in a dictionary for the definition of this word "thrill?" It is very revealing and helps me understand why there is never enough. According to Websters 1828 dictionary, a *thrill* is "a sharp shivering sensation running through the body." It means "to give a rush of pleasure, to penetrate the body with intense sensations." Thus, the whole idea of more and more thrills is sensual in its roots. Worldly men are working overtime to come up with another thrill that is a little higher than the last one. And the masses are running after them as fast as they come out.

There is never enough; 200 mph is not fast enough. The old rides at the amusement park are not good enough. The rush is gone, and the crowds must have another one. Now, they tie a rubber band around the waist and jump off the side of a mountain. The rush they get is the feeling of free fall onto the rocks below. What perversion!

We watch over the thrill level of the children at our house. Oddly enough, the children still get a thrill out of going to McDonalds for a meal together or riding bikes. We are teaching our sons and daughters to be excited with more basic things in life.

Reading Material
Most children are avid readers. It seems as though they can never get enough books to read. This presents a real challenge to parents. We are the ones responsible to screen their reading material. I encourage you to stick to the true and the real and to stay away from the imaginary. America is being overrun with "Christian novels" these days, and the church is eating up these books by the millions. They have either a story of romance or a fast-paced drama in them.

The romance novels are read mostly by ladies and girls. I feel these books are dangerous for our daughters and wives to read. They present an unreal, fuzzy kind of love affair that is not true to real life. A girl's lust for romance is stimulated while reading these books. Dozens of times I have heard of girls reading till three o'clock in the morning to finish such a book. Let us read the Bible till three o'clock in the morning. Our daughters get an unrealistic idea about what love is, and then they are disappointed with their marriage because it is not like the book. Fathers, guard their hearts and keep them for the one man whom God brings into their life.

Foolish Playmates

Proverbs 13:20 says, *"He that walketh with wise men shall be wise, but a companion of fools shall be destroyed."* This scripture is not written to children, but it certainly applies to them. There is a mentality among parents that allows nonsense and foolishness in small children when they play. This is very dangerous. I have learned, sometimes the hard way, that foolishness breeds worse things when parents are not looking. Choosing playmates for your children is not a small matter.

Computer Games

A caution about these "innocent" games has been raised in the past few years because of all the high school shootings. Even the secular media is raising questions about the connection between the practice of these games and youth walking down the halls of the school shooting their classmates. Because of "progress," these games are getting more realistic all the time. You actually feel as though you are in the game, standing before an enemy when you blow his guts out. The blood even flies everywhere when you shoot. You may say, "We don't go for the ones that are that bad." Okay, I'm glad for that, but who wants to participate in of any of it? Remember, your children are practicing for real life as they play. The golf games got boring and gave way to the killing games long ago.

The Internet

We have Internet access at our house. It is fast becoming a tool for every kind of business and activity you can imagine. Although we do use the Internet, our usage is very limited, and no one is allowed to log on without someone else in the room. The children are not allowed access to the Internet at all. We use it a few times in a week to gather information about a subject or product of interest.

The first issue I see with the Internet is the time issue. The amount of time wasted on this one thing alone is staggering. The main issue, however, is the filth available to those who go looking for it. It has been the greatest curse to American men. It has revealed the low level of spiritual strength to which Christian men have slipped. The dangers to our children are obvious. There is some really good software available that protects the family from this evil. Don't wait until you have a tragedy to do something about it. Do it now. Develop some kind of accountability to cover your family.

"Christian Rock" Music

When Balaam could not curse Israel because of God's blessing on them, he thought of another way to curse Israel indirectly. He counseled Balak to destroy them from the inside. He sent sensual women down into the camp of Israel, and the rest is history. This is the story that comes to my mind when I consider the destructive influence wrong music has had on the youth of America.

That would be sad enough, but the influence has reached over into the Christian realm, and now the church is dancing to the world's music, with some sanctified words thrown in. Even the subtitle I have used is a misnomer. Those two words do not go together anymore than the words "Christian gambling" or "Christian beer" go together.

I want to encourage you fathers to stand at the gate and check out the music your children are listening to. We spoke about authority in an earlier chapter. Here is where the rubber meets the road. Sit the family down; and get a clear understanding from all that you will be checking their music.

Silly Bible Stories

Some time back, maybe twenty years or so, it came into the minds of Christian educators that children learn better if the material is funny. Well, the children did really sit up and listen as they laughed their way through the Bible story. From there, the educators went to silly puppets, which really made everyone laugh. By now, it is the norm. Most material for the little ones is full of this "nonsense" method of teaching. Moses is a funny little man with a big round nose and eyes that look like those of a Precious Moments baby instead of a prophet. Where are they going with all this? Do you really think this is the way to pass on "the faith" to the next generation? I hardly think so. Now they have put the characters in animated cartoons with silly voices, and have distorted the prophet Moses. These "creative educators" have now come up with the greatest perversion of them all. King David is a cucumber playing his harp. This whole thing is the devil's device to water down the word of God and His testimonies. How do we ever expect these children to tremble at the story of Moses when he has been introduced to him through all this.? I feel this is a poor choice of babysitters and an even poorer choice of teachers.

These are the evil teachers we have invited into our homes to entertain our children while we do "better things." I am deeply burdened about all this. Most of these poor choices have happened because fathers have not been watching the gates. Many fathers don't even know that they are the ones responsible to deal with all these influences. Maybe you feel I have been too strong. I'm sorry. It is not my desire to offend. Leonard Ravenhill says, "Prophets are for crises hours." Forgive me, but I feel we are in one.

Dear fathers, are the walls and the gates of your home broken down? Have you directed your family with holy standards? I pray that God will give you the strength and courage to cleanse your home of anything that defiles. Don't be harsh. Don't act like a bull, but with calm quiet authority cleanse your house. Have a family burning in the back yard. Sing a few songs, read some Scriptures, and burn that stuff in Jesus Christ's name.

I want to say a word to all the wives who are reading this. Your husband needs your support as he attempts to rid his house of all uncleanness. Stand behind your man. You do unwisely if you resist his actions concerning these things. Many a father has been stopped from eliminating evil from his house by the pleadings of the children and the pressures of his wife. Remember, you are the one who prayed that God would make your husband a spiritual leader.

25

The Fulfilled Woman

> *Who can find a virtuous woman?*
> *for her price is far above rubies.*
>
> *Proverbs 31:10*

This verse is no doubt one of the most powerful verses in the whole Bible. Many treasures are hidden in it and the verses that follow in the chapter. There is a warfare raging for God and His Kingdom, for the souls of men, and for our families. This war has strategies that Satan does not want us to find. He knows if we find them, they will be his doom. The powerful woman, proclaimed in the opening scripture, is one of those strategies. Her affect on the outcome of this war is staggering. I am sure none of us know just how influential she really is. But Satan knows, and he also knows *woman*. He knows very well how to deceive her.

It seems he has come to her again in the last days with a questioning spirit, a seducing spirit, saying, *"Yea, hath God said?"* She, like Eve of old, has again been convinced to take a bite of the new fruit, not realizing that it is the old fruit with the old curse hidden in it. To Eve, the way looked pleasant to the eyes, and she was assured of an exalted position and wisdom she never knew before. O, the confusion that has come by the choices she made!

We are focusing on a godly seed, and this fall that even Christian women have made is greatly affecting the generations of children being born. We cannot aim for godly children if we are not willing to come to grips with the role of women in the home.

For the next few chapters, I want to address the sisters concerning this beautiful woman of whom we have lost sight. My desire is to raise the calling of women back up to the high, high place God intended it to occupy. I know I could lose my head over some of the lost principles I am going to bring back into the light. That is okay with me. I cannot help but speak. The eternal Word speaks so clearly about this powerful woman in so many places that I feel a little like Amos the prophet, who said, *"The Lord God hath spoken, who can but prophesy."* (Amos 3:8b).

Our "Christian world" is changing so fast these days that I will probably seem like an alien to some. You know how they say, "What planet did he come from?" There are many hidden forces working overtime to bury the glorious revelation of a Christian woman forever. I plan to dig it back up, clean the dirt off it, and put it on display for all to see again.

Sometimes things happen (mysteries) that I a minister of the Gospel don't understand. At such times I just hide the mystery in my heart, hoping I will understand it later. You, dear sisters, are one of those mysteries to me. I haven't had many opportunities to speak to sisters, but I have had a few. Each time I do, an unusual awe and burden comes over me. Something unusual goes on inside my heart. It is the same whether I speak or write. I have often wondered, "What is this deep sense of awe all about?" Even as I sit here typing before the computer, the same burdened anointing to minister to you and affirm you in your calling has come upon me. I believe it is because you are very special to God. I believe it is because you are a powerful force in this holy war, and God is calling to you.

My desire is to enlighten you, inspire you, and activate you in such a way that you will never again feel as though you are "just a woman." You are very important to God. He has a special work for you to do, and He has already given the methods that produce the work. Yes, it is true that in this life most of you will not stand in prominent places. You will not move the crowds with the preaching of the Word and rise to places of public praise and honor. However, eternity will reveal the power of your hidden position. Eternity will show it.

A Paradox

In considering the influence and role of a godly woman, we must recognize from the start that we are dealing with one of the paradoxes in the Bible. You know many of these paradoxes: the way up is down; give away and you will receive; lose your life and you will find it. A paradox challenges our logic, but remember, God's ways and man's ways are very different.

The role of a Christian woman is supportive, hidden, and many times unknown to others, yet her power and influence often exceed those of a man in public ministry. Remember dear Susanna Wesley. Consider the New Testament path to greatness that Jesus taught. Greatness comes as we live the life of a servant. Jesus illustrated this path by the example of washing someone's feet. This is a beautiful picture of serving others. Can we carry this principle over into the life of a wife and mother? I think we certainly can. God has called you women to a life of greatness, but it is a paradox.

Did you ever consider the life of the angels? Their life is hidden. Most of the time they are never seen. Most of the time people don't even know that they did anything. God gets all the glory from these magnificent heavenly creatures. They are concealed from human view, yet they do a myriad of different tasks.

Think about the work of angels for a moment. An accident is about to happen. Angels are on the scene, yet invisible. They grab the steering wheel and guide the car to safety. When the car stops, and we know we have been spared, we bow our heads and thank God for His care over us. We say not a word to the angel. God gets all the glory. Oh, purify our motives, dear Lord, and give us eternal eyes to see our service as unto the Lord as the angels do. There is something beautiful hidden here for you sisters. Your lives and ministry are very much like theirs. Do you see it? Keep looking. It will begin to shine if you keep your eyes open.

Think about the life of Joshua. For forty-two years he served Moses faithfully. Very little is mentioned about him until Moses died. Do you think Moses could have served God the way he did if he hadn't had a Joshua to serve him and support him?

Earlier I mentioned the raging war about us. Every military man knows that if he doesn't have a solid support unit working behind the scenes, he will not be able to win the war. This is a good way to describe the role you sisters play. In fact, if the soldier doesn't have that secluded unit of support in place, he will not even go out to the battle. Today's modern woman has a problem being the support unit that God intended her to be. Shall the support unit say, "If I can't be on the front, then I won't be in the war?"

My father was a medic during World War II. That is the job he was given to do. What if he had said, "I won't do that job." What kind of battle could have been fought without a medic to care for the wounded? Is the man on the front lines more important than the medic? Of course not. We all know this to be true. But somehow, when it comes to the roles of husband and wife, or the parts to be played by father and mother, we have lost our way. Our God, who is the Creator, has made this world and given order to it according to His wisdom. He has robed greatness in the form of a servant and promised exaltation on the path of humility. God is calling the Christian woman to lose her life, to throw it away by taking the secondary and supportive roles in His order.

God's Ordained Purpose for Woman

> *Who can find a virtuous woman? For her price is far above rubies. The heart of her husband doth safely trust in her, so that he shall have no need of spoil. She will do him good and not evil all the days of her life.*
> *Proverbs 31:10-12*

"*Who can find a virtuous woman?*" This is given not only as a question, but also as a clarion call, as if to say, "Where are they?" This call is becoming a cry in America that gets louder and louder. If this cry for a virtuous woman was needed in Solomon's day, how much more is it needed in this our day. Where do you find this kind of woman today? I do rejoice that more and more women are "coming home" and finding sweet peace and fulfillment in supporting their husbands. Still, it is hard to find women who are willing to stay home and guide the household for their husbands.

Where do you find women who will be hidden, supporting their husbands, women willing to hide in the shadows, pray for their husbands, be a blessing to them, and honor them all the days of their life? I know the heart cry of you sisters. You want be that virtuous woman for your husband, and I want to remind you that you are highly valued by God. Many times when I preach on this subject, men come up to me after the service and tell me, "Brother Denny, I have one of those virtuous women. I don't deserve her, but I have one." If you are one of these men, you have a treasure that cannot be measured. If you've found one of these women, you have something more valuable than a whole handful of rubies.

The verses at the beginning of this section picture a beautiful woman whose life is all wrapped up in being a helpmeet to her husband. His heart safely trusts in her, and he doesn't have a worry. He knows she will never leave him. Her commitment to him is sure, and he has confidence in her. He knows she will be his loving, supportive wife *"all the days of her life."* She will be the mother of his children *"all the days of her life."* We see a woman whose heart's desire is to live for him, and please him. *"She will do him good, and not evil."* How long? In contemporary terms, "till death do us part." He can count on her and trust her with his money. He knows what her responses will be in the thick and thin of life. He knows she will guide the home according to his heart when he is away. This woman pictured here is valuable, a priceless jewel, a crown to any husband.

Dear sisters, this is a foundation stone that must be laid in every godly home. This is God's revealed purpose for woman, plain and simple, and to the point. You will never see the godly children you are longing to have if you cannot, or will not, nestle down in this beautiful purpose for which you were made. From a man's perspective, with this kind of supportive wife a man can do anything. She is a hidden source of strength that continually charges his mental and emotional batteries.

Wo—man: Taken Out of Man

It may surprise some of you sisters to know that God did not make you to raise your children. That was not His primary purpose for creating Eve. Although childrearing is one of the duties most of you will have in your life, it was not God's first purpose.

God made you for your husband. That is why you are here. If God had not seen the need of man for a helpmeet, there would be no women. I cringe a bit to make this statement because public opinion is so contrary to this. Yet God's Word clearly reveals why you were made.

Many a mother finds her primary fulfillment in her children. To live for her children is her joy, her blessing, and her fulfillment. This is a bit out of order. It is a little like serving people without having a relationship with God. It is good, but it is out of sync with God's beautiful plan for us. Although it is true that much of your life is filled with those precious blessings God has given (and they are fulfilling), your greatest satisfaction will come from being a helpmeet to your husband. You will experience the height of joy, contentment, and blessings in doing what you can do to bless the life of the man that chose you to be his wife. Look at what God says about you in Genesis 2:18, 21-23.

> *And the LORD God said, it is not good that the man should be **alone**; I will make him an help meet for him...And the LORD God caused a deep sleep to fall upon Adam, and he slept and He took one of his ribs, and closed up the flesh instead thereof; and the rib, which the LORD God had taken from man, made he a woman, and brought her unto the man. And Adam said, This is now bone of my bones, and flesh of my flesh: she shall be called Woman, because she was taken out of Man.*

These verses are very revealing if you believe them, and I do believe them. This is the recorded account of your naming. Adam gave you your name. His name was "ish" (man) and he named his wife "Isha" (woman) "because she was taken out of man." Do you see your very name reveals why you are here.

The Fulfilled Woman

Let us picture these verses for a few moments. Part of meditation is to picture what is being said. There are some awesome scenes before us in these Scriptures. Here we have God watching over His creation and observing Adam whom He had made. He begins speaking to Himself in the Godhead: *"It is not good that the man should be alone. I will make him an help meet for him."* Then, it seems as though the scene switches. All the animals are brought before Adam, and he gives them their names. Adam watches them come by: male, female, male, female. They come two by two. When Adam finishes, there is not found a female for him. It seems God was preparing Adam for the gift he was about to receive.

God caused Adam to sleep, and the first surgery was performed. A rib was taken out of his side, and from that rib God formed a female, Adam's counterpart. He took the woman He had made and brought her to Adam. Can you imagine how he must have felt that day? Here is a woman. She is like me, yet not like me. She was made from me and made for me. Oh, he must have been delighted that day! He must have been filled with joy that day when all of a sudden he woke up and found that God had given him a helpmeet (a wife).

Have you ever stopped to think about how Eve must have felt? This is pretty awesome too. She was not, and then all of a sudden, she was, she found herself existing. There she was, standing before Adam and God. Maybe she had that unspoken question on her face, "Why am I here?"

Perhaps God explained to her: "You've been made for this man. Adam is his name. You were needed for him, so I made you." Can you imagine how that must have settled down over her heart? Do you think she had any problem getting in her place before the Fall? She had to think, "I am here because of Adam! If it weren't for him, I wouldn't even be here." Her place as a helper was clear. Her place under his authority was clear. Her place of gratitude also was clear. Oh how beautiful!

Here is the true spirit of marriage, isn't it? If we could take those two pictures and just meditate on them, it would greatly enhance our marriages. The spirit of this revelation in the Scriptures is the heart of God for marriage. The man says: "God has given me a gift." The woman says: "God has made me for this man, and I am a gift for this man, to be his helpmeet."

Ah, that is a blessing! The full revelation of this reality was upon Eve, and it needs to be upon each one of you sisters also. This is your purpose. This is the reason why you are here.

This teaching is not just some archaic idea extracted from Genesis. You will also find it clearly revealed several places in the New Testament. Nothing has changed although six thousand years have passed by. This revelation, as it sinks down in your heart can change your life, if it hasn't already. Sister, don't pass it off too quickly. Think about it. Put yourself in Eve's place for a while. Think thoughts after her. Think about how she felt and feel the same things. God wants you to drink deeply from this revelation of His purpose for creating you. It will absolutely transform your life and your home. Your life will explode with meaning as you come to grips with this revelation. The women who have done so are the happiest, most fulfilled women on this earth.

Prayer

Dear Lord Jesus, I pray for the dear sisters who have read this chapter. Speak deeply to each one of them. Lord, the devil has lied to them and blinded them from the greatest purpose of their lives. Open their eyes to see the power and the beauty hidden in that great purpose. In Jesus name. Amen.

26

The Hidden Woman

*Her husband is known in the gates,
when he sitteth among the elders of the land.*

A virtuous woman is a crown to her husband.
                                                Proverbs 31:23; 12:4a

Have you ever made the connection between the woman mentioned in Proverbs 12 and the beautiful description of a godly woman found in chapter 31. The Bible defines itself, and these two passages are no exception. If a man has found himself a virtuous woman, like the one defined, she is a crown of glory to him. Even as it says in I Cor. 11:7b, *"The woman is the glory of the man."* Proverbs 31 clearly shows that the role of this woman is a supportive one. She is involved in the important things of her husband's household. It is also clear from verse 23 that her supportive activity propels her husband into places of influence and leadership. This is a good illustration of the powerful effect that a woman has on her man. Hidden influences are at work here that bring blessings, encouragement, and moral strength to a man. These are secrets known only by godly women who have dared to believe, trust, and obey, women who have tasted the fruits of obedience as their husbands have risen to bless them and thank them for their practical love.

Behind Every Great Man Is a Hidden Woman

A famous proverb in our land is often quoted in the context of history: "Behind every great man, there is a great woman." This saying has a worldly origin, but probably was coined with the right understanding of the woman's place in relation to the man.

But let me tell you what this proverb means in our modern context. It is believed that every great man has a woman behind the scenes pushing him, challenging him, and telling him to go, that there is a woman making him great, motivating, driving him, and causing him to rise up and become a great man. This is the worldly interpretation of the statement.

Despite this wordly view, I do believe this proverb. However, we need to give it a biblical interpretation.

A woman does have a powerful influence on her man, some positive and some negative. In fact, she probably is the most influential person in his life. So, what is this "great woman" behind this great man like? I think a change of one word in this proverb will sanctify it and put it in godly order. "Behind every great man, there is a *hidden* woman." We have already seen what the Bible calls greatness, so, *hidden* fits very well. A hidden woman, as Proverbs describes, is one who has found her place and her power before God and her husband in a supportive role. Yes, it is true that behind every great man, there probably is a godly woman, praying, supporting, loving, and admiring her man.

Mothers and daughters, this is true greatness. I encourage you to open your heart and ask God to fill it with the spirit of this teaching. Make it the longing desire of your heart to become, yea to develop the characteristics of a virtuous woman, the characteristics of a hidden woman.

Mrs. J. Frank Norris

When I think of a hidden woman my mind goes to the illustration of J. Frank Norris. Most of you probably don't recognize him. He was a famous Baptist preacher who lived in the 1930s during the Prohibition days. Back in the early days of his ministry, J. Frank Norris was a dud. He was a flop, a powerless preacher. When he preached, souls were not saved and lives were not changed.

The Hidden Woman

Evaluating his life and ministry, he decided, "I'm not effective. God is not using me. I am going to get out of the ministry." This is how he was feeling. But J. Frank Norris had a wife who was a hidden woman. She didn't tell him he was a dud. She didn't sit him down and tell him what a flop he was. She didn't remind him on Sunday afternoon that no souls got saved when he preached that day. She didn't do that. She was a hidden woman. She was a wise woman who carried a burden for her husband's need. God laid it upon her heart to pray and fast for her husband three days. She didn't know that he was planning to resign his position and get out of the ministry.

As the story goes, Frank had some meetings in a certain town in Texas. He decided, "I'll go to these meetings, and when they are over, I'm done. I'm quitting."

Well, that happened to be the very week that God had burdened Frank's wife to pray earnestly for her husband. O, how she prayed! She prayed day and night. She prayed without ceasing, with a fervent heart, and God began to move.

On the last night of the meetings, Frank stepped into the pulpit, ready to preach the last sermon of his ministry. As he was standing behind the pulpit, something happened to him. God began to move upon his heart in a mighty way. God's Spirit began to prevail upon him, and he preached in a way he had never preached before. The anointing of God fell on the meeting, and revival broke out in the church. Hardened sinners came down the aisle. Families got right, and there was brokeness everywhere. He dealt with people until midnight that night.

After the meeting was over, he called his wife. He could hardly contain himself in telling her what had happened. He kept trying to tell her, yet he repeatedly broke down and cried.

Finally, he managed, "Oh, Honey, God poured His blessing out tonight, and I'm a changed man. There is hope for me."

They rejoiced and praised God together for His sweet deliverance.

Mrs. Norris wasn't at all surprised by the good news. She had been fasting and praying, and she had prayed through to victory. She had an answer from God that He was going to bless her husband. Praise God. I don't know how that fits your theology on prayer, but we need more sisters who have learned how to pray through till they get an answer for their husbands.

Dear sisters, Frank's wife was a hidden woman. She was just like that angel I mentioned earlier. She knew what she had done, but she stood silent, and joined her husband in thanking God. J. Frank Norris had a jewel, doing him "good and not evil all the days of her life" (Pro. 31:12).

Frank came back from that meeting with a new courage in his heart and a blessing on his ministry. He went on to pastor two large churches at the same time: one in Fort Worth, Texas, and one in Detroit, Michigan. Both churches grew by evangelism until five thousand people were attending each. Frank traveled back and forth every two weeks between the two congregations for many years.

Let me ask you a question. In eternity, do you think Mrs. Norris will receive any rewards for her hidden work? We all know the answer. Do it again, Lord, do it again.

Great Men and Their Wives

As I pondered the influence that great women have had on their husbands, I thought of several other well-known men who were "known in the gates." I'm sure there are exceptions to this principle, but most of the time you will find one of these godly, hidden women behind the scenes. There they are serving, praying, and supporting their man as he becomes great.

> **D. L. Moody** had Emma, who traveled with him, teaching the children on the road and setting up housekeeping dozens of times. According to him, she was one of the most stabilizing influences in his life. She was full of gracious kindness, and her example slowly turned the great evangelist into a compassionate winner of many souls.

> **Robert Moffat** had his Mary, who sacrificially established his household in a mud hut, surrounded by jungle. Her faith in God and her confidence in Robert became a continual

source of encouragement to him. The time was 1820, and pioneer missionary life was very difficult. It didn't matter to her. She aided her husband, and together they established one of the most prosperous mission stations for hundreds of miles around.

John Bunyan had an Elisabeth, who stood beside him in loyal support while he was locked up in jail for twelve long years. She cared for his five children including one blind daughter, and visited him in the jail faithfully. She never tempted him to compromise so he could come home. Only eternity will reveal the place she played in the writing of *Pilgrim's Progress*.

Adoniram Judson had Ann, the first of his three missionary wives, and the most famous one. They were pioneer missionaries to Burma. Together they endured many hardships to plant the first church in Burma. She was wife, mother, translator, and servant to her husband while he lay in prison for about two years. It is hard for us to imagine the role of a missionary's wife. Her husband faces so many hardships in the work. The smiling face of a believing wife is priceless.

The Power of Reverence

I receive many letters in the mail through our church's tape ministry. One of the most often asked questions I read in these letters is from sincere sisters. They hear "The Godly Home" tapes, and long for their husbands to rise up and take their place as the leader in their home. Here is the question: "Brother Denny, how can I encourage my husband to be the leader in our home? He is just not tuned in to his responsibilities." This is a sincere question that reveals the greatest need among Christian men. I will take some time here to answer this often asked question.

First, I want to say quickly, if you want to "change your husband" you probably have a selfish motive. God doesn't bless "sanctified" manipulation. I want to show you how you can encourage your husband and let God make him a man of God, providing he is not a rebel. Yet, according to 1 Peter 3, there's hope for him even if he is a rebel. There is a way to see your husband change. It may be an entirely different way than you might think, because God's ways are not like ours. Paul said it all in one small statement in a verse of Ephesians that many women have overlooked to their own hurt. Let's dig deep and see what treasures we can find.

The wife see that she reverence her husband.
Ephesians 5:33b

The last verse in Ephesians 5, is kind of a summary covering all the verses that preceded it concerning husbands and wives. We will address only the part that ministers to wives. Whereas the last verse is a summary of all the other verses, there actually is one word that gives the summary. That word is "reverence." This is one of our English words that is slowly vanishing away. Webster's 1828 dictionary gives this word a definition striking to our modern minds: "fear, mingled with respect, and affection." I know that a word such as "fear" will cause many a modern day lady to cry out in opposition. Some women have fallen so far that their heart moves with disgust at the thought of fearing their husband. They say, "How can I fear him when I am better than he is, smarter than he is, or more able than he is?" I know I am writing to sisters in the Lord who do not feel this way, but it is good for us to see how far things have fallen in our world. Many times, the Christians are not far behind. This attitude is part of the reason why men are in the sad condition we see.

I will show you how you can help your husband to become "known in the gates." There are a lot of words hidden in this one word "reverence." They are effectual words of influence for the wise woman. You see, a lot of women approach their husbands in a totally unbiblical way. They think if they nag their husband, and pressure him, he will straighten up. Not so sisters, not so. And by the way, it hasn't worked has it? You must do it God's way. He wrote the rules, and reverence is the highest rule. There is power in reverence, wonder-working power. If we search out this word in the *Amplified Bible* (an expanded paraphrase), we find a whole list of words to consider. Let's look at them. I will give the sense of the words from Webster's 1828 dictionary.

Submit to him: "to yield or surrender to the power, will, or authority of another." This word is deeper than the word "obey." The command to obey can be done as an outward thing. This word "submit" requires an inward attitude of surrender with the obedience.

Notice him: "to observe with the eye, and consider in the mind; the act by which we gain knowledge of someone." Dear sisters, turn your eyes upon your husband with attentive interest in what he is doing. He should feel your interested eyes looking at him when he is around.

Regard him: "to give a focused attention; to consider seriously; that view of the mind that springs from value." This is so important, especially when your husband speaks. Do you want a leader? Quiet down and look attentively at him, genuinely valuing what he says. He will talk more; he will lead more; and he will rise up to his responsibilities.

Honor him: "any expression of respect or high estimation by words or actions; to adorn, ornament, or decorate." It is the same word used in references to honoring the king. Sisters, decorate your husband with expressions of respect by word and action. You will never be sorry.

Prefer him: "to bear or carry in advance; to consider one to be better than you are." In practical language, it means to place his desires, his opinions, and his ideas ahead of your own. You can't imagine the confidence that this builds in a man.

Venerate him: "to give him much worth; to respect, and to worship." I know wives are not supposed to worship their husbands. Only God deserves this. But when a man senses that his wife values him, what he does, and what he says, this affects his leadership ability.

Esteem him: "to prize; to set a high value on someone; to have a high opinion of someone; to give a high place of honor."

Defer to him: "to yield to another's opinion or judgment because of respect and honor." This is a most beautiful quality of character for a wife to have. She can display this confidence builder often, because there are lots of opinions in marriage.

Praise him: "to prize or value with words; to lift or raise another with words of value, and gratitude." This word is a good practical outward expression of many of the aforementioned attitudes. Praise is fuel on the fire of your husband's heart.

Love him: "to be pleased with, and regard with strong affection." Noun: "a prompt, free, willing desire for someone; ardent friendship springing from high esteem." This is a word of endearment. Aside from God, the love of a woman is, without question, the strongest motivation in a man's life. It will cause him to do and be far beyond what you might imagine.

Admire him exceedingly: "to hold up; to stop and behold with wonder; to regard with strong affections." This is a pleasant respect with wonder.

And let the wife see that she reverence her husband.

Beloved sisters in Jesus Christ, this is quite a list of words to consider. There are three ways you can respond to this challenge. You can be careless and indifferent, just passing it off with little interest. You can be overwhelmed by it and give up in discouragement. Finally, you can be stirred, motivated, and convicted, rising up in faith with a will to do as God has said. I pray that you will do the latter with vision and purpose.

All Bible principles are effectual. They have an effect. They have an influence. The law of sowing and reaping begins to operate when we obey. We cannot cancel this process. If you choose to sow reverence upon your husband's life, you will receive a bountiful harvest. The opposite is also true. We cannot get away from this principle. God Almighty, the Creator, has set these laws in motion, and they move according to our choices.

Many times the effect of a Bible principle is hidden. It is a concealed treasure full of many rich blessings. There it lies, waiting for anyone or all to pick it up, obey it, and experience the wealth of its contents. I encourage you to do just that with the principle of *reverence*.

Read over the list of words again. Can you see how these actions and attitudes will have direct influences on your husband? If you begin to honor him, defer to him, and submit to him, his desire to lead out in the home will be increased. His confidence in his leadership will rise to new heights. I have been amazed to watch weak men blossom into leaders, in homes where these principles were believed and practiced. I also have seen this work in our church fellowship. Let me explain.

When there is a need for more leadership in our church, we choose out a leader from among us. The brother selected through prayer and fasting has not been a leader in the church. As he begins, he hangs back at first, unsure of himself previously. During this time, the church is admonished to respect and honor their new leader. We practice these very principles with the new leader. We come along side of him and bless him for the sermon he just stumbled his way through. We write him notes of thanks for the way he handled a hard situation. We step out of the way and give him room to lead, and even room to fail. We follow much of what I have just written to you sisters. Do I need to tell you what happens to that brother as time goes on? In a year or two, we see a responsible, confident leader emerge who will bless the church for many years to come.

These precepts work the same way in a husband-wife relationship. Oh, if only I could somehow show you ladies what could happen if you would go about this whole thing God's way, you would heartily agree.

In the church, we do not do these things to manipulate the new leader. No, that would be evil. We encourage him out of a desire to see him prosper in his new role as elder. This should be your heart also. You should want your husband to be a blessed leader in your home. Therefore, you come along side of him and esteem him, praise him, and hear his words with interest. When the elder flourishes, we are the ones who recieve blessings from it. It is the same in the home. Your encouragements to your husband will bring blessings on your head.

The Pursuit of Godly Seed

I mentioned earlier how many letters I receive from wives about their husbands and their needs. Well, I also read many letters of praise and victory from sisters who have heard a sermon on this subject, repented of their human ways, and begun to change how they relate to their husbands. They are letters of gratitude with miraculous reports of changed husbands. The statutes of the Lord, they work.

I think it would be good to ponder the negative side of this subject for a few moments. Let me tell you how you can make your husband a weak, timid man, one who sits in the corner and doesn't talk very much, one who is afraid to lead out in conversation or make decisions, one who always looks to you to see what you think before he speaks.

Here is how it works. Set yourself to disregard what he says, and don't notice him when he is around. When he comes home from work at night, don't go to the door to meet him. Disregard what he says when he is talking and look the other way or bring up some other subject. Dishonor him and belittle him as you walk through life together. Don't fulfill his desires for the home, and push him to get your way. Find fault with him, and let him feel your silent disapproval all his days.

If you do these things for about five years, I guarantee that you will have a husband like I just described. No wife wants that kind of husband. Deep down in her heart she wants a man who will be a man. I have seen men with tremendous potential turned into mice by these kinds of activities. We must be careful what we try to make happen in ourselves. Abraham attempted to help God with the promised son, and he left behind an Ishmael. The world is paying for his human reasoning to this day.

Remember the new church elder. What kind of leader will he become if the church follows the aforementioned patterns? He will become a puppet, that is all. And the church will become a desert, dry and fruitless. I can give you a few real-life examples of churches that cut their own throats by treating an elder this way.

This is not a small issue for you sisters. We are dealing with beautiful blessings or devastating desolation. I am describing a place of power and influence, where you can stand, that will bless your husband. That powerful place to stand is beneath your husband's authority, a hidden place of encouragement and support, but not an insignificant place. Only eternity will reveal how important your place really is.

Dear Sister Jane

Years ago, when I was in Bible School, I had responsibility over a large part of the bus ministry at the First Baptist Church in Hammond, Indiana. I had oversight of about three hundred Bible school students. Among these students, one young lady stood out to me above the rest. She was a single girl studying to be a school teacher. Her name was Jane. She was a godly young lady. She had been guided with some godly principles as she was growing up. She knew the principles that govern a hidden woman and practiced them very effectively. She practiced the art of staying in the shadows and encouraging leaders. She was not married then, so she gave herself to the ministry of support for many leaders at the school.

This young lady was a blessing to me as I served in the bus ministry at the Bible school. It just seemed as though she always knew what to say at the right time. She knew when to write a little note. She seemed to know when it was time to pray. Somehow, she had the sensitivity in her heart to know how to encourage a leader to lead out and not hold back. At just the right time I would get a little note from her when I was facing a battle. "Dear Brother Denny, God bless you today. I prayed for you today. God be with you. Jane." I often thought, "Some young man is going to get a jewel when he marries this girl."

Well, one day she came to me to seek some counsel about her future. There was a young man at the college who was asking if he could spend time with her. At the Bible school, that meant more than just a date. It meant he was considering her for marriage. She said, "Brother Denny, I would like to know what you think about him. Would you please check into his life and see what you think of him?" This was a smart girl.

I agreed to do this, and began to make inquires about him around the school. I didn't know him very well, but other leaders who worked more closely with him gave him a good report. He seemed like a nice young man, but he was just kind of a mediocre young fellow in the school. He hadn't been there long, and was just beginning to mature. I thought to myself, "Jane is such a godly young lady, she could have someone much better than this." His life was clear according to all I asked, so I gave her my blessing for her to move ahead if she felt God was leading.

This couple started courting. Their relationship began to prosper, and within the year they were married. Well, guess what happened to that unknown preacher at the Bible school? His wife knew the principles of being a hidden woman. She got under his authority and began to look to him and bless him. All those notes that I used to get, I didn't get anymore. He got them. All those prayers, he got them. All those words of encouragement, he got them. Her submissive spirit that was such a blessing to all in the bus ministry, it all fell on him. She poured all her strength, all her prayer power, and all her spirituality on her new husband. She poured it all into that man, loving him, encouraging him, supporting him, and lifting him up.

Two years later, he was a different man. He was known in the gates of the school and had risen to a place of leadership there. He had become a young man of God, a fine preacher, a leader, a man of direction, a man of purpose, one who was easy to follow. I watched this young man blossom as the months passed by, and I knew why. His desire was fueled by her admiration, and a man of God emerged. Sister Jane knew the principles of a hidden woman. She was a master of them and turned all her gifts and abilities toward her husband.

Dear sisters, you must master this holy art. You have been specially designed by God to be all of this to your husband. Turn your energies and your creativity loose on your husband. There is as much power available to you as there is to any man who stands in the pulpit to preach. Jane lost her life and identity in the life and identity of her husband. She had all the potential to rise to her own place of prominence, but she hid it all in her husband. The day will come when she will shine as stars *"shine as the brightness of the firmament"* (Dan. 12:3).

A Fish Out of Water

When God the Creator made Eve, He designed her for a specific purpose, just as He did for everything else that He made. She was made to be a helpmeet for Adam. The first man was a farmer, so Eve willingly became a farmer's wife. Things have really been twisted by the Fall, so it is good to go back to the garden to refocus. When I ponder the "modern woman" and what she is trying to do, the illustration of a fish out of water comes to mind. The modern woman is a career woman. She is bold, she is aggressive, and she wants to make a name for herself. If you believe the creation account, as I do, these dear ladies are like fish out of water. They were not made by God for that.

Did you ever watch a fish out of the water? It is very interesting. First of all, its gills start going in and out very fast because it's trying to get oxygen. Now God didn't make the fish to get oxygen out of the air. God made fish to get oxygen out of the water. The fish flip flops around, trying to get oxygen. If kept out of the water long enough, it will slow down and eventually die. This fish out of water is a mighty uncomfortable fish. It is very discontented, and unhappy. But if you take that same fish and drop it back in the water. O what a beautiful picture you see! The fish starts swimming away through that water like a contented fish, free and breathing again.

These are the pictures I see when I come in contact with the dear ladies who are feminists. These women who believe in liberation of the female are like fish out of water. Do you remember Mary Pride? Years ago she wrote a book about her departure from corporate America entitled *The Way Home*. I didn't read it, but Jackie did, and it was a great help to her.

In this very interesting book, Mary Pride gives her testimony as a career woman. She shares what was really going on inside her while she was in Corporate America. She was gasping for air, and hurting on the inside. She was unfulfilled, empty, and unhappy even though she was seeking to be a career woman and all that goes along with it. When she finally got "back home," it so fulfilled her life that she was motivated by the Lord to write a book so that other career women could find their rightful place.

The Pursuit of Godly Seed

There are many curses and a multitude of confusions falling upon these dear "fish out of water" who have lost their way. In the past thirty years, a new group of diseases has appeared: fibromyalgia, chronic fatigue syndrome, environmental illness (allergies), and others. For the most part, these diseases plague the women. Doctors are discovering that these new diseases often are caused by fear, anxiety, and stress. Consider my thoughts on this for a moment. The ladies have taken on more than they can handle and things they were not designed to handle. Their being is not at peace, but under continual stress, and the body is breaking down under the load. Maybe they just need to come home, jump back into the water, and breathe again.

Conclusion

God made you for your husband. He made you to reverence your husband, to bless and encourage him, and to be a helpmeet to him. He made you to breathe the cool fresh air of a supportive life.

I wonder, are you a fish out of the water? If you're trying to make your man do it, you are a fish out of water. If you are trying to do it instead of him doing it, you are a fish out of water. If you are out in corporate America, you are a fish out of water. Your environment is to be in the realm of the home, blessing your husband as Jane did. In that place, life will spring forth for you, God's grace will flow in you, and you will swim right through life with the greatest of ease, freedom, and blessing.

Prayer

Father in heaven, I thank You for Your beautiful plan and purpose for women. How excellent is Thy wisdom. How can we question it? I pray for all the dear ladies that who have read this chapter. Please, Lord, pour out Your Spirit upon them this very moment. Witness in their hearts what is right. Speak peace to them and lead them back home, back to reverance, and back to that safe place under their husband's authority. In Jesus' name. Amen.

27

My Lord and My lord

Wives submit yourselves unto your own husbands as unto the Lord
Ephesians 5:22

Even as Sarah obeyed Abraham calling him lord
I Peter 3:6a

The book of Ephesians gives us glorious, heavenly vision of the Christian home. Many undiscerning couples use this revelation to correct each other, each using it to show the other how the other should be. In most cases, this is very counterproductive. Although it is true that all Scripture is given for correction, I don't believe that was Paul's original intent for this Scripture.

The verses found in chapter five express Paul's spiritual vision of the New Covenant marriage. This is how the home should function as two people live under the power of the Holy Spirit. When this grace is flowing between a husband and his wife, it makes a powerful, joyful marriage. The focus of this book is on godly children, not marriage, but it is very hard to raise a holy seed in the midst of a troubled marriage. One of the greatest gifts you can give your children is a happy marriage. I am addressing a happy home from the sisters' perspective and will encourage the men later.

I will describe an imaginary scene to illustrate verse 22. Almost every one of your homes has a chair or two where your husband sits. I have one where I sit in at my house. We call it "Papa's chair." Everybody in the house knows that I sit in that certain chair. When I have been away for a few hours, I walk into the house, sit down in my chair where I always sit, and visit with the family. I want you to picture the chair that sits in your house, the chair where your husband sits when he comes home in the evening. You know the scene. It happens all the time, and is easy to imagine.

Now, to help you understand the meaning of the verse at hand, I want to change this imaginary scene a bit. Instead of your husband walking through the door, greeting everyone, and sitting down in his chair to visit, I want you to picture the Lord Jesus Christ in his place.

It is evening time. Suddenly, the door opens up, and the Lord Himself walks into your house instead of your husband. He gives everyone a kind warm greeting and tells you He is taking your husband's place for the evening. He feels right at home, walks right over to that special chair, and sits down. Wow, what an exciting surprise!

We can easily imagine what is going on inside your heart by this time. Thoughts of reverence spring up in your mind. You think, "The Lord walked into my house today! He is sitting in the chair where my husband usually sits! How can I serve Him?" Think about it a moment. The Lord is sitting in your house. How are you going to respond? Let me write the imaginary script for a few minutes. I think you will agree with my choice of words.

You (the wife) ask, "Lord, is there anything I can get You tonight?"

He (the Lord) responds, "Well, yes, yes there is. I would like a cup of tea."

You (the wife) "What kind of tea would You like Lord?"

Him (the Lord) "A cup of mint tea sounds good to me."

You (the wife) "Yes, Lord, I will make it right away."

You go back into your kitchen thinking, "Glory! The Lord is in my house! The Lord is sitting in my husband's chair, and He wants a cup of tea! What a privilege I have!" O you will be so excited to

My Lord and My lord

make that cup of tea. You will get the best water you can find. You will choose the best tea you have, and you'll make that cup of tea for the Lord. And all the while you're making it, you know what your thoughts will be: "The Lord is in my house. Wow! I can't believe it." "I get to make a cup of tea for the Lord!"

Let us go on with our imaginary story. When the tea is ready, you joyfully serve it to Him. I don't think you will quickly walk away as you usually do. What do you think you would do? I think you will linger there near the chair with your eyes on Him as He drinks some tea.

"Lord, is the tea okay?"
"Well, it is a little hot."
"Oh, I'm sorry Lord, I will get an ice cube to cool it down."
And off you go, for an ice cube, doing it with all your heart.

You think again as you are walking back with the ice cube, "Oh, the Lord is in my house." You have prepared supper, and it is on the table. You were expecting your husband at five, and all things are now ready. So a word is given to the Lord about supper.

"Lord, I have supper on the table. Would you like to eat?"
"Yes, I am hungry. I'm sorry, but I have a phone call I need to make. Could you hold the supper a little while until I get done with my phone call?"
"O sure, Lord. I will gladly do that. I'll just put it back in the oven and keep it warm. You take Your time and make Your phone call."
"Thank you for honoring me in this way."

That is what you would say, isn't it. I don't think you would even think some of the thoughts that normally go through your mind when your husband makes such a request. All you would think is that the Lord is in your house, and He can do whatever He wants. You would adapt around His desires because He is the Lord. It would be your delight to wait on Him, look to Him, and hang on His every word.

The Pursuit of Godly Seed

Beloved sisters, this is a picture of what Ephesians 5:22 means: *"Wives submit yourselves unto your own husbands as unto the Lord,"* or as if you were serving the Lord. Could we say, "Inasmuch as you have done it unto your husband, you have done it unto Me?" I think we can, just as we would in reference to the poor and needy. Your husband would surely rank higher than "the least of these my brethren."

Maybe you are thinking by now, "Is this guy crazy or what? My husband isn't the Lord, and he surely doesn't act like the Lord!" Let me encourage you to be careful not to react, or you may miss a very important life-changing principle. Remember, Paul is giving his vision of a Spirit-filled marriage. Don't react, but dream awhile. I will address the husbands in later chapters.

May I give you an assignment? Take this simple, imaginary exercise and use it to reflect upon your home life. Use it as a plumbline to examine your actions, reactions, and attitudes toward your husband. You can place the Lord in that chair at your house with dozens of different situations. It is not the how-to that I am after, but rather the spirit of this imaginary story. If you get that, you will live it out in many areas of your marriage.

As I sit reflecting upon this scenario, here is my thought: "I don't deserve that kind of treatment." None of us deserves that kind of treatment. I know that. But, let me ask you sisters some questions. Do you think such treatment will make us better men or worse? Do you think it will encourage us or discourage us? Many a wife gets fearful of creating a selfish tyrant. Let me share from my own experiences.

A husband who gets this kind of treatment will sit in that chair and say, "I don't deserve this. I am not worthy of this kind of treatment. What can I do for my wife? How can I show her how grateful I am for the way she serves me so lovingly, so sweetly, and so submissively?"

This is what usually happens. When I preach a sermon like this, I usually give the hearers an opportunity to respond at an altar. I have been surprised to see men weeping at the altar. They hit the altar, expressing attitudes of unworthiness and longings to be a better husband. We are uncovering a hidden secret in this illustration, one that an arrogant self-willed woman will never see, one that will release your husband to grow, to dream, to rise up in confidence, and to take the lead. Do you see it? Don't miss it. It is too important to miss.

The Power of a Submissive Spirit

Likewise ye wives, be in subjection to your own husbands; that if any obey not the word, they also may without the word be won by the conversation of the wives while they behold your chaste conversation coupled with fear.

I Peter 3:1-2

As we continue to consider the influences hidden in the glorious roles of a woman, we dare not pass over the amazing text found in I Peter 3:1-6. There we find wealth of treasures lying just below the surface for those seeking souls who are diligent enough to mine them. I do not have the space to cover all the treasures in this book on raising children. It deserves the attention of a whole book. However, we must look for a moment at the amazing effect a woman can have on her husband if she will trust in the Lord and follow His ways.

I am seeking to change your view of woman's place in the kingdom of God. In some ways, the woman's role can be more effectual than that of a man. Consider Christ again. He laid down His life, an utter failure in man's eyes, and provided the way for mankind to be changed absolutely forever. It is in this manner that God uses some of His choicest servants. The Spirit of the Lord came upon Christ, and He willingly submitted to the will of His Father, which was the failure and humiliation of the cross. He is the example given to you sisters in these verses. One of the words in this passage is "likewise." It refers to the example of Christ in the verses before (see 1 Pet. 2:21-25). Our text says, *"Likewise ye wives."* It means, "in like manner." In the same way that Christ laid down His life, ye wives, let the Spirit of the Lord come upon you and lay down your lives for your husbands.

The Pursuit of Godly Seed

How is this done? God is very practical here in these verses. He is not calling you to suffer in a martyrs' prison somewhere. He says, "Be in subjection to your own husbands." As I mentioned earlier, these words mean much more than obey. They are words describing an attitude of the heart. And this is where the power lies. God has told us right in these verses how you can have the most influence upon your husband.

The word *subjection* means "adapt yourself." Ladies, adapt your lives, adapt your thoughts, and adapt your desires to your husband. Herein lies great power and influence.

The word *adapt* means "to make something fit." Make your life fit your husband's life. Webster's dictionary (1904 edition) gives this broader definition: "to change oneself so that your behavior, attitudes, and will conform to new circumstances." This is a good way to describe a wife beginning a new life with her husband. You are putting on your husband's life, and you are adapting your life to fit into his. Remember Eve? Adam was a farmer, so Eve became a farmer's wife.

Consider the power of such submission. There is such potential in this attitude that God says it can win a lost husband to Christ without the wife saying a word. Many wives whose husbands are lost make the human mistake of trying to convert them with many words. They preach, plead, even nag at times in hope of turning him. Usually, it has the opposite effect, driving him away. Often, the motive is wrong when these methods are practiced. Dear sisters, come let us reason together. If there is enough power here to win a wayward husband, think about how much more influence you could have on your believing husband by living this way.

Many times Christian wives have followed the tactics of nonbelieving women who nag and manipulate to change their husbands. It doesn't work for them, and if you are honest, it hasn't worked for you either. I know that we men have a lot of needs. Some of us are the products of absentee leaders in the home for two generations. We need to change, but there is a right way and a wrong way to change us. Your posture should not be "I'm going to change my husband," but rather, "How can I be his helpmeet?"

The spirit of submission and the potential influences it has are found everywhere in 1 Pet. 3:1-6. Let's skim them for a moment.

- ❖ First, we have the powerful example of Christ's submission, which we are to follow. The influence of His submission is staggering (verse 1).
- ❖ Second, the word "subjection" gives us clear insight into the attitudes of a godly wife. She should adapt her life to her husband's life (verse 1).
- ❖ Third, this brings forth a whole life of meekness and submission, which is seen by the husband (verse 2).
- ❖ Fourth, this life is coupled with reverential fear toward the husband, which has a powerful effect upon a him (verse 2).
- ❖ Fifth, this manifests the life of Christ in the hidden man of the heart and becomes a most beautiful, magnetic draw upon a husband. He is drawn as he sees Jesus in his wife (verse 4).
- ❖ Sixth, we are given a reminder that this is the way godly women adorned themselves in the past (verse 5).
- ❖ Finally, Sarah is given as an example of one who called her husband "lord" (verse 6).

You can greatly influence your husband without preaching to him by simply living this beautiful anointed life before him. You become a living translation of the Word of God in your home. Jesus Christ comes to live in your home through you. This is God's way. Who will do it? Who will believe these words enough to act on them and see the results? You will never change your husband by trying to change your husband. It won't work. It is contrary to God's way.

Tirshatha

Charles Spurgeon was a famous Baptist preacher in England during the latter part of the nineteenth century. He was called the prince of preachers because of his eloquent gift of expounding the Word. This godly man had a very unusual wife named Susana. This godly lady was a profound example of a hidden woman who adapted her life and talents to those of her husband. She was a very gifted person, and her life in the Lord could have stood all on its own. She had mastered the Greek and Hebrew languages and could read them just as you read English. She was a good expository preacher's wife. As a helpmeet to her husband, she assisted him in his sermon preparation.

Spurgeon would seek God for a Scripture text on which to base his sermon, then call for his wife to come and help him. He would sit back in his easy chair and listen while she read out loud every commentary he had on that text. They would work their way through each one, sharing, pondering, and searching for the sense of the verses. Picture it: lord Spurgeon just sitting there listening while she read to him for several hours. Then he would get alone with God again and seek God for an outline and the flow of the sermon. Every helpmeet is different, and God gave him a helper meet for him.

Spurgeon's wife had a special name that she called her husband, which I would like to share with you sisters. She called him "Tirshatha." When she greeted him in the morning, she would say, "Good morning, Tirshatha." It was a special name between the two of them. They were both Greek scholars, and she found a name that expressed her heart to her husband.

Tirshatha is a Greek word that means, "my reverence." Imagine greeting your husband in this way: "Good morning, my reverence. How are you this morning?" O, can we glimpse the spirit of those words? You see, they were not just words. There was a heart attitude behind those words. There was a spirit of honor, a spirit of love, and a spirit of respect and reverence in those words "Good morning my reverence."

Sarah called Abraham lord. When she met him in the morning, I can imagine she greeted him with, "Good morning, lord." This word *lord* means "master, leader, and guide." It is very clear from the text that Sarah felt reverence for Abraham because she called him lord.

Now, it doesn't matter to me what name you call your husband. The spirit behind the words is what we are after here. We have here another example of a hidden woman who served her husband in submission and reverence and helped him become *"known in the gates"* of the city of London. I realize that I am addressing a wide range of sisters who are on many different levels of relationship with their husbands. Maybe you don't even have a sweet word that you use when you address your husband. However, God's Word instructs you to let the spirit of reverence come out of your heart and mouth to your husband.

What was Mrs. Spurgeon saying when she said, "Good morning Tirshatha"? She was saying

"Charles, I love you."

"Charles, I highly esteem you."

"Charles, I care about what you say."

"Charles, I like to be under your authority. I like it so much that I will call you a name that speaks of authority."

"Charles, I'm here for you, and my life's desire is to live for you."

That's what she was saying. What do you think that did to Charles? It made him a king in his house. Every man ought to know what it feels like to be a king. He should never walk around with an attitude that says "I am a king." No, he needs to be a servant leader in his house. But he ought to know what it feels like to be a king by the way his wife reverences him.

Mrs. John Rice, a Holy Example

Mrs. Rice went on to her reward many years ago now, but my memory of this queenly lady is very vivid. I must share a little about this saint because she was a lovely hidden woman. Her husband, John R. Rice, was a man of God. He was a famous Baptist evangelist, the editor of a successful periodical, and the author of fifty books. All over the country, he was known to be a family man. Together he and Mrs. Rice raised six lovely daughters who are serving God today. But John R. Rice was a busy man who traveled often. He would be gone for a few weeks, and then be home for one week. This is the life of an evangelist. This was God's call upon his life. There was no way he could practice consistently all that I am sharing with you in this book. When he was home, he was a good and godly father, but he was gone a lot. However, there was one thing he had going for him.

John Rice had a wife who was a hidden woman. Mrs. Rice honored him from her heart and before those six little girls. When he left for a preaching trip, she would gather all the girls around in a circle of prayer in the living room, and they prayed for Daddy.

All the girls would hear Mama pray, "Oh, God, bless Daddy. We thank You, Father, that Daddy is out winning souls. We thank You, Father, that Daddy loves You. We thank You, Father, that Daddy is in the work of God, and that he cares about people." She would pray this kind of honoring prayers, and the girls followed her example.

Mrs. Rice preached Daddy all the time at home, not out of duty, but from a true heart of reverence and respect. The girls caught this spirit of submission from their mother. They never knew that he probably was too busy. They never knew that he should have spent more time at home with his family. He was so full of zeal for souls, he might not have known either. All of them turned out to be fine Christian ladies who rose up to serve the Lord and raise their own families for Christ. One of the daughters wrote a book, *Me Obey Him* (Elisabeth Rice Hanford).

This dear lady was a hidden woman who filled up the gaps in the home, lifted up her husband, blessed him, and honored him. The Lord let her live to be 94 years old. She spent her old age speaking to women all over the country. Do you know what she told them? She encouraged them to love their husbands, to build them up, and to submit to them.

Is Honor Based on Perfection?

The New Testament says a lot about honoring others: kings, magistrates, parents, husbands, wives. It even says we are to honor all men. Let me ask you a question. Are we supposed to honor only those who are honorable? We all know the answer if we stop and think about it. According to the Bible, honor is based on position, not on perfection.

If you are driving down the road and in your rearview mirror you see red lights flashing on the car behind you, what do you do? You pull over and wait for the officer to come over to the side of your car. An attitude of respect settles over you as you see

My LORD and My lord

him coming. Why is this? It is because he is a police officer, and we have learned to respect policemen. This particular policeman might be a man who drinks too much when he is off duty. He might be known for some shady deals in the town. But when that officer approaches your vehicle and asks for your license, you say, "Yes sir" with respect. He will sense honor and respect coming out of your spirit. The policeman gets his due honor because of his position.

If the president or the governor knocked on the door of your house, and you opened up the door and saw him standing there, what would you do? He probably would get the same treatment the Lord got in the chair a little earlier. Your words would be clothed with honor as you spoke to him, even though he is not a perfect man.

Honor is not based on perfection. It is based on position. Sisters, we must grasp this truth for the sake of our homes. We see it with the policemen and with government officials, but for some reason we miss it in our homes. We tell the children with our mouths *"Honor thy father and thy mother,"* but we don't teach them by our example to honor father. Let us teach them by our example.

Not one of us brethren is prefect. Not one of us is always worthy of honor, but God calls us to honor, reverence, respect. If you feel free to complain about your husband to the children when he leaves, Woe! Woe! Woe! That is big stuff. There ought to be a line inside your conscience that says, "I will never speak evil about my husband."

A Sad Story of Generational Sin

I live in Lancaster County, Pennsylvania. It is a very unique place to live for many reasons. Some families have lived in this area for two hundred fifty years, generation after generation. It is not unusual to find four generations of one family still living here. I have been blessed at times to look into the faces of four generations and see the resemblances. However, there are other family traits that are not so beautiful. People who have lived here for decades know the family flaws very well. In some cases these flaws are common conversation (such talk is not right, but they do it). The story I am going to share is a true one. I have made it into a story out of kindness.

Once there was a nagging woman who lived in Lancaster County with her husband. He was not the best husband, so she often dishonored him. She picked at him. She fussed at him. She nagged him and said to him, "You're dumb and can't do anything right. You're a good-for-nothing." This is the way she treated her husband. Somehow, she thought she could get him to straighten up if she shamed him and degraded him, but it only made things worse.

This woman had little girls who grew up in her house. These little girls loved their mama and watched her every action with admiration. As little girls do, they were thinking in their hearts, "I want to be just like Mama when I grow up." But this mama wasn't very careful what she said in front of them. These girls watched that mama tear their father apart with her words day after day after day.

It came to pass, as time went on, that these little girls grew up and became young ladies. When things didn't go right at home, they felt the freedom to sit their father down and tell him all about it. O, it hurt him when he saw the same thing he was getting from his wife coming out of his daughters. They would correct him, frown at him, and find fault with his leadership every passing day. They did the same to their mother, and she was so displeased with the way they were acting. She often said to her friends at the church, "I don't know what has gotten into my daughters. They are so rebellious. It must be a stage they are going through." This was the way life was at home during those youthful years.

The years went by quickly and all the girls found husbands and left the home. They put on their brightest dress and a pretty smile and found husbands. Mama also put on her happy smile as the young men came to the house to court. The weddings came and went one by one, and everyone seemed pleased at the good fortunes that had come to them.

As time went on, the girls were not happy. They didn't like the way the husbands did things. Their smiles soon became frowns of disapproval. Words came out of their mouths, familiar words that degraded and discouraged their husbands. This was the way they talked to their husbands.

God gave them a couple of little girls. They were so happy when the little ones were born, and were filled with good dreams for each one. The little girls were innocently watching Mama and thinking what all little girls think, "Oh, when I grow up, I'm going to be just like Mama." We all know by now what they were watching and what they were becoming as the days passed by.

In some cases, this sad sad story has gone on for many generations. Because the families stay closer together in Lancaster County, one can often see the patterns. I have heard ministers say with burdened hearts, "That is the way the women in that family have been for generations." It has become common knowledge that the ladies in that family disrespect their men.

Sisters, let me ask you a question: who is going to stop this sin and break its chains? Your little girls also are watching their mama, and saying, "I'm going to be just like Mama." And they are going to be just like mama. Someday (and it will be sooner than you think) they are going to get married. What kind of home will they have? What will their husbands think after all the smiles and good will are past. I challenge you sisters to rise up and conquer this land now in your generation. Save the next generation from the curse of this sin.

If you will not deal with this curse, or others like unto it, then please warn the young man of the coming confusion that will descend upon his home. It is not right just to put on a smile and act as if everything is fine when this sin is lurking in the character of your daughter. He needs to be allowed to make a choice with his eyes open.

Proverbs 14: 1 says, *"Every wise woman buildeth her house: but a foolish woman plucketh it down with her hands."* The wise woman who builds her home is the wife who joins hearts with her husband to build the lives of her children. The foolish woman literally tears it apart, and destroys it by fighting against the unity of the home. The women described in the story above are foolish women, tearing down their husbands, and thus tearing down their homes.

Give yourself completely to the Lord and to your husband, and let the Lord build your house, your family, and your marriage. If we are not willing to meet God in these basics, then we labor in vain as we build. I have seen many a house built on the sinking sand described in the preceding discussion because the parents were not willing to yield to the Lord. The house on the sand went smash, and great was the fall of it.

But My Husband Is Not Right
God bless you, dear sisters. Some of you probably are feeling a bit overwhelmed by now. You have sat and read three chapters all about a woman's place. Please don't think that I am putting the whole load on you. Remember how much I have said to your husbands already, and I will say more. I know that a lot of us husbands are not doing very well. I'm sorry if you feel condemned. That is not my purpose. God's plan and picture for the home must be changed, and this will not happen unless we decide we are going to make the changes God's way. This is my burden in these chapters written to the sisters. Your husband needs your support desperately. The principles I have shared are life-changing, home-changing principles. Don't try to change him. Get on his team and build.

Maybe you are the stronger of the two in your home. This is the case in many homes of this day and age. I see it everywhere. Weak men are part of the curse on those who turn away from God. Are you stronger? Do you have more insight? Are you the more spiritual one in your house? I often see homes in which the wife is alert, praying, and quick to speak up for God. My sister, God did not give you all those spiritual blessings so you could run ahead of your husband, take charge of the home, and lead out. Whatever strength God has given you is yours so you can get under that husband and pour all your spiritual energies into him. This is your position. This is the environment (the water) in which God has placed you as a wife and mother. Be a loving wife to your husband. Honor him, bless him, and support him. If you will take this sanctified approach, then all of heaven will be on your side.

My LORD and My lord

God's Spirit is moving upon women, pleading with them to believe the Word, obey it, and reap the blessings of a changed husband and a godly home.

A Prayer

Our Father which art in heaven, hallowed be Thy name. Thy kingdom come and Thy will be done on earth, Lord, in each of our homes, even as it is in heaven. Father, help the dear sisters who long after You and long for a godly home with a dedicated father leading it. Give them the desire of their hearts. Teach them this holy art. Cause them to have a clear vision and a lively faith to believe all that You have said in Your Word. In Jesus Christ's name. Amen.

Meditations

HOME

Home is the holy of holies of a man's life.
There he withdraws from all the world,
And there shutting his door,
He is alone with those who are his own.
It is
The reservoir of his strength.
The restorer of his energies.
The resting place from his toil.
The brooding place of his spirit.
And the inspiration for all his activities and battles.

S.D. Gordon

28

Motherhood: The Highest Place of Honor

Who can find a Virtuous Woman? For her price is far above rubies.

Many daughters have done virtuously, but thou excellest them all.
Proverbs 31:10 & 29

When God calls a prophet, He gives him a prophet's anointing. When God calls an apostle, He gives him the anointing of an apostle. As these men walk out the reality of their calling, they will find their hearts being strengthened to do the task. Paul was speaking about his apostolic anointing when he penned these words: *"By the grace of God I am what I am, and his grace which was bestowed upon me was not in vain; but I labored more abundantly than they all; yet not I, but the grace of God which was with me,"* (I Cor. 15:16).

When God calls a woman to be a wife and mother, He also gives her the measure of grace she needs to carry out her calling. As it is with the prophet, so it is also with a mother. When a mother lives out the reality of her calling, she will find that she is being anointed and strengthened by God to fulfill the task. I don't know how many of you believe that God's grace flows to a mother in this way, but I do. It is a power available to mothers that most are not aware of; however, it is still there for all who will believe and receive. Just like the prophet loses his anointing if he walks away

The Pursuit of Godly Seed

from the task God gives him (e.g., the prophet Jonah), so also a mother will lose her anointing if she turns away from family to seek "better things." Selah (Stop and think about this).

Proverbs 31:10-31 is worthy of a whole book of chapters. I consider it one of the most important texts in the Bible. I can only skim the text for some of the jewels that are laying on the surface and hope that many will take their own pick and shovel and go deeper.

This portion of the Bible is a prophetic word from the Lord for our day. It is a clarion call, flowing out of heaven to a fast and furious society. It was spoken by a prophetess to her son, who happened to be a king. Picture a woman clothed in modesty and humility standing on the street corner in down town USA. Hundreds of ladies are passing by, and she lifts up her voice as the Spirit of the Lord comes upon her, and cries, *"Who can find a virtuous woman? Who can find a virtuous woman?"* Crowds of ladies gather as the words stir their interest. Think with me as this prophetess continues down through this prophetic word, explaining what this woman is like, what do you think the response will be? From this, we can see how far we have fallen. Even as I sit here preparing to write about what God says about mothers, it feels a little archaic. This troubles me. How can it be that motherhood and all that is involved in motherhood feels old and out of date? Do we just sit back and let mothering pass away, as we let farming pass away? Is it merely a cultural issue, and now our culture has changed? God forbid! We are not the first nation that let issues like these pass away, calling them a change in society. What is our response to this lady's prophetic word? There are other nations who have vanished from existence because of issues like these. Will we be next? I pray not.

It only seems right for us to look a little closer at the glorious place of a mother as we consider pursuing a godly seed. It is my conviction that we will never see a godly seed until we restore motherhood to its rightful place. There are twelve precious jewels that the prophetess covers in this text. Let's listen to her for awhile and see what we can learn. I have emphasized the text in some places to enhance your personal meditations.

Motherhood: The Highest Place of Honor

__Who can find a virtuous woman?__ For her price is far above rubies. The heart of her husband doth safely __trust in her,__ so that he shall have no need of spoil. She will do him good and not evil all the days of her life. She seeketh wool, and flax, and worketh willingly with her __hands.__ She is like the merchants' ships; she bringeth her food from afar. She riseth also while it is yet night and giveth meat to her __household,__ and a portion to her maidens. She considereth a field and buyeth it: with the fruit of her __hands__, she planteth a vineyard. She girdeth her loins with strength, and strengtheneth her arms. She perceiveth that her merchandise is good: her candle goeth not out by night. She layeth her __hands__ to the spindle, and her __hands__ hold the distaff. She stretcheth out her __hand__ to the poor; yea, she reacheth forth her __hands__ to the needy. She is not afraid of the snow for her __household:__ for all her __household__, are clothed with scarlet. She maketh herself coverings of tapestry, her clothing is silk and purple. Her husband is known in the gates, when he sitteth among the elders of the land. She maketh fine linen, and selleth it; and delivereth girdles unto the merchant. Strength and honor are her clothing; and she shall rejoice in time to come. She openeth her mouth with wisdom, and in her tongue is the law of kindness; she looketh well to the ways of her __household__, and eateth not the bread of idleness. Her children arise up and call her blessed; her husband also, and he praiseth her. Many daughters have done virtuously, but thou excellest them all. Favour is deceitful, and beauty is vain: but a woman that feareth the Lord, she shall be praised. Give her of the fruit of her __hands;__ and let her own works praise her in the gates.
Proverbs 31:10-31

The Virtuous Woman

She is a mother

I know we all know this, even from a light reading of the text;

however, it seems we have allowed this major point to fall into the background, as if it was not very important. She is a mother, and nothing stands out more clearly. Most of the other attributes that we will consider are given in the context of a wife and mother. I have seen these verses used to justify real estate agents, corporate executives, and world-traveling ladies. This is an application out of context. She is a mother and has submitted to all that it costs to be a mother. This involves the bearing and caring for children. This involves staying home and turning the focus of all her abilities onto her home. It's not that she has no talents, or that she has no intelligence; no, she is very gifted. But she has chosen to turn all of these gifts toward her husband, and those most precious, eternal souls under her care. This is sacrifice at its best. God bless you sacrificing mothers.

She lives out her husband's vision

Her heart beats with the goals and dreams of her husband. She has carefully discerned his desires for her and the children. She has meditated on those desires and then translated them into everyday details that please him. Her husband—ah, he trusts in her; he has no worry even if he goes away for a few days. He knows assuredly that, everything will go on as he has directed while he is gone. Her life is hidden in her husband's dreams, and she shall be rewarded not many days hence.

She honors her husband

Her husband is highly esteemed in his home. She talks highly of him when he is away and preaches Daddy to the children. She will do things in his name, and give him the credit for it. This is no problem for her, for she understands the order that God has ordained. As a mother, she knows that the more she honors him, the more the children will follow his teachings and example. She stirs up excitement when Daddy comes home, and rejoices to see the eyes of her children light up for him. Truly, truly, his heart does safely trust in her.

Motherhood: The Highest Place of Honor

She is a keeper at home

Notice in our text, the word *household* appears four times. It is very clear that this unsung hero's life is centered in her home. Many mothers express the feeling of "being tied down" because of the many home responsibilities, but we must remember, it is all a matter of perspective. Ask the mother bird if she feels tied down, ask the mother hen if she is bored with sitting on those eggs all the time. We know they are living out their God given instincts. There are so many verses in our text refer to the home or allude to it. *Home, home, home* everywhere. This is the realm of the godly woman's domain, and God calls her virtuous because she is a keeper at home.

She Is a Hard Worker

In our text, there are eleven references to what she does with her hands. This is honorable. She has strong hands and arms because she works hard. We are slowly losing this point of character among our young ladies. The prim and the proper are taking precedent over the hard working lady. But the Bible does not spell *godly woman* that way. We must sanctify our hearts and our vision with the Word. *"She worketh willingly with her hands."* Most of what a mother does is done with her hands. Lord, preserve the working hands of our sisters, please. Consider the list of honorable activities done with her hands. Washing the dishes. Preparing and cooking food. Cleaning the house. Changing the diapers and caring for children. Washing clothes. Keeping the garden and canning the harvest. Sewing clothes. You say, "this is servants work," this is well said, but remember the words of our Lord Jesus Christ, when He said, *"But he that is greatest among you shall be your servant"* (Matt. 23:11).

She is productive

She will use her abilities and energies to help her husband with the family finances. As the children get older she will turn her focus on ways to help, and ways the children can help meet the needs. She will make things with her hands, she will grow extra produce in the garden, or even expand the garden, to help. This is not to gain money for her own plans or future; no, her heart is for her husband. She will use her creativity to find ways to save money for the family budget.

She is a spiritual woman
This dear lady is more than a good cook. She walks with God. Remember, at the start of this chapter we acknowledged that God gives an anointing for the sacrificial task of motherhood. If mother is born again and sets her heart to love and know God, she will be becoming spiritual. She gives to the poor, she is filled with inner strength, she flows with words of wisdom, and she fears God. Many mothers settle for the outward parts of mothering and neglect the more important aspects of prayer, prophesying, and serving God. As mothers come in brokenness to God throughout their day, He will pour into them His very life. This is the pinnacle of true motherhood.

Her testimony is a crown to her husband
She is highly esteemed in her community—a true mother in Israel. Just as the men become elders who sit in the gate, the virtuous woman's life gains her a place of honor in her sphere. This whole testimony, the testimony of motherhood, crowns her husband with honor. We have said much about this already, so I will refrain from repetition.

She has a vision
This dear lady smiles at the future and rejoices in the time to come. She knows where she is going and sees clearly as she looks down the road of life. She is not merely doing housework—she has a vision. She sees beyond the diapers, and all the work that goes into raising children. When she holds her baby in her arms, she sees a fine young man, walking with God. This vision is what fuels her fire when her life threatens to become commonplace. Then she remembers, "I am raising children for the kingdom of our God." When she looks at her little diamonds in the rough, she sees the diamond way more than the rough. Oh dear sisters, God needs to give you more of

the vision that goes along with mothering. It is easy to get bogged down in the everyday things, and lose sight of what you are really doing. This is where many mothers have lost hope. They lost their vision, then the work was no longer sanctified, and soon they left home for "better things."

Her words are powerful

Grace, grace, grace flows out of her mouth. These kind words set the spirit of her whole household. Her loving ways create a lovely atmosphere in her husband's home. He loves it there, the children love it there, and even the visitors find it a haven in a weary land. Her kind words of love and wisdom mold the very soul of her children. As she prophesies into the hearts of her children, their dispositions are formed into the same kind and caring ways. At nursing times, at changing times, and at many other times, she is speaking words that mold the fabric of each one of her little ones.

She is a household organizer

Yes, she is a manager (an executive if you please), one who can keep several things going all at the same time. As her family grows and her little helpers grow older, she becomes a manager of others. She oversees all of the household duties and projects. A houseful of growing children is enough to keep a few people busy, but they must be ordered, directed, and trained in new tasks. But this busy mother will not agonize over it; she will organize, delegate, and look well to the ways of her household.

She excels them all

In our text, verse 29 is the crowning verse of the whole chapter. The prophetess has made many statements of purpose in these verses. From a natural standpoint, we might think, "Oh well, just a mother and a long list of home labors." But this is not how God looks at this list. This is not a list of duties; this is a description of the godliest woman of them all. Who are the many daughters who have done virtuously, mentioned in our text? All we can do is guess, however, some of those daughters are recorded in the testimonies of scripture. Sarah, Debra, Esther, and Ruth are a few that have been recorded, in the Old Testament. These were women who excelled in virtue, enough to be listed as examples to us. But this woman who fears God in this way is praised above all of the others.

As we stand in the crowd on the street corner in downtown USA, what is our response to the message of the prophetess? Do we think, "This sounds like something from another planet!" Or, maybe we just feel she is being a bit old-fashioned. I personally shudder at the thought of what the typical American lady would do with a message like this. I know that many a lady in our land, would not rejoice at the thought of giving her life talents, and abilities away to such a "second rate" cause. So many have "progressed" way beyond this job description. This is very sad to me. While many look down on the most honored role that a lady could play in life, at the same time, our homes are falling apart en masse. There are more divorces in the Christian setting than there are in the secular. The children are maladjusted, not knowing to whom they are to give their loyalties.

This book, and especially this chapter, are a clarion call to some to come home. God is calling you to a step of faith. To some, it is as major as when God said to step into the river Jordan. You may not realize the impact that your decision will make for a few years, but that is what faith is all about. To others, this chapter is a strong word of affirmation. You are going the right way, mothers. You did make the right choice back there a few years ago. Don't give in to those lying voices that are telling you, "You were all wrong." God will vindicate His Word to you; stay faithful. Ye shall reap, if ye faint not.

Prayer

Father in heaven I pray for these words that are written. Put Your prophetic breath upon them. Make them quick and powerful and sharper than a two edged sword. Reveal the hearts Lord, uncover the motives, and bring the women home. Lord I also beg You to pour encouragement into many a struggling mother, who has lost heart. Affirm them, inspire them, give them fresh courage to keep on keeping on. In Jesus' name. Amen.

29

Where Are the Men?

*I sought for a man, among them
That should make up the hedge, and stand in the gap before me
For the land, but I found none.*

Ezekiel 22:30 adapted

God needs men, as this verse clearly declares. All through the pages of the Bible, we find the Lord looking for a man, or men. He has ordained it that He would work through men to lead His people. The exciting part of it all is that God is no respecter of persons. He will use anyone who is willing to make himself available. I think all of us who know anything about church history would agree that the early church was filled with men, godly men, who were leaders. In those early days of God's glorious power, the church did not lack for men. It was as was prophesied in Psalms 68:11, when the presence of God will come. *"The Lord gave the word; and great was the company of those that published it."* This word *company* means, army. Picture it: a whole army of men prophesying. That is exactly the way it was in the days of the early church.

Yes, God needs men, lots of men, dedicated men who will deny themselves to serve their God. It is also evident in the Scriptures that God is searching for these men. His eyes go to and fro throughout the whole earth, seeking men with upright hearts. But where are those men? This is the question that I raise here in this chapter. The title of this chapter is more than a question. It is a question given with a clarion call to the men. The opportunities of a life time are everywhere, but where are the men?

This little question has become almost a household phrase among many of us. I wonder how many times I've heard people coin this phrase in the last several years of my life. I have heard it in living rooms on a Sunday afternoon when an opportunity for service is mentioned, and there is no one to take it. It gets quiet for a moment, and then someone will say, "Where are the men?

Paul said to Timothy, "The things that thou hast heard of me, the same commit thou to faithful men who shall be able to teach others also." In Paul's day, it wasn't hard for Timothy to find faithful men to whom he could commit his treasures. In 2 Timothy 2:2, we see four generations of leaders: Paul is the first, Timothy is the second, the *"faithful men"* are the third, and the *"others also"* are the fourth generation. It was through faithful men like these that God continued to propagate the faith from one generation to the next in the early church. We know as we study church history, that Timothy did find faithful men, and those faithful men did commit the things that they learned to others also.

A Burden is Born

The words, "Where are the men," and the burden that flows out from these words began to dawn on my heart over twenty years ago. Before that, I was sort of shielded from the need by the Bible school I attended. At Bible school we had the best young men from all over the country—hundreds of young men aspiring to the work of God. They were on fire for the Lord and earnestly seeking Him through prayer, the study of the Word, and Christian service. It wasn't until I was away from the Bible school, and into regular church life, that the burden began to grow. There was one particular meeting where the Lord set me up for a lesson that would affect my whole ministry.

I was traveling with Lou and Ralph Sutera, serving them in their revival ministry. We were in Morden, Manitoba at the

Alliance church there. About three weeks into the meetings, Ralph said to me, "We are going to have a ladies' meeting, and I would like you to speak to the ladies." I had never preached to a group of ladies before; I wasn't too sure about it, but I consented. This is where I first began to sense a special burden for ladies. I believe it was on a Tuesday evening, four hundred ladies gathered together in the church auditorium. It was an experience that I will never forget. I stood up before all these sisters, trembling, with an unusual burden on my heart. We had been having meetings every night for three weeks, and these ladies were in tune with God. They were like sponges that draw out the Word.

I preached to these dear ladies on the power of a submissive spirit. I shared with them the same basic principles that I have shared with you in this book. I told them that God has power for their lives, and that they need to get in their God-ordained place in order to experience it. I told them that they could have a tremendous influence on their husbands' lives, if they would find that place of power underneath his authority. I encouraged them to quit trying to change their husbands and to give God a chance.

I had tremendous liberty as I preached and then I gave an invitation. All over the auditorium ladies stood up and started making their way down to the front. They filled the altar, two hundred of them, as well as every aisle. This went on until there was no more room to put them. These dear ladies hit the altar. They were weeping! And they were wailing! They were crying out to God for their failures, broken over the needs in their lives. I must admit, I was somewhat surprised and shocked. I did not expect such a response.

Two days later, we had a men's meeting. The design of the meeting was the same as for the ladies. A special message was given to the men, challenging them in their areas of responsibility.

Again, this was after the meetings had been going on for three weeks. The men were supposed to be revived by then. I was not speaking at this meeting, but went to hear the message. When the message was over an invitation was given, and three men went to the front. I sat there in shock, (this is where the title for this chapter first flowed up out of my heart). My heart cried out, "God, where are the men?! Why aren't they up here?!"

You see, I had caught the tears of all the ladies two nights before. They stood in line to ask me questions when the service was over. With tears running down their faces they said, "I don't know what to do. My husband doesn't seem to love God. He doesn't seem to be a spiritual leader, and I don't know what to do. Would you please help me?" I had caught all their tears, and now, to see how unconcerned the men were to respond to the call that was given to them was almost more than I could bear.

This is not an isolated case; I wish it were. It is now twenty-three years later, and I have had several opportunities to preach to the sisters about their place of power, under their husband's authority. I have seen the whole story lived out again and again. In one meeting where this message was given to a mixed group, we sat for 25 minutes and listened to one sister after another stand to their feet with tears running down their faces, confessing their sins. They were pleading for grace to live according to the message that was just given. It was again a real blessing to my heart to see their soft, tender hearts.

Then, a short time later, the men were given a challenging message about God's place for them. The meeting was opened up afterwards for any of the men who would like to give testimony or make confession. Nobody stood up. Nobody. And again my heart cried out, "God, where are the men? What is wrong with the men?"

In my travels, I find myself in a lot of different homes. As Jackie and I sit together in homes and have fellowship with other couples, we often notice something about the couples. We have noticed that the men seem to be sadly lacking for spiritual fervor, interest, and desire. At the same time, we have found a real hunger and many questions coming from the ladies in the room. Many times when we drive away from a place like that I look over to Jackie, and she looks over to me, and we almost say in unison, "Where are the men?" In all of these situations, the men were there, but yet the men were not there. There were men filling their spots, but not their role as leaders.

Dear men, you hold in your hand the knowledge and wisdom to transform your whole life. God's Word is powerful. Maybe you are feeling a bit dejected right now as you come to grips with where you are with God and your family. God can change it all my brother; rise up and believe. All this has the potential of affecting your children to the third and fourth generation.

For Judgment, God Takes Away the Leaders

Okay, the question is, "Where are the men?" There are probably a few answers to this question, but I believe we have a couple of answers in Isaiah 3. When men turn away from God and His ways, God judges them and their families by taking precious spiritual things away from them. This is part of the New Testament principle of *"to whom much is given, of him shall be much required"* (Lk. 12:48). If you have something and you are not using that which you have, God will take even that which you have away. But, if God has given you something, and you use that, God will add more to it (see Matt. 13:12).

> *For behold, the LORD, the LORD of hosts, doth take away from Jerusalem the mighty man, the man of war, and the judge, the prophet, the prudent, and the ancient, the captain of fifty, the honorable man, and the counselor, the cunning artificer, and the eloquent orator. And I will give children to be their princes, and babes shall rule over them.*
>
> Isaiah 3:1-4 (adapted)

Now, these are some very interesting verses in light of our question, "Where are the men?" I believe we have some answers in the text above that will deal with our present dilemma. God took some things away from Israel because Israel (specifically, the men of Israel) turned away from God. They turned away from God's ways and God's voice. The judgment that He brought upon the people was that He took away all the leaders. Do you know what happens to a people or a family if you take away the leaders? Chaos! Could this apply to the situation here in America. It is hard to find leaders, isn't it? I have been grieved over the lack of character, even in some of our presidents.

The Pursuit of Godly Seed

God said to Israel, "You went your own way; you didn't hear My voice. I warned you, I sent prophets your way, but you wouldn't hear them." What could God do but judge them? He took away their bread and water, but He took away much more than that. He took away the leaders, the most important thing they had. All those strong pillars in Israel—they were gone. The eloquent preacher, and the wise judge—they were gone. That problem-solver and the wise old men—they also were gone. So what did they have left? Children to rule over them.

This sounds like America to me. I don't believe that verse four is talking about little babies, but rather young men who should be following wise old men. Even so, it still reminds me of those three year olds who rule their fathers and mothers in the grocery stores. Verse five goes on to prophesy how *"The child shall behave himself proudly against the ancient."* The whole description reminds me of America. Now we dump all the ancients in the rest homes and forget about them. We go and see them once a year, maybe twice. This is what happens, and why does it happen? Because America is turning away from God and His Word.

This whole scenario has fallen upon us as God's people. Isaiah prophesied that the time would come when men would say, *"make me not a ruler of the people"* (see vs.7). He warned of day when men would say, "I don't want to be a ruler, you do it!" This is the way it is today. In fact, in many of the churches, if a man is called by God to lead out he complains, "Oh no, I have to be the leader! Now what?" It is no longer an honorable thing to be a preacher of righteousness and a minister of the gospel. What is wrong? Nobody wants to be the leader.

I had a real eye-opener twenty three years ago that illustrates the reality of this dearth in the churches. I sat in a home with a bunch of men on a Sunday afternoon. They were all sitting around trying to decided who was going to have devotions that evening at church and nobody wanted to do it. I was sitting there listening to these men pass the ball back and forth. (And remember, I love to preach.) This is how it went.

"Well, brother, you have the devotion tonight."

The other brother said, "No, let Brother So-and-So have it."

And Brother So-and-So said, "No, I don't have anything. You do it."

These pillars of the church did this for ten minutes. Finally, one man succumbed to the task and all the rest breathed a sigh of relief. I didn't say a word, but in my heart I was saying, "I'll take it! Give the ball to me! I would be delighted to have devotions at the church."

It is hard to find very many men who will rise up and say, "Give me the ball. I will be glad to carry it." The reason why nobody wants to pick up the ball and run with it is because they don't have the unction of the Holy Ghost. They don't have the life of God burning within them. It is hard to find men who are willing to rise up and submit to the discipline that it takes to pray, read the Word, and get some fresh bread to give to everybody else. Nobody wants the responsibility; it is too much work. I tell you, it is a judgment from God because we are leaving His ways.

Then the Women Fill In

When men turn away from God and His ways, then God takes away their anointing. He strips them of their spiritual authority and leaves them void of wisdom. He takes away their internal strength, and there they stand, trying to be husbands, fathers, and church leaders, without the goods. This is what happens. All those blessed gifts from God leave. The children turn against their fathers, authority issues get distorted, and leadership is lacking. With all this lack, then the women step in and try to fill in the gaps, right? I wonder how many times I've heard women say, "Should I just step in and do it? My husband won't have devotions, but he doesn't mind if I have them."

How do I answer questions like this? She is being so careful how she words the description of her husband's irresponsibility. My heart hurts for the mothers and the children. They are Christians, and they want to have the proper respect for Daddy, but the truth is, he is a tire without air. I tell the sister carefully, "Hey, if he doesn't mind you having devotions, then, Go for it!" But at the same time, I'm thinking, "Brother, wake up! Why don't you get some bread to give to your children?"

The Pursuit of Godly Seed

Why should the wife be the one who has to gingerly lead the family, being careful not to hurt her husband's ego? That father ought to hang his head in shame, repent, and turn back to God. There is more than one problem with the feminist movement, but, this is one of the problems. Two generations of absentee men, and, finally, the women step in and start filling in the gaps.

Somewhere back there our forefathers failed the Lord. And as they failed, they lost their power and their authority. Then, a generation of boys grew up underneath the plague of no leadership. Then another generation of boys grew up underneath that. Now, here we are, and many of us don't have a clue how to lead our families.

I believe this is one of the answers to our great question. I am not blaming you men, I'm just saying that this is the situation in which we find ourselves. Many of us are not the leaders we ought to be. Brethren, we have got to break the chain! We must shake this thing off! We need to get honest with ourselves and acknowledge the need of our heart. We need to "Rise up, O men of God!" and "Have done with lesser things."

I wonder how many times I've caught the tears of a woman as she spoke these words, "How can I help my husband be a spiritual leader? He is a good provider, he has given us a good home to live in, he pays the bills, but he won't take any leadership." It is easy to handle these material things (We live in America) but it takes a clear, clean, spiritual man to do the other.

I give them the right counsel; brethren, I do. I tell them, "Sister, you get in your place, learn how to pray, and honor your husband." But I must admit, sometimes I cringe inside when I give that counsel because I know that some of the men are going to step all over them.

Dear brothers, it isn't right to tell them all the humbling things they should do if you aren't going to take the lead in all this. It isn't right to keep telling the ladies to overlook all your needs and give honor. Some of these dear sisters have been trying this "hidden woman" stuff for ten years. When are we going to wake up and get right with God? We are too proud, brethren. I've noticed that for years, even in revival meetings where God is moving in a mighty way. The sisters are quick to break their hearts and confess needs, but the men are very slow to do the same. Are we so spiritual that we don't need to confess-or are we too proud? Maybe it is time to have an old-fashioned revival meeting at home. You know, when the father sits down with the family and says, "I've failed! I've failed! I've failed! Will you forgive me? I've put everything else ahead of you. I haven't put God first in my life. Please forgive me."

Leaders Raise Leaders

There were days in the history of Israel when the nation was full of leaders. Have you ever read the list of David's mighty men? There is quite a hall of fame listed in 2 Samuel 23. David was an anointed leader, and leaders produce leaders. This principle works, whether it is with a father and his sons, or a leader and his men. This is the reason why there were so many leaders in the nation of Israel at one time. The men of Israel were leaders; and their sons grew up to be leaders, even their servants became leaders.

Brethren, there are two ways that this dearth for leaders can be changed. First of all, we need a heaven-sent revival. Just like in days of old, when the Spirit of God is poured out upon men, then we have an abundance of leaders. This would stem the tide.

The second way is closer home to each one of us. We men need to have a personal revival in our hearts and take our place as leaders in the home. This will produce a whole generation of young men who are leaders. You see, when a boy grows up in a home where Father is a leader, he catches the spirit of leadership. His role model is Father. He grows up at his dad's feet, and catches leadership from him. This is something that each one of us men can do. We men have the potential to turn this whole thing around in one generation. If we will rise up and take our place, and be faithful, God will give us a generation of young men who are leaders. God is seeking men today. He is looking for men who are willing to stand in the gaps and make up the hedge This begins at home. There are many men who are aspiring to the work of God. I thank God for every one of them, but we must remember, God's work begins at home. There you have a house full of waiting disciples. There you have a wife who needs nurture. There you have a training ground for future ministry.

God wants each of you men to become a mature man. A mature man is a man who has learned to walk with God, a man who is willing to be sensitive to the Spirit of God. A mature man is a man who is filled with the convictions of the Word of God. Nobody needs to tell him what to do; he does it by conviction, out of his own heart's desire.

A mature man is a man who has made commitments to God; he has learned to walk in the light. As God gave him light, he said, "Amen" (or "so be it"). Then, God gave him more light, and he said, "Amen" again. As the years went by he kept on saying, "Amen," to the will of God, and he matured. This kind of man is *"able to teach others also."*

A mature man is one who has learned how to handle his finances. It is God's will that you become financially stable. For some of you, that means making some major changes, so that you can get out of debt. I am not referring to a wise debt (like a house), but credit card debts and the like. It is an honor to God if you are financially stable. This is part of true leadership.

A Church Full of Godly Men

Now, let's dream a bit. All these thoughts about leaders stirs my heart: What if all of us men would get serious about this whole matter of leadership? Oh, what a church that would make a whole church full of men who are sold out to God and walking in leadership. That would be a powerful church. That would be a New Testament church. It would be an apostolic church, like the early church was in the days of the apostles.

In the early days of Christianity, as the Spirit was poured out upon all, many leaders were raised up. The church was full of godly leaders. It was the norm. Maybe you think the standard is too high, but consider for a moment. These descriptions of a mature man are the biblical requirements for church leaders (1 Tim. 3:1-14). I believe all of us men should be aspiring to take our place as leaders in the church. That means we should all be working on these requirements. We should be mature men who walk with God. We should be men of convictions, having financial stability. We should be men who have our children in order, with faithful wives. The list goes on, but the point here is that we should aspire to these leadership qualities. In time, this will give us churches full of godly leaders—and this is New Testament church life.

It ought to be the normal thing for the church to be filled with men of God. The church should be filled with prophets, teachers, exhorters, evangelists, and men of wisdom who can lead. Today, most churches have one or two dynamic men in them, and the rest just sit there in the pews. This is not New Testament. May God give every family a man of God for a daddy. All the children should have a papa, who brought a hot word from God today in devotions. But where are these men?

God Honors Men

Now God honors men. From the beginning of creation God established His order. He made Adam the king of the earth and put him in charge of everything. For the most part, and in most situations, God leads through men. God has ordained that the church as well as the home be led by men. There is much responsibility that goes along with this truth, and I think we men need to wake up to it.

All through the Bible we see God using men. Even the context of the Bible was written to men. Even though it is written for us all, still, it was written to the brethren. I am not saying that God dishonors women; I have already explained how God has placed His order for them. But from the beginning it was God's plan to place men in authority and give them more responsibility.

But, brethren, where much is given, much is required. I have often said to people as they were struggling with being under authority, "I would rather be under authority than in authority any day, because of the heavy load of responsibility that falls upon you when you're in authority." Nevertheless brethren, the mantle has fallen on us. God is calling us in this hour to rise up and stand in the gap. We are the men.

Meditations

Marriage: The Finest Friendship

Friendship is unselfish love between two hearts.
It is the finest weave of any tie that binds human hearts.
It is the thoughtful outgoing
of one's whole nature to another.
It is an act of the will, though unconsciously so.
It is not essentially an emotion,
Though it sweeps all the emotional powers of a human.
It is not of the heart primarily,
though it absolutely controls it.
It is wholly in itself a matter of choice.
The will gathers up all the information at hand.
Displays it skilfully before the heart,
Until it is enraptured and completely swept along.

adapted S.D. Gordon

30

Happy Radiant Wives

> *Husbands love your wives*
> *even as Christ also loved the church,*
> *and gave himself for it.*
>
> *Ephesians 5:25*

The marriage relationship is by far the deepest relationship that humans can have. This statement holds true even on a natural level, but it involves an even greater reality for those joined in Christian marriage. The influence of this Christian union on the next generation is beyond measure. There are so many different ways that your marriage affects your children, yet God sums it up in one small phrase in Malachi: *"Wherefore one? That he might seek a godly seed"* (Mal. 2:15). There are many deep reasons why God made man and wife one flesh, but one of those reasons is the powerful influence that this union has on the children born to them.

The greatest gift that you can give your children is a happy marriage. Children should grow up in the secure atmosphere of parents who love each other deeply. That love should be so evident to them that they can testify, "My father and mother love each other." O the devastation of living in a home where arguments break out regularly. The children have a feeling of foreboding lingering over them: "Will my parents stay together or divorce?" This breeds insecurity at all levels of development. The stress and strain of a divided home undermine so much of the good parents try to do through training. In previous chapters, I addressed the sisters and the part they play in maintaining a happy marriage. Now it is the men's turn.

Thus Saith the Lord

Husbands, love your wives, even as Christ also loved the church, and gave himself for it; that he might sanctify and cleanse it with the washing of water by the word, that he might present it to himself a glorious church, not having spot, or wrinkle, or any such thing; but that it should be holy and without blemish.

So ought men to love their wives as their own bodies. He that loveth his wife; loveth himself. For no man ever yet hated his own flesh; but nourisheth and cherisheth it even as the Lord the Church.
Ephesians 5:25-29

Many of us men are missing a wonderful crown upon our life because we neglect to give the proper care to our wives. As I understand the language of Proverbs, we are missing a beautifying ornament that draws attention to us as a men and leaders. That ornament is a wife who knows she is loved and cherished by her husband. It is a wife who walks in holiness, serving her husband out of love. *"A virtuous woman is a crown to her husband"* (Pro. 12:4a).

The picture in this text is tremendous. As Paul seeks to illustrate the beauty of a New Covenant marriage, he draws from a most profound spiritual example. He turns our attention to the relationship of Christ and His church. We see the blessed result of all Christ's care for the church. What is that result? It is a glorious, shining, spotless, and blameless bride for Himself. We see a bridegroom who is grooming his bride for a glorious wedding day, and a union that will last for all eternity. Hallelujah! His methods of grooming are worthy to follow, and we will look at them later. But first, let us look at the bride.

A Radiant Woman

In verses 26 and 27, God gives us the most beautiful picture of the church in all the Bible. There she stands, radiant, spotless, and waiting for her husband. There is much here that we can glean for our marriages. Just as Christ's wife is to be radiant (glorious), our wives should be the same. A glorious church is always a crown to Jesus Christ. We see this so clearly in the book of Acts. Revival history also verifies this repeatedly.

A shining, happy wife provides the same crown for us men, and we are the ones responsible for this glow. Our wives should have the "glow-ry" shine on their faces. It is a shine that comes up out of the heart and manifests itself on the face. In the Christian context, this shine is much more than happiness. It is the manifestation of many beautiful things within the heart. Consider a few of the colors that make up this glow.

- It is a heart, "cleansed with the washing of water, by the word."
- It is a heart, showered with the love of a husband, bursting forth with joy.
- It is a heart, manifesting the godly character of Christ.
- It is a heart filled with mature wisdom and judgment.
- It is a heart with no major spiritual problems.
- It is a heart where the presence of God does shine.
- It is a heart that manifests a clear conscience.

Brethren, this kind of inner beauty makes a wife radiant, and this kind of radiance is a crown on our head. Its silent message cries to a world full of hurting marriages. It says, "My husband loves me and cares for me." As we look over this rainbow of qualities, it is easy to see that we husbands have a lot to do with most of them. This woman is radiant because she is receiving ministry from her husband. Her life is happy, fulfilled, and charged with meaning because of the spiritual care and direction her husband gives her.

Ephesians clearly teaches us to conduct this ministry in the tenderness of our Savior's example.

Laying Down Our Lives
I am so glad we have a clear revelation of Christ's example to follow. He laid down His life for the church. God tells us to love our wives the way that Christ loves us. How tenderly He guides us along the heavenly way, patiently giving us room to grow! He is longsuffering as He waits, sometimes years, until a change takes place. This is how the Savior deals with us. It is amazing how He continues to love and bless us while He waits. Oh, Lord, make us like Jesus with our wives. We need to smile upon them from our hearts while we see needs in their lives with our eyes. We need to take away the furrowed eyebrow and replace it with a smile.

Likewise, ye husbands, dwell with them according to knowledge,
giving honour unto the wife, as unto the weaker vessel,
and as being heirs together of the grace of life;
that your prayers be not hindered.
I Peter 3:7

This verse gives us more insight into what it means to lay down our lives for our wives. In this verse, God connects the example of Christ with practical ways we can love our wives. The connection is revealed through the word "likewise," which means, "in the same manner." This word appears twice in this chapter. In both places, it refers to the example of Christ given to us in Peter 2. If you want to grasp the full thrust of this verse, you should go back and read 1 Peter 2:21-25, and then read the verse preceding this paragraph.

God is speaking to us husbands about suffering in a redemptive way as we dwell with our wives. As I read all these verses together, I picture a husband full of faith, dwelling patiently with his wife. There are no arguments in this home and no retaliation for failures. The word "dwell" is a deep word. It means much more than living in the same house. The depth of this word is beautiful. The picture is that of a husband communing with his wife with a patient, understanding heart. We should be husbands who know enough about our wives to discern their needs and how much they can bear. *"Dwell with them according to knowledge."*

God admonishes us men to honor our wife as the weaker vessel. However, what does God mean by "weaker vessel?" This is one of those phrases that men use in many unscriptural ways. It does not mean the wife is dumb or lacking in wisdom. It is not right to push her aside by simply saying, "She is the weaker vessel." Many of us men use this phrase out of context. God is telling us to honor our wives, to give them a place of special esteem, such as we would give to our eyes. We take special care of our eyes because they are a sensitive part of our body, a part we do not want to lose. Likewise, our wives are a very important part of us, and they require special tenderness and care. Give them honor, give them extra attention, and you will be the better for it. If you lose your eyes through neglect, you will stumble your way through the rest of your life. If you lose your wife, you also will stumble your way through the rest of your life. *"Therefore take heed to your spirit, and let none deal treacherously against the wife of his youth"* (Mal. 2:15b).

The Lord adds strength and balance to the words we have already considered by proclaiming husband and wife to be equals. We are fellow heirs of the grace of life, washed in the same blood. We stand together in God's kingdom, under the same canopy of grace. *"Be not high minded, but fear"* (Rom. 11:20b).

There is no place for an arrogant display of authority by the husband over his wife. Again, I plead for a calm, quiet authority led by the gracious Spirit of God. Remember, the Holy Spirit is gentle. We are brothers and sisters in Christ, bound to the many gracious principles of brotherhood in the New Testament.

The husband and wife are a powerful prayer team, and Satan knows this. I wonder how many couples have an effective prayer ministry, warring together against the enemy. I am afraid that more times than not, their relationship is so strained they don't even pray together. God is admonishing us husbands about how we can eliminate that strain. Lay down your life for your wife. This is God's way.

If a man is preparing for the ministry, the Bible says he is not ready for the ministry unless he has had an effective ministry in the life of his wife. The ministry of washing, encouraging, teaching, cherishing, praying, and discipling his wife prepares a man for future work. These are qualifications for leadership. A leader must have a sanctified wife. A man who has made a disciple of his wife will be able to make disciples in the church. This happens in many practical ways. I will cover some of them in the remainder of this chapter.

Husbands Love Your Wives

The Powerful Emotion of Love

This first point needs some definition because everything I will mention falls under the category of love. There is a difference between the acts of love and the emotion of love. Ideally, the many acts of love should flow out of the deep commitment and emotion of love. This kind of love is one of those phenomenons that stretches beyond understanding. In Song of Solomon 8:7 we read, *"Many waters cannot quench love, neither can the floods drown it: if a man would give all the substance of his house for love, it would utterly be contemned."*

This is the power of love. Love is an unexplainable force that works to produce all the rest of what I share in this chapter. Christ did not die merely out of obedience. His love for us compelled Him to lay down His life and die for us. I know of no other thing that will cause a wife to radiate from within like love. Genuine love has commitment and emotion. We dare not separate these two with our wives.

Some time ago, I saw a beautiful illustration of this at a church gathering. One of the courting couples had just announced their engagement. She was radiant. Why was she all aglow? The young man had not had much time to disciple her yet, but she was beaming because of his love and favor flowing to her heart. The most powerful influence you can have on your wife is to love her.

A Student of Your Wife

This point naturally flows from the preceding one. When we love our wives, we will want to understand them. We will seek to know them in deeper and deeper ways. God made the woman very different from the man. His plans and purposes for her are not the same as those for the man. It is very important that we understand this in a positive way. These differences are beautiful variations. Yea; she is *"fearfully and wonderfully made"* (Psa. 139:14). When men make foolish statements about women such as "Women, who can understand them?" they are showing their ignorance of God's purposes in creation. These differences, learned in a joyful and positive way, can change your marriage. She is an amazing creation made very different from you. We men need to take the time to get to know our wives. We should be enjoying our wives unique qualities. They are a balance to us. Just as Christ seeks to know us, His bride, we also should seek to know our wives.

A Spiritual Leader

Christ is the initiator of the relationship He has with His bride. He loved us first and laid down His life to draw us to Himself. He is the initiator. We are the responders. This is a lovely picture of spiritual leadership. Most Christian wives long for a husband who tenderly leads out in their home. This kind of initiative brings great security to the heart of a wife. Her heart becomes loyal and respectful, and submission is easy. The opposite is also true. When men do not take the lead in their homes, problems arise, and there is unrest in the home. Have you ever seen an insecure woman sparkling?

A Wise Financial Manager

Christ is the provider of all that His bride needs. She doesn't have a worry or care when He is near. We husbands are to follow this pattern in the home. Statistics show that financial conflict is one of the top reasons for divorce in America. I am not inferring that we must be rich, not at all. But we must be free. A wise manager relieves the pressures of money from the home. He will not spend money for unneeded things or things that he wants. This kind of mismanagement is a wound in your wife's heart. If your family finances are out of order, it is time to take some aggressive measures to bring things into balance. A lot of good material on Christian finances is available to men today. We need to take advantage of this. Foolish debts are not Christlike. I cannot see Him doing anything like this. You must free yourself of all these debts and bring peace to your home.

Praise and Attention

Christ's continual care for His church is the fuel that keeps the fires of love burning in our hearts. This works the same in marriage. Let your wife be the object of much praise and attention. We have a proverb at our house that goes like this, "A little bit of love goes a long way." Take the time to show your wife how important she is to you. If you stop and think about it, there are dozens of things that you appreciate about your wife. She needs to know how you feel. Write her a note. Send her a card, or think of some creative way to say "I love you." Stop for a moment and think what it would be like if your wife died. Think of all the things about her that you would miss. This little exercise will bring a host of things to your mind. Then act on some of them by expressing praise and appreciation.

Quality Time

An intimate relationship is the key to a happy marriage. I mean more than a physical relationship when I make this statement. Actually, the physical relationship flows out of the intimate relationship. As husbands and wives, we need time to focus on deep heart type sharing. Use your creative abilities to find ways to help you share like this. Jackie and I have a date every Tuesday. The whole purpose for the date is to spend sweet time together. We may sit in a restaurant and talk for two hours or walk hand-in-hand in the park. We dream dreams together, laugh about some lovely thing the children said, or make plans for future events in the home. Just as intimacy with Christ takes time, so it is with our wives. Do we really want to get to know them? If we do, we will make a way to spend the time and direct that time into intimate sharing.

"Honey Do" List

Do you have one of these lists at your house? We call our list the "Honey Do" List. It consists of things Jackie would like me to fix. Attention to the list is lacking a bit while I am writing this book. This list of things that need to be done is not a little issue in your marriage. Many wives are vexed daily by the nagging neglect of dripping faucets and squeaky doors. There is a silent message here that you do not want to give to your wife. You are saying, "I don't care what bothers you." Many times we undo every sweet word we say by that faucet that keeps on running for days and weeks and months. I often find organizational helps on the list at our house. Our wives are gifted organizers. God has made them detailed creatures. They need our help to carry out many of their plans to keep an orderly home. Help them, brethren. Do it now. Do not wait any longer.

Protector

When Christ is by our side, we have nothing to fear. When we are under His wings, all is well. This should be the experience of our wives. We are their covering. There are responsibilities that go with this position. We need to be alert to the dangers and pressures that our wives face and cover them. Sometimes they have fears. We need to draw these things up out of their hearts, and then help our wives with them. It might just be prayer that is lacking, or maybe we need to change an activity she is facing. An alert husband will sense that something is wrong and draw it out with tenderness. Wives love a good listener. Learn to ask concerned questions that draw the issues up and out, and then just listen as she shares. If a solution is needed, we should act upon it and clear her pressures whenever possible.

Good Manners

The Bible uses the word "courteous" to define good manners. This word means, "manners for the kings court." I like that. Manners vary in different cultures, but all civilized cultures have manners. We men know what they are, and we used them very well when we were courting. We took a bath and brushed our teeth. We spoke with kindness and gentleness. We said "excuse me" and "thank you." Good manners say "you are important, and I care for you." We need to cultivate courtly manners. I am afraid that some of what we call "manliness" is simply bad manners.

A Disciplined Man

A disciplined man is a Spirit-controlled man. When our wives see us living a consistent, ordered life, it gives them confidence in our leadership. Personal devotions are at the pinnacle of all the disciplines because it is a daily exercise. It is much easier for them to trust in our judgments when they see us reading the Word of God and praying every day. Every husband should pursue these goals. Overcome your bad habits by the grace and power of God. Ask your wife what things bother her, and change them. All this reveals a man who is in control of his own spirit.

Humility

I hear a statement often in marriage counseling that I wish I could change right here today. The woman says, "My husband never says, 'I'm sorry'." This is a very sad commentary on Christian manhood. Our wives live with us through the thick and the thin. They know we make many mistakes. It seems so wrong never to admit our errors before our wives. This one flat spot can blot out many good things we try to do. Our integrity is at stake here. Tell her you were wrong and with a sincere humility ask her to forgive you. You may think you will lose respect for this, but actually, the opposite is true. Her respect for you will rise way above the norm when you take the low road of humility in your marriage.

Making Changes Together

Many men, in the name of leadership, damage the spirit of their marriage by making major decisions alone. This is a dangerous way to lead your wife. I have seen many homes derailed this way. All along the husband thought he was "exercising leadership." Brethren, you do not just walk into the house after work one day and say, "God told me to quit my job." You must bring your wife along with you, so she is at peace with such a change. Prepare her ahead of time, and seek her counsel about it. A wife's counsel is one of the most valuable insights you have when making major decisions. She knows you as no one else does. You two are one flesh. This union requires a oneness of heart in major changes. When a man refuses to seek the counsel of his closest companion, he wounds the spirit of his marriage. He gives his wife a silent message that says, "Your opinion is not important." In God's order, the man is the visionary, whereas the wife lives more in the immediate present. You could never dream dreams if you didn't have a wife who lives in the now. When men make impulsive decisions on their own, it is like shooting themselves in the foot before they run a new race. A man must be sensitive to the feelings of his wife and must not spring new things on her without some unifying counsel.

The Dangers of Comparing

The apostle Paul warns us about the dangers of comparing ourselves with others (2 Cor. 10:12). There is, however, a greater danger than this. When a husband compares his wife with another woman, it has a devastating effects on his marriage. Many husbands make this foolish mistake, and they are not even aware that it hurts. It usually comes at the same time that a correction is given, and that is worse yet. To complain about the messy house, then mention another sister's clean house is not productive. This is a sharp wound in the emotional heart of your wife. It tells her that you are not happy with her, and that you have been thinking about another woman. You need to be a one-woman man, and your wife needs to know it is that way.

Affirmation of Her Ministry

We live in a day when it is not popular to be a wife and mother. We men rejoice in the many sisters who have "come home."

I know that our wives have chosen to do this out of deep conviction of heart, and they are firm in their stand. Praise God for their commitment. However, they face many adversaries. They are bombarded with negative input about their sacrifices. We need to affirm our wives in their calling, and do it on a regular basis. If we believe this is God's highest call for them, we will inspire them on to deeper levels of home keeping, and child training. We stand in danger of taking their commitments for granted, forgetting the sacrifices they make for the family. With all the negative voices shouting at them, this is a grave mistake. We need to pass on the vision to our wives and stir them on to prepare for a future teaching ministry as they become the "aged women."

Comfort and a Listening Ear

Our wives are going to fail. We need to give them the freedom to fail and learn. We all know from our own experiences that much learning comes through failure. It is so easy to give them correction, but that usually is not what they need when they have failed. How often would you come with your failures if you received correction each time you came? There are times when correction is needed. However, with a woman, in most cases, it should come later. When your wife has failed, she needs a good listener and some comfort. Try it sometime, and see how she responds. When she comes, sympathize with her and give a listening ear. She already knows a failure has taken place. Just listen.

Sanctified Discipleship

As I look over the list of practical ways to love our wives, it seems they all flow to this one. All these varied acts of love and concern open up the way for a husband to wash his wife and mold her into a true disciple of Christ. This is where spiritual ministry takes place and character is formed in the inner man. A whole book needs to be written on this one point alone. It can be devastating to a wife if her husband tries to exercise this type of ministry without the loving care in place.

However, if the care is there, a husband can take his wife to higher planes spiritually.

Unconditional Acceptance

This final point flows from the previous one. In Christ, we are "accepted in the beloved" (Eph. 1:6). I am so grateful for this reality. This is a tremendous motivation for growth and sanctification. This whole principle works the same way in marriage. The focus of our initial text is that of a pure and holy bride. The husband is the savior (sanctifier) of the wife. This process of discipleship works best in an atmosphere of love and acceptance. When we accept our wives just the way they are, we lay the foundation stones for Christian growth. We also pass the test of impure motivations. It is very hard to sanctify your wife if she senses that you don't like the way she is.

There is so much more that should be written on this subject. I feel I have only begun to scratch the surface. As a husband, you may be thinking, "What a long list of things to do." I want to encourage you to take another attitude about what you have read. Remember, if you care for your wife in ways such as these, you actually are polishing your own crown.

Brethren, Take Care of Your Glory

> *[The man] is the image and glory of God: but the woman is the glory of the man. But if a woman have long hair, it is a glory to her.*
> *I Corinthians 11:7,15a*

There are many beautiful truths in the whole of this Scripture portion. I encourage you to meditate on all of it. However, for the sake of our teaching in this chapter, I will focus only on these two verses.

Three glories are mentioned in 1 Corinthians 11, and one of them is the crown I mentioned at the beginning of these thoughts on marriage. The word glory means "the outshining that brings attention." Man, as the image of God, is God's crown. He is the first glory mentioned in this text. He is the reflected glory of God, and he should bring attention to God. Woman was made after the image of the man. God formed her with a rib taken out of Adam's side. She is the glory of the man, and the second glory mentioned in the text. She is the outshining that brings attention to the man. She is the man's crown. The third glory revealed in the text is a woman's long hair. It is her glory, or that which brings attention to her.

In each of these examples, someone is responsible to care for the glory. God is responsible to care for the man, that He, God, might be glorified. Man is responsible to care for the woman, that he, the man, might receive glory. The woman is responsible to care for her hair, that she, the woman, might receive attention from her hair. Do you see the picture? I have only one thing to say to the men. Men, take care of your glory. Your wife is your glory. Take care of her. Your care for her will only bring brightness and attention back onto you. As your wife glows, you shine. For what more could you ask than that?

My wife takes care of her glory. I appreciate this. At night she lets down that beautiful long hair and brushes it out to keep it healthy and growing. She is no dummy. She cares for that which brings attention to her from me. I love her long hair, and it always turns my head when she lets it down to brush it out at night. Brethren, take care of your glory. You are cutting your own throat if you don't.

When you neglect to care for your wife, her shine begins to dim. The character of Christ begins to fade, and her heart gets cloudy. Many times your wife has a deep need, and God is waiting on you to minister to it. You are going to have to get spiritual. It is not right for you to think the preacher can do it. You are her covering, not the preacher. God's ministry to her will flow through you if you will let it.

O brethren, if we could grasp the revelation of this, it would change our marriages forever. If your wife is not radiant, glowing with love and care, you are the one who is missing the crown. Furthermore, one of God's eternal pictures is distorted, and the world is missing one of the clearest expressions of Christ on the earth. Let's take care of our glory.

31

The Spirit of Law and the Spirit of Grace

*And the Word was made flesh, and dwelt among us,
and we beheld his glory, the glory as of the only begotten of the Father,
full of grace and truth. . . .
And of His fulness have all we received, and grace for grace.
For the law was given by Moses, but grace and truth came
by Jesus Christ.*

John 1:14,16-17

This whole matter of raising children is a very spiritual thing. By this I mean we must be spiritual persons if we want to do all this right. I have tried in many different ways to say this throughout this book. This chapter is another attempt at encouraging you unto the spiritual rather than the carnal, or natural. This is the place where you will find the most effective use of all that I have been teaching.

By my use of the word *spirit* in the title of this chapter, I mean "temper, or disposition of mind; the attitude or nature of our actions; the motivating factor behind our actions." There are many uses of this word in the dictionary, but this is how I use it in this chapter. The other key words of significance in the title are "law" and "grace." These two words appear together fairly often. Many theological discussions have centered around them, and many more will. I don't claim to understand the proper balance of the two, but I do believe it would be good to consider the subject and how it relates to child training.

One thing I have enjoyed about writing this book is the opportunity it has afforded for sharing all my favorite verses with you. The verses that open each chapter all are dear verses to me. They are in my heart, engrafted there, abiding there, and they are the joy and meditation of my soul. The opening verses in this chapter are no exception. O how sweet are these words about the incarnation of Jesus Christ! A wealth of wisdom is hidden in them, as well as a lifetime of fresh drinks from the wells of salvation. I pray that we can get a drink from them here that will bless our families for many days to come.

The apostle John wrote these words near the end of his life on earth, when he was about ninety-five years old. As he wrote this fourth gospel, he was a dear old man who had walked with Christ for about sixty-five years. We are catching some of the overflow of this walk in these verses.

First of all, John gives some of his testimony and his experiences with Christ. He says in awe, *"We beheld his glory."* When John says *"beheld,"* he means way more than just seeing. He means, he had gazed upon him with deep meditations. Then he goes on to describe what he saw. He says, *"The Word was made flesh, and dwelt among us. . . full of grace and truth."* When God uses the word full, it means overflowing. Christ, the anointed one, was full and running over with both grace and truth. This is a beautiful description of the Son of God, and of a perfectly balanced life. I long for this in my own life. I want to be like Jesus-- full and running over.

John goes on to give his personal testimony, as well as the testimony of many others. He shares some of the effect that this Christ has had on him, and remember, he is looking back over sixty-five years. When he says, *"And of his fullness have all we received,"* he is saying, "This incarnate Son of God, who was full and running over, has filled me to the full." Then the apostle uses a phrase to explain this fullness which is fitting to describe boundless grace. *"Grace for grace"* is the phrase he uses. It means, "grace upon more grace upon more grace, an ever-increasing flow of boundless grace." This is a really encouraging word for mothers and us fathers as we look to God for help in time of need.

Two Very Different Ways

In verse 17, John makes a most amazing statement that deals with the two covenants: "The law was given by Moses, but grace and truth came by Jesus Christ." There is a lot of difference in the manner whereby these two ways have come to us. Let us consider how the law was given.

Mt. Sinai was full of fire and smoke, and it literally trembled from the presence of God. There was thunder and lightning. The people actually heard the audible voice of God. Everyone was afraid, and they all trembled just as the mountain did. This is how the law came.

Now when grace and truth came, it was very different. They came by Jesus Christ. He came as a beautiful example, full of the Holy Ghost. He came with gracious words flowing out of His mouth. He came with an inviting spirit, which caused the publicans and sinners to want to be around Him. This is very different. This second way is what we all are intent upon applying to our homes. I wonder which words our children would use to describe the way we guide our homes. Would they say it is Mt. Sinai or Jesus?

The apostle Paul referred to these two ways as two different ministries in II Corinthians 3. He used the word ministration, which means "ministry." The law had a ministry of death, condemnation, and fear. This flows right along with the coming of the law at Mt. Sinai, which brought fear and trembling. The way of grace and truth has a ministry of life and ability, a ministry of inward revelation and transformation. We could also call the first way the way of religion and the second way the way of true Christianity. Again, we want this second way to operate in our homes. It is obvious which way will get better results. Consider what the word *ministry* means: "the effect or influence that we have on someone." This is what home life is all about: effect and influence. The sad note here is that the way of law has a ministry also. However, we do not want this kind of influence in our homes. There is a vast difference in the effects of these two ways. One can be devastating, but the other drops like heavenly dew upon the lives of our children.

The way of grace and truth operates in our homes as long as we parents choose to walk in the Spirit. It is just that simple. The saddest part of this whole story is that many parents are not committed enough to walk in the Spirit. So, most of the time, they have a home that moves in the operations of law. With small undiscerning children, it is easy for parents to function in this way. However, the laws of sowing and reaping are in effect.

You will have a very different kind of child if you raise him under the operations of law instead of grace. Therefore, it is very important that we give some clear characteristics of each way to help you divide between the two. I want to define clearly how the spirit of law functions in everyday home life, and then show how the spirit of grace functions as well. This is the burden and purpose of this chapter. I give these distinctions with a burden that you will flee from the operations of the law and cleave unto the Lord, and to His grace.

The Spirit of Law Exposed

The Spirit of Law Condemns: When we condemn our children, we bring feelings of failure and judgment upon them. A spirit of accusation is in operation here. We all know that Satan is the accuser of the brethren. I am sure none of us want to enter into any of his work. When we accuse the children, this leaves them in despair, with no way out of their problem. At this point, many parents say things they do not really mean, to the devastation of the child. Verbal corrections done in the flesh often are condemning. Continual nagging often has the same effect.

The Spirit of Grace Convicts: Discerning parents knows that they are not alone in their task of parenting. The Spirit of God is their helper, and He will convict the child in his conscience when the parent makes a correction. When we know this, we do not need to raise our voice or use strong words to show the child how bad he was. I earlier spoke of calm quiet authority.

The Spirit of Law and the Spirit of Grace

This is one of those times when you can choose to minister to your child in his heart by the Spirit. You can lovingly correct without condemning.

The Spirit of Law Discourages: This word *discourage* is an interesting word in light of raising children. It means "to take the heart out of, or to dishearten." God warns us about affecting our children in this way. It is a very dangerous thing considering their natural desire to please us. As parents, we need to ask ourselves, "Do I leave my child disheartened after I have related to him?" If your child loses his desire to do right and to please you, something is wrong. Lord, please open our eyes.

The Spirit of Grace Encourages: Grace, on the other hand, fills the heart with desire. This is very different from what law does. We need to come alongside of our child and egg him on in the right ways of God. A synonym of this word encourage is "*to cheer.*" I like this. That is what I want to be for my child, one who cheers him on when he does right and picks him up when he does wrong, so he can keep on going. The grace of God inspires us to do the will of God. I want to be like God, inspiring and leading my children to go the right way. This is training the palate of my children by exciting them in the right paths.

The Spirit of Law Is Never Good Enough: With law, you never quite measure up. You could always do better. It seems that you never reach a place where what you do is accepted. This is the nature of law. I think of the Pharisees in this context. By the time of Christ, they had developed a whole book of Sabbath laws. Law operates this way. It always demands more. They even felt they were righteous because they wrote more laws for the Sabbath. Attitudes such as these are very hard on children who want to please their parents. Many parents do the "silent disapproval act" on their children when they do not measure up. What a miserable way for the children to grow up. Some children spend the rest of their lives trying to be good enough, but never making it. Under the law, mistakes are not allowed--period.

The Spirit of Grace Blesses Each New Step: First of all, grace is not dependent on every little action. However, as we look at the actions, grace is excited over each new step of obedience. This excitement stirs the child on to higher ground. Remember, there should be nine pounds of praise to one pound of correction. When a child knows he is not being judged by every little action, he is freed up to please his parents out of love. This is the Bible way. You will see that the way of grace produces much better fruit, with much better motives. Under grace, the children can even make mistakes. Parents should give their children room for failure. If they do, the children then can learn from their failures in freedom instead of condemnation.

The Spirit of Law Binds: It gives you more than you can bear all the time. Remember Bunyan's Pilgrim. The burden that Pilgrim had on his back pictures the bondage of the law. When we weigh our children down with more than they can bear, we bring them into bondage. They become slaves to our insensitive demands. We should always remember the carefree attitudes of a little child. This is what the kingdom of heaven is like. God forbid that we should be guilty of binding our precious children with heavy burdens they cannot bear.

The Spirit of Grace Brings Liberty: When a child is led into the right by encouragement and praise, he finds life full of freedom. A child's innocent life is supposed to picture the glorious kingdom of God. We have a lot to do with this childhood experience by the way we order the children's young lives. If we walk in grace, we will not be loading them with more than they can handle. We will be careful to measure the task according to the ability. If we lead the children into right paths, they will begin to receive blessing and freedom from those right paths. We must be committed to full-time parenting for this to happen.

The Spirit of Law Curses: A person who is cursed is one who is forsaken. He is left alone to bear his punishment for wrongs he has done. Jesus bore our curse in just this way. A person who

The Spirit of Law and the Spirit of Grace

is cursed is one who has had curses pronounced over him. This is a despairing state of being. Many children feel just this way when they are sent to their room with harsh words. They are to sit there under the curse, waiting for punishment. In addition, when parents curse their children with words, this leaves the child in despair. Many children never free themselves from the verbal curses their parents put on them. A curse often has an element of the future in it, and can be prophetic. Most parents do not mean it when they speak this way, but the words have a powerful influence on the children.

The Spirit of Grace Blesses: Earlier, I wrote about blessing your children, yet I feel it is worthy of another reminder. We need to see that blessings flow from the heart that walks in grace. Words of blessing naturally flow from an abundant heart. Encouraging words have fire in them. They inspire, motivate, and strengthen our children to do right. It is Godlike to bless. Look through the Bible and see how many times God and blessings are mentioned. God is obsessed with blessing His people. O God, make us like Thee in this holy act.

The Spirit of Law Criticizes: When we as parents are always finding fault, we are moving in the realm of the law. This is an easy trap to fall into because we want our children to do what is right. However, if we neglect the positive leading aspects of training, we slip into the critical or nagging aspects of the law. None of us like to be the nag. It makes all who are involved miserable. It even affects those who have to listen to it repeatedly. Dear parent, if you catch yourself always finding something wrong, then you probably are operating in the law and not in the grace of God.

The Spirit of Grace Gives the Benefit of the Doubt: This is such a beautiful description of grace. Do you know someone who is like this? They are always refreshing company. The golden rule comes in here: "Do unto others as you would have them do unto you." We want people to give us the benefit of the doubt. This is very different from looking first for the worst and expecting to find it. I think of the words from the "love chapter": *"[Charity] beareth all things, believeth all things, hopeth all things, endureth all things"* (1 Cor. 13:7). Too often we look for the worst first. This is a great discouragement for the children.

The Spirit of Law Exposes Sin and Remembers It: This happens in parent-child relationships when proper correction is not given. We expose the sin, complain about it, remind the child of it, but never do anything about it. We do not attempt to clear the heart and bring the issue to a close. This is what the law did. It had no remedy for sin. Then, to make things worse, we remind the child repeatedly of what he did wrong. There is no mercy in this conduct at all. When a child is in this state, he is miserable and has no hope.

The Spirit of Grace Forgives and Forgets: When a child does something wrong, our heart should be redemptive. We should seek the best possible means to clear the issue and forget it. *"Love covereth all sins"* (Pro. 10:12b), and God has provided the way for parents to do this. When we lovingly spank our child and help him clear his conscience, we free the child to forget the wrong. This kind of conduct is full of mercy and forgiveness. There is not better way to teach a child what God is like than to say from your heart, "You are forgiven; go and sin no more!" When we remind the child of it again, we are acting like Satan.

The Spirit of Law Tends to Details: I cite the Pharisees again as an example of this characteristic. They were extreme in their demand for details, while missing the more important matters of the law. It is a great burden to our children when we demand detailed perfection of them. Our exacting nature weighs them down to the point of giving up. Worse yet, they will become perfectionists like us and have to live with this bondage all their days.

The Spirit of Grace is Flexible: When we are moving in grace, things do not have to be exactly the way we want them. The spirit of a law is good enough. There are at least five ways to take out the garbage, and it does not have to be my way. The law says: take out the garbage, but there grace allows flexibility about how to do it. I have had to learn this firsthand with my business. As I am writing this book, my son Samuel is operating the family business. He does things differently than I do. I give him the freedom to make judgment calls according to his discernment. He is doing a good job, even though it is different from the way I would do it.

The Spirit of Law Is Performance Oriented: This point has many sad stories to go with it. When parents place actions and detailed performance at the top of their list, they develop a theology of works. In a theology of works, you never know if you have done enough to be accepted. Children who grow up under this theology usually carry it into their adult life. They can spend the rest of their life performing to get a blessing. We all know that this blessing comes and goes because we don't always perform rightly. This is bondage. When parents train children this way, the children feel rejected when they don't do right. It is a tragic reality that many children receive love and acceptance only when they perform right. Is God like this? Is this what the grace of God is like? We all know the answer.

The Spirit of Grace is Relationship Oriented: The highest goal in the grace life is relationships. Everything in the New Covenant points to relationships, first with God and then with others. The foundation of these relationships is unconditional love. We are Christians, and we are accepted in the Beloved because we have turned to God through Jesus Christ. This kind of theology should permeate our homes. Our children should know deep in their hearts that we love them no matter what. They should feel our love and acceptance even when we are spanking them. This is grace.

In Conclusion

I want to define my use of the word "law" at this time. I believe in using law at my house. The children are under tutors and governors until they come to Christ. However, all this is to be in operation by the grace of God. The motivation is to bring the child to a saving knowledge of Christ, and then to teach the child to walk with Him. The question is "What will I be?" Will I be a loving parent who guides and trains, or a demanding law that shows no mercy? If we lean heavy on the law side all the child's days, we will raise a worldly rebel or a Pharisee. If we lean heavy on the grace side, we will raise a loving disciple of Jesus Christ.

I close this chapter with a story. Some years ago I was sitting in my office counseling a young couple about their home. They were very concerned about their firstborn child, who was three at the time. They were having many obedience problems with her. The father had absolutely no relationship with his daughter. He was not walking in the grace of God in any solid way. As we sat in my office sharing, I could not help but notice the little girl. Every move she made was with a fearful eye on her father. I could tell that she had been corrected for every little thing she did. I also could tell that she received spankings often for many of these little actions. My heart broke as I watched this relationship between father and daughter.

Finally, I broke down and shared my heart with him. I said, "You are operating under the law as you seek to guide your child." I tried to help him see the robot he was slowly creating by his methods. God opened his eyes right there in my office. He broke down and wept like a baby as the revelation of what he was doing dawned upon him. We had a sweet time of repentance, and his family was forever changed.

Maybe this is what you feel like doing as you finish this very probing chapter on relationships. Go ahead and weep. It is better to weep now than to keep on going the wrong way. I often say, "Weep now or weep later, take your pick."

Prayer

Dear Lord, give us eyes to divide between the Old Covenant and the New. For the sake of our dear children who suffer from our ignorance, please open our eyes. Teach us to walk in the Spirit and find our homes full and running over with the Grace of God. Amen.

32

Youth: Anointed Disciples of Jesus Christ

And it shall come to pass in the last days, saith God,
I will pour out of my Spirit upon all flesh:
and your sons and your daughters shall prophesy,
and your young men shall see visions,
and your old men shall dream dreams:
And on my servants and on my handmaidens
I will pour out in those days of my Spirit; and they shall prophesy.
Acts 2:17-18

As you parents come to the reading of these powerful verses, you are in many different stages of your parenting. Some of you may not have a child in your arms yet. Some of you may be just beginning, and your hearts are full of dreams. You may be somewhere in the middle of all this process, wondering how it all works out. Wherever you find yourselves, these verses are for you in this very moment in time. They are timeless promises given to the saints centuries ago, yet they apply to you.

I want you to take a moment, shut your eyes, and dream with me. Envision your children standing somewhere in the world, serving God. They are twenty years old, full of the Spirit of God, and serving God with their whole heart. They open their mouths with boldness and speak out the mind and will of God with unction. Their life and service is such that they are *"known among the*

Gentiles" and by all people. *"All that see them shall acknowledge them, that they are the seed which the Lord hath blessed"* (Isa. 61:9). Their testimony is clear, and everyone can see that the blessing of God is upon them.

This is God's heart and will for your children. Remember, He is a God who *"calleth those things which be not as though they were"* (Rom. 4:17b). He is a God who calls us to see, believe, and move toward that which is in His heart. God sees your seed, anointed with the Holy Ghost and living as witnesses of His life-changing power.

Although this should be our vision all through the years of child training, there is a point in time when this vision of dedicated youth must be actively pursued. We have looked at the awesome reality of God dwelling in our children. We have considered the great blessing that falls on them if we preserve them from evil and guide them down the right path. In this chapter, I consider the maturing process that takes place in our youth from the time they say "I am the Lord's" to the time when they have become like the youth I have just described--the joy and consolation of a parent's heart.

To have youth who are filled with God is a great asset to any home. To have youth who are learning to walk with God is a refreshing addition to any family. This is the goal. I assure you, it is one worth striving to attain.

I remember the first time it dawned on me that the spiritual level had risen in my house because of our young people. The older children were moving into this "dedicated disciple stage," and revival fires were burning continually. It changed the atmosphere of our home. Seasons of revival began to burn during family devotions. It was like the firstfruits of a harvest yet to come. The reality of what I described earlier was just beginning to grow. Jackie and I were pleasantly astounded by the added benefit this brought to our home. We were encouraged by this to press on with each of our children and see them through to a solid walk with God. We have not been disappointed for our labors.

Dear parents, this is a very crucial time in the life of your child. Many parents are shortsighted on this point. Somehow they have the idea that once their child has been soundly converted, the job is done. This is a grave mistake that many undiscerning parents make. I have dealt with many young people who were left to their own ways after conversion. We get them in the prayer room at the age of seventeen years, and they have totally lost their way. This becomes a confusion to them, because they question their earlier experience. This chapter covers this whole process of raising up spiritual youth who are **anointed disciples of Jesus Christ.**

Make a Disciple

Jesus told His disciples to go and make disciples in the same manner that they were trained. This is what we must do. Each converted youth is to be made a disciple of Jesus Christ. We must carefully take our newly converted babe in Christ and teach him how to walk with God.

As parents, we should have the same attitude toward our newborn Christian in the home that we would have in the church. I don't know why we separate things with our children, but we often do. In the church we fuss over all the new babes in Christ. We check up on them. We ask them questions. We spend time in prayer with them, and many other things. Why do we do this? Because they are babies, and we know they must be established in the faith. It is the same with our children. We need to arm ourselves with the same mind concerning our own. This whole process should be a major focus for the next few years until we can see clearly that our child is walking in the grace of God.

You Must Be Spiritual

A spiritual person is one who has learned to walk with God and who walks in His ways. We cannot enter into the task of making a disciple until we have become a disciple. I am not saying this so you can take a back seat and leave the job to the pastor. Rather, I want to provoke you to an earnest seeking after God. As I have mentioned already, many parents neglect the responsibility of making disciples at home. I am afraid the reason why this is neglected, is that parents can't make a disciple if they are not disciples themselves. It is a very sobering condition to have a child who has given his heart to the Lord, yet to be in no shape to help him along his way. Paul said to Timothy, *"The husbandman that laboureth must be first partaker of the fruits"* (2 Tim. 2:6). We can take our children only as far as we have gone in the Lord.

You probably are wondering when I am going to get off your back. I'm sorry if this troubles you, but your precious young people are at stake here. I don't write this to condemn you, but to provoke you to seek the Lord. I have caught a lot of tears from young people who started out in their new faith with high hopes, but fell into many hurtful sins later. They have to bear these scars all their days.

We must be spiritual. I have spent much time convincing you of how important this is for your little ones. It is doubly important for your youth. If you have a young person who has come to faith in Christ, in spite of your weak commitment, now is the time to get serious with God. *"Be thou an example of the believers"* was the challenge that Paul gave to Timothy (1 Tim. 4:12). They need your spiritual guidance desperately.

Young Adults

Your young people are no longer children. This is something that we can see with our eyes, but we don't always realize it in our relationship with them. I like the term "young adults." This helps me to remember that I am moving into a different level of relating. They are not children anymore. They are blossoming adults. Your child is now your brother or sister in Christ. This demands a change in how you relate to him or her. You don't speak with frustration in your spirit when you converse with a brother in the church, do you?

We as parents need to start thinking differently. When the children were young and undiscerning, we could get away with this. But now they are gaining insight into who we really are. This changes everything. If you treat them unkindly, it will wound them because they will know you were unkind. Now we must go and make these things right, or they will be hindered by us. This kind of conduct was wrong when they were young, but now they see it more clearly. We must deal with it.

I have shared some of our failures in this area already. As Jackie and I sat down to hear the hearts of our youth, these were-some of the things that came out. We were offending them by treating them as small children. We slowly learned that we could not just tell them what to do, no questions asked. They had to be treated with respect, and they needed to know it was okay if they had a question about something. We shifted from commanding to leading, from quick words to conversation and explanation. There was a learning curve in this new way of relating to our youth, and there were a few times when we had to go back and say, "We were wrong, please forgive us."

Help Them Keep Their Conscience Clear
We must now help our youth move into the lessons of learning to walk with the God who just saved them from their sins and washed their hearts clean in His own blood. The whole purpose of salvation is to bring man into right relationship with God so that he can walk with Him. This then must be our top priority. This is the most important aspect of being a disciple. A disciple must be, literally and personally, a follower of Jesus Christ. It is our job to see that this close connection is nurtured.

Our son Joshua was recently born again. What a beautiful time for the whole family as his heart was cleansed and changed by the blood! Not long after this, he did something wrong. I knew that his conscience would be bothering him, so I took him aside, and we had a lesson on clearing the conscience. I explained to him that he now has a new responsibility to keep his conscience clear. This was about a week after his conversion, and he had been full of joy all week. But his conscience had become clouded, and the joy was gone. He didn't know what to do, so I instructed him. Then we got down on our knees together, and he repented of his sin. You should have seen the joy on his face when we got up from praying. He understood the lesson very clearly. I have come alongside him a few times since to remind him that he needs to deal with some things in his heart.

It has been beautiful to behold a whole new relationship between me and my son. You see, he is a new Christian who wants to learn to walk under God's blessing, and I am his father who knows how to help him attain this. He comes to me often just to counsel about things that are happening in his new heart. I love it. I'm not the fellow who is correcting him when he does something wrong. I am the man who knows how to encourage his faith and help his joy. We are buddies in a new way that we have never been before.

Establish Their Devotional Life

This is an area that we are quick to cover with a new convert. We know that if the new babe in Christ spends time in the Word and in prayer, he will grow. And we want him to grow. This is of utmost importance, and we check up on the new convert to see how he is getting along.

All this kind of care should be applied to your child. He needs parents who watch over him and help him get on his feet spiritually. If your child doesn't have a regular time to seek God each day, help him get it in concrete. Now is the time to go after this one. It is a natural. He is expecting you to speak about it. Help him get up in the morning, and check in on him to see how things are going.

I am always floating around the house in the morning, checking on all my little lambs to see how the morning is going. I ask them what they are reading. I ask them to share what they are getting from God. I ask them how their prayer time is going. All this is assumed, so no one feels threatened. They feel loved when I ask. By keeping close contact here, I get a constant glimpse into their walk with God. What a joy to see them grow and express fulfillment in knowing God!

Talk Time and Accountability

Young people need to talk. Communication is one of your key methods for guiding them and monitoring their progress. Sometimes this can be serious conversation, and sometimes it can just be good old family-time talk. Everything does not have to be heavy. Natural humor is always appreciated in the family setting. We often enjoy popcorn Sunday night as we sit around and discuss the sermon that morning and how it applies to each of us. The point here is that you as parents must keep your hand on the pulse of your youth's heart. The youthful years are formative years. The young people are finding their way with personal convictions. They need to talk all of this out with someone, and it is best if that someone is you.

This flow of communication naturally opens up to some accountability for them. If relationships are right, this accountability is perceived as loving protection. And that is what it is. Maybe your young people go to a special meeting for the youth. You should have the freedom to ask them how the evening went and what they talked about. You should be one of their friends, and you should be able to ask them how they are doing morally. This should be a willing free flow of information so you can help them through the battles of coming to maturity.

I have seen dozens of young people prosper and gain great victories in the area of self-abuse simply by being accountable to Mom or Dad. Communication opens the door for them to share on these deeper levels. Nothing will stunt their growth in grace more than these moral struggles. The opposite also is true. If a young person can walk in victory in these areas, it seems as though God picks them up and uses them in many ways in their youth.

The Blessing of Human Authority

I have been young in the ministry, and now I am getting old in the same. I have watched the lives of many young people in the past twenty-five years. The ones who really prospered in every way had some blessed human authority in their lives as they grew in the Lord. In the Christian context, there is no greater power available to mold a young disciple into maturity.

Think about it a moment. How can there be any discipleship if there is no submission to authority? A parent knows his child as no one else could. The parent has more loving concern than any others could possibly muster. Blessed are the youth whose parents watch over their souls through these formative years, directing their steps, and even telling them no.

I wrote of this authority already in a previous chapter. However, it was applied there in the context of small children. Obviously, if you do your homework while the child is young, you will have very little problem moving into this vital aspect of making a disciple. The rules are the same because the principle is the same. The principle is that of the older and wiser directing the younger in the way he should go, with the younger, inexperienced one submitting to the older and receiving much benefit. As I stated earlier concerning the small children, the great need is for calm, quiet, authority. This is most important with young people. They are beginning to question issues in life. They are beginning to make decisions on their own. It is vital that you as a parent be firmly established in your authority. There should be no arguments, no debates, no raising of the voice at all in your relationship. This is always counterproductive. As the child learns to give up his will on an adult level, there may be times when he will disagree with your direction. It is very important that you stay calm, firm, and loving. "In quietness and in confidence shall be your strength" (Isa. 30:15).

Young people need to be told "no" at times. This is your job. They need oversight as they learn to live in a real world. We need to come alongside them and help them learn to live. Where they are doing well and seem to be clearly in control, we can let up. But where they are not doing well, they need the restraints and directions of a wise parent. Remember, the goal is a young person who clearly is walking with God. When you get there, you will know it, and everything will change.

I remember when our son Daniel came to this place. He was nineteen years old at the time, and had been in Africa for six months. God gave him some precious, sweet times of grace while he was there, and also six gruesome weeks of hepatitis, during which he could hardly eat anything. In the midst of all this, God brought him to that place of full surrender.

When Daniel arrived back home, we knew something was different from day one. He had always been a good boy, but now there was a humility, a surrender to God and his parents that was fresh and new. I remember how my heart slowly changed toward my son Daniel. I knew he was walking after the promptings of the Spirit. I began to say in my heart, "He doesn't need my authority anymore." At the same time that I was feeling this way,

Daniel was thinking, "I want to be under my parents authority in everything I do." This is a perfect balance. From there, everything went quite well at home. It was a good foundation for his future marriage.

Godly Friends

We hear a lot about peer pressure these days, and it is a right concern. However, there also is good peer pressure, or better said, the godly influence of close friends who love the Lord. This is an important aspect of making disciples of Jesus Christ. I know as I am writing this that some of you don't know how to live this point out. You are in a less than ideal situation, and don't know how to find the right kind of fellowship for your youth. Let me encourage you. Until you can find better fellowship for your family, you be their best friend. You must get close to them and fill in this gap. I personally believe you should be one of those good friends.

When parents are intimate friends with their youth, and the youth also have close, godly friends, this becomes a winning combination. It is such a complementary help when youth have friends who tell them the right things. When the voice of their peers agrees with the voice of their parents, this is a great blessing. Through the years, we have always sought out older youth for our children's fellowship. When Rebekah was sixteen years old she had a nineteen-year-old friend who helped her sort through difficult learning experiences. This friend was very supportive of our authority. She became positive peer pressure in Rebekah's life. Praise God!

God, in His wisdom, has provided all of this and more in His church. It is His will that we find like-minded fellowship for ourselves and our families. "God setteth the solitary in families" (Psa. 68:6). I know that there is much confusion these days and a departing from the Word in many parts of Christendom. Yet, it is recorded in the Scriptures that blessings, wisdom, strength, and many other benefits are designed to flow from the church to its individual members. This is God's plan. I want to encourage you parents to seek God's help and direction for your family in this.

When the children are small, it is easier just to keep them at home and do it alone. But when they get older, it is not that easy.

It is not good to be alone too long. Many families are missing vital Christian life experiences because they have been alone much too long. It is God's best if we have our families in a church made up of people who love the Lord with all of their heart. It is good to stand alone in the world, but God would have us stand together in a church as we stand alone in the world.

My heart goes out to many of you who have visited twenty churches before giving up to start "home churching." I don't mean to be judgmental toward anyone. That is not my heart as I address this delicate subject.

I am not alone in my concerns. I receive many periodicals from a wide range of believing denominations. The leaders of all of these groups are crying out with grief over the churches that are departing from the Word, and over the scattered sheep without a shepherd. We must seek God in earnest for the great need of revival. May God give each father the wisdom to lead his family through these difficult times.

Help Them Get Involved in God's Work

As your young people begin to experience the fullness of the Spirit in their lives, they must have an outlet for this river. This is a major principle in the New Testament and a vital key to your task of establishing them in the faith. Your youth must be doing something for God. We all are saved to serve. God has called us to Himself that we might serve Him, the living God. There must be a giving out even as there is a flowing in of God's grace.

God's fullness is maintained through several means that we have been considering. But this is one of the most important of them all. Your children need to experience the blessed joy of being a channel of God's grace. This will happen as they are allowed opportunities of service. We as parents must help them find a place to serve in God's kingdom.

Many parents are shortsighted on this point. They think that youth must mature first and then serve. They think that service is for the mature adults in a congregation, and that the youth must maintain a holding pattern for awhile till they grow. I feel this is a wrong approach to take with young people. If they are born again, (as defined in chapter two), then they must get busy for the Lord.

You likely have heard the Sea of Galilee and the Dead Sea used as an illustration. The Sea of Galilee is a living sea. It has fresh water flowing into it and out again. It is always receiving and giving. Because of this, it is alive with fish. But the Dead Sea is not like this. It has water flowing into it, but that water never flows out again. Therefore, the water is dead. There is no life in it. Our young people should have an outlet for their new life. The joy and blessings that they experience in this way are addictive. They get hooked on serving God. Remember the house of Stephanas. The whole family was addicted to the ministry of the saints. They all were hooked, and I believe it was because Stephanas got them all involved.

A life of living for others is what Christianity is all about. I think many youth lose their way because they don't have anything to do. They will miss out on many growing experiences if we just let them sit for the first few years of their new life. This may stretch some of you parents a bit also. Maybe you have no outlet in your life. You should seek an outlet of service for everyone in the family. Then you can experience this bliss together.

Remember William Booth who took his children out on the front lines, where they all got thoroughly addicted to the work. I send my children to Africa when they turn sixteen years old for a short-term mission trip. It is a tradition around our house, and one that every child longs to experience. Hannah recently turned sixteen and she is eagerly anticipating her trip in January. This little mission trip changes their lives forever. Their perspective on life and what is really important is totally altered during one trip to a poor country. Let me give you a few suggestions of involvements you can initiate to encourage your young people.

Rest homes

The youth can go to a rest home to minister to the dear old folks. There are many beautiful lifemolding opportunities at a rest home. The youth can conduct a service in which they sing, and even preach to the people. They can connect with different souls there, then return to minister to the deeper needs. They can share the gospel with them. They can go and feed the patients who need extra care. Wow! There is a lot to do at a rest home, and most rest homes are begging for someone to come and minister. These dear old folks are a forgotten people group.

City Children's Ministry

This ministry has been a life-changing experience for many of our youth. They go into the inner city and minister to the poor children that live there. It is so good for our youth. They get first-hand experience working with the real needy, rejected ones. They build relationships with them, teach them Bible classes, and even get involved with the parents of these children. So many of the young people at Charity have given testimony of how their whole life was redirected because of this service. They will get involved when they are fifteen years old during those formative years.

Soul winning

It is good to provide opportunities where your young people can get out on the streets, witness, and lead souls to Christ. Nothing will fuel their fire more than this. Fishing for men is most exciting. It far surpasses fishing and hunting. They can go door to door, or just go out on the streets and enter into conversations with people. Once they lead a soul to Christ, they will be hooked, and the joy of souls will carry them through many hard areas of service.

Shut-in ministry

This is a lovely chance to bring sunshine to those who can't get out. Our youth will take a Sunday afternoon and go from one house to another, singing and visiting the people who are not able to get out and go to church. This can be anyone in your community. These people don't care what denomination you are—they are lonely.

New York City trips

This is something that we have done for many years. We load up in a couple of buses and head into the city for a day of witnessing and open-air services. What a day we have, and what a blessing to the youth. We all go together, parents and young people. The day is full of blessings: three hours of singing and fellowship on the bus as we travel there. Then we spread throughout a park to do personal work. We have three open-air meetings where all are allowed to sing, give a testimony, quote poems, and even preach. Many of our people have learned to preach in this way.

Short term mission trips

Twice each year someone takes a team of ten young people on a six-week missionary journey to a poor country. These are life-changing experiences. I have never seen one youth whose life was not radically altered during those six weeks of front line warfare. These trips are not tourism; we are not into that. But rather, the youth really get their feet wet in the service of God. They do village evangelism, open-air preaching, personal soul winning, and much more. The trips are designed by us leaders to put our youth into full time service for six weeks. Once they have tasted the Lord in this way, they are never the same. That is what we want.

There are many more ideas that I could share with you, but I have given you a few so you can understand the importance of getting your young people busy for God. These activities give our youth many varied opportunities to be stretched and grow. Contrary to what some may think, service brings maturity. They will learn the Bible as they are forced to use it. They will learn to pray as they get burdened for a needy soul. They will develop convictions as they seek to answer the questions of seeking souls.

Conclusion

As I sit here and reflect over all I have written, much more comes to my mind. However, I have shared enough different ideas, for you to understand the principles involved in raising up spiritual youth. If you will pick up this burden for your young people when they are fourteen and walk them through some of these growing exercises, they will be well on their way to becoming anointed disciples of Jesus Christ.

Daryl and Rebekah Nolt

Daryl and Rebekah have been on the mission field since 1998. They are doing church planting work and evangelism among the Dagomba tribe, which is an unreached tribe in the hot part of northern Ghana. They have two children, Rachelle and Dwayne. Daryl currently oversees several workers who are taking the gospel to more than 50 villages. They are also training native leaders for churches in these villages.

Daniel and Christy Kenaston

Daniel and Christy are missionaries to the Konkomba tribe, in Ghana, West Africa. This tribe is one of the last unreached peoples in the Sub-Sahara area in the north. They live in a round mud house with a grass roof, and do the majority of their evangelism by bicycle. One of Daniel's main burdens is to plant indigenous churches led by local brethren They started the work there in January 2000. Their little ones are Abigail and Nathaniel, both born in Ghana.

Andrew and Elisabeth Weaver

Andrew and Elisabeth, (and daughter Jenny), began mission work in January, 2003 along the Pomeroon River in Guyana, South America. They are in the beginning stages of a church planting endeavor. They live in a 17x20 wood house on stilts along the river. Their only form of transportation is a small boat because everyone lives on the river. They are expecting another little one in November 2003.

33

Joining the Next Generation

Let thy fountain be blessed; and rejoice with the wife of thy youth.
Let her be as the loving hind and pleasant roe;
Let her breasts satisfy thee at all times;
and be thou ravished always with her love.
Proverbs 5:18-19

The pursuit of godly seed is not a one-generation thing. If our hearts are filled with God's burden for sanctified children, we will look way beyond our present generation. I have made this clear all through the pages of this book. I hope by now you have caught the vision of what God is longing for. God is pursuing a godly seed with all His heart, and this burden reaches into the realm of marriage partners for our children. I have one more strategy to consider in my presentation of God's heart for godly generations.

If we stop and think about it, we all know this is no little issue. You can lose much of the work you have invested if you stand idly by, and allow your children to "fall in love" with whomever their affections happen to land on. I have been a pastor for twenty years now. I have seen this a few times, and it is a great burden every time I see it. I have seen the whole next generation lost by a foolish "love affair," that ended in a marriage that Mom and Dad did not want. It seems like utter folly to me that, after you have spent twenty years training your child, you then send them out into a mixed-up Christian world to find a partner all on their own. This is folly. They say that the divorce rate is now at 50% in the "Christian church." Could this be part of the reason for all this devastation? I think it is.

The Scriptures are full of examples of a sweet and happy marriage. The text at the beginning of this chapter is one of them. I believe there are things we parents can do that will help our children to have the reality of this blessed picture. The whole appeal of these verses is to stay with the wife that you chose in your youth and enjoy a happy marriage.

The word *fountain* is referring to the children of that union. That which comes forth from your loins will be blessed if you stay with the wife of your youth and enjoy her all your days. This is consistent with what God speaks in Malachi 2:15. He makes them one flesh and pleads with them to stay together. Why? *"That he might seek a godly seed."* Let us parents set our sights on holy unions for our sons and daughters.

Parents: Please Get Involved

The whole issue of parental involvement is coming back out of the closet in the last fifteen years or so. I for one am very happy about this. There are several voices in our land calling us back to the old paths of Bible courtship and parental involvement. I am one more of those voices. This chapter can by no means cover all the issues of godly courtship; however, I desire that it will at least stir your interest. Most of our children are not able to seek their life-long partner without some outside counsel. There are simply too many gray areas that undiscerning youth cannot see through. They need your twenty plus years of experience to guide them through the maze. I mean no offence to the youth, but it is harder than you might think.

In the Bible, we learn that the father exercised his influence when his child was ready to marry. Abraham arranged a bride for Isaac. It seems this was common in his day. When a young man was seeking a wife, he sought permission from her father. In addition, the father gave the word to his son when it was time to go and get his bride. The parents were involved; this is clear. There are several reasons why I feel it is urgent that you parents take an active role in joining the next generation of children. Let's look at some of them, and see if you don't agree with me that they are urgent reasons.

False Christians: We live in America, the "Christian" nation. Millions stake their claim on the Christian faith, however, many professors are not possessors of the real thing. Sincere youth are tricked into marriage, only to find out later that there is no substance to their partner's Christianity. This is a life-long tragedy. The parents are the ones who can stop it. These false professors sound very good when you talk to them. They can wax eloquent and theological when questioned about their faith in Christ. Our young people are not mature enough to discern all this; they need our help. We parents, through proper teaching, should lay the groundwork for this kind of involvement. A mutual understanding on this point is imperative. Lead your child to covenant with you, "I will not release my emotions without your blessing." Then, when the issue arises, you will have a free and open voice in the whole matter.

Divorce Is Very Common: I wish it was not like this, but it is. The possibility of a partner breaking the marriage vows is very high today; it happens all the time. It must be stopped. The Christian ideals of marriage have dropped very low, and the binding power of the vows is gone. Dear parents, I think most of us still believe that marriage is for life. We must protect our children from these tragic separations. If we are not alert, it will spoil the next generation. I meet many Christian men who are afraid to get married because they don't trust the commitments of the ladies anymore. This situation is worse yet for the ladies. Our children need our discernment in these things. We must get involved. We must learn how to get involved. We must teach our children that it is right for us to get involved.

Emotions Are Powerful: There is a lot of truth in the old adage "love is blind." Once the heart falls in love, it is almost too late to try to change things. The youth cannot see straight anymore. This is the power of emotions. It is from God; He made the human emotions to function in this way. When these emotions are released in a proper relationship, it is most beautiful. There is nothing quite as lovely as the first love of a man and a woman. As a pastor, I never grow tired of seeing a godly couple on their wedding day. When these emotions release on the wrong person, they are just as powerful. It is hard to stop your child if he or she has reached this level of love. Again, because of this, it is imperative that we secure an understanding with our children. Our counsel can stop them from making a life-long mistake.

Not Compatible: I have given some very strong reasons up until now, but this one is not so strong. Sometimes a couple is simply not compatible. There may be many different reasons for this. If their convictions are very different, this can hinder a marriage. If they have been raised in a different culture, this can make problems in the marriage. Young people need help in discerning all of this. Parents bring their many experiences into this discerning process.

The Rewards of a Happy Marriage: This is the most urgent point of all that I have made. All the rest were negative; this one is very positive. If our children find godly mates with like-minded convictions, they will prosper all their days together. Because of this prosperity, their children will also flourish in this stable atmosphere. This is the greatest motivation for parental involvement. We want blessings on their marriage, and their children. Remember the young man and the young woman I desribed in a previous chapter? We must pray and labour to bring that kind of youth together in holy matrimony. Joy and blessings will fall on that kind of couple. We can have a part in this joy, if we will get involved. I now have a long list of couples who have followed the old-fashioned-way to get married. Without question, they enjoy a blessed marriage. It may be hard for you to imagine the power and stability that comes into a marriage, when the couple is totally dedicated to the Lord Today, there are hundreds of these couples scattered around the country. I can hardly wait to see their children in about fifteen years. Parents, help your children find a godly mate.

Preserving Their Hearts for One

And the rib, which the Lord God had taken from man made he a woman, and brought her unto the man. And Adam said, this is now bone of my bones and flesh of my flesh. She shall be called Woman, because she was taken out of Man

Therefore, shall a man leave his father and his mother and shall cleave unto his wife: and they shall be one flesh.
Genesis 2:22-24

I have already commented on these verses when we were looking at the role of the woman in God's economy. I would like to meditate on them further as we look at God's heart for our marriages.

God prepared Adam to see and feel his need of a helpmeet. This is evident as we read the flow of the context in chapter two. Adam named all the animals before God gave him a wife. The text says, "but for Adam, there was not found an help meet for him" (Gen. 2:20). I can imagine that a sense of loneliness settled over him as he realized he did not have a counterpart like all the animals.

The Lord God caused a deep sleep to fall upon Adam, and He performed the first surgery in human history. He took a rib from Adam's side. From the rib, God made a woman. She was like Adam, but then she was not like him. I want you to use your imagination again as we drop in on a very sacred scene. The Lord God *"brought her unto the man."* God gave Adam his wife. She was beautiful, she was unique, and she was just what he needed. It was love at first sight I am sure.

It was the same for the woman. She was not, and then she came into being, created especially for Adam. God gave Eve a husband, and she knew it. It is still the same today, if we will let God have control of our lives. He has provided a mate for each of our children that are to be married. The seeds of every happy marriage spring forth from this text. The Lord God performed a very informal wedding that day, and the universal pattern of marriage was set in motion.

Adam became a one-woman man that day, and Eve became a one-man woman. This may sound silly to you, but God could have easily given Adam two wives, if that would have been the best for him. The permanency of their relationship is very clear in our text. From the beginning, the pattern is one man and one woman for life. We Americans surely have lost our way on this one, but God's heart has never changed. The beauty of what Adam and Eve had is still possible, if we follow a few godly principles.

They entered into their marriage from a place of utter innocence. They were both virgins, physically and emotionally. The emotional fountains of their hearts found release for the first time on their God-given partner. I believe this is the foundation of a happy marriage. We parents have a responsibility to preserve the hearts of our youth for the glorious day when they marry.

It may seem radical to some of you, but it is possible for your children to come to the marriage altar with a heart that has never loved another man or woman. It is possible; I have seen it many times in my twenty years of pastoral work. They can come to the altar with a heart that is not being motivated by fleshly desires. They can come with a heart that says, "What can I give?" instead of one that says, "What can I get?" This can happen, if we will guide them down a clear path and watch over their hearts while they mature.

The Spirit of a Virgin

I would like to use this term to describe the beautiful state of innocence that Adam and Eve had in the beginning. What ever happened to the word *virgin*? We lost it somewhere in the rubble of free love. A few men have pulled it out, dusted it off, and found a beautiful glittering diamond; praise God for them.

The root meaning of the Greek word is "unknown." There are many implications in this meaning. The word *virgin* in the Bible describes a maiden who has not known a man, and a young man who has not known a woman. Other words that describe its original meaning are "fresh, new, and unused." These words portray the lovely purity of Adam and Eve's marriage. It is our duty as parents to keep our young people fresh, new, and unknown in the area of love. It is possible.

In Bible days, a true virgin was fresh and unknown, physically and emotionally. I praise God for every young person who has determined in his or her heart that they will not have sexual intercourse before getting married. This is commendable. However, there is a higher plane than this. To have a heart that has never known romantic love is that higher plain.

Virginity is sacred and something to be highly esteemed. We need to guard over our children that they do not lose this sacred treasure prematurely. I believe the heart is just as sacred, yet overlooked by most parents and young people. I believe this oversight is the reason for many a sensual failure with young people. You see, God has designed our human emotions of love to lead to sacred physical love, and holy children. Many youth play with these emotions before it is lawful, and sensual sin is the result.

To bring a virgin heart to the marriage altar is powerful. We have fallen so far that it is hard to imagine what this would be like. Parents, let your imagination drift and dream a bit. Imagine it: young people entering into courtship with the one they are going to marry, and they can say to them, "I have saved my heart for you." There is much more to be written on this subject, maybe I will write a book about it later.

Touchy Applications

This all sounds wonderful, dreamy, and much like a storybook- but how do you make it happen? We will have to change a few things to attain such high ideals. Allow me to stretch you a bit on this whole subject? Consider of few practical issues which have emerged in our modern world.

The Dating Game: Dating is a temporary, romantic relationship with the opposite sex. This is what the dictionary says about the word. It is very common in our society; however, it is relatively new. You have to go to a modern dictionary to get a definition. Through the means of dating, a young person can "fall in love" several times before they marry. They think that it is great fun, but they do not know what they are playing with. They do not realize that they are playing with two of the most powerful things in their life. They are playing with the heart, which is the most powerful part of their being, and with the emotion of love, which is the most powerful emotion in man. They do not realize the depth of what happens inside of them when they "break up." It is like a mini-divorce each time they do it. Remember what I said about play in an earlier chapter. Play is practice for future living. Each time young people "break up," they tear holes in their sacred emotions. These wounds leave scars of fear, mistrust and vengeance which hinder their marriage for life.

Flirting: The definition of this word is very revealing. Look at this definition in the light of what I presented in the previous point. *Flirting:* "to court triflingly; to express emotions of love without serious intent; to play at love; and to toy with love." This word does not sound so innocent after reading its true definition. These definitions are relatively new. The old dictionaries only allude to them. The modern dictionary calls a flirting woman "a loose woman." If we are saving our heart for one man or woman, we will stay far away from this activity. The Bible calls it *defrauding*. It is stirring up desires that cannot be lawfully fulfilled.

Sensuous clothes: Many different motivations lay underneath the world of fashion and provocative dress. For most of our youth it is the desire to draw attention. They want to be noticed, they want the boys or the girls to look their way. These three points flow together like sisters. Think with me; let us reason this one out together. If we are saving our hearts for only one, we will not have any interest in drawing the attention of others. When you put the three of these together, you can have some very destructive failures. Let's sum it all up together.

Joining the Next Generation

Sensuous clothes
+ Flirting
+ Dating Game
Fornication & Divorce

The sad part of all this premature play at love is the immorality that it breeds among those who claim to be Christians. This brings more devastation into the marriage. The guilt and wounds that moral failure brings into marriage are almost irreparable. Many of us parents can testify to these damages, and how hard it is to overcome them, even though we walk in grace and forgiveness. It is heartbreaking to look at all of it together.

Imagine this scenario. Two young people come to the glorious day of their wedding. They are filled with hopes and dreams of a good life together, and everyone is happy for them. They both have some of the above baggage with them as they enter into marriage. The hurts are there from previous relationships. Fear and mistrust are standing right beside the hurts, remembering the pain. They have plenty of fleshly desires cultivated during the many fun days of "playing the field." In addition, they both have their ideas about what a man or woman is "really like" filed away for future responses. The knowledge of all this baggage does change this happy scene a bit. Will they make it? Do they have enough Christian commitment to go through the hard times?

By God's grace, some will make it through all this, and secure a happy marriage. They will knuckle down and work through the many issues that come up, and they will make it. On the other hand, many will not make it. We all know the statistics.

Parents, we have some responsibility in all of this. We can save our children years of heartache, if we will get involved and direct them through these crucial years. I give this chapter to encourage you parents to search out this subject further, and to whet your appetite for more meditation and discussion.

Daryl and Rebekah
Nolt , January 3, 1998

Daniel and Christy
Kenaston, March 13
1999

Andrew and Elisabeth
Weaver, September 23,
2000

34

Eternal Tragedy: Offending the Little Ones

Woe to that man by whom the offence cometh.
Matt. 18:7b

How different are the laws of God's kingdom than the laws of our human kingdoms! Wherever the natural man dominates, he quickly sets out to establish his pecking order. Who shall be at the top, or rather, more truthfully, who will be under me? It seems the disciples were not free from this human Adamic tendency, even though they walked in the midst of the Savior, who came to save them from their sin.

In Matthew 18, our Lord Jesus was seeking to enlighten them to the higher laws of an eternal Kingdom. He chose a little child as the object lesson for His class. Picture the scene with me for a moment. The eternal Word, God incarnate, is desiring to teach them how things are in heaven. Jesus calls a precious little child and set him in their midst. Can you see him sitting there, bright, open, and innocent, full of trust, with a happy countenance? This is what heaven is like, and this is what heavenly greatness is all about. Humble yourselves as this little child, and you will be great in the kingdom of heaven. This was His message to them, in Matthew 18:1-4.

But then He changes the subject and turns the focus of His teaching onto the child. We have to remember that this is God who is expressing Himself here. As I see it, His heart begins to overflow because His Father's heart is doing the same. Jesus explained this experience many times. He said, *"The words that I speak unto you, I speak not of myself, but the Father that dwelleth in me"* (Jn. 14:10b).

His heart begins to utter a revelation of the Father's value of the little child. He shares the Fathers concern for the little lambs, and out of that flows a revelation of the judgement that shall fall on those who offend them. I encourage you to study the whole of verses 1-14, but I would like to focus specifically on the verses that speak without question about the little ones. Let's read them slowly out loud.

> *Whoso shall receive one such little child in my name receiveth me. But whoso shall offend one of these little ones which believe in me, it were better for him that a millstone were hanged about his neck, and that he were drowned in the depth of the sea. Woe unto the world because of offences for it must needs be that offences come but woe to that man by whom the offence cometh.*
>
> *Take heed that ye despise not one of these little ones; for I say unto you that in heaven their angels do always behold the face of my Father which is in heaven. Even so it is not the will of your Father, which is in heaven that one of these little ones should perish.*
>
> *Matthew 18:5-7 & 10,14*

This is a very sad chapter, and one that I would rather not write. On the one hand, I wish we could just skip over this material; on the other hand, I dare not. America is sinning against its children in so many ways that it makes me weep to ponder it. I have mentioned already that the fathers have turned away from their children, and the children have turned away from their fathers, and God has smitten our land with a curse. To put it in modern slang, God says, "Don't mess with the children." The bottom line issues

Eternal Tragedy: Offending the Little Ones

are not abortion, and child pornography, no, the real issues go deeper than that. The American people have a defiled, and darkened view of the value of a child. We do not see them the way God does anymore. These two issues are not a problem among true believer's in Christ. Thank God for that, but, we do have some tragic problems that sadly, need to be addressed. The needs that I must address reveal that even among Christians, there is a defiled veiw of children.

As we read the first fourteen verses of chapter 18, a very sobering spirit settles down over us. This cannot be helped if you take the words seriously and don't pass them off to some unknown group of people besides us. They were written for you and I, and all the force of them is given out of God's love for our children. While we find these verses sobering, at the same time, I see again, that God places a very high value on children. He is expressing it here in His warning of judgment if we despise them.

I believe it was Bill Gothard, who coined the proverbial definition of wisdom: "Wisdom is seeing all of life from God's perspective." I have always relished this simple yet very practical definition of wisdom. You can apply it everywhere, and we have the Bible to give us God's perspective on just about everything. In this text we see our dear children from God's perspective. He highly values each one of them. If you are one who is offending the little ones, I plead with you to get help, to get right, and to change your ways, lest the judgment mentioned in these verses fall on you.

Offend

Before we get into some of the practical ways that we can offend our children, it would be good for us to understand the word *offend*. It means, "to cause to stumble, to violate, and to scandalize." One of the definitions was quite revealing, in light of offending our children. It said, "to make angry." If we take these definitions of the word *offend* and look at the context of these verses, it becomes very clear. God is warning us, first of all, that we can cause our children to stumble and not follow the Lord. And then secondly, that if we do cause them to stumble and depart from Him, judgment will be upon us. The verses are very clear if you take them for their simple face value. Go back and read the verses again, slowly. Read them as if God were speaking them to you. I would like to draw our attention to several major areas where Christian children are being offended. I am sorry I have to bring these up, but it is such a great need, I cannot be silent.

Lukewarm Christianity

When Jesus Christ was revealing needs to the seven churches, He labeled the Laodicean church as lukewarm—not hot and not cold, just kind of in the middle (see Rev. 3:14-22). In today's language, it could mean, "religious." We go to church, we go through a lot of the motions, but Christ is on the outside of the door knocking, and wanting to come in and fellowship. We feel pretty good about our faith and don't see our deep needs. This kind of lukewarm faith usually neglects the training of the next generation. The worldly-minded parents don't have time to do the important things that count.

This kind of faith is not very palatable for the next generation. They look at an exciting, stimulating world that is calling to them to come and have fun. They look at Mom and Dad's faith, and it is pretty dry. It is very much in the "we have to" mode. You know, you do your Sunday thing and get it over with, then on to your own life the rest of the week. The children are in the evaluation stage as they are growing, and the world wins out as much more interesting.

So junior starts making his choices one by one, and by the time he is twenty, he is fully in the world and not interested in the faith of his father. Junior has been offended. There was a time in his boyhood when he loved Jesus. He sang the songs and wanted to go to church. But now, he is not interested at all. I meet dozens of these on planes as I travel. They all give the same basic story of growing up in church. They are offended. This may seem like strong language to some of you, but let's be honest, lukewarm Christianity has slain its millions of youth.

Beating in Anger

Deep wounds and utter confusion follow the child who is beaten in anger while he is growing up. The perversions he receives are many. The definition of love is twisted. The roles of father and mother get distorted, and most of all, who God is becomes defiled. How do you come to a God of grace and mercy if you view Him as a tyrant? It is very difficult for the child. Many are afraid to come to Jesus in repentance.

When we spank our children in anger, we pass on to them a spirit of bitterness and anger. They grow up to be hateful, rebellious, and defiant. These children are being offended. They are being beaten with unkindness, and they are stumbling away from the faith. Someone must answer for what is being done to their hearts. Many of them end up in a prison; others do come to Christ, but they suffer from the scars most of their lives. Only a very few break through the emotional barriers to find God as all sufficient for them. They have been offended.

Divorce and Remarriage

This is a curse of the American church. I say that in a general sense. How can the true apostolic followers of the suffering Lamb be filled with divorce (that is bad enough), and then remarriage (that is worse yet). It is not fitting to address this whole issue here in this book. My burden here is to stop it from happening any more. This whole scenario is totally destructive on the next generation. I don't know of any issue that is offending the next generation of Christian's like this is.

Where there is divorce, there is division. Where there is division, there is a tearing away at the emotional base of the children. This is the best way I know to build your house on the sinking sand. The spirit of divorce is usually at work in the home, long before the papers are served. The poison seeds of hatred and bitterness have been germinating in the children long before they hear the dreaded news. Then the lawyers increase the hatred by pitting the couple against each other even more. Once the divorce takes place, then the children have to decide who was right and who was wrong. This is utter foolishness. A six-year-old must choose Mom or Dad. This child is being offended. Then to add insult to injury, in comes the new lover. These new lovers are often provided by the new divorce facilitator in the local church. Oh, the pain and the confusion of all this! When will it ever end?

The child gets a new parent, new brothers and sisters, new grandparents, and a whole new set of problems to work through. Then we try to tell them to come to Jesus. I know this probably sounds very strong, but remember, I am trying to stop you from being the next divorced family. This devastates the children. They cannot come through it all without major problems. We have lost sight of the value of our children. Humility, brokenness, openness, and repentance are the need of the hour—not a new partner.

Verbal Abuse

This one is a great burden on my heart. Many children grow up under the verbal curses of their father and mother. How foolish it is when parents just shoot out hateful words to their child. Many times, if they would stop and think about what they said, they would probably say, " I didn't mean all that I said." But the problem is, they say it, again and again. This is very destructive. Proverbs rightly says, "death and life are in the power of the tongue" (Pro. 18:21a).

Some of you parents are speaking death and destruction over your children. You are prophesying failure and curses upon their precious lives. This is abuse; it is evil, and a deadly poison. I deal with the wounds of these words in the counseling rooms all the time. It is hard for me to imagine that parents say these things, but I know they do. Not just a few, many of them.

Imagine saying, "You stupid idiot, you will never amount to anything." Imagine them saying, "I wish you had never been born!" It hurts me to even write the words—I'm sorry. Children who grow up hearing curses like these, tend to grow up and fulfill the very words their parents preached to them. These children are offended, they are being scandalized. The words parents speak are not just words—they come true. Parents are speaking prophetic curses over their children. Unless the children have a mighty transformation by the power and love of Christ, most of them will not make it.

If a parent were to cut off the leg of their child, the authorities would rightly put him in jail. But what is worse: a leg or a forever-wounded heart? I catch a lot of tears in the prayer rooms while ministering to the youth. Some of them are absolutely devastated by harsh words. Sometimes I wonder if we are putting the right ones in the prisons. It is time to repent. I know I am coming across very strong, but what about your children?

Molesting the Children

My heart hurts to bring this offending monster out of the closet, but I must. When a parent drops so low in the darkness of his or her own heart, that they can justify sexual advances with their own flesh and blood, this is utter heathenism. A father lusting after his daughter, a mother lusting after her son—oh, how dark can you get! Then you go to church on Sunday and play the part. The wounds that incest brings are criminal. Children very rarely fully recover from these abuses.

I have preached many revival sermons and worked in the prayer rooms dealing with the struggling souls who want to walk with God. Here they come: forty, or even fifty years old, not able to get this whole Christian thing to work for them. You start asking questions, and here it comes again: sexual abuse when the person was a child or a youth. It was a father or a mother, or some trusted uncle or friend of the family. I get angry, righteously angry, as I help them weep their way out of the maze they are in. Some of them will sob and wrench their soul out for thirty minutes: the pain is so deep. These children have been offended, and somebody needs to repent.

Dear father or mother; is your eye or your hand causing you to offend one of God's precious little lambs? It is time to get utterly broken before God. It is time to go and get some help. God has a millstone waiting for you: I promise you, except you repent. You are the greatest key to the fullest healing of the offended child. The deepest healing will come when you are broken to pieces asking for forgiveness. I know I am using some very strong words to wake only a few people up. Please forgive me. If I stop one parent from offending one more little one, it will have been worth it all. Okay, I have said my piece. Now I can go take a spiritual bath, wash all the ugly pictures out of my mind, and go on.

Provoking Them to Anger

One of the definitions of *offend* is "to make angry." This sin is addressed very clearly in Ephesians and Colossians. There are many ways that this takes place in a home. If parents rule their home in the spirit of law instead of grace, children become frustrated and angry.

Some fathers enjoy teasing a son until the son gets angry and comes out swinging. The dad just laughs at the dilemma that he has his son in. This is very unkind. It is almost impossible for a child to honor and respect when they have this kind of treatment. Father beware, you are raising a bully who will soon rise up and get his fun out of doing the same to others. How can this be called Christian? This gives the child a distorted picture of God. To him, God is a bully.

I think the greatest cause of provoking children to anger is the simple neglect of training the children. The parents have just enough knowledge of how things should be to make life frustrating for the child. Think about it. There is no real desire to "go for the gold" in child training, yet the parents know that children should obey. They have no grit to learn how to spank properly, yet they know the child should be spanked. So here is what happens.

The child is left to himself most of the time and does what children do. The parent finally gets tired of nagging, and in a burst of emotional words, they lash out at the child. Abusive words, grave warnings, and a good twist of the ear is what the child gets. We know that this will not change anything; it will only compound the problems. Soon they are back at it again, and the parent finally spanks them in frustration and even anger. This kind of neglect does provoke the children to anger. When parents rule by reaction, this breeds confusion and discouragement. We parents need to decide what we want and get off the fence.

Conclusion

I think I have given enough examples to bring some accountability and, hopefully, some repentance. I have never heard a sermon on this text. I think it is time for every pastor to rise up and cry out against this kind of oppression and evil. The effects of this kind of

Eternal Tragedy: Offending the Little Ones

conduct are devastating. Forty-year-old people still carry debilitating emotional hang-ups that were dumped on them when they were children. Many adults are dying premature deaths from diseases caused by life-long bitterness toward one of these predators. And what about the eternal effects? It is an "eternal tragedy" to offend our little ones. Eternity is a long time for the effects of our evil and neglect to last, but that is what God says. I trust that for most of those reading this book, nothing of the kind will be named among you.

Prayer

Heavenly Father I thank You for the clear revelation of Your heart for children. I pray for all the hurting children who are victims of man's evil lusts. Lord, help them to come out of the closet with their wounded, devastated lives. I prayer for the fathers, mothers, and any other close relative or friend, who is involved in this kind of oppression. Lord Jesus, force them out into the open, where they can get help. And last, I pray for the many wounded. Heal them O Lord, spirit, soul, and body. In Jesus Christ's holy name. Amen.

Meditations

Training Christian Soldiers

Little Samuel, four years old, all ready to go soul winning in New York City. He has his grandma's old Bible in hand, about as big as he is, and some wooden crosses that he made during homeschool activities. All of the children grew up learning how to face people with a gospel tract at an early age.

35

Fighting For the Next Generation

*But my servant Caleb,
because he had another spirit with him, and hath followed me fully,
him will I bring into the land whereinto he went;
and his seed shall possess it.*

Numbers 14:24

As I draw near to the end of my long treatise on the home, I feel the Lord would have me pick up some of the strain of challeging vision again. We have covered a lot of material so far, and many of you may be tempted to be discouraged. May the Lord use this chapter about Caleb, to lift the eyes of your hearts upward. You can do it. God will help you, just as He helped him.

Caleb is one of my heroes in the Bible. I want to be like him. The words recorded above are few but packed with meaning. God uttered these words in the midst of an intercessory prayer that Moses made for the children of Israel. They had failed to enter into the Promised Land because of their unbelief. Caleb, however, was different.

God said that Caleb had another spirit with him that was different from all the rest of the people. Caleb had a spirit of faith and victory. He was a pioneer with a fighting spirit. The Lord said, "He followed Me fully — not halfway. He followed the fullness of the revelation that I gave Him of My person." There is a secret for us in Caleb's testimony.

Those of us who want to go on in our Christian life must be like Caleb. We must have a spirit of faith that says, "Come on, let's go. God will help us. Let's go in and take some of that land. Give me that mountain! It's mine, I want it and I'm going to have it." Words like these express the heart attitude of a Caleb. The Lord gave a prophetic promise to Moses about Caleb. He said, "I will bring him into the land." God promised Caleb the land that he saw and walked upon. We see in the book of Joshua that this land was not obtained without a fight, and that is how it is in our Christian lives also.

The Lord made another statement of promise about Caleb in the same verse. It holds some thrilling inspiration for us parents. God said, *"His seed shall posses it."* This promise has tremendous applications for our homes this very day.

Our Children Shall Possess What We Have Fought For.
If we were to visit Hebron, the mountain Caleb possessed, in the early days of the book of Joshua, we would hear the noise of battle. We would see the strain of war and hear the sound of prayers. We would see Caleb, the man of war, standing there leading others in a battle for the land. We would hear Caleb saying, "God said He will give me this land. And bless God, by His grace, I'm going to take this piece of land." He was eighty-five years old, but he had the strength, fire and zeal of a young man. His faith in God and his desire to provide for his family caused him to rise up as a warrior and fight. We need the same kind of heart, as we consider our homes.

If, however, we were to visit the mountain of Hebron twenty years later, we would find a totally different scene. We would find Caleb's children and his children's children there on that mountain, working in the fields and living in peace. There they would be, plucking olives off the olive trees, picking grapes, grazing the sheep on the hillside, gathering the honey and milking the goats. They would be enjoying all of the things God said that they would find in the land that flowed with milk and honey.

This is a beautiful picture, but it would not have been so except for a man named Caleb, who was willing to fight for his inheritance. He was willing to fight for the land God said he could have. If it were not for Caleb, you would not see all of those children living in all the good of the land. His children possessed what he fought for. It is the same for us today. Caleb was a pioneer. There's something very stirring about being a pioneer. There's something very challenging and adventuresome. There's something adventuresome about being a first generation Christian looking down the road and saying, "Bless God, I'm going to fight for everything I can get for the sake of the children that live in my house. I want them to start their lives with far more than I started with."

I know that not everyone is a first generation Christian. A first generation Christian is one that has no Christian heritage. You were lost. You were undone. You had no thought of God. You found yourself face to face with the reality of God. Your eyes were opened, and you were born again. That's where my wife and I found ourselves thirty years ago. We were standing on the good side of the river Jordan, just gazing out over the land. Ah, there it was! All that land! We had nothing—absolutely nothing—but we were born again. We saw so many things as we gazed over the land of Canaan. We saw the beautiful land of the disciplined life. We saw the beautiful land of love. We saw the beautiful land of the character of Christ. We looked out there and saw the beautiful land of a happy marriage and a godly home, and our hearts said, "I want that mountain."

There were preachers along the road who said, "You can have it! It's God's will! Go in and possess." We started our Christian life very undisciplined in probably every area. Marriage didn't go too well. We didn't know how to be a husband or a wife. We were not doing too well with our children. We didn't know much about raising them. Leadership was terrible. Finances were a struggle. I could give you a big long list of the failures in which we needed to grow thirty years ago when we gazed at the land.

The children in my own home have been saved and salvaged from so much. Some of the older ones know the battles and fights that took place, but the younger ones—all they know is a happy mom and a happy dad. All they know is order in the home. All they know is sweet fellowship around about the table. All they know is order, discipline, leadership, and fellowship. They don't even know there was a war to get those things, but there was a war to get every single one of them. We fought with the enemy for everything we have. By the grace of God, we fought for it. The children in my home today are literally possessing what we fought for. The little ones are growing up in a home where there is a sweet spirit of love and kindness. They know nothing of anger and arguments. They don't know any of those things. They are just simply possessing a sweet spirited home.

But, brothers and sisters, that didn't happen by accident. We fought for every bit of it. By that I mean we wrestled with God. We wrestled with the devil. We wrestled in prayer. We wrestled with each other. We argued sometimes. It didn't always go the way it should have, but we saw the piece of land. We knew that God wanted us to have it if we were willing to keep on fighting. By God's grace, we do possess that land. The children just grow up in the midst of it, as if that was the way it always was. That's exactly how God wants it to be. God wants our children to grow up in peaceful habitations. Yes, we can tell them, "It hasn't always been this way," but they will never know the strife, the fight, the battle and the struggles that we went through, because they were safely born in the midst of the things we fought for. What a beautiful truth. What a stirring thought that is to my own soul.

We Set the Battle in Array

As I look back over the battles during the last thirty years, I think about the strain. I think about how the enemy tried to discourage and destroy and try to get our eyes off the Lord. Through the years God kept drawing our hearts to keep our eyes looking ahead at the beautiful land. We saw the land of a happy marriage, of harmony in the home, of a disciplined life and of prayer that's real. We saw the land of godly character and of loving attitudes. We saw them and said, "I want them! I want that mountain! I will have that mountain!"

I remember what I was like before conversion. I used to hate children. I couldn't stand them. "Get them out of my sight! I don't want children around! They're a noise, a bother. They're just trouble." Imagine my children possessing that, but they know nothing of it. They don't even know it ever existed unless I tell them. I used to hate old people. I would not give them the time of day, but now they are the dearest people to me. My children know nothing of that. I fought for that piece of land, and my children know nothing of the other. My life was filled with insecurities and negatives. That's the way I was. That's the way I looked at life. I wouldn't try anything new. I was full of negatives. Some of my children know what that's all about, but the little ones know nothing of it. They grew up in a land filled with confidence in God, with positive attitudes and with an uplifting anticipation of what God can do today. That is all they know, because I was willing to fight for a piece of land back there years ago in my Christian life.

Paul wrote to Timothy about this subject of advancement in the Christian life, in I Timothy 4:15. He said, *"Meditate upon these things; give thyself wholly to them; that thy profiting may appear to all."* Maybe we should call it "taking new ground."

I would like to look at one word in this verse. It is the word *profiting*. This word means "pioneer advance." A pioneer advance is taking new ground. It's heading down a road that you've never been down before. It's standing there in a covered wagon with Mama beside you and two little children in the back of the wagon, looking out over a vast wilderness out in front. And, oh, you dream of a California you've never seen, but only heard about. It's standing on the edge of that wilderness, dreaming about California on the other side of the mountains and saying, "We're going to California. Whatever it takes." That's what a pioneer advance is. It's taking new ground that you've never taken before. That's what the word profiting means. Consider the context of this word in I Timothy 4:12-16.

Let no man despise thy youth; but be thou an example of the believers, in word, in conversation, in charity, in spirit, in faith, in purity. Till I come, give attendance to reading, to exhortation, to doctrine. Neglect not the gift that is in thee, which was given thee by prophecy, with the laying on of the hands of the presbytery. Meditate upon these things; give thyself wholly to them; that thy profiting – thy pioneer advance – *may appear to all.*

Paul told Timothy, "Don't stay where you are. Be an example to the believers in every area of your life. Give attendance to reading and exhortation. Give attendance to doctrine. What do I mean by giving attendance? Meditate upon them. What do I mean by meditate? Mill it over and over and over again. Give your heart wholly to the things you are meditating upon, so that everybody can see that you are advancing in your Christian life—that you are taking new ground that you never had before." As we give our whole heart to the words of Scripture, we will be changed, and all will know it.

Pioneers
In our Christian lives we stand looking ahead. You don't know what's ahead, but you read the Bible and see that there is much more land to posses than what you already have. There you stand in the little wagon, with your wife beside you, with a couple children in the back, and you look out ahead and say, "Let's go for it." You husbands look over at your wife and say, "Honey, let's go for it. Let's not stay here. Let's go on. Let us go forward. Let us pioneer. Let us advance. Let us go in and possess. Let us go and take that little mountain over there." Maybe today, your marriage isn't going too well. Brother, sister, there's land up ahead. It's beautiful land, and God wants to change that marriage of yours. And for the sake of those two children in the back of that wagon, go for it with all your heart! Maybe there is chaos in your home. There is disarray. There is strife. There is fighting. For the sake of those children, you need to go ahead. Fight for that piece of land. Your children shall grow up in the midst of that beautiful land with all of its milk and honey and with all its fruits and grapes. They can grow up in the midst of that, knowing nothing else, if you are willing to keep on persevering. It doesn't have to be the way that it is.

There is something stirring and adventuresome in that whole thought to me. As I look on down the road of my Christian life, I realize that there is much land yet to possess. I want to take my children in the good of everything I am willing to fight for. When it's time for them to take their own little wagon, I want them to look out ahead and say, "Bless God for all the land we obtained from Mom and Dad, but let's not stay here. Let's keep on going." I don't know a better way to teach the children about how to fight and possess the land than to teach them by example. We aren't going to stay on the riverbank. There are too many beautiful things out there that God wants us to inherit. We aren't going to stay on the riverbanks. We are going to keep on going.

I tell you every piece is worth fighting for. Think with me. It is the will of God that our children grow up in the midst of the things that we fought for. Let it be that way. Some are just married. Go for it, newlyweds. Keep everything you have; go for everything you can get. Your children will just grow up in the midst of everything you get. They will not know anything else. "Fighting? What is that? Angry words? I don't know what they are." Your children can just grow up in the midst of the things you are willing to fight for. I don't know what it is. Maybe there is fighting in your home? God wants you to possess a better land. Maybe there is chaos? Don't settle for that. Maybe you're an undisciplined, lazy person? Don't let them grow up in the midst of that. Let them grow up in the midst of a diligent home. They can grow up not knowing anything else. It is all in your hands today.

That happy marriage you need to have, it's worth fighting for. It will be worth straining over. It will be worth crying about. It will be worth every struggle and every energy you put into it. It will be worth every hour that you spend pondering what a happy marriage should be. It will be worth every hour you spend praying, meditating and facing your needs. It will be worth every bit of it when you look at it in light of the children who just grow up in the midst of this happy home.

We will close with the words of Caleb. He was standing in the midst of all of God's people. He was listening to them, and they were settling for less than what God wanted them to have. They were struggling over the giants. They were complaining about how hard it was. They were even talking about Egypt. They were saying, "Maybe it would be better if we weren't here. Maybe it would be better if we didn't follow the Lord."

Caleb, who was victorious and had a great heart, said along with Joshua, "*The land, which we passed through to search it, is an exceeding good land. If the Lord delight in us, then He will bring us into this land, and give it us; a land which floweth with milk and honey. Only rebel not ye against the Lord, neither fear ye the people of the land; for they are bread for us: and their defense is departed from them, and the Lord is with us: fear them not."* (Num. 14:7b-9)

Let me apply Caleb's words to us today? All the land that God promises us concerning our homes is there. Let us go in and possess it. Don't give in to those discouraging thoughts that are in your minds. Don't listen to those demons, those lying spirits, who come to lie to you and fill your mind with unbelief, doubt and discouragement. They tell you how it will not be worth it, and you cannot have it. Don't listen to them. If the Lord's blessing is upon you, if heaven is open over you, if God's grace is upon you, surely He will give you all of the land—all the land that you want."

What do you want? What do you need? What are you willing to fight for, that your children can grow up in the midst of the good land? What you are willing to fight for is the heritage you leave your children.

> *Have not I commanded thee? Be strong and of a good courage be not afraid, neither be thou dismayed: for the LORD thy God is with thee, whithersoever thou goest.*
> *Joshua 1:9*

Prayer
Dear Heavenly Father, In Jesus' name help each parent. Baptize them with faith and courage. Rebuke every lying unbelieving spirit away from them and let them believe. Help these parents to put on the mind of soldiers, and fight. Amen!

36

Revival and Godly Homes

*And the Redeemer shall come to Zion,
and unto them that turn from transgression in Jacob. . . .
As for me, this is my covenant with them, saith the Lord;
My spirit that is upon thee,
and my words which I have put in thy mouth,
Shall not depart out of thy mouth nor out of the mouth of thy seed,
Nor out of the mouth of thy seed's seed...from henceforth and for ever.
Isaiah 59: 20-21 adapted.*

We have come to the last chapter of this book. I know of no other way to finish a book filled with things to do than to appeal for revival. In this last chapter, I make a clear connection between a godly home and revival. I don't believe you can have one without the other.

Don't misunderstand me. If you apply what I have shared thus far, you will get some good results. I have written about many things that can bring positive changes in your lifestyle. A home business or homeschooling may be on God's agenda for you. These are good, and they bring good results. But if you apply all this and unite it with the power of the Spirit, you will get overwhelming results and generations of godly children. This is my burden for this last chapter.

Through these past fifteen years of preaching on the home, I have found that many parents are feeling a bit overwhelmed at this point in the discussion. I am sure the feelings are somewhat the same at the end of this book because I have lifted the standard high and clear throughout its pages. Your heart may be saying, "I can't do this." This is a normal response that does not need to be negative. However, if you let these feelings cause you to give in to discouragement or to give up, this is not good. Your feelings of helplessness are right. You can't do it. *"With men, this is impossible, but with God, all things are possible"* (Matt. 19:26b). If you feel utterly helpless, this is good, *"Blessed are the poor in spirit"* (Matt. 5:3a).

You see, it comes down to how we view the Christian life. Is it a life of things that we do, or is it a life accomplished by the grace of God working in us? According to the one view, we can take a shot at it ourselves. The other view requires a total surrender of our all to God every day. I hope you will take the latter approach and give God a chance to show Himself strong on behalf of your family. Look at this paraphrase of II Corinthians 9:8 applied to the home.

> *God is able,* (He is full of power) *to make all grace abound toward you in your home that you may always have all the power you need for every situation in your home, that good things may burst forth everywhere in your home.*

This is what God wants to do for you as you come to Him bankrupt, empty, and needing His grace to work in your home.

Other parents come to the end of a series of teachings ready to go for it. They have gotten lots of new ideas, and they are anxious to try them out. I want to encourage you zealous ones also. The answer is not the new things you have learned. The answer is, first and foremost, Jesus Christ. He is the reviver of every parent and the inspirer of all sincere ones. Look to Him as your sufficiency. It is good to rise up and implement what you have learned, but do it by the grace of Christ. You need a vibrant, Holy Spirit-filled Christian life to live out all these teachings.

Revival and Godly Homes

Those Who Turn from Transgressions

The text I have chosen for the beginning of this chapter is another one of those precious promises the Father gives us for our homes. It is also another portion of Scripture that defines the effects of repentance in a person's life. Have you noticed how many times God refers to our homes in the context of repentance and revival? God promises that He will come personally and visit those who turn from transgression. I picture someone on his knees crying out to a holy God in repentance. Whenever God finds a seeking soul down on his knees turning from sin, there He visits, because the purpose of redemption is to make man holy.

The Lord goes on to declare a covenant that He will keep with those who turn. He promises to put His Spirit upon them. This is a picture of salvation, and it is also a picture of what revival is: a pouring forth of God's Spirit upon the believer. Another good verse that helps us to see what God is saying here is Proverbs 1:23. God says, *"Turn you at my reproof: behold, I will pour out my spirit unto you, I will make known my words unto you."* This is also a good verse for those of us who have been examining our hearts as we moved through the chapters of this book.

This verse also agrees with the next part of God's promise in our text. God says He will put His words in us "when we turn from our transgressions." This is beautiful. It is what I need to be a godly father: God's Spirit upon me and His words planted in my heart by revelation.

The Lord goes on to give us a promise about our generations. As we turn, God says He will keep His word in the hearts of our children, and in the hearts of our children's children. This generational blessing is not some mysterious blessing. It is cause and effect. When "the love of God is shed abroad in our hearts by the Holy Ghost" (Rom. 5:5), that holy influence affects the next generations of children. The Holy Ghost is the oil that makes all these methods work smoothly. God, who made our children and knows His plans for each one of them, is ever present in our homes through the Holy Ghost. When God's presence is real in our homes, that is revival, and revival makes a godly home.

The Pursuit of Godly Seed

There are many enemies that fight against a godly home, but God even takes care of these adversaries. When you are under God's covenant, He fights against your enemies. Notice the verse just before our text, *"When the enemy shall come in like a flood, the Spirit of the Lord shall lift up a standard against him"* (Isa. 59: 19b). O, if only we could get a glimpse of the simplicity of the Christian life, we would believe that Christ is literally all we need. Let's look at another revival text and see what God has planned for our children.

Those Who Are Directed in Truth

> *I will direct their work in truth, and I will make an everlasting covenant with them. Their <u>seed</u> shall be known among the Gentiles, and their <u>offspring</u> among the people: all that see them shall acknowledge them, that they are the <u>seed</u> which the Lord hath blessed.*
>
> Isaiah 61:8b-9

The whole of Isaiah 61 is a thrilling prophetic promise of blessings to come through the Messiah, the Anointed One. The fruits of the anointing are listed here to the joy of all God's people. The aforementioned family blessing is one of the many fruits of the Spirit promised here. Again, we see that this covenant has conditions. Those who love the truth and allow themselves to be directed according to truth are the ones who will find a blessing upon their seed, their offspring. These covenant people shall be blest. They will have the Spirit of the Lord upon them because they are directed in truth. The overflow of this blessing will fall upon their children. The results of this blessing on the next generation will be spiritual influence on the world around it. It is clear in our text that the results of these blessings are expressed in tones of evangelism and witness. What else could the phrases *"known among the Gentiles"* and *"among the people"* mean?

In my studies for Home Histories in *The Remnant*, I have noticed this evangelistic result in every example. The fruit of the blessings that fall on the children is God's use of them to win the lost. Think about the offspring of godly families: Hudson Taylor, William Booth, John Patton, Amy Carmichael, and Andrew Murray. The list could go on and on. In every case, these offspring of godly parents all are *"known among the Gentiles,"* and others are still looking at them and saying, *"This is the seed that the Lord hath blessed."*

Do you see what I am seeing? Is this for me, and can I expect God to use my children? I think I can. There is a lot of work to be done in the kingdom. God is always short on laborers. The point here again is that continuous revival produces a blessing on the next generation. God promises these things to us as parents if we are consecrated enough to walk in this revival.

O dear parents, let us march to the beat of a different drum! God has us all in a corner. This whole thing will not work out right unless we as parents get back to the basics. God wants all of our heart, not half of it. He has ordained in His wisdom how this whole thing of raising children will work. We need to get in line with His way of blessing, and not wait another day.

A Family Revival

Allow me to make a healthy suggestion to you parents at the close of this book? Through the years, I have noticed the response of many parents at the end of teaching such as this. They are ready to make some major changes in their homes. My suggestion is that you start with a "family revival." If you quickly start making changes without bringing the children along, you may get some unnecessary reactions from them. Spend some time preparing them.

It is always good to make changes from a posture of humility. The fact is that many of you have missed the vision for your homes. It is best to approach your family in this way, instead of rising up with zeal to start changing things. If the family sees the father and mother broken over their mistakes, it will be much easier, for example, to throw the TV away. On the other hand, if you just walk into the living room and carry it out of the house, you may get a reaction. Bring the family along with you through confession and brokeness. I want to walk you through the steps that could give you a sweet heaven-sent revival in your home and cause your family to rise up in unity and say, "Let's make some changes."

Father Leads the Way

Revival in your life is the place where all of the changes must begin. You must be sure you are rightly related to God in your own heart. There must be no more half-heartedness. You also must be rightly related to all that you have been reading. Obviously, you cannot lead the family in all the rest of what I will say here unless your heart is saying, "I see where I have failed, and I want to change." You must have a personal time with the Lord during which you get it all out in the open and clear your life. I address this more fully at the end of this chapter.

Mother Follows Along

If father is the first one to read this book, then the next step is for the mother to read the book also and catch the vision. The order may be different, but either way, if you want to have a family revival, then mother must be in tune with what God is saying to her and to her husband. All that I address at the end of this chapter applies to the sisters also. This is a good time for the two of you to get things clear with each other if you haven't done so yet.

Call a Solemn Assembly

This is not snack time or family time. This is a time of sadness. You should set aside a couple hours for this meeting. You don't want to rush anyone. This kind of meeting cannot be put on. There must be a sorrow of heart in both parents for the family to respond properly. The children should sense the grief as they gather for the meeting.

Confess Your Faults

Again, it is good if the father leads out in this to set the proper stage for the rest of the family. You should begin by telling the family what God has been doing and saying in your heart. "I have failed the family" are good words to express as you open up to them, followed by some of the vision that God has put in you. Then you mothers should follow with the same kind of openness to the family. Ask the children to forgive you for your failures in the home.

Have the Family Do the Same

Once the two of you have cleared things with the family, it is time to open up the meeting for the children to share. They will have a response to all they have just heard you share. Just sit and listen, allowing each one to express his or her thoughts, even the young ones. This is a whole-family revival meeting. Most of the time, the family will want to get on board and allow Dad to redirect the home.

Get Right With Each Other

Dad, you need to lead out in this also. Open the suggestion by stating your own failures again: "I know I have hurt some of you." If you open the meeting up like this, the family will follow your lead and begin to confess and ask the others how they have hurt them. Take as long as you need on this point. The clearer the better.

Pray Together

After everyone has gotten right with each other, it is good to get the family down on their knees. It is time to take a spiritual bath and be cleansed in the blood of Jesus. Pray around the circle, with each person talking to God about all that has just transpired. They may pray for Daddy. They may confess their own sins, or even join in your heart vision with prayer.

Make a Family Altar

While all are still on their knees, and after they have cleared everything with God, there is something else that is important to do. Lead the family to make an altar in their mind, and let each one get up on that altar and sell out to God. This will mean different things to each family member, and even the younger ones can get involved in this. You are coming to God as a family and giving Him the place He deserves in your home. He is the King.

Ask the Lord to Pour Out His Spirit

This is the last part of your solemn assembly. Using one of the many promises I have shared with you, show the family how God wants to keep His side of the covenant. There should be faith in your words. Then lead the family in a prayer for God's promise of His Spirit on your home. Ask God to come and release healing in every heart, so all can rise up leaving the past behind and trusting God for His blessings on the future

If you can do this in sincerity and in truth, your home will never be the same. We have had more than one of these family revivals through the years, and each one brought great blessing down upon our home. The challenge then is to keep the channels open between God and each other as the days go by. If you do this and walk in the reality of the clearing, this is revival. You will sense God's Spirit hovering over the home daily. Reconciliation is the goal here in this whole exercise. Two hearts smiling upon each other, two hearts walking together in harmony, this is what you are after. If you have this kind of harmony in your home, you can take the family anywhere you want to go. Oh for God to release His blessings on our families through us as yielded vessels!

Jesus Loves the Children

Suffer the little children to come unto me, and forbid them not...For of such is the kingdom of God.

And he took them up in his arms, put his hands upon them, and blessed them.
Mark 10:14b,16

The picture in this text is one from which I many times have drawn insights about children. Here we have some discerning parents who realized that there was a blessing that flowed through Jesus. So they brought the young ones to Him that He might lay His hands on them and bless them. The undiscerning disciples thought that His time could have been better spent at more important things, but they were wrong. We see the heart of God coming out again as Jesus expressed the value of these children. I know that if I had been a parent in those days, I would have loved to bring my children to Jesus for a blessing.

Have you ever imagined what it was like that day? I have many times. I imagine the Lord Jesus with a warm inviting smile on His face saying to the parents, "Bring the children to Me." I can see Him greeting the little ones with the same warm smile as His eyes and His face light up while they come. I think His heart of love rose up and overflowed toward those precious children.

How do you think He blessed them? I believe it was in a warm and gentle way. The Bible says He put them on His knee. Imagine being one of those little girls or boys. He probably spoke to them to set them at ease. What kind of words do you think He spoke over each child? They undoubtedly were good words with a blessed future in them. Then He prayed for them. I wonder what He prayed? O to hear one of those prayers! O to have Him pray a prayer over one of my children! I'm sure we all would like that blessing.

Yes, Jesus loves the little children, all the children of the world. He loves them whether they are red, brown, yellow, black, and white. They all are precious in his sight. Jesus still loves all the little children of the world. He hasn't changed a bit from that day when He blessed those brought to Him.

There is only one problem. He has no hands that He can lay upon them. He has no face to shine their way. He has no eyes to beam upon them, and no mouth to invoke the blessing that they need. He has none, for He sits in heaven at the right hand of His Father. He has none unless He uses our hands, our eyes, and our mouths. Yes, Jesus longs to bless the children, but He needs fathers and mothers as willing, yielded vessels to do it. We must grasp the utter need for an absolute surrender of our lives to God. He wants to shine out His love upon the children through us. He wants to speak out a blessed future over them through us. Will we give him a yielded vessel through which He can flow? I hope we will.

I Can't Do It

Okay, here we are on this point again. I want to approach this issue from an entirely different perspective for a few moments. You are right. You can't do it.

I remember a young man who came into a prayer room where I was counseling with seekers after an altar call. He was weeping uncontrollably, and I had the privilege of helping him. As I sat with him, he burst out with a whole row of frustrated words. He said, "I quit! It doesn't work! I can't do it! I am tired of trying, and I give up!" He was crying while he said all this.

Well, I shocked him by what I said to him, and maybe I will shock you too. I looked him in the eye and said, "Good, this is wonderful! I'm glad to hear this."

I am sure he was expecting me to comfort him a bit and tell him to get up and try again, but I didn't. I told him he was in a very good place. I told him that God had been waiting for him to say all this for a long time. Maybe that is the place where you are at the end of this book. That is okay. God has a remedy for your problem.

I went on to tell this young man, "Now that you have given up, God has a chance to show you what He can do." I went on to explain that he must yield his life totally to Christ and let him have the reins from now on. You see, he was trying to do this Christian thing and still live the way he wanted to live.

Many parents are in the same place. They are trying to make this "home thing work." This will not do. God has already planned how the Christian life is supposed to work. He also has set many hidden things in motion for those who think they are going to do it their way. You will always end in frustration and failure until you lay your all on the altar of sacrifice. This is God's way. God dwells with the broken and yielded, and they shall be revived again and again. God said it so beautifully through the prophet Isaiah.

Revival and Godly Homes

> *For thus saith the high and lofty One that inhabiteth eternity, whose name is holy; I dwell in the high and holy place, with him also that is of a contrite and humble spirit, to revive the spirit of the humble, and to revive the heart of the contrite ones.*
>
> Isaiah 57:15

So, if you think you can't do it, that is great. I know Someone who can. Paul testified that the Spirit was working in him mightily. This is what we fathers and mothers need. We need the Spirit of God to work in us mightily in our homes. Somehow we have gotten the idea that the grace of God worked like this for Paul, but it will not work this way for us. This is terrible theology. Paul was a broken man, and God revived him daily.

This is the counsel I gave to the young man who came to the prayer room. I told him that he needed to crawl up on an imaginary altar and die there, to give up his whole life, to sell out lock, stock, and barrel for the Lord. Then I told him that he must be willing to fall on the rock daily, yielding his heart, his plans, and his every choice to the Spirit's leading. This is how the Christian life works, and this is the only way it works.

An Altar of Stones

One of my dear friends, a minister in a growing Baptist church, came to this place some years ago. I will never forget what he did. He was a successful businessman, but God was calling him to give all his future plans up and enter the work of the ministry full-time. This was no easy choice. He had a promising future, good pay, two cars in the garage--the whole American dream. But God said, "Give all this up, and trust Me." He wrestled for days with his decision.

One day as he was out walking in the woods, he came to the place in his heart where he was ready to sell all and follow Christ. He did something very beautiful out there in those secluded woods. He started to gather large stones into a pile and built an altar. This took him a while, but that was no problem. He was building an altar in his heart all the while. He wept as he laid each stone in place. When he was finished, he crawled up there on that stone altar and wept like a baby. He was there for a long time, repenting, yielding, and opening his heart to God. When he got down off the altar of stones, he was a changed man.

O fathers and mothers, my heart weeps just picturing it again. Some of you may need to do this for your family's sake. Beloved, I have brought many challenges to you through this book. Those challenges had real-life issues in them for each of you. The issues are different for each person. The Lord knows your heart. He knows what is hindering you from having a godly home. I believe, if you will lie quietly before the Lord with an open heart, He surely will show you what the issues are. If you will respond, think of what might happen. If you could just get it all right this very day, and then lead the family to do the same, what might happen?

O the potential of a whole family sold out to God: Dad walking under the anointing, being led by the Word; Mom filled with wisdom and pursuing a fervent prayer life; Young people anointed with the Holy Ghost, living as we described earlier, and children, guided by their parents into sound principles from the Word. This is a godly home. This is how you pursue a godly seed for His glory. Think of the potential to be found in a church made up of families like this! Dear fathers and mothers, I plead with you. Let us go for a revival like this, one that transforms our homes and secures generations of godly children, to the praise of His glory.

A Final Prayer

Our God and Heavenly Father, we come to You in the name of Jesus again. We cry out from the depths of our heart, have mercy on us. We have sinned. O God, "Where are the men" who will take this challenge and raise up a family this way? God, we know what has happened. We know that our fathers turned away, dear God. They didn't take You seriously! They didn't walk in Your ways. They stopped hearing Your voice. They quenched the Spirit of God in their lives. God, some of them went on in their traditions, but had no power. We acknowledge their transgressions and ours, for we have followed them in many ways. God, we are asking You to break the chains of past disobedience and set us fathers and mothers free. We know we are needy, but we pray that You will give us a godly generation of children, whatever that costs. In Jesus' name, Amen.

Bibliography

Barrett, Ethel "The War for Mansoul" Christian Light Publications 1998

Bounds, E.M. "The Complete Works of E.M. Bounds on Prayer" Baker Books 1999

Bramwell-Booth, Catherine "Catherine Booth" Hodder and Stoughton 1970

Choy, Leona "Andrew & Emma Murray – An Intimate Portrait of Their Marriage & Ministry" Golden Morning Publishing 2000

Collier, Richard "The General Next to God" Collins 1965

Crosby, Fanny – Heroes of Faith "Fanny Crosby" Institute in Basic Life Principles 1995

Ezzo, Gary & Anne Marie "Preparation for Parenting" Growing Families International 1995

Gothard, Bill "Men's Manual Volume 1" Institute in Basic Youth Conflicts, Inc. 1984

Hanford, Elizabeth Rice "Me, Obey Him?" Sword of the Lord Publishers 1972

Harvey, E.F. & L. "Soul Sculpture" Old Paths Tract Society Inc. 1994

Hyles, Jack "How to Rear Children" Hyles-Anderson Publishers 1974

McMillen, S. I. "None Of These Diseases" Pyramid Publications 1974

Murray, Andrew "How To Raise Your Children For Christ" Bethany Fellowship, Inc. 1975

Murray, Andrew "Abide In Christ" Whitaker House 1979

Murray, Iain H. "Jonathan Edwards" The Banner of Truth Trust 2000

Nee, Watchman "The Release of the Spirit" Christian Fellowship Publishers, Inc. 2000

Pearl, Michael & Debi "To Train Up A Child" 1995

Phillips, Phil "Turmoil in the Toybox" Starburst Publisher Inc. 1986

Pride, Mary "The Way Home—Beyond Feminism—Back to Reality" Crossway Books 1987

Ravenhill, Leonard "Why Revival Tarries" Ravenhill Books 1974

Smalley, Gary & John Trent "The Gift Of The Blessing" Thomas Nelson Inc. 1993

Stevens, Abel "The History of Methodism" Carlton & Porter 1859

Taylor, Dr. & Mrs. Howard "Hudson Taylor-Volume 1" Overseas Missionary Fellowship 1989

"The Amplified Bible" Zondervan Publishing House 1987

Webster, Noah "American Dictionary of the English Language" Foundation for American Christian Education

Wilkerson, David "The New Covenant Unveiled" Wilkerson Trust Publications 2000

Yohannan, K. P. "The Road to Reality" GFA Books 1988

New Book

Coming Soon (2004)

Households of Zion

By Denny Kenaston

Biographical Studies of Godly Homes in Christian History

In this book, Brother Denny outlines in depth studies of the homes of several heros of the faith, investigating principles of child training and household order. Hudson Taylor, John Patton, D L Moody, and John Wesley are a few examples. Many biographies focus on the great exploits of Christian leaders of the past, with very little emphasis on the homes that made the leaders. Brother Denny takes you behind the scene for a close up look at their homes. Very informative reading.

200 pages   Softcover $ 9.95 plus shipping

Home Fires Publishers
P.O. Box 256, Reamstown PA 17567-0256
www.homefirespub.com

Charity Tape Ministry

Audio Messages by Denny Kenaston

The Godly Home Series 28 messages on the home

Other Messages...
Courtship-Marriage
Dedicated Youth
Solid Bible Preaching
Revival

Many other speakers

Inquire for a free catalogue

Charity Ministries
400 W. Main St. Ste 1, Ephrata PA 17522
www.charityministries.org
1-800-227-7902

All tapes are by freewill donations

Home Fires Publishers

Where revival fires burn, toward the hearts, toward the homes, and unto the uttermost parts of the earth.

Books Published by Home Fires

The Pursuit of Godly Seed	Softcover	$17.95
The Pursuit of Godly Seed	Hardcover	$21.95
Households of Zion	Softcover	$9.95

Quick Order Form

Fax orders: Fax this form to *717-336-5756.*

E-mail orders: *sales@homefirespub.com* Please send all information on this form.

Online orders: *www.homefirespub.com* You can view all our products and books online.

Postal orders: Mail this form to: *Home Fires Publishers* P.O. Box 256, Reamstown PA, 17567-0256

Please send the following books, tapes, or CD's. I understand that I may return any of them, in new condition, for a full refund — for any reason, no questions asked.

_____
_____
_____

Name _____
Address _____
City _____ State ____ Zip_____
Telephone _____
Email Address _____

Sales tax: Please add 6% for products shipped in Pennsylvania.

Shipping
U.S.: $4.00 for first book or disk and $2.00 for each additional product.
International: $9.00 for first book or disk; $5.00 for each additional.

Payment: ❑ Check Enclosed ❑ Credit Card
❑ Visa ❑ MasterCard ❑ Discover

Card Number _____
Name on Card _____ **Exp. Date** _____